In Search of *The Thin Man*

ALSO BY PHILIP ZWERLING
AND FROM MCFARLAND

The Theater of Lee Blessing: A Critical Study of 44 Plays (2016)

*The CIA on Campus: Essays on Academic Freedom
and the National Security State* (2011)

After-School Theatre Programs for At-Risk Teenagers (2008)

ALSO OF INTEREST
AND FROM MCFARLAND

*Eyes on Havana: Memoir of an American Spy Betrayed
by the CIA* (by Verne Lyon with Philip Zwerling; 2018)

In Search of *The Thin Man*

Dashiell Hammett, William Powell and the Classic Film Series

Philip Zwerling

McFarland & Company, Inc., Publishers
Jefferson, North Carolina

LIBRARY OF CONGRESS CATALOGUING-IN-PUBLICATION DATA

Names: Zwerling, Philip, author.
Title: In search of the Thin Man : Dashiell Hammett, William Powell
and the classic film series / Philip Zwerling.
Description: Jefferson, North Carolina : McFarland & Company, Inc.,
Publishers, 2024. | Includes bibliographical references and index.
Identifiers: LCCN 2023059562 | ISBN 9781476686578 (paperback : acid free paper) ∞
ISBN 9781476651026 (ebook)
Subjects: LCSH: Thin Man films. | Hammett, Dashiell, 1894-1961—Film adaptations. | Detective
and mystery films—United States—History and criticism. | BISAC: PERFORMING ARTS / Film /
History & Criticism | LITERARY CRITICISM / Mystery & Detective | LCGFT: Film criticism.
Classification: LCC PN1995.9.T485 Z94 2024 | DDC 791.43/6556—dc23
LC record available at https://lccn.loc.gov/2023059562

BRITISH LIBRARY CATALOGUING DATA ARE AVAILABLE

ISBN (print) 978-1-4766-8657-8
ISBN (ebook) 978-1-4766-5102-6

© 2024 Philip Zwerling. All rights reserved

No part of this book may be reproduced or transmitted in any form
or by any means, electronic or mechanical, including photocopying
or recording, or by any information storage and retrieval system,
without permission in writing from the publisher.

On the cover: (left to right) Dashiell Hammett
and William Powell (MGM/Photofest)

Printed in the United States of America

McFarland & Company, Inc., Publishers
Box 611, Jefferson, North Carolina 28640
www.mcfarlandpub.com

for Clare

Acknowledgments

I want to thank the Mendocino County Library system for their help. I live in a little city of 7000 on the Pacific Coast, a four-hour drive north of San Francisco. Our entire county consists of 100,000 souls. We have no research library or university at hand. Somehow the public library responded to my requests and supplied me with well over 200 books without which I could not have written this one. I want to thank Amelia Hiseley, senior library technician at the Ukiah branch of the Mendocino County Library, and Daniel Hess, branch librarian at the Fort Bragg branch of the Mendocino County Library, for all their help in keeping my research habit well supplied. The extra sauce in all this was something called Zip Books, a statewide project of the NorthNet Library System funded by the California State Library. It delivered book after book to my front door.

Let's always protect our local libraries for the knowledge they preserve and share.

Table of Contents

Acknowledgments vi
Preface 1
Introduction 3

1. Nick Charles and *The Thin Man* 5
2. Dashiell Hammett, Acts I and II 20
3. The *Thin Man* Movie 32
4. William Powell 59
5. Myrna Loy 82
6. The Rest of the Cast and Crew 101
7. *The Thin Man* and Race 110
8. *After the Thin Man* and *Another Thin Man* 127
9. Hammett, Act III 142
10. Three More *Thin Man* Sequels 154
11. Hammett, Act IV 170

Epilogue: Who Was the Thin Man? 191
Chapter Notes 193
Bibliography 213
Index 223

Preface

I need to admit how much fun I had researching and writing this book. I proposed the idea to my publisher with visions of seeing old movies and reading detective stories during the Covid-19 lockdown. I got to do that and a whole lot more. Each research track I entered led to another and then another; paths running parallel and then crisscrossing, then doubling back in new and unexpected ways. Nick Charles led me to the Continental Op, Sam Spade, and Philo Vance. Dashiell Hammett led me to Lillian Hellman, Senator Joe McCarthy and Walter Winchell. Winchell led me to Josephine Baker, who took me from the Folies Bergère to the March on Washington. William Powell led me to Carole Lombard and Jean Harlow and Myrna Loy. Loy led me to Clark Gable, Spencer Tracy and (again) Senator Eugene McCarthy.

The field kept expanding. Follow the lines: Jean Harlow to *Red Dust* and *Red Dust* to the War in Vietnam. Louis B. Mayer to Irving Thalberg to Upton Sinclair. William Powell in *Libeled Lady* led me to actor Otto Yamaoka (1904–67), who led me to the World War II internment camps for Japanese Americans. I had begun with no thought of writing about racism but there it was, on the screen and in your face in *The Thin Man*, *Test Pilot*, *Princess Tam Tam* and so many others. Race, whether as Critical Race Theory or being woke or anti-woke, is at the forefront of arguments today, but this is not a contemporary concern alone; Adolf Hitler, Henry Ford, and the Hays Office made sure it stood front and center 90 years ago as well. But most important, I discovered Dashiell Hammett didn't stop writing in 1934, as his biographers claim, and I discovered why he didn't and how he made another U-turn in a life filled with zigs and zags. I could write a book about what I learned, so I did.

I had the time of my life weaving individual strands of lives, careers, films and history into the uniquely American story they form. I hope you'll enjoy taking that journey with me.

Introduction

Samuel Dashiell Hammett wrote *The Thin Man*. He drew the plot and characters for this, his fifth and final novel, from his imagination and also from his real-life professional experiences as a Pinkerton detective.

Hammett's fictional hero, Nick Charles, retired from detective work when he married the rich, smart and beautiful Nora Charles, who matches him in her capacity for nonstop drinking, witty remarks and marital lust.

Metro-Goldwyn-Mayer bought *The Thin Man* and turned the novel into Hollywood gold, then spun it out across five sequels.

After kicking around in the moving picture business for years in silent films, usually as the villain, William Powell appeared in all six *Thin Man* movies and became a star.

Thousands read the *Thin Man* novel but millions saw the six *Thin Man* movies. Nick and Nora Charles and their dog Asta will be popularly remembered as portrayed onscreen by William Powell, Myrna Loy and Skippy, seen here in a publicity shot for *The Thin Man Goes Home* (1944).

Myrna Loy, formerly a dancer and exotic screen vixen, starred as Nora Charles, adding a level of charm and sophistication rarely seen on screen.

Skippy, a male Wire Haired Terrier, and his lineal descendants played Asta. (In the novel, the Charleses' dog was a female Schnauzer.) Asta added a level of comic relief. The threesome captured hearts and entertained millions.

MGM mogul Louis B. Mayer, screenwriters Frances Goodrich and Albert Hackett, director "Woody" Van Dyke and hundreds of actors of every description brought the adventures of Nick Charles to multitudes of moviegoers over the last 88 years, from the depths of the Great Depression to the cataclysm of World War II and the ensuing Cold War. The Thin Man films can still be seen on Turner Classic Movies and in revival houses and are sold in DVD box sets.

In real life, Van Dyke put a bullet in his brain, Goodrich and Hackett threw down their typewriters, MGM fired Mayer, Powell retired—and Loy entered politics. Hammett went to jail and died a pauper … and a hero.

People born in the 19th century made movies in the 20th century that we enjoy in the 21st century. *The Thin Man* lives as a cultural touchstone and a political dividing line, as American as a martini.

1

Nick Charles and *The Thin Man*

Nick Charles and *The Thin Man* first appeared in print in the December 1933 issue of the women's magazine *Redbook*. The story was reprinted the following year in a hardcover anthology, *Six Redbook Novels,* along with other works that appeared in the magazine that year. Founded in 1903, *Redbook* published new short fiction, much of it by women authors.

A lot happened in 1933: The world had settled deep into the Great Depression and America inaugurated Franklin Delano Roosevelt as its new president. Roosevelt narrowly escaped an assassination attempt before taking office, then closed the banks and proclaimed a New Deal. In Germany, Adolf Hitler assumed power, one part of a fascist wave sweeping across Europe and even into the United Sates. Americans embraced the end of Prohibition. The Lone Ranger premiered on radio and *King Kong,* with Fay Wray and a great ape, played on movie screens throughout the country.

Hollywood actor (and future Thin Man) William Powell turned 41 and appeared in three movies that year, including one as detective Philo Vance. Myrna Loy had seven movies that year but she and Powell had yet to share a screen, as they would later, 14 times in all, beginning with *The Thin Man*.

Lillian Hellman began her career in 1930 reading play scripts and novels for Metro-Goldwyn-Mayer, at a salary of $50 a week, with an eye to finding her bosses, the studio producers, material for future movies. In Hollywood, she met Dashiell Hammett in 1932, beginning a relationship which lasted until his death in 1961. In 1934, Hellman's first play *The Children's Hour* premiered on Broadway, launching her decades-long career and placing her among the first rank of American playwrights.

And Hammett, the creator of our Nick Charles, turned 39 in 1933 at the apex of his writing career and craft with *The Thin Man* appearing as his fifth and final detective novel.

America had first given the world the new literary genre of detective fiction through the pen of Edgar Allan Poe (1809–49). Eighty years later, Hammett brought the detective story to its greatest popularity. His rise and fall all too closely followed Poe's own trajectory. Poe, like Hammett, considered himself a poet, but both found real fame and financial success with fiction. Success turned to excess for both: They both turned to drink, both suffered ill health, both stopped writing.

Poe's first detective story, "The Murders in the Rue Morgue," like Hammett's *The Thin Man,* appeared first in a journal, *Graham's Lady's and Gentleman's Magazine,* in 1841. Poe's was a tale of crime, but also a tale of ratiocination. It had a brutal murder as its subject but it had a paragon of crisp logic for its detective hero. It was the world's first detective story. Thousands, perhaps hundreds of thousands, followed down to the present day.

Poe followed "Murders" with two more detective stories, "The Mystery of Marie Roget" and "The Purloined Letter"; all three featuring his fictional Parisian detective C. Auguste Dupin. Poe wrote these three detective tales and then no more, though they had each sold well. And while he lived another five years after the last one appeared, he did not return to the genre. He died, supposedly in the throes of alcohol poisoning, after being found passed out at a Baltimore tavern. His death is still as great a mystery today as any he created.

Poe not only wrote the first detective story, he laid down the model for its protagonist. Detective fiction has had a definable shape and substance fairly recognizable since its origin: A crime is committed. A detective, professional or amateur, gets involved, often with a sidekick as narrator (think Dr. Watson from the Sherlock Holmes yarns) and they follow clues left by the perpetrator and finally unmask the villain. The reader participates vicariously by trying to solve the crime before the detective can. The genre continues to be as popular now as 150 years ago and the success of new authors depends upon how they expand, embellish or innovate on its basic framework. Poe is credited with inventing 32 conventions of the mystery story (e.g., the perfect crime, the innocent accused, the bungling police, etc.), conventions followed all too loyally by those who succeeded him.[1]

Early on, we had many straight white male detective writers like Erle Stanley Gardner (Perry Mason), S.S. Van Dine (Philo Vance), Arthur Conan Doyle (Sherlock Holmes) and the team of Frederic Dannay and Manfred Bennington Lee writing collaboratively as Ellery Queen. Popular female detective writers included Anna Katherine Green (1846–1935), sometimes called "the Mother of the Detective Novel"; Mary Roberts Rinehart (1876–1958), called "The American Agatha Christie"; Carolyn Wells (1862–1942) and the great Agatha Christie (1890–1976), the author of 66 detective novels.

More recently we've also had detectives who were gay, lesbian, physically challenged, black, Asian, short, tall, autistic, child, canine (and more). Few, however, brought to the genre the air of authenticity that Hammett brought to his detectives like the unnamed Continental Op, Sam Spade and Nick Charles. After all, Hammett, unlike these other writers, had earned his living as a professional detective for many years and knew his way around a lowlife bar, through the criminal underworld and around police procedures. Most importantly, he had developed a practiced ear for the street patois of his seemingly realistic characters. His follower in the new "hard-boiled" detective field, Raymond Chandler, creator of Philip Marlowe, noted, "Hammett took murder out of the Venetian vase and dropped it into the alley."[2]

In Howard Haycraft's literary history *Murder for Pleasure: The Life and Times of the Detective Story* (1941), he celebrated what he termed the "Golden Age of Detective Fiction" and singled out certain writers as masters of the "classic detective story": Agatha Christie, Dorothy Sayers, E.C. Bentley and others. In December 1944, in an essay in the *Atlantic Monthly* called "The Simple Art of Murder," Raymond Chandler fired a broadside against Haycraft's primarily British tradition. This narrative form, Chandler claimed, failed to provide, among other things, "lively characters, sharp dialogue, a sense of pace and an acute use of observed detail." The murders in these stories, he wrote, are implausibly motivated, the plots completely artificial, and the characters pathetically two-dimensional, "puppets and card-board lovers and *papier mache* villains and detectives of exquisite and impossible gentility." He called the authors of this fiction ignorant of the facts of life, "too little aware of what goes on in the world."[3]

As the last quotes suggest, Chandler accused the writers of Haycraft's Golden Age of failing to be true to the world we experience every day: "[I]f the writers of this fiction wrote about the kind of murders that happen, they would also have to write about the authentic flavor of life as it is lived."[4]

In his essay, Chandler singled out Dashiell Hammett as the person who rescued the genre by bringing it back to the real world: "[Hammett] tried to write realistic mystery fiction."[5] Hammett knew exactly what he was doing and he made clear his disdain for the writers and their detective protagonists who preceded him. He sought a new commitment to the reality of the mean streets he had himself patrolled as a Pinkerton detective. One of these previously successful fictional detectives, featured in a series of 12 books and 15 movies, was Philo Vance, a creation of Willard Huntington Wright, writing under the *nom de plume* S.S. Van Dine. In 1926, Wright introduced Vance to the world as a young aristocrat, educated at Oxford and owner of a villa in Florence, but solving crimes in America.[6] His appearance, with monocle screwed firmly in place, in Wright's second book *The Canary Murder Case*, "broke all modern [1927] publishing records for [sales of] detective fiction."[7] Wright, according to Haycroft, was a dilettante, like his sleuthing hero, and both dabbled in art, music and criticism.

In 1907, Wright had become literary critic for *The Los Angeles Times*. To write detective fiction, he created the name S.S. Van Dine, explaining, "I rather feared ostracism if I boldly switched from esthetics and philologic research to fictional sleuthing, and so I hid behind an old family name [Van Dine] and the Steam-Ship initials."[8] For a few years, Philo Vance was the best-known fictional sleuth on the globe.[9]

Hammett found this state of affairs absurd. Critiquing Vance as he appeared in *The Benson Murder Case*, both the book and the movie, Hammett wrote,

Willard Huntington Wright, under the pseudonym S.S. Van Dine, was a best-selling writer of detective fiction. Between 1926 and 1936, he penned 12 novels featuring his sleuth Philo Vance. Ten were turned into feature films. William Powell portrayed Vance in film versions of four of the novels including *The Canary Murder Case* (1929).

> This Philo Vance is in the Holmes tradition and his conversational manner is that of a high school girl who has been studying the foreign words and phrases in the back of her dictionary. He is a bore when he discusses art and philosophy, but when he switches to criminal psychology he is delightful… [H]e manages always, and usually ridiculously, to be wrong. His exposition of the technique employed by a gentleman shooting another gentleman who sits six feet in front of him deserves a place in a "How to be a detective by mail" course.[10]

It is therefore quite ironic that actor William Powell portrayed both Philo Vance in the movie version of *The Benson Murder Case*, *The Canary Murder Case* and two other Vance movies, and Nick Charles in the six Thin Man films.

We catch a whiff of Philo Vance's superciliousness in this brief quote from Wright's *The Benson Murder Case*:

> As I was ushered into the living-room that morning by Currie, a rare old English servant who acted as Vance's butler, valet, major-domo and, on occasions, specialty cook, Vance was sitting in a large armchair, attired in a surah silk dressing-gown and grey suède slippers, with Vollard's book on Cézanne open across his knees. "Forgive my not rising, Van," he greeted me casually. "I have the whole weight of the modern evolution in art resting on my legs. Furthermore, this plebeian early rising fatigues me, y'know."[11]

Such upper-class puffery led Ogden Nash to write, "Philo Vance needs a kick in the pance."[12]

Hammett came from a different world, in which the detectives of his experience did not wear silk dressing gowns. Haycraft returned Hammett's antipathy: "Hammett's lean, dynamic and unsentimental narratives created a definitely American style, quite separate and distinct from the accepted English pattern."[13] And Haycraft damned him with faint praise: "[His novels] miss being Literature, if at all, by the narrowest of margins."[14]

Hammett did indeed aim to create literature. In the words of writer Ross Macdonald, "Hammett was the first American writer to use the detective-story for the purposes of a major novelist, to present a vision, blazing if disenchanted, of our lives."[15] Hammett did so in some 40 short stories and in his five novels: *Red Harvest*, *The Dain Curse*, *The Maltese Falcon*, *The Glass Key* and *The Thin Man*.

The plot of *The Thin Man*, his last novel, is fairly mundane: A man, Clyde Wynant, disappears; his secretary and lover, Julia Wolf, is found murdered, and a witness to her murder, Arthur Nunheim, also turns up dead. A detective steps in and solves the crime. The plot seems not to offer much novelty. But the characters do.

In *The Thin Man*, Hammett added to his own detecting experience in gritty mining towns and dark alleys, the creation of Nick Charles, Nick's wife Nora and their pet Schnauzer, Asta. Nora has inherited wealth, both a lumber mill and a railroad, and she and Nick move seamlessly from alley to penthouse suite, patronizing illegal speakeasies and Broadway shows with equal aplomb. And while we've seen many detective duos from Sherlock Holmes and Dr. Watson to Batman and Robin, Hammett created a duo bound by the holy bonds of matrimony, not mere friendship or implied homoeroticism. A husband-wife team was new in 1933, although later writers of detective fiction replicated the formula again and again.

Marriage added a patina of respectability and ethical inhibitions to Nick Charles that had not applied in Hammett's previous novels which often featured the shadowy, brutal and unattached Continental Op or the oily dick on the make, Sam Spade. But we see more here as well: On one level, Nick and Nora are loving and well-matched, living life on both coasts with enough money to enjoy the finer things in life. But behind the hotel rooms, Broadway shows, stylish gowns and bright repartee lies a hollowness, a lack of direction and engagement, a Nick and Nora who are a bit lost and lonely, and for whom alcohol becomes simultaneously celebration and crutch. This dissipation of family ties appears writ even larger in the relationships of the Wynants, Clyde, Dorothy, Gilbert and Mimi, a family devoid of loving bonds. According to George Thompson, "The novel suggests the almost total alienation of modern man."[16] Hammett pursues this theme of alienation on three paths throughout the novel: sex, alcohol abuse and the collapse of American society.

The story of *The Thin Man* is told in first person by Nick Charles. It establishes its novelty in the opening paragraph: "I was leaning against the bar in a speakeasy on Fifty-Second Street [a few days before Christmas]."[17] A beautiful young woman, Dorothy Wynant, approaches and asks Nick's help in locating her father, Clyde Wynant. Nick once did some work for Wynant, a gaunt man who stands over six feet tall, the "Thin Man" of the novel's title. Nick hasn't seen him in many years and remembers Dorothy as a child sitting on his knee. Now she's all grown up, gorgeous and, as we'll see, a bit unmoored. Nick suggests she contact her father's lawyer, gives her a name and lends her a nickel. She calls and arranges to meet the lawyer.

Then the unexpected occurs. Just as this beautiful young woman asks Nick, "Look, why don't…"[18] Asta the dog enters the bar and jumps up on him. We don't know just what Dorothy was about to say; was it "Why don't you come with me to see the lawyer?" or "Why don't you have a drink with me?" But Nora holds the end of Asta's leash and Nick introduces the two women. Dorothy returns to her own table and Nick and Nora sit at another.

Nora said: "She's pretty."
"If you like them like that."
She grinned at me: "You got types?"

Dashiell Hammett's *The Thin Man* was serialized in *Redbook*, then published by Knopf as a standalone book in 1934. That same year, MGM turned it into a high-grossing movie with William Powell and Myrna Loy.

"Only you darling—lanky brunettes with wicked jaws."
"And how about the red-head you wandered off with at the Quinns' last night?"
"That's silly," I said. "She just wanted to show me some French etchings."[19]

In the opening of this short novel (135 pages), Hammett has not only deftly introduced three of the main characters but nicely delineated Nick and Nora's easygoing, seemingly egalitarian, teasing and loving relationship without ever having used any of those words.

This first of 31 short chapters also introduces us to the recurrent theme of alcohol. We've met Nick and Nora for the first time in a bar. At the top of Chapter 2, when Clyde Wynant's lawyer, Herbert Macaulay, calls Nick for a meeting, Nick is too hung over to go out but helps himself to two more drinks in his room before lunch. His drinking is prodigious, either impressive or frightening depending on your point of view. In Chapter 3, Nick asks Nora for a drink but when she suggests they have breakfast first, he responds, "It's too early for breakfast"[20] (but apparently not too early for alcohol). Nick drinks in just about every chapter; usually Scotch and soda, but suffers no ill effects except for occasionally feeling "tight" or suffering a hangover. Other drinkers in his orbit, like the married philanderer Harrison Quinn and Dorothy Wynant, often act drunk or pass out or need to be put to bed, often by Nick and Nora. But Nick is a high functioning alcoholic, much like his creator Dashiell Hammett. In the novel, the word "alcoholic" is never spoken and no one suggests that Nick has a problem.

After 13 years as the law of the land, Prohibition ended in December 1933, the same month and year *The Thin Man* first appeared. Drinking, legal or not, had never gone out of style. The prohibition on the manufacture, sale and transportation of intoxicating liquors by the Eighteenth Amendment to the Constitution in 1919 capped a decades-long campaign by temperance movements across the country. In 1920, the Anti-Saloon League optimistically welcomed Prohibition as the beginning of "an era of clear thinking and clean living."[21] If only. In fact, Prohibition in one fell swoop turned previously law-abiding Americans into criminals; anyone having a drink with alcohol was breaking the law. At first, national liquor sales decreased, but many observed alcohol abuse increasing as the Depression worsened. When sociologists Robert and Helen Lynd published their groundbreaking study of Muncie, Indiana, in 1929 under the title *Middletown*, they reported that a businessman told them, "Drinking increased markedly here in '27 and '28, and in '30 was heavy and open. With the Depression there seemed to be a collapse of public morals.... There was much drunkenness—people holding bathtub gin parties. There was a great increase in women's drinking and drunkenness."[22]

To meet this illicit thirst, organized crime became a major force in the American economy. Gang violence increased, as did political corruption.[23] *Madam,* a recent biography of Polly Adler, tells her story as a teenager who emigrated from Russia to New York and rose to prominence in the 1920s as the owner of a successful brothel just opposite Columbia University. With the advent of Prohibition, "speakeasies sprouted 'like mushrooms'" and there was "manic, uninhibited revelry" everywhere in the city. "When the Depression hit," we are told, "Polly was able to turn away 40 young women for everyone she hired." The literati collected at her doors and Polly and Dorothy Parker would chat "while the men [of the Algonquin Round Table] availed themselves of the services [upstairs]. [Gossip columnist] Walter Winchell used Polly's services extensively."[24] No wonder then that when Nora asks Nick, "Why don't you stay sober today?" Nick has a ready answer: "We didn't come to New York to stay sober."[25]

In his book *Nick and Nora: The Couple Who Taught America How to Drink*, Michael Turback notes that in the novel, "Nick downs 33 drinks, about one every six pages."[26] Turback adds that for Nick and Nora, "[a]lcohol is as much a part of the marriage as the couple is."[27] He believes that the Charleses "taught the men and women of post–Prohibition America how to drink."[28] If so, Hammett had a much greater impact than he could ever have imagined.

Hammett pursues his interwoven themes of sex, alcohol and social dystopia through a fairly conventional plot with one big surprise. The novel's Inciting Incident is the mysterious disappearance of eccentric inventor Clyde Wynant, divorced from Mimi and father of two estranged adult children, Dorothy and her even stranger brother Gilbert. In fact, the Thin Man himself never appears in the eponymous novel. The Inciting Incident is that event in any fictional work which occurs prior to the beginning of the drama. For example, the death of Hamlet's father is the Inciting Incident in the play Hamlet. The Point of Attack refers to the event that starts the action of the drama moving. In *Hamlet*, it is the appearance of the ghost asking Hamlet to avenge his father's murder: everything that happens in the play results from Hamlet's quest for vengeance. In *The Thin Man*, the Inciting Incident is the disappearance of Clyde Wynant. Nick, retired from detective work at the Transamerica Detective Agency (just as Hammett was himself retired from the Pinkerton Detective Agency), is reluctant to get involved in the affairs of the oddball Wynant family, but happy enough to spend his time looking after Nora's wealth. He is drawn in to find the missing Clyde Wynant at the behest of a desperate Dorothy, a seemingly concerned Macaulay and a money-hungry Mimi, all the while egged on by a curious Nora who wants to watch her husband crack the case. Nick's involvement is the Point of Attack.

Nick starts detecting, and murders follow. All of these murders happen offstage. We never see them but rather hear them described after the fact. This feels like a return to the classic Greek theater where all violence occurred offstage, leaving it to the audience's imagination to picture the horror of Oedipus gouging out his own eyes, or his mother-wife Jocasta hanging herself.

Hammett packs in a lot of plot. The first of *The Thin Man*'s three offstage murders occurs the day after Nick and Nora meet Dorothy, when the papers report that Clyde Wynant's former wife Mimi has discovered the "bullet-ridden"[29] body of Clyde's secretary Julia Wolf on Christmas Eve. We later learn of an even earlier killing. Suspicion for Julia's death falls upon Wynant and the police begin searching for him. Setting the plot of *The Thin Man* between December 23 and December 31 provides us a tight window for all the action and helps ironically juxtapose murder and mayhem against the usual family gatherings and holiday parties celebrating the birth of the Prince of Peace. Clues keep coming and the list of suspects grows.

Hammett drops in allusions to contemporary political and cultural events. Nick hears one cocktail party guest forecast a coming revolution when "we'll all be lined up against the wall…"[30] just as many Americans expected a class revolt to emerge from the Depression. Nora is in bed reading "Chaliapin's memoirs,"[31] a reference I had to look up. Feodor Chaliapin was a world-renowned Russian opera singer of the time. Nora's choice of reading material reflects an intellectual bent and mirrors Hammett's own: A biographer once revealed that Hammett had recently read that book himself.[32] On Christmas Eve, Nick and Nora take in a show at Radio City Music Hall, probably seeing the Rockettes, who began their long run performing there that very year.

We also learn that Nick's ancestry is Greek, the family name changed at Ellis Island from Charalambides to Charles, making him one of the mass of common folk renamed to fit the American WASP standard. At one point, Nick tells Nora, "Everybody trusts Greeks," which sounds fine until we recall the story of the Trojan Horse.[33] Later an angry Nora calls him a "Greek louse"[34] and "a Greek liar."[35] Nick's ethnic identity was scrubbed away in all the subsequent Thin Man movies.

Sexual innuendo abounds. When Dorothy visits the Charleses and gets so drunk she needs to be tucked into bed, Nick helps Nora undress her, a job I would have imagined Nora taking upon herself. Sure enough, Nick tells us (but not Nora), "[Dorothy] had a beautiful little body."[36] When Dorothy's mother Mimi comes looking for her on Christmas Day, her (Mimi's) new husband Christian Jorgensen accompanies her and we learn he has a waxed mustache and a heavy Teutonic accent, perhaps reminding readers of his countryman, Adolf. When Christian and Mimi leave their apartment, Nora declares to Nick, practically swooning against the closed door, "Jesus, [Christian's] a handsome guy."[37] In fact, Nora goes to parties and to the theater with other men while Nick works the case. She appears as liberated as he. A cop named Quinn clearly has the hots for Nora.

Earlier, in mixed company, Mimi asked Nick if he liked the recently murdered Julia Wolf as well as he had liked her (Mimi), alluding to an earlier unspecified romantic involvement between the two. In the best line of the novel and the cruelest putdown imaginable, he answers, "You mean those couple of afternoons we killed?"[38] Some time later, when Nick leaves Nora to pay a visit to Mimi, Nora advises him: "Keep your legs crossed."[39] When Mimi tries to physically attack Dorothy, Mimi and Nick tussle and land on a couch. Nora throws water in Mimi's face to end it all. Nora later asks Nick, "When you were wrestling with Mimi, didn't you have an erection?" Rather a risqué question for 1933, as is Nick's answer: "Oh, a little."[40] *Redbook* cut that exchange when they printed the novel but Knopf put it back for the book and made sure everyone knew it via a *New York Times* ad reading: "I don't believe the question on page 192 had the slightest influence on the sale of the book,"[41] so that everyone who read the ad would be sure to buy the novel and turn immediately to page 192. This sexual banter and the rather informal morality of Nick and Nora's marriage got the book banned in Canada.[42]

We learn from Nick's underworld acquaintances that Julia Wolf, her body now full of lead, had a checkered past of many amours: Kicked out of high school for an affair with a teacher, she took up with "Face" Peppler, spent some time with another guy when "Face" went to prison, took up with the wealthy, much older Clyde Wynant while waiting for "Face"'s release, all under various aliases. The police inform Nick she once did time "on a badger-game charge."[43] The badger game is a form of blackmail usually involving a pretty woman luring a married and/or wealthy man into a compromising sexual position only to be discovered *in flagrante delicto* by her jealous boyfriend or husband, perhaps "Face," who holds off on thrashing the mark or informing his wife in return for a discreet payoff.

As the novel unwinds, we face a slew of suspects: Dorothy; Mimi; Christian Jorgensen (hiding a secret past as Clyde Wynant's former partner Kelterman); Gilbert, Clyde's creepy son; Shep Morelli, gangster and friend of Julia Wolf; Arthur Nunheim, who claims to know who killed Julia; Wynant's lawyer Macaulay, and, of course, the missing Clyde Wynant himself, whom people claim to have seen here and there and who occasionally sends letters to Nick and Macaulay. Nunheim winds up dead as well, shot with the same gun that did in Julia Wolf.

For my money, Hammett has drawn Mimi as the most vivid character: capable of beating her own daughter, trying first to seduce and then to slander anyone who might help her get her hands on Clyde's money. Dorothy seems too neurotically unhinged for a reader to grasp; Morelli plays the tough gangster and drug abuser to the hilt; and Gilbert intrigues us, always hanging around, eavesdropping, pretending to know more than he does. The scene where Nunheim's squeeze Miriam packs a bag and walks out on him as Nick and detective Guild question him is priceless:

> [T]he bedroom door opened. The big woman came out carrying a suitcase. She had put on street clothes.
> "Miriam," Nunheim said.
> She stared at him dully and said: "I don't like crooks, and even if I did, I wouldn't like crooks that are stool pigeons, and if I liked crooks that are stool pigeons, I still wouldn't like you."[44]

That dialogue made it into the movie untouched.

Gilbert initiates the oddest part of the novel when, out of the blue, he asks Nick if cannibalism exists in the U.S. Hammett had foreshadowed this when, hung over and needing to eat, Nick and Nora phone from their hotel room to order food from a deli. Nora asks for a raw chopped beef sandwich with lots of onion and some coffee. Sounds gross but it is a thing; a traditional holiday food of the season and known as a "Cannibal Sandwich." It's so popular that the Wisconsin Department of Health Services annually warns people against it for the danger of "Salmonella, E. coli O157:H7, Campylobacter and Listeria bacteria," which sickens hundreds of Wisconsinites each year.[45]

Thirty-six pages after Nora orders the sandwich, Hammett returns to the subject of cannibalism to answer Gilbert's question about cannibalism in the U.S. Nick hands Gilbert a copy of *Celebrated Criminal Cases of America*, a real book by Thomas Duke; he says Nora picked it up in a second-hand book store.[46] (The book was previously seen in the possession of Sam Spade in *The Maltese Falcon*. Did Nora buy Sam a copy also?) Nick opens the book to the crimes of one Alfred G. Packer, "The Man-eater,"[47] who killed and ate several of his fellow prospectors out west in the 1870s. The entire entry is reprinted here in the novel at some 2000 words. On the surface the story seems to have nothing to do with anything that has occurred or will occur in *The Thin Man*. It does not foreshadow future action, it does not reveal character, it seems to serve no purpose at all. So why does Hammett devote space to it in *The Thin Man*? According to Richard Layman's Hammett biography *Shadow Man*, a writer asked Lillian Hellman, after Hammett's death, why she thought he'd included the story. She replied that Hammett, used to writing so many short stories, simply included it to lengthen the novel.[48] You would think any editor worth his salt would have removed this filler. In her master's thesis at Harvard, Anne Kelly says the Packer story "needlessly pads the novel."[49] William Marling, a Hammett biographer, writes that the story's "thematic importance is slight."[50] And Dennis Dooley in his biography calls the Packer story "an odd insertion ... which has no ... connection with the rest of the novel."[51]

Unless Hellman, Kelly, Marling and Dooley err and this book excerpt is, as I believe, not padding, not extraneous to the theme but is, in actuality, the key to the novel and to Hammett's intent in writing it. He included this interlude and he did so thoughtfully and deliberately. This is his indictment of a society in which everyone around Nick and Nora is a cannibal just like Alfred Packer, metaphorically speaking. Each character selfishly wants something from the others at whatever cost to their personhood: Macaulay literally kills people. We see Mimi as a man-eater who also beats her daughter. Julia Wolf used sex to extort men for money. Dorothy seeks physical experiences regardless of their harm to other people, as she carelessly destroys the marriage of Alice and Harrison Quinn. Only the strongest, the one who murders, or eats another first, will survive in this dystopian society. As an inversion of the American Dream, what we have here is an allegory of the unbridled capitalism of the Old West: The winner, whether the biggest landowner, the richest miner, the fastest gun, wins by literally eating their competitors. As we shall see, it is this grim vision which elevates *The Thin Man* and Hammett from the usual run of detective fiction.

People will tell you that *The Thin Man* is minor Hammett. They'll point you to *The Maltese Falcon* or *The Glass Key* or *Red Harvest* as the real Hammett. But they just mean Hammett did something different in his last novel. He moved away from the amoral lone wolf detective hero (the Continental Op and Sam Spade), away from the gore and bloodshed (*Red Harvest*), away from the femmes fatales who litter a hundred other noir yarns. And so he did. But he moved not just away from the old ways but also towards something new. Though some of his critics see *The Thin Man* as a dead end, the last of his detective fiction, I think it might be fairer to see it as a culmination of this period of his work. In this, his last novel, he took the genre as far as he could. He had earlier blazed a new path in hard-boiled fiction, created unforgettable macho loners, and then turned rather dramatically to domestic tranquility with Nick and Nora, paralleling his own personal growth in his relationship with Lillian Hellman. He created a novelty: the new genre of detective fiction that combined mystery with a comedy of manners. Yet it retains and enlarges, for all its humor and fun, Hammett's devastating critique of contemporary American society as evidenced in his earlier novels and stories. When he finished *The Thin Man*, he was again ready for something completely different. He had moved from a sense of nihilism (nothing can be done) in his earlier work to detachment and personal indulgence in this his final novel. But he had one more transition to make, to political commitment which would come outside of his fiction and invade his personal life, seeking to answer one question: If things are so bad, what is to be done? His answer would be political organizing.

The big reveal at the end of the novel comes when we learn that Clyde Wynant, the Thin Man himself, was the very first murder victim. On several occasions, Nick has suggested to the police that they search Wynant's workshop and when they finally do, they unearth his body "sawed up into pieces and buried in lime"[52] beneath freshly poured concrete. All the reported sightings of Wynant (by Macaulay and Mimi) were bogus, as were the various letters to Nick, Macaulay and Gilbert supposedly signed by the deceased. In the denouement, Nick fingers Clyde's lawyer Macaulay as the murderer since he had the most to gain by having all of Wynant's funds in his hands, and the one who repeatedly lied when he claimed to have seen Wynant alive. And when Macaulay makes a move to escape, Nick puts him down with a left to the chin: "The punch was all right, it landed solidly and dropped him…. 'What do you want me to do?' I growled at Guild [the cop]. 'Put him in Cellophane for you?'"[53]

Solving the mystery and apprehending the killer is all seemingly neat and tidy, as usual for this genre, but the final paragraphs come with a little existentialist philosophy. Nora asks how they can know that Macaulay is really the killer and if justice is being served. Nick has little fervor for justice, saying: "You find the guy you think did the murder and you slam him in the can and let everybody know you think he's guilty

... the District Attorney builds up the best theory he can on the information you've got ... [people] come in and tell you things about him and presently you've got him sitting on the electric chair."[54] Nora feels that while all this evidence may be good enough to convict Macaulay, it still "seems so loose"[55] and "not very neat."[56] Then Nora asks Nick: "What do you think will happen to Mimi and Dorothy and Gilbert now?" He answers: "Nothing new. They'll go on being Mimi and Dorothy and Gilbert just as you and I will go on being us.... Murder doesn't round out anybody's life except the murdered's and sometimes the murderer's."[57]

The truth will out, or some version of the truth, or the truth we tell ourselves, Nick implies, but the truth neither changes people nor improves society. To which Nora responds, in the very last line of the novel, perhaps speaking for all of us: "That may be ... but it's all pretty unsatisfactory."[58] A murderer has been caught, but murder continues. Indeed, it is the very foundation of our society, a capitalist society where murder is just the most naked form of economic acquisition.

The Thin Man works on many levels. Hammett tells a large part of the story in dialogue and this conceit works well. Multiple pages feature nothing but conversation. Dialogue, when done well, reveals character and salts the novel with the unique patois of different classes ranging from the gangsters like Studsy and Shep, to tough cops like Guild, professionals like Macaulay and women trying to play femmes fatales like Mimi and Dorothy. It also makes the reader feel present in the moment as if eavesdropping on real-time conversations, like a fly on the wall observing the action. The reader doesn't

A lobby card for the film version of *The Thin Man* (1934).

have to take the author's word for anything; the reader hears what's happening and weighs its value.

The dialogue frames scenes of violence. Though we do not see the three murders, we do see Shep Morelli and Studsy beating up Sparrow in a speakeasy, Nick hitting Macaulay and, my favorite, Nick knocking out Nora. That unlikely event occurs when Shep bursts into Nick and Nora's bedroom. Armed with a gun, Shep wants to convince Nick he didn't murder Julia Wolf. At that moment, says Nick: "I looked at Nora. She was excited, but apparently not frightened: she might have been watching a horse she had bet on coming down the stretch with a nose lead."[59] As the police rap on the locked door and Shep points his gun at Nick's chest, Nick acts: "I hit Nora with my left hand, knocking her down across the room. The pillow I chucked with my right hand at Morelli's gun."[60] Nick takes a bullet to his side and the cops bust in the door to take Shep down. Nora takes five minutes to come to. It's a nice scene highlighting Nick and Nora's equal toughness. Nick revives Nora after knocking her out:

> **NORA:** "You darn fool! You didn't have to knock me cold. I knew you'd take him, but I wanted to see it."
> **LT. GUILD** [*LAUGHS*]: "Jesus, there's a girl with hair on her chest."[61]

Screenwriters Albert Hackett and Francis Goodrich riffed on Hammett's dialogue in this scene for the film, adding (as the police search their room) Nora asking, "What's that man doing in my drawers?" The next day reading the newspaper accounts of their brush with death, Nick reads one story aloud:

> "I'm a hero. I was shot twice in the Tribune."
> **NORA:** "I read where you were shot 5 times in the tabloids."
> **NICK:** "It's not true. He didn't come anywhere near my tabloids."[62]

Hammett also crafts brief but evocative physical descriptions, especially of the minor characters. He tells us Arthur Nunheim, later murdered by Macaulay, has a "nose … peculiarly limber, a long drooping nose, apparently boneless."[63] He describes Nunheim's girlfriend Miriam as "a big boned, full-fleshed, red-haired woman … handsome in a rather brutal, sloppy way."[64] His writing is crisp and terse, Hemingwayesque before Hemingway; his stories unsentimental and gritty. He invents the hard-boiled detective story writing that will be emulated by so many writers to follow.

I want to reflect on some of our own contemporary issues, especially misogyny and racism, through the prism of first the novel and then the series of movies that followed it. Everyone with official power in the story, the several cops, the lawyer and the stockbroker, is male. Most of the women do not come off well. Nora shines as a paradigm of intelligence and curiosity but she stands alone and in the other women, from the vicious and avaricious Mimi, to the ditzy Dorothy, to the blowsy Miriam, we see a series of ugly female stereotypes. In Hammett's favor, we must admit that the men, Shep, Nunheim, Macaulay, Guild, etc., are equally unattractive; so we see the author cast an unflattering light on all his characters without gender discrimination.

Alice, wife to the philandering Harrison Quinn, first draws our sympathy as the abused wife but then pushes back brutally. When Nick brings Harrison home drunk, she tells Nick, "Bring it in." And then: "You know I'm only staying with him for his money, don't you? It may not be a lot to you but it is to me."[65] Cannibalism here is attached not so much to human flesh, as in the case of Albert Packer, as to cold hard cash. In fact, Nick theorizes that all of the murders are economic in nature: Having suffered reversals in the stock market of those Depression years, Macaulay has been using his power of attorney to steal from Clyde Wynant and then must kill Wynant, Julia Wolf and Nunheim to cover his tracks.

We see no African American characters in the novel at all. None. Hammett's characters, from the bars to the parlors, move in a completely white world. If we read only *The Thin Man*, we might think Manhattan devoid of black, Hispanic and Asian people, which, we know, it was not. I thought for a moment about the Charleses' visit to Rockefeller Center on Christmas Eve.[66] They must have seen the Rockettes preforming there in the first year of what is now a 91-year run. My parents took me into Manhattan to see that show when I was ten or so. Looking back, we know that the show Nick and Nora and I saw, though in very different years, was an all-white revue; the Rockettes included no black dancers until 1987.[67] Black people are simply erased from a white world, whether it is the fictional world of the novel or the real world of Radio City Music Hall.

The issue of race comes up directly in the novel only once in an especially dismissive, ugly and brutal throwaway. The cops follow a clue that someone spotted the missing Clyde Wynant in Allentown, Pennsylvania. It turns out to be a case of mistaken identity: Detective Guild reports that the man is "a fellow named Barlow ... that got shot by a nigger trying to stick him up."[68] Why did Hammett write those words? What did they add to his story? Years later, Hammett led an organization to defend the rights of African Americans and even went to prison rather than divulge the names of the group's financial supporters. We can only guess that Hammett's audience, his white readers, had no problem with these sentiments in 1933. Discrimination, segregation and violence against black people was endemic in 1930s America. The Library of Congress reports: "Lynchings, which had declined to eight in 1932, surged to 28 in 1933,"[69] the year *The Thin Man* appeared. So here Hammett both reflects and reinforces America's deadly prejudices. We'll see where this thread leads us.

The Thin Man was well-received. The critic Isaac Anderson in *The New York Times* wrote of the novel:

> Dashiell Hammett is in a class by himself.... In this new story Mr. Hammett is at the top of his form ... [T]hose who enjoy a good story, racily told in the sort of language that a roughneck detective might be expected to use will find in this story a welcome relief from the neatly patterned solutions of the miracle men of detective fiction.[70]

The Saturday Review rated it "Extra Swell": "It's the telling more than the tale that counts here and both are better than earlier Hammetts."[71] The *New York Herald Tribune* reviewer said of Hammett: "This most unusual author, darling of brows both high and low, has come through with a new hard-boiled opus worthy of standing beside the best of his other works."[72] In London, however, *The Times Literary Supplement* complained, "This American detective story is told largely in dialogue, of which the object is rather to amuse with the smart phrase than to advance the movement. In fact there is little movement in it, if we deduct what goes to the getting of drinks and the making of telephone calls."[73]

Certainly *The Thin Man* is not a great novel on the level of Dostoevsky's *The Brothers Karamazov* or Joyce's *Ulysses*, although it may be more widely read. But it is a well-written, clearly conceived and intriguingly plotted story filled with characters who hold the reader's interest from start to finish. Hammett elevated his chosen genre by, ironically, lowering its tone to more accurately create realistic characters who might believably be murderers and murder victims. Raymond Chandler, another master of this craft, wrote: "[Hammett] wrote at first (and almost to the end) for people with a sharp, aggressive attitude to life. They were not afraid of the seamy side of things; they lived there. Violence did not dismay them; it was right down their street.... He was spare, frugal, hard-boiled, but he did over and over again what only the best writers can ever do at all. He wrote scenes that seemed never to have been written before."[74]

Hammett mashed together multiple genres to create something new and fresh; mixing detective fiction with romance, screwball comedy, farce and comedy of manners. To this mix, he added the novelty of Nick and Nora, who will live forever as a certain paradigm of a married couple: committed to each other, able to tease and laugh at each other, intellectually curious, and always entertaining. Here marriage isn't a goal or a problem, but a continuing partnership with surprises, good and bad, along the way, that they work out together without ever questioning their basic relationship or sacrificing their own identities. Hammett highlights their relations in contrast to those couples around them:

- Alice and Harrison Quinn; Alice stays with her husband for his money and Harrison chases other women
- Mimi and Christian Jorgensen; Christian has assumed a false name and married Mimi to seek revenge on her former husband Clyde
- Clyde Wynant and Julia Wolf, whose affair has broken up Clyde's marriage to Mimi while Julia herself, under an alias, waits for her real lover's release from prison, stealing money from Clyde and having another affair with Macaulay.

These other intimate relationships, in contrast to Nick and Nora, are dysfunctional, constructed mostly on the contempt of one partner for the other. They constitute a daisy chain of guilt, lies and betrayals: a story of social breakdown as seen in what should be its foundational building block: the family. It is, in Hammett's telling, a society of cannibals feasting on each other. Nora and Nick escape this moral morass through alcohol, safe in their numbed cocoon. But the comic surface of the novel upon which they skate cannot hide the tragic chaos below: the prevailing corruption of family and society which only sugarcoats the poison.

Hammett knew what he'd created with the Charleses and faced it with ambivalence. After working on the script for the second movie sequel, *Another Thin Man*, Hammett bailed on future projects and sold his rights to Nick, Nora and *The Thin Man* to MGM for $40,000. At the time, he wrote to his companion Lillian Hellman with his usual level of cynicism: "There may be better writers than I am, but nobody ever created a more insufferably smug set of characters than the Charles [sic], and they can't take that away from me, even for $40,000."[75] He also called The Thin Man "a charming fable of how Nick loved Nora and Nora loved Nick and everything was just one big laugh in the midst of other people's trials and tribulations."[76]

Where did Hammett get these two iconic characters? All writers mine their personal experience for their work and catalogue the people and places they encounter. Hammett's 30-year companion and sometime lover, Lillian Hellman, wrote in her memoir:

> It was a happy day when I was given half the manuscript and told that I was Nora. It was nice to be Nora, married to Nick Charles, maybe one of the few marriages in modern literature where the man and the woman like each other and have a fine time together. But I was soon put back in place—Hammett said I was also the silly girl in the book [Dorothy] and the villainess [Mimi]. I don't know if he was joking.[77]

Years later in a *Rolling Stone* interview, Hellman elaborated:

Some of the dialogue is almost direct quotation from me, but she is Hammett's picture of me. I don't see myself. Some of the dialogue is exact because it amused him.... It's an affectionate portrait of a woman; but what pleased me more than anything else was that it was an affectionate pair of people. A man and woman who amused each other and got along. Nora often tries to get Nick involved in various detective cases and I think he once said she was always trying to get him in trouble. He used to accuse me of doing that. I was interested in his past detective career and I was anxious for him to go back to it occasionally. He never went back to it.[78]

Hammett dedicated *The Thin Man* to Hellman.[79]

In his book *Dashiell Hammett and the Movies*, Prof. William Mooney makes the point that the evolution of female characters in Hammett's detective fiction, from stereotypical femmes fatales to erudite and powerful characters like Nora, parallels Hammett's own widening experience of the world as he moved from San Francisco to New York and became familiar with creative women like his lovers, the journalist Nell Martin (for whom he left his wife and family), Hellman and his new friend Dorothy Parker. Women had won the vote in 1920 and the flappers of the Roaring '20s epitomized society's openness to newly empowered women. Though the other female characters of the novel (Dorothy, Mimi, Julia, Miriam and Alice) are self-absorbed users (cannibals) of those around them, Nora transcends the usual wife, clearly as smart, independent and loving as our detective protagonist himself.

And the dog, Asta? Such an odd name. The story is that Laura Perelman, wife of humorist S.J. Perelman and sister of Nathaniel West (author of *Miss Lonelyhearts* and manager of the hotel where Hammett locked himself in to write *The Thin Man*) had a dog named Asta. Hammett and Laura may have had an affair as well. Asta made it into the book and there may be a bit of Laura Perelman in Nora.[80]

In the end, it is not the mystery of the murders but the verve of the characters that make the novel. Nick and Nora remain alive and vibrant 90 years after they first appeared on the page. The names Nick and Nora have a nice alliterative ring to them. Could Hammett have taken the name "Nora" from Nora Helmer in Ibsen's *A Doll's House*, who struggles for her freedom against male domination? Was "Nick" chosen for its moral ambiguity, calling to mind both good St. Nick, Santa Claus and "Old Nick," the Devil? We don't know, but it is Nick and Nora, living, breathing man and woman, who make *The Thin Man* special. Who else but Nora could tell Nick after a drunken night in a speakeasy (highlighted by encounters with thugs and criminals), "I love you Nicky, because you smell nice and know such fascinating people."[81]

To make these unique characters come alive on the cinema screen would require a pair of very special actors as well as an unusual director and two screenwriters who understood gender dynamics and marriage from the inside out.

2

Dashiell Hammett, Acts I and II

There are a few things people don't know about Samuel Dashiell Hammett. For one, most of us, including me, have been mispronouncing his name; it is pronounced Da-sheel, from the French, on his mother's side, not Dash-el. Most people called him "Dash" and that sounded sufficiently macho to match his hard-boiled detective fiction. This is an American writer who put most other writers to shame by turning out over 40 short stories and five novels in just over a single decade, from 1922 to 1933.[1]

All from the son of a drunk who became a drunk himself, who dropped out of high school at 15 to help support his impoverished family and never went back, who read and studied on his own while knocking about from stevedore to messenger to freight clerk, to nailing boxes together in a factory,[2] to Pinkerton detective. Then by sheer commitment, he willed himself into becoming one of the great American writers of the first half of the 20th century and eventually, almost accidentally, a political martyr to American freedom.

The thing that perhaps no one knows about Hammett is why, after his prodigious output of stories and novels, and his great literary and financial success, he stopped writing for the last 27 years of his life.

As a playwright used to structuring stage plays, I'd divide his life into four Acts and call them: Act 1 Struggle, Act 2 Success, Act 3 Dissipation and Act 4 Redemption. It is a story, as Hollywood would say, that writes itself.

Act 1: Life began badly for Hammett. His youth included a mother often bedridden with tuberculosis, a father drinking and chasing other women, frequent family moves from Maryland to Philadelphia and back to Baltimore, jobs he hated and took only for the little bit of money they paid. Of his spotty employment record, he said: "Usually I was fired."[3] His was not quite, but almost, a Horatio Alger story of overcoming adversity.

Born in 1894, he grew through his teens as a high school dropout without economic or familial stability, without prospects, without good health and without dreams he had any hope of attaining. By age 20, he was drinking too much and treating his first of many cases of gonorrhea. With not much to lose, he enlisted in the Army in World War I and joined the Ambulance Corps. As the driver of an ambulance filled with wounded soldiers returning to the States, he somehow overturned the vehicle and vowed never to drive again; he honored that promise for the rest of his life.[4] He contracted the flu in the Pandemic of 1918–19 and saw it morph into the debilitating TB he had earlier pitied in his own mother. His life became one bout of respiratory illness after another: flu, TB, pneumonia, bronchitis, each destroying a bit more of his lungs. At various times in his life, the Army labeled him 25 percent to 100 percent disabled.

He did meet and marry a pretty Army nurse, Josephine Dolan, at a TB sanitarium, fathered two children, and then abandoned his little family. After Hammett's death, his executor Lillian Hellman claimed that the first child, Mary, was not Hammett's and that he assumed paternity only to protect Josephine's good name. I have found, however, no evidence to support this claim. It does demonstrate the sort of conflicting narratives indulged in by writers like Hammett and Hellman (and studio flacks and gossip columnists, as we shall see). As the curtain closes on Act 1, we can only wonder if this sickly young man, now married and a father, with no real career and few prospects, will ever amount to anything at all.

Act 2 dramatically answers this question. Two years before his Army service, Hammett had responded to an enigmatic newspaper recruiting ad and found himself working for the Pinkerton National Detective Agency. Founder Allan Pinkerton, born in Glasgow, Scotland, in 1819, and immigrant to the U.S. in 1842, had written: "The eye of the detective must never sleep."[5] The company's symbol, an open eye above the motto "We never sleep," gave us the term "private eye." Pinkerton became a "name synonymous with protection and security."[6]

In 1861, Pinkerton secured his fame by discovering a plot to assassinate President-Elect Lincoln in Baltimore as he journeyed by train to his inauguration. In his history of the Pinkertons, James Mackay describes in great detail the nefarious plot and how Pinkerton foiled it[7]; in his own book on the subject, S. Paul O'Hara questions whether any such plot existed at all.[8] Both agree, however, that agents, whom Pinkerton called "operatives," did serve as spies for the Union during the Civil War, returning from behind enemy lines with tallies of Rebel troop strength and deployments. After the war, these operatives turned their attention west to chase outlaws for the banks and railroads plagued by highwaymen. By the 1880s, they had become hired guns in the labor wars in places like the Homestead Strike in Pennsylvania and the Haymarket Riot in Chicago, "armed guards for capital"[9] and "a private army on the side of the industrialists."[10] *The Nation* called them "a band of mercenaries."[11] The strategy was best expressed by "Robber Baron" Jay Gould, who hired Pinkertons to break the 1885 Great Southwest Railroad strike, and said he could "hire one half of the working-class to kill the other half."[12] Pinkertons, wrote Hammett biographer William Marling, "broke strikes, beat up strikers, burned their headquarters, and safeguarded the 'scabs' who crossed picket lines."[13]

The American labor wars involved dirty tricks, false identities, frameups, beatings and lynchings. As Leo Huberman reported in his book *The Labor Spy Racket*, it was also big business. Drawing from testimony heard before the Committee on Education and Labor, Subcommittee Investigating Violations of Free Speech and the Rights of Labor, 1936–1941, Subcommittee Chair Senator Robert La Follette, Jr., of Wisconsin found that in 1935 alone, "the Chrysler Company paid $72,611.89 for all its undercover operative spying on the labor movement at Chrysler and Dodge auto plants."[14] The capitalists had many tools to choose from in their attack on labor: the William Burns International Detective Agency, operating in some in 43 cities, Pinkerton's National Detective Agency with offices in 35 cities, and some 230 smaller agencies with up to 135,000 operatives. According to Huberman, there was a spy in every union local.[15] The big companies paid a total of $80,000,000 for labor spies[16] who "sold a unique service—Union-Prevention and Union-Smashing."[17] The La Follette Committee also found that 47 paid Pinkerton spies secretly held offices in labor unions and six served as union presidents,[18] though such subterfuge was a violation of the 1935 Labor Relations Act.[19] These spies submitted daily reports to their agencies: Lists of union members were turned over to employers, who then fired those workers. The Agency operatives were instructed to report "radicals, with the customary agency definition of a radical—a man who belongs to a union."[20] Some labor spies simply robbed the union bank treasuries, putting the union out of business.[21]

In later chapters we'll see where Hammett's evolving political beliefs led him but as early as 1921 he'd had enough of the dirty game with Pinkerton's to quit the Agency for good. He had seen service in San Francisco and Seattle, tailing suspects and capturing thieves, but had his eyes opened about such detective work when assigned to Butte, Montana, where the mine owners confronted union-organizing campaigns from the Industrial Workers of the World. The IWW, or Wobblies, sought "One Big Union" of working men and women that would overthrow the exploitation of the capitalist class. The mine owners imported scab labor, occasional Federal troops, and met workers' demonstrations with clubs and guns. Historians Philip Taft and Philip Ross wrote, "The United States had the bloodiest and most violent labor history of any industrial nation."[22]

One horror too many finally soured Hammett on the job. Most gut-wrenching was the lynching of Frank Little, a union organizer and IWW Executive Board member. After a fire at the Butte Speculator Mine claimed the lives of nearly 200 miners and revealed the shockingly unsafe conditions under which they labored, the miners went out on strike. The Wobblies sent Little in to lead them, even though he had a broken leg and hobbled about on crutches. The mine owners struck back. In his autobiography *Wobbly*, Little's friend Ralph Chaplin wrote that six armed men, wearing masks, broke into his hotel room, beat him and carried him away:

> They dragged him by a rope back of their automobile to the [train] trestle on the outskirts of Butte.... They tossed the rope over the trestle, pulled Frank Little up by the neck, and left his half naked body dangling to the stars.... No attempt was ever made to locate or punish the killers. Instead the streets of Butte were flooded with heavily armed private guards and state militiamen.[23]

Did Dashiell Hammett have a hand in this atrocity? Historians disagree over Hammett's own claims of tangential involvement. In her memoir *Scoundrel Time*, Lillian Hellman wrote:

> I remember ... listening to him tell me about his Pinkerton days when an officer of [the] Anaconda Copper Company had offered him five thousand dollars to kill Frank Little, the labor union organizer. ...I said, "He couldn't have made such an offer unless you had been a strike-breaker for Pinkerton." "That's about right," he said. ...I came to believe ... that it was a kind of key to his life. He had given a man the right to think he would murder.[24]

Some have speculated that Hammett did not turn down the $5000. The report of a slim young man among the six killers fits a general description of Hammett.[25] Another biographer, Nathan Ward wrote that Hammett was in Butte at the time of the murder.[26]

The murder of Frank Little changed Hammett forever. As Hellman said: "I think I can date Hammett's belief that he was living in a corrupt society from Little's murder. In time he came to believe nothing less than a revolution could wipe out the corruption."[27]

Hammett did turn his real-life Pinkerton experiences into his evolving writing craft, somehow churning out 25 published stories in 20 months[28] in 1923–24, and developing across many stories and two novels a unique protagonist: the fat, middle-aged, balding detective known as the Continental Op. This forerunner of Sam Spade and Nick Charles works for the Continental Detective Agency, a stand-in for the Pinkertons.

Hammett took the name Continental from the Continental Building which housed Pinkerton's Baltimore office when Hammett first worked there. "The Op" was not a mere reasoning brain like a Sherlock Holmes solving a complex puzzle, but a flesh-and-blood protagonist, a man of action whose tough exterior often masked a well of deep human and ambivalent feelings. He sometimes solved a case by squeezing the suspects, male or female, until they broke.

Hammett's Continental Op, the detective with no name who might do anything for his employer, emerged as something new in the detective fiction genre. Critic J.A. Zumoff wrote,

> Hammett's Op stories are extremely violent. Although there is violence in traditional detective stories, it is not their core. Instead, the puzzle, the mystery—and hence the struggle to return the world to rationality—is what the novel is really about. Hammett changed this. Violence—and violent people—are Hammett's real subjects…. In the Op's world violence, rather than justice or truth, is the core of society…. His is a society fundamentally corrupted, and the reader is left without the rational ending of a [Sherlock] Holmes story.[29]

Certainly Hammett explores that corruption in his fiction, even revels in it. If you knew early on that Hammett would eventually join the Communist Party, you might claim to find clues to his future ideology in his early work. But I think that would be a mistake. Hammett critiques his society, even condemns the system in which he lives, but it is clear he is searching for some answer to the injustices of his time, political corruption, state violence and widespread poverty, affecting one response and then another, without settling upon a single analysis for action until much later. His time with the Pinkertons dirtied his hands without offering a way to remake a decadent and deadly society. As another biographer, Joe Gores, put it: "He was a strikebreaker, and he was a very good strikebreaker. Then, I think, he had a gradual, genuine revulsion and turned around."[30] And turned around again. And again.

Hammett's failing health factored in as well. He often found himself too ill to get out of bed. Nineteen twenty-one was a particularly tough year. After his hospital discharge, the pretty nurse he had been dating wrote to tell him of her pregnancy. He proposed marriage. Soon they had their first child, and he searched for a new career and a means to support a family of three. He enrolled at Munro's Business College in San Francisco and began studying writing and advertising. To get by, he wrote newspaper advertising copy for a jewelry store and, often too weak with lung disease to pursue even that, began writing short stories from home, knocking out detective tales for the pulp magazines. At home at night, he wrote at the kitchen table. During the day, when well enough, he worked at the San Francisco Public Library.[31]

He began by turning out colorful tales at a penny a word for monthly pulp magazines like *Black Mask*. Successors to the dime novels of the period from 1860 to 1910, the pulps enjoyed great popularity with the masses in the 1920s, '30s and into the '40s. Printing copy on inexpensive pulpwood paper and selling their magazines cheaply for a lower class and lower-brow reader, these genre fiction magazines of detective stories, romance and Westerns sold for ten cents a copy while the "slicks," printed on smoother, treated paper, aimed for a higher class of reader. Five hundred or more pulps filled the newsstands. Their writers, mainly white straight men like Hammett, aimed for the tough, the sensational, the violent and the sexy in their writing. As Neely Tucker wrote, "Their primarily blue-collar male readers understood certain truths: that bad things should happen to bad people, beautiful women are a problem, sex is dirty, violent crime can be funny and whiskey is our friend."[32] The writers for the pulps churned out stories at a penny a word (or less).[33] Some pulp writers worried about getting by and putting food on the table but some, like Hammett, had higher aspirations.

Black Mask was founded by the unlikely but hugely successful publishing duo of H.L. Mencken and George Jean Nathan. Mencken, a *Baltimore Sun* reporter, grew into a memoirist, editor, social critic and satirist, earning the honorific "The Sage of Baltimore." Nathan combined forces with Mencken on *Black Mask, The Smart Set* and *The American Mercury*. He became the most influential American theater critic of the first half of the 20th century.

Mencken cultivated the pugnaciousness of the city streets while Nathan reveled in the intellectual elevation of Broadway theater, championing the careers of Eugene O'Neill and George Bernard Shaw, while liking few others. Together Mencken and Nathan formed for an era American literary and artistic opinion. Both of their reputations have suffered in our own time: Mencken's for the racism and anti–Semitism of his writing and Nathan's with charges that he traded positive Broadway reviews for sexual favors.

Printed on poor-quality paper ("pulp" rather than "glossy"), magazines like *Black Mask* presented lurid tales that appealed to a largely lowbrow male readership in the 1920s and '30s. *Black Mask* published Dashiell Hammett short stories and serialized several of his novels.

A satirical poem, Berton Braley's "Mencken, Nathan and God," summed up the hold Mencken and Nathan had on the literary standards of their day, imagining them more powerful than God Himself:

> There were three that sailed away one night
> Far from the maddening throng;
> And two of the three were always right
> And everyone else was wrong.
> ….
> And the two they talked of the aims of Art,
> Which they alone understood;

> And they quite agreed from the start
> That nothing was any good
> ....
> When God objected they rocked the boat
> And dropped him into the sea,
> "For you have no critical facultee."[34]

But Nathan and Mencken liked Hammett—his spare prose, cynical characters, gritty settings and moral ambiguities—and they launched his writing career. His two years of Pinkerton adventures, cross-country travel, and interactions with crooks in high and low places gave him 12 years' worth of writing material in which he produced those many short stories and five novels from 1922 to 1934. Hammett yearned to raise detective fiction to the level of literature. "In the pulps," wrote Claudia Roth Pierpont, "Hammett developed not just a literary style but the style of an era."[35]

Otto Penzler, publisher and editor of numerous books of mystery fiction, wrote of Hammett:

> The argument could be made that the most influential writer of the twentieth century was Dashiell Hammett. As writers turned from the rotund style of Henry James and his Victorian predecessors to lean and swift prose, later scholars have pointed to the undeniably profound force of Ernest Hemingway. But who influenced Hemingway? Hammett did.[36]

Penzler supports his conclusion with two facts: Hammett's first Continental Op story was published in *Black Mask* on October 1, 1923, while Hemingway published his first book, *In Our Time*, in Paris in 1924 and in the U.S. in 1925. However, it must be admitted that Penzler cannot show that Hemingway read Hammett prior to publishing his own work.

Hammett traded on his personal experience in detective work. One of his earliest magazine pieces, "Memoirs of a Private Detective," appeared in Mencken and Nathan's *The Smart Set* in 1923 and contained 29 pithy entries such as these:

- (2) A man whom I was shadowing went out into the country for a walk one Sunday afternoon and lost his bearings completely. I had to direct him back to the city....
- (8) I was once falsely accused of perjury and had to perjure myself to escape arrest....
- (18) Pocket-picking is the easiest to master of all the criminal trades. Anyone who is not crippled can become adept in a day....
- (28) I know a man who once stole a Ferris wheel.[37]
- Hammett claimed to have found that stolen Ferris wheel at the only place one might expect to find one ... at another carnival.

Hammett's stories were a good "fit" for the pulp magazine market with their atmosphere of authenticity found in the smells and grittiness of the city streets, leavened with the omnipresent possibility of violence and the banality of tawdry sex. He appeared first in *The Smart Set* and then in *Black Mask*, which billed itself on each monthly cover as containing "Western, Detective & Adventure Stories." After some eight issues, they sold out and were succeeded as editors by others, most notably Philip Cody and Edward Shaw. Though Hammett wrote first under the *nom de plume* Peter Collinson, derived from old theater slang where a new employee is sent on the prank errand of finding a non-existent Peter Collins (Peter Collinson is the son of a non-existent person),[38] he soon felt confident enough to publish under his own name. Asked to introduce himself to *Black Mask* readers, he wrote: "I am long and lean and gray headed, and very lazy. I have no ambition at all in the usual sense of the word; like to live ... in the center of large cities, and have no recreations or hobbies."[39]

Stretching the detective genre, he crafted longer stories, serializing them in *Black Mask* and then publishing them in book form. At first, he was earning only $1000 a year which, even with his veteran's disability pension, made for a tight budget for a sick man with a wife and child.[40]

His first novel, *Red Harvest* (1927), features the Continental Op traveling to Butte, Montana, to look into a murder. The action recalls Hammett's work in Butte during the labor wars and Frank Little's murder. As the Op narrates the backstory:

> The strike lasted eight months. Both sides bled plenty. The wobblies had to do their own bleeding. Old Elihu [fictional owner of the equally fictional Personville Mining Company] hired gunmen, strike-breakers, national guardsmen and even parts of the regular army, to do his work. When the last skull had been cracked, the last rib kicked in, organized labor in Personville [Hammett's name for Butte] was a used firecracker.[41]

Hammett somehow shoehorned 34 murders into the 140-page novel, eliminating characters with pistols, knives and explosives. But Hammett offered more than cynicism, violence and gore; he could tell a story and touch a reader, using spare and direct prose to transport them to places they had never visited. *Time* magazine included *Red Harvest* in its 100 Best English-Language Novels from 1923 to 2005, and author-critic André Gide called it "a remarkable achievement, the last word in atrocity, cynicism, and horror."[42]

The Op enters Personville, which has been owned for 40 years by an industrial capitalist: "Elihu Willson was Personville, and he was almost the whole state."[43] Willson controls Congressmen, city

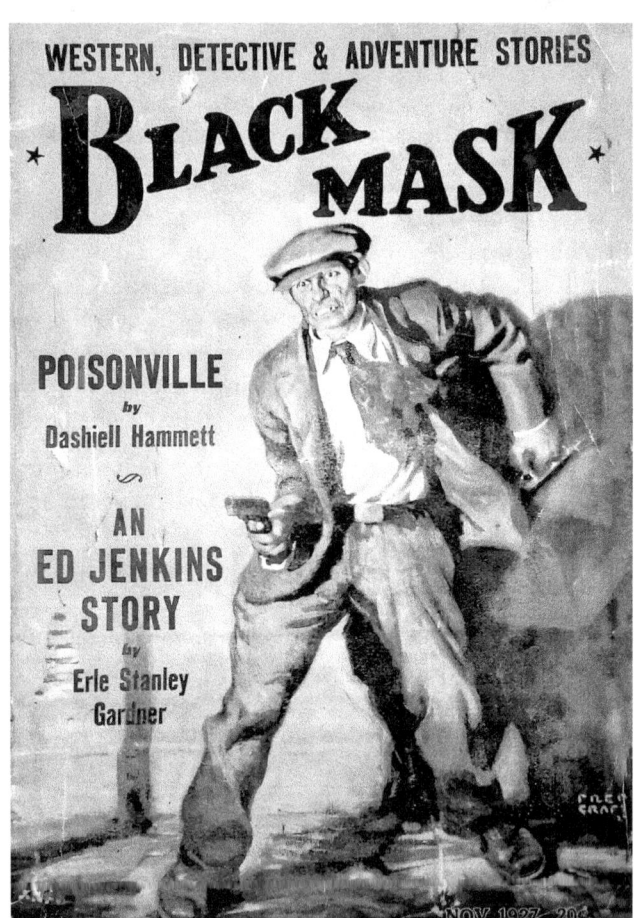

The opening installment of Hammett's very first novel *Red Dust* appeared in *Black Mask* in November 1927 under its original title: *Poisonville*. After two further installments, Hammett sold the rights for the novel to Knopf, where editors convinced him to come up with a new title.

officials and the police, but at the opening of the novel, his hold over the town is in jeopardy. To break a strike by the mineworkers, he called in thugs connected with the mob. After brutally suppressing the strike, the gangsters refused to leave and took over the town, occupying its offices and businesses. When the Continental Op arrives, an uneasy peace prevails in a thoroughly corrupt town, as rival gangster factions carve out their territory.

The police are bought off casually; they even supply getaway cars for criminals. At one point, thugs are let out of jail to commit a midday bank robbery; they later use their incarceration as an unimpeachable alibi. In short, the world of the novel is thoroughly and completely dishonest. As one critic noted, "In *Red Harvest* we never meet an honest businessman or an honest policeman, and the only lawyer is a blackmailer."

The Op cleans up Personville not by solving crimes but by muddying the waters, convincing criminals of each other's guilt, setting gangster against gangster, and letting them kill each other off. In the "real world" of Hammett's fiction, gangsters wield political power, people are not who they pretend to be, justice is not served, and "law and order" are polite fictions. "Cleaning up the town" becomes for the Op a euphemism for systematically eliminating its various players[44] by stratagems and lies and sending them all to Hell. But the violence and crime are so endemic, the rot so deep, that even the Op is corrupted, telling his passing love interest Dinah Brand near the end of the novel: "Poisonville is right. It's poisoned me."

But Personville is more than a stand-in for Butte, it stands as an analogy for America writ large, which Hammett saw as a moral cesspool which no hero, not even the Op, could clean up.

At first look, Hammett's fictional detective seems to fit in with this scheme. In all the Op stories, he remains nameless, simply "The Continental Operative," an agent wholly identified with his agency: "When I say me," he tells Elihu Willson, "I mean the Continental."[45] The Operative is simply his function, a worker, with "no commitment, personal or social, beyond the accomplishment of his job." Anna Kelly wrote in her Harvard thesis that in *Red Harvest*, "The Op's disillusionment with American society reaches a dramatic peak."[46]

But unlike the mostly hack writers who produced filler for the pulps and quickly cashed their checks, Hammett had higher aspirations. "I'm one of the few ... people moderately literate who take the detective story seriously," 33-year-old Dashiell Hammett wrote New York publisher Blanche Knopf in 1928, two years before the death of Sherlock Holmes creator Arthur Conan Doyle. "Some day somebody is going to make 'literature' of it ... and I'm selfish enough to have my hopes."[47]

The 1920s ushered in Prohibition and its attendant law-breaking as many thirsty Americans refused to give up alcohol and turned to the speakeasies and bathtub gin often proffered by organized crime and sometimes violent bootleggers. At the same time, President Warren Harding, busy impregnating his paramour Nan Britton in a White House closet,[48] chose corrupt cronies for his cabinet; they solicited bribes for public lands that culminated in the Teapot Dome Scandal. In a sense, the decay and corruption Hammett described in the Butte of *Red Harvest* was a microcosm of the political corruption in the nation at large. The carnage American boys had encountered in World War I trenches also affected the psyche of a nation. Given Hammett's emerging political consciousness, *Red Harvest* could also be read as a tale of capitalist exploitation and violence directed against the working class even as the capitalists, the criminals, devoured each other.

Hollywood picked up the novel, repackaged it as *Roadhouse Nights* and released it in 1930. They changed the characters and plot and turned it into a musical-comedy gangster movie, crediting the story to Ben Hecht (1893–1964), later famous for the films *Scarface, The Front Page* and *Gunga Din. Roadhouse Nights* did not make this illustrious list. It starred Helen Morgan, Fred Kohler and, in his film debut, Jimmy Durante. Nowhere in the credits was Hammett mentioned. He cashed his check and moved on.

However, Hammett was hitting his stride and money and fame followed—as did booze, broads and blackouts. In 1931, Paramount released *City Streets,* written for the screen by Hammett. The movie starred Gary Cooper in a rare gangster role with Sylvia Sidney as his love interest. Hammett cashed another check.

The Continental Op appeared as the first-person narrator in Hammett's second novel, *The Dain Curse,* serialized once again in *Black Mask* and then released as a stand-alone novel in 1929. This time Hammett mixed murder with drugs and a religious cult. His third and most famous novel, *The Maltese Falcon* (1930) introduced the iconic and ruthless detective Sam Spade, bearing Hammett's own first name, who lives by his own code of justice. *The New York Times* reviewer wrote, "If the locution 'hard-boiled' had not already been coined it would be necessary to coin it now to describe the characters of Dashiell Hammett's latest detective story."[49]

Hollywood outdid itself making three movies based on *The Maltese Falcon* in 1931, 1936 (retitled *Satan Met a Lady*) and in 1941, putting money in Hammett's pocket each time. The 1941 version, starring Humphrey Bogart and directed by John Huston (his directorial debut), is considered the gold standard for film noir. *Variety* wrote of the movie: "This is one of the best examples of actionful and suspenseful melodramatic story telling in cinematic form. Unfolding a most intriguing and entertaining murder mystery, the picture displays outstanding excellence in writing, direction, acting and editing—combining in overall as a prize package of entertainment for widest audience appeal."[50] The film garnered three Oscar nominations.

For Hammett and other writers, the 20th century private detective in film and novel took certain tropes from the popular Western of the previous century. Like the brave sheriff standing up for the law all alone while others slink away (think Gary Cooper in *High Noon*) or the stranger, new in town but drawn to help the law-abiding and ordinary citizens defenseless in the face of criminal forces (think Alan Ladd in *Shane*), the private detective risked life and limb for his own moral code, brave enough not to back down, and tough enough to prevail. Sam Spade epitomizes the lone protagonist standing out in an ethically murky and decadent society, sticking to his moral code, like Shane, but with an automatic instead of a revolver. "The core of Hammett's art is his version of the masculine figure in American society," wrote critic David T. Bazelon.[51] That tough, masculine figure stood alone, always brave, protective of women and children, and always prevailing against the forces of evil.

Or so it was until Hammett created Nick and Nora. While the Western mythological hero usually rode alone, some had sidekicks: the Cisco Kid with Pancho, the Lone Ranger with Tonto. None I can think of had a wife as his partner in adventures, excepting Grace Kelly to Gary Cooper in *High Noon*, and that didn't premiere until 1952. Hammett played around within an increasingly stereotyped and limited genre when he created Nora Charles to complement Nick in his very last novel.

Writing one novel after another, Hammett had the marketing formula down: Write a detective story, get it serialized in a monthly magazine, revise the story as a short novel, and then make a quick sale to Hollywood. A year after *The Maltese Falcon*, he followed this now familiar route with his fourth novel *The Glass Key*. This time the protagonist, Ned Beaumont, investigates a murder for a friend who just happens to be a crooked politician. Serialized in *Black Mask*, it appeared as a standalone best-selling novel (and birthed two film adaptations).

Dorothy Parker (1893–1967) wrote of both *The Glass Key* and *Red Harvest* in her *New Yorker* magazine review "Oh Look—Two Good Books":

> It seems to me that there is entirely too little screaming about the work of Dashiell Hammett. My own shrill yaps have been ascending ever since I first found *Red Harvest*, and from that day the man has been, God help him, my hero.… All I can say is that anybody who doesn't read him misses much of modern America.[52]

Hammett sold the *Glass Key* movie rights to Paramount for $25,000,[53] the equivalent of $373,000 in today's dollars. Hammett sent money, *some* money, *sometimes*, to his wife, Josie, and two little girls in Los Angeles. But after 1929 he was only intermittently a family man. When Hammett left California and family in 1929, he went to New York with his lover, writer Nell Martin. Martin (1890–1961) also wrote detective fiction—both novels and short stories. She sold her 1928 novel *Lord Byron of Broadway* to MGM, which made a film of it in 1930. Hammett's wife, abandoned and out of funds, appealed directly to Hammett's publisher Alfred Knopf in a heartbreaking letter dated 1932: "For past seven months Mr. Hammett has sent me only one hundred dollars.… I am desperate—the children need clothing and are not getting the right food–& I am unable to find work." In his reply to Josie Hammett, Knopf had to admit he didn't know the whereabouts of his bestselling author.[54] Growing up with an often absent dad, Hammett's younger daughter Jo wrote many years later about finding her parents' love letters: "My parents' romance didn't last long. They were together for less than eight years, but it's nice to be reminded as they started out as sweet and romantic, as playful and loving, as any couple anywhere."[55]

Some time in late 1930 or early 1931, a still married Hammett, 36, crossed paths with a married Lillian Hellman, 24, and so began a long, combustible relationship that left its mark on American letters and politics. Samuel Marx (1902–92), who oversaw Hellman's work as a $50-a-week reader at MGM, recalled her then as "a skinny, bony slip of a girl before our gaudy spree of the 1930s. She had rust colored bobbed hair and an unpretty face that was in a state of perpetual indignation about the human condition."[56] Marx soon had reason to regret hiring her: "She called on readers to strike for shorter hours and the organization of union. She made anti-capitalist speeches during lunch hours."[57] Marx, who may have borne the name of a historical anti-capitalist but who enjoyed his job and salary at MGM, soon fired her.

Hellman fell for Hammett on first sight, calling him "the most interesting man I ever met."[58] She described their first meeting: "We met … in a restaurant in Hollywood. The five-day drunk had left the wonderful face looking rumpled, and the very tall thin figure was tired and sagged. We talked of T.S. Eliot … and then we sat in his car and talked at each other and over each other until it was daylight."[59] They spent the next 30 years both together and then apart and together again as lovers, friends, partners, co-creators, emotional supporters and, sometimes, adversaries, critiquing each other's work and challenging each other to become better writers. Sometimes they cohabited and sometimes they went their separate ways but they never lessened their intimate contact. When drunk, Hammett could be "cruel, heartless, violent."[60] and, when sober, hard-working and intellectual. Hellman drank to keep up with him. She took female lovers and invited Hammett to join in or just watch.[61]

Hammett biographer Sally Cline often relied upon material presented by Hammett's daughter Josephine to tell her story. Josephine seems to have adored Hammett and despised Hellman. "Lillian," she wrote, "was the Boogie Man of my childhood."[62] At some point, Hammett suggested Hellman read William Roughead's *Bad Companions,* a collection of criminal case histories, and drew her attention to *Closed Doors, or The Great Drumsheugh Case,* the story of a lesbian scandal at a girls' school, as material for a good play. He had toyed with the idea himself but thought Hellman might do a better job of it.[63] Lesbian love, then taboo in practice and even conversation, became a theme of Hellman's first play *The Children's Hour,* on which Hammett collaborated. Hellman dedicated it to him, writing, "For D. Hammett with Thanks,"[64] Her later play *The Autumn Garden* is similarly dedicated: "For Dash."[65] Hellman later said in an interview: "I'm not at all sure I would have written without Hammett.... I had stopped writing.... It was he who teased me back into writing, baited me back into writing, And then watched for as long as he lived."[66]

He became her first reader and prime critic, and occasionally he rewrote some of her scenes. *The Children's Hour* ran for 691 performances on Broadway; it was banned in Boston, Chicago and London for its focus on lesbianism. The play secured Hellman's reputation and standing among America's greatest twentieth century playwrights.

In 1933, a civil suit caught up with Hammett and he had to pay out $2500 (over $50,000 in today's money) to actress Elise De Viane, who had accused him of sexual assault in 1931. The Associated Press reported that De Viane had been "bruised and battered in resisting the asserted fervid love making of Dashiell Hammett."[67] Hammett did not contest the accusation and lost the case without appearing in court.[68] By all accounts, Hammett could be a nasty drunk. At times, friends found him passed out in the gutter. He ran up bills at fancy stores and restaurants and failed to pay. He seems to have given away money to anyone who asked for it, and lost more money playing poker and betting on the ponies. Almost broke from boozing and partying, Hammett stopped drinking for a few months in 1933 to write his fifth and last novel, *The Thin Man.*

While writing *The Thin Man,* Hammett was holed up first at the swanky Hotel Pierre in Manhattan, then skipped out without paying his bill to take up residence at a cheaper hotel in midtown managed by Nathaniel West, who was then working on his own novel *Miss Lonelyhearts.* (West cooked the hotel books in order to offer his literary lodgers free or reduced rates.[69]) Said Hellman: "The locking-in time had come and nothing was allowed to disturb it until the book was finished. I had never seen anybody work that way: the care for every word, the pride in the neatness of the typed page itself. The refusal for ten days or two weeks to go out even for a walk for fear something would be lost."[70]

Hammett created a new kind of detective in Nick Charles: "drunk, famous, and accompanied usually by his charming (and rich) wife," in the words of one biographer.[71] Disappointment set in when his agent circulated the manuscript among the usual magazines and received a host of rejections because of its racy nature. Finally he sold it to *Redbook* for $5000[72] which included rights to censor it as they chose and to include it as a giveaway to new subscribers in the special year-end volume *Six Redbook Novels.* Knopf then brought it out, uncut, in January 1934, selling 34,000 books in the first 18 months;

on the jacket was a picture of dapper Hammett with his walking stick. Readers confused the tall and thin Hammett in the photo with the Thin Man of the title. MGM paid Hammett $21,000 for the film rights.[73] In the Hammett biography *Shadow Man*, Richard Layman estimates that Hammett earned over a million dollars off the novel, follow-up movies and radio shows between 1933 and 1950.[74] The novel stayed continuously in print to the present day, interrupted only for a few years by the McCarthy anti–Communist witch hunt which plunged Hammett into penury.

MGM released the movie version of *The Thin Man* in 1934. The movies kept coming: Universal bought a Hammett script titled *On the Make*, rewrote it and released it as *Mister Dynamite* in 1934. RKO brought out *Woman in the Dark* in 1934 from Hammett's same-name story. Paramount made versions of *The Glass Key* in 1935 and in 1942. For a time, Hammett enjoyed fame and fortune. Wrote Hellman:

> When I first met Dash he had written four of the five novels and was the hottest thing in Hollywood and New York ... [T]he ex-detective who had bad cuts on his legs and an indentation in his head from being scrappy with criminals was gentle in manner, well educated, elegant to look at, born of early settlers, was eccentric, witty, and spent so much money on women that they would have liked him even if he had been none of the good things.[75]

In all, Hollywood made 19 films from Hammett stories.

But in 1934 he stopped writing and went back to drinking. He was, in the words of Steven Marcus in his Introduction to *The Continental Op*, "casually self destructive."[76] His youngest daughter Jo, who never ceased loving him, felt that his recurrent bouts of illness had convinced him he would not live to enjoy old age. She wrote: "Tuberculosis marked and stiffened him. His illness caused him to conclude that it was useless to take good care of yourself."[77] And so he didn't.

Gertrude Stein wrote in her book *Everybody's Autobiography* that upon her return to America, she sought to meet two people, Charlie Chaplin and Dashiell Hammett. She wanted to meet Hammett, a man and a writer quite unlike herself, because she liked detective stories and "I liked somebody being dead and how it moves along and Dashiell Hammett was all that and more."[78] She had that right.

3

The *Thin Man* Movie

The great commercial success of Hammett's *Thin Man* novel and the controversy around its risqué content quickly attracted Hollywood's attention and MGM bought the film rights for $21,000. The studio pushed the film into production and it appeared in theaters the same year Knopf brought out the novel in standalone book form.

MGM hired the husband-and-wife screenwriting team of Albert Hackett and Frances Goodrich, who knocked out a shooting script in just three weeks. Then they put the project in the hands of veteran director Woodbridge Strong Van Dyke II, known in the business as "One-Take Woody" for his quick work behind the camera. Remarkably, Van Dyke filmed it in 18 days.[1] To film so quickly, "[Van Dyke] would have one set [already constructed] behind the camera and one in front of it. As soon as he finished shooting the scene in front of the camera, he would have the crew turn around and the cast change positions and shoot until that scene was finished while the other stage was being readied for yet the next scene."[2] Van Dyke had to talk MGM studio boss Louis Mayer into making the picture. Then, having gotten Mayer's reluctant okay on what he (Mayer) considered a potential B picture at best, Van Dyke had to work quickly.

The movie cost $231,000 to make and returned MGM a profit of $729,000. By comparison, *Manhattan Melodrama*, released the same year and also starring Powell and Loy, took 24 days to shoot and made a profit of $415,000.[3] Some film critics said Van Dyke worked so fast to catch the freshness of the first take on screen while others said he simply "had no time for perfection."[4] Certainly his quick work and cost-cutting endeared him to his boss Mayer and to Mayer's boss Marcus Loew. Contrast this *Thin Man* shooting schedule with the usual shooting schedule of a Hollywood movie in 2018 of 106 days.[5] Or the 56 weeks Stanley Kubrick took in 1980, with his taste for as many as 127 takes for a single scene, in *The Shining*.[6]

All the filming was done on the MGM stages and back lot, expending no money on location shooting. Studio management didn't consider the film a major movie event for the year and assigned it a B film budget and schedule. In fact, MGM worried about the success of the entire project. Samuel Marx, head of MGM's story department, had brought *The Thin Man* to Van Dyke. Marx said: "I'd bought this sprightly detective story … and we had no idea if this kind of comedy would go. It had two unprecedented elements … they were having fun with murder, and they were a married couple who acted with total sophistication … [T]he matrimonial combination … even that was a risk, because in those days you got married at the end of the movie, not at the beginning. Marriage wasn't supposed to be fun."[7]

Once MGM realized they had a winner, they moved quickly to schedule bigger-budget sequels. Loath to tamper with a winning formula, they brought back

On the set of *The Thin Man*, director W.S. Van Dyke gives instructions to Myrna Loy and William Powell as cinematographer James Wong Howe stands by his camera. More crew members are in the background, preparing to film the penultimate scene which gathers the suspects and reveals the murderer (MovieStillsDB.com).

the lead actors for all five sequels. Each sequel feels like a return of old friends. Hammett enjoyed the *Thin Man* movie and its success: "They made a pretty funny picture out of [the *Thin Man* novel] and it seems to be doing good business wherever it is shown."[8]

The film deviates from the novel in numerous notable aspects. Some script changes improve the storytelling but others lose the striking originality of the novel. Overall, the novel has its rougher edges smoothed down, its violence muted, and its raw sexuality excised. The changes begin in the very first moments of the script. In the movie we actually see Clyde Wynant, who never appeared in the novel, at work in his shop. He is developing some weird electrical apparatus fitted out with electrodes and flashing lights, which is never identified or explained but simply offered as a visual mark of his work as an inventor. A workman interrupts him, causing the whole experiment to fizzle. Then his daughter Dorothy enters, but rather than the unbalanced woman of the novel, partying in speakeasies with various young beau including a married man, she is quite prim and proper and trailed by her respectable fiancé, Tom. She wrings from her father a promise to attend their wedding, scheduled for December 30. Wynant reveals he is leaving town but promises Dorothy to return by Christmas. As Dorothy and Tom leave, lawyer Macaulay arrives. He tries and fails to get Wynant to tell him where he is going. Wynant leaves Macaulay in charge of his affairs in his absence.

Wynant takes the elevator from his basement shop upstairs to his office to check his safe for the wedding present he intends for Dorothy. He finds the safe empty; $50,000 worth of government bonds are gone. Working nearby, Wynant's assistant Tanner (a character not in the novel) suggests that Julia Wolf has taken them. When Wynant visits Julia in her apartment, he encounters the small-time gangster Morelli having a drink with her. Wynant gets angry and Julia sends Morelli on his way. The script describes Julia as a pretty tough customer herself: "She is in very elaborate lounging pajamas, her hair is too well waved, her nails too red, her eyebrows too delicately arched. But she has the look of a hard businesswoman underneath it all."[9]

When Wynant threatens to call the police about the missing bonds, Julia confesses to taking them. She claims to only have $25,000 and so Wynant suspects an accomplice has the other half. While they argue, Julia receives a call from Nunheim, who hangs up as soon as Wynant answers the phone. Wynant claims to know who the accomplice is but doesn't name him. Julia asks him what he plans to do. Wynant goes to the door, turns with a "terrifying smile"[10] and exits without answering. In the next shot: "Wynant strides down the street, his long, lean, narrow form casting a long shadow on the snowy pavement. THE CAMERA HOLDS IN A RUNNING SHOT ON THE SHADOW as it elongates still further, and finally disappears."[11]

All of these opening scenes are original to the film. They work well and quickly set the stage for the action to come. In the film, we get to see Wynant, who never appears in the novel. We see him as an inventor, doing "inventor type" experiments; we see him as a father to Dorothy, and as a lover to Julia. We understand the motive for any foul play to come: the stolen bonds. We meet suspects Tanner, Macaulay, Morelli, Julia, Nunheim, Dorothy and Wynant himself. Finally we see how this story got its title as Wynant's shadow elongates longer and longer in the snow. Wynant, not Hammett, nor Nick Charles, is the true Thin Man.

To this point, we see and expect a typical detective film noir. The brief scenes have sketched out suspicious characters and criminal motivations. But then the film upends our expectations and takes us to Nick and Nora. At the very beginning of the novel, but now several minutes into the movie, we enter a well-lighted and noisy speakeasy decked out for the Christmas season. Nick stands behind the bar, tipsy, his speech sometimes slurred, and in dialogue not found in the novel, he instructs the bartenders on how best to make a martini: "The important thing is the rhythm. Always have rhythm in your shaking. Now, a Manhattan you shake to fox-trot time, a Bronx [a gin cocktail with orange juice] to two-step time, a dry martini you always shake to waltz time."[12] Hard to believe, but this bit of business was improvised. According to director Van Dyke's biographer Robert C. Cannom, Van Dyke told Powell, "Bill take this cocktail shaker ... go behind the bar ... and just walk through the opening scene. I want to check sound and light before we make a take."

> Bill stepped behind the bar, the other members of the cast took their places, and one of the most beautiful ad libs ever enacted came off perfectly. "That's it!" Van Dyke said, as he snapped his fingers. "Print that." William Powell turned, "What did you say?" "Print it," Van Dyke repeated. "Do you mean to tell me you shot that scene?" "I sure did, and it was the best take you ever made, you big stiff."[13]

As Nick teaches a course in mixology, Dorothy spots Nick from across the room and goes to introduce herself and her fiancée. She tells Nick that her father is missing and Nick suggests she call his lawyer Macaulay and gives her a nickel for the call. Then

At a speakeasy, Nick and Nora encounter Dorothy Wynant (Maureen O'Sullivan, right). Her request for Nick to find her missing father Clyde Wynant (the "Thin Man" of the title) sets the action into motion.

Nora enters the bar, dragged by Asta. In the novel we read "Asta jumped up and punched me in the belly."[14] The movie greatly embellishes this scene and plays it for all it's worth. We see Nora enter the bar balancing a high pile of Christmas gift boxes, a pile so high we cannot see her face. As Asta yanks on his leash, the boxes fall and Nora, wealthy and well-bred, falls face first onto the barroom floor. To get the shot, Van Dyke put a camera on the floor and a mark where he wanted her to land. Loy said: "We shot it without any rehearsal. I must have been crazy. I could have killed myself, but my dance training paid off."[15]

The restaurant majordomo rushes forward to Nora to inform her that dogs are not allowed. Nick calms him: "It's all right, Joe. It's my dog…" Then, as an afterthought, he waves his hand at Nora. "And my wife."

Nora: "You might have mentioned me first."[16]

At this moment, we know this will not be a typical detective film. Nick orders Nora a martini and when she asks him how many he's had, he says he's on his sixth. Nora quickly asks the waiter to line up six martinis for her so she can catch up. Of course, Nora wonders about Dorothy:

> **Nora:** "Who is she?"
> **Nick:** "Oh, darling, I was hoping I wouldn't have to answer that."
> **Nora:** "Come on."

NICK: "Well, Dorothy is really my daughter. You see, it was spring in Venice and I was so young, I didn't know what I was doing. We're all like that on my father's side."
NORA: "By the way, how is your father's side?"
NICK: "Oh, it's much better, thanks. And yours?"[17]

The next scene takes place the following morning. Nora is in bed in their hotel suite with a hangover. Nick applies an ice pack to her throbbing head. She tries to get out of bed and slips back down. She asks Nick, "Hey, what's the idea of pushing me?" We see that Nick hasn't touched her.

Van Dyke, happily married himself, said he had chosen to film *The Thin Man* because of the teasing, loving Nick-Nora marital relationship. He told screenwriters Goodrich and Hackett, "I don't care anything about the mystery stuff—just give me five scenes between Nick and Nora."[18] Van Dyke saw the novelty of the relationship: "There had been so many stories, novels, and screenplays about puppy love that audiences sickened of the overdose. Romances among mature people are as old as the universe itself, but apparently they had been obscured by the petting parties of flaming youth on the screen."[19]

Nick, age 41, and Nora, age 27, and married for four years, carry the story from beginning to end. Beneath the banter and teasing, we also see the love. As Nick heads out to investigate a murder:

NORA: "Take care of yourself."
NICK: "Why, sure I will."
NORA: "Don't say it like that! Say it as if you meant it!"
NICK: "Well, I do believe the little woman cares."
NORA: "I don't care! It's just that I'm used to you, that's all."[20]

To fully appreciate the innovative impact the movie makes on the detective film genre, step back one year to 1933 when Warner Brothers released *The Kennel Murder Case*. William Powell stars in that movie also, his fourth in the long series of Philo Vance films based on the S.S. Van Dine series of detective novels. Also present is Mary Astor, who will reappear eight years later opposite Humphrey Bogart in *The Maltese Falcon*. Oddly enough, in *The Kennel Murder Case* we first encounter Powell's Vance at a Long Island Kennel Club event showing his prize black Scottish Terrier, MacTavish, who prefigures the unnamed black Scotty who cuckolds Asta in *After the Thin Man*; and some of the wire-haired terriers at the dog show look a lot like Asta. Here the films' similarities end. Though there are two murders and a cast full of suspects, the emphasis is not on the people and their personalities and relationships, it's on the clues: the murder weapons (gun, knife, fireplace poker), the puzzle of how a dead body in a locked room could indicate murder and not suicide. In fact, we learn little about the characters at all and little about Philo Vance either.

Powell has Vance's foppish accouterments from the novels: white gloves, cane, flower in his jacket buttonhole. But he seems without personality. He does not drink, though he joins everyone else in smoking up a storm, and he does not joke. He makes a single reference to "psychology," the supposed Vance superpower, when he suggests "psychology" indicates that dead man Archer Coe would not commit suicide. By this we suppose he means that a cold, patronizing, abrupt and all-around nasty man like Coe directs his violence outward rather than inwards as suicide. I know about as much psychology as Philo Vance and this just doesn't hold water. For example, we know nothing of the stresses Coe may have been facing: financial setbacks, the end of an intimate relationship, feelings of guilt for past misdeeds, etc., all of which might lead someone to contemplate self-harm.

Rather, Vance solves the crime the traditional Sherlock Holmes way, like an intricate puzzle. When the movie ends, you feel cheated in the sense that nothing has changed, you haven't learned anything, and you still don't know these people you've spent 73 minutes with. The film has a mind but not a heart. Vance's only semi-friendly relationship is with detective Heath (Eugene Pallette) and even here, Vance merely invites us to patronize the self-aggrandizing policeman. They have one decent bit of funny dialogue:

> **PHILO VANCE:** "What do you think of the suicide theory now, sergeant?"
> **HEATH:** "Well, it's slightly complicated since the man shot, slugged and stabbed himself—especially in the back."[21]

But, overall, Vance comes across as your soft-boiled detective. One year later, in *The Thin Man*, Powell is back and with the same pencil mustache but now his Nick Charles has a heart, a wife, a drinking problem and, when we forget the intricacies of the mystery, we will always remember the personalities on the screen.

Notably absent from the film version of *The Thin Man* are many of the novel's details. There is no scene in Studsy's speakeasy where tough guys save Nick from a fight. No one orders a cannibal sandwich, there is no story of Albert Packer and cannibalism. No one mentions Nick's Greek ethnicity. There is no talk of a past relationship for Nick and Mimi, no attempt by Mimi to seduce Nick, no physical tussle between the two of them and no talk of an "erection."

Major scenes, original to the movie, are added: Nick actually goes to Wynant's shop and discovers his body after Asta starts digging at the fresh cement covering his grave. "Asta," Nick tells him, "you're not a terrier, you're a police dog."[22] Asta gets much more to do in the movie than in the novel. At times Hammett seemed to forget all about the dog but Van Dyke milked all the cuteness he could from the cuddly terrier who replaced Hammett's depiction of Asta as a Schnauzer. In the novel, Asta is female; in the movie, Asta is male. In the film, Asta sits up, runs in circles, and is alternately brave and cowardly in the face of danger. At one point, Nick tells a crook: "Don't make a move or that dog will tear you to shreds." At those words, we see Asta run out of the room and hide under the bed. As Nick heads out to search Wynant's shop, Nora tells Asta, "If you let anything happen to him, you'll never wag that tail again."[23] The film launched a career for Skippy, the canine actor portraying Asta, and a national craze for wire-haired terriers made him even more popular than President Roosevelt's Fala, a Scottie.

The movie's central party scene, a ten-minute take in a film of otherwise briefer scenes, is a visual and audio knockout as all kinds of folks invade the Charleses' hotel suite for a Christmas Eve gala. Some are members of Wynant's family but the majority are people Nick once had a hand in jailing, cops, a boxer as well as folks who just wandered in to party. The action occurs simultaneously across multiple rooms. Nick welcomes one guest at the door, saying: "Shed the chapeau. Divest yourself of raiment and join the Yuletide revelers."[24] Nora, seeing the suite filling up, calls room service: "Send me up a whole flock of sandwiches."[25] Nora instructs one waiter: "Waiter, will you serve the nuts? I mean, will you serve the guests the nuts?"[26] As the party ends and drunken

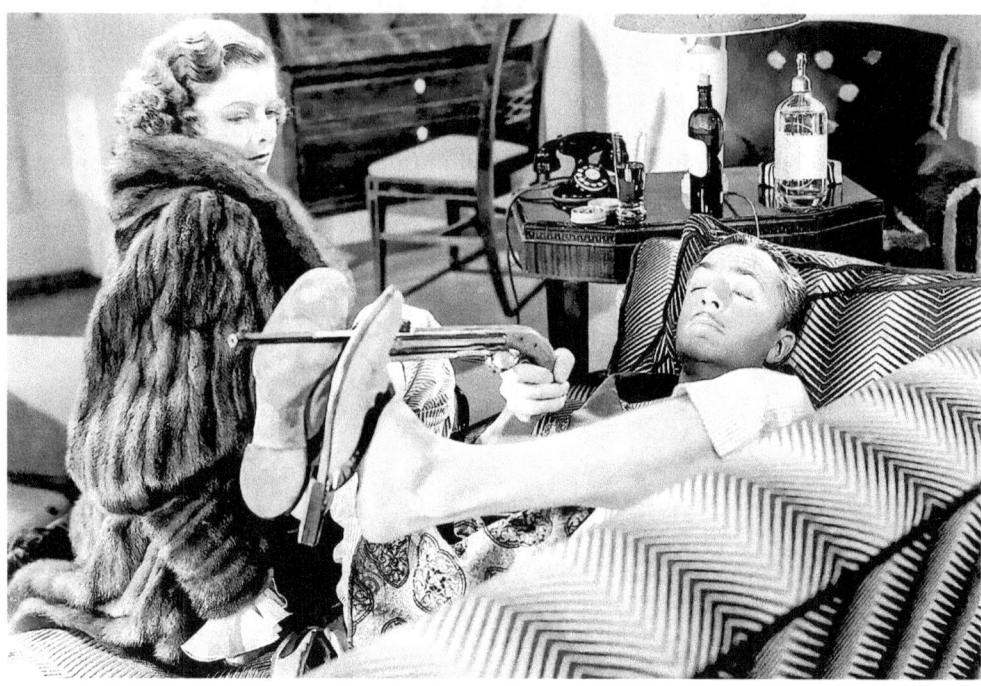

When director Van Dyke saw William Powell killing time between takes with a BB gun, trying to knock ornaments off the Christmas tree on the set, he had the actor recreate his actions in this scene in the film.

revelers sing carols, Nora says to Nick: "Oh, Nicky, I love you because you know such lovely people."[27] And we fall in love with both of them.

Also original to the movie is a penultimate big scene with all the suspects invited to dinner. Policemen in waiters' uniforms have to be reminded to hide their guns in their aprons as Nick prepares to unmask the killer. The setup allows Nick to build suspense and announce to the assembled company: "The murderer is in this room. Sitting at this table. You may serve the fish."[28] The waiters serve the company oysters, and here Van Dyke's usual directing speed let everyone down. According to Myrna Loy, the oysters were real and reused for take after take: "They wouldn't bring fresh ones, and under the lights, as shooting wore on, they began to putrefy. By the time we finished the scene, nobody ever wanted to see another oyster."[29]

After Nick fingers the killer, the film brings our focus back to the loving couple at its heart. In the final scene, Nick and Nora share dinner on a railroad car with newly married Tom and Dorothy, and then adjourn to their private sleeping car. Nora suggests Asta sleep in the lower berth with her. But Nick says, "Oh, yeah?" and tosses Asta into the top berth. The film fades out as Asta covers his eyes with his paws. We get the picture.[30]

The movie, like the novel, treats alcoholism as an amusing foible. Alcohol can be subversive (literally and symbolically) when it accompanies and allows sexual freedom and liberation from old norms and customs. In this last year of Prohibition, there were speakeasies (columnist Walter Winchell called them "upholstered sewers"[31]) on every corner of New York City. MGM's story editor Samuel Marx noted: "Nightclubs flourished although Prohibition authorities raided them and padlocked them regularly....

A padlocked club simply moved a few doors down the street and reopened the next night. The customers followed."[32] In speakeasies and hotel suites, Nick keeps drinking and Nora struggles to keep up. When Nora asks Nick to pass her drink to her, Nick asks, "What are you drinking?" Nora: "Rye." Nick picks up her glass and drains it, "Yes," he says, "that's rye," as he hands her the now empty glass.[33] Here the adventures of a functioning alcoholic are played for laughs. "What hit me?" Nora asks as she wakes up with a hangover.

"The last martini. How 'bout a pick-me-up?" asks Nick with drink in hand.

"No!" exclaims Nora.[34]

And when a reporter asks Nick, "Can't you tell us anything about the case?" he replies: "Yes. It's putting me way behind in my drinking."[35]

Life imitated art. Woody Van Dyke directed some 90 films, most of them for MGM, over a 25-year career and, according to one crew member, "Van Dyke came to work with a flask of gin in his pocket, from which he regularly sipped and which would be refilled a few times during the day."[36] Samuel Marx remembered, "Van Dyke enjoyed gin for breakfast and suffered miserably [on location] in Tahiti and Africa when forced to imbibe warm martinis."[37]

There was a lot less on-screen drinking in the *Thin Man* sequels, even one (*The Thin Man Goes Home*) in which Nick goes on the wagon and fills his flask with nothing stronger than apple cider.

Like the novel it is based on, *The Thin Man* does not send its characters on a personal journey from ignorance to knowledge. The static nature of the two main characters may have been what caused their creator to call them "smug" in a letter to Lillian Hellman. Nick and Nora have no desire to change and, more importantly, Hammett and screenwriters Frances Goodrich and Albert Hackett do not provide any plot points or personal crises to force them to change. They simply are a couple suspended in space and time, as things happen around them. Consider another Powell-Loy vehicle, *Double Wedding* (1937), directed by Richard Thorpe. Jo Swerling wrote the screenplay of this forgettable comedy in which opposites attract and, after a series of misadventures and misunderstandings, get married. It paired Powell and Loy as co-stars for the seventh of their 14 movies together. Powell plays a bohemian artist named Charles. We know he is a bohemian artist because he wears a French beret and an unflattering horizontally striped shirt reminiscent of a Venetian gondolier. Loy plays Margit, a hard-driving, no-nonsense businesswoman. We know this because her blouses and dresses all button up to her chin. Each would seem to have no interest in the other if not for the indefinable, unpredictable, cinematic value of love. How can they wind up together by movie's end? Each must change to get what he or she wants. Charles gets a little more respectable and loses the beret and Margit loosens up a bit and unbuttons a few buttons. By the end of the movie, they are not only together but they are not the same people they were at the beginning. Nick and Nora, however, simply go on, unchanged, by all the tumult surrounding them.

Double Wedding may be forgotten today but *The Thin Man* is not. Some iconic actors identify with specific roles and we can't imagine another in their place: Sean Connery as James Bond, Clark Gable as Rhett Butler, Audrey Hepburn as Holly Golightly … and William Powell as Nick and Myrna Loy as Nora. As director Van Dyke said in explaining the success of the characters on screen: "They played [Nick and Nora] beautifully, because Powell was just Powell and Loy was just Loy, both of them wisecracking all the time and clowning right through the picture."[38] You can see the fun between takes bleed into the movie. The dialogue sparkles:

> NICK: "[If something happens to me] you wouldn't be a widow for long."
> NORA: "You bet I wouldn't."
> NICK: "Not with all your money."[39]

Or Nick's line to an armed gangster: "Hey, would you mind putting that gun away? My wife doesn't care, but I'm a very timid fellow."[40]

Sometimes Hackett and Goodrich take lines from the novel and expand them into a joke. In the novel, when detective Guild discovers an old pistol Dorothy left in the Charleses' hotel suite, he asks: "You heard of the Sullivan Act?" Nick responds: "Yes."[41] But in the movie, Guild asks: "Haven't you two ever heard of the Sullivan Act?" Nora responds, "That's okay, we're married."[42] The joke here is that the Sullivan Act covered illegal possession of guns, while the Mann Act covered illegal transportation of an underage person across state lines for sexual purposes. It's a sophisticated joke.

The women do a little better here than in the novel. Mimi, Julia and Miriam are still conniving and double-dealing vixens but Dorothy has been redeemed. In the novel, she's a neurotic member of the Wynant stable of nutcases; in the movie, she's a woman of stable mental faculties. Nora stars in both novel and movie as a strong woman who can hold her own with any man. At one point, Nick tricks her into a taxi which he dispatches to Grant's Tomb to keep her out of his investigations. When she later returns, he asks: "How'd you like Grant's Tomb?" "It's lovely," she replies. "I'm having a copy made for you."

She is not intimidated. In bed at the end of one active day of murder and mayhem, she asks:

> NORA: "Nick? Nicky?"
> NICK: "What?"
> NORA: "You asleep?"
> NICK: "Yes!"
> NORA: "Good. I want to talk to you."[43]

A scene of Nora doing some sleuthing on her own (searching a warehouse dressed as a man) wound up on the cutting room floor.

Hammett's novel contained no black characters with speaking parts; the only one even mentioned is dismissed with a racial slur. The movie omits the "N" word but also omits all black people; all people of color, for that matter. There are none on the streets of Manhattan (shot on the MGM back lots), none among the pedestrians we see on the sidewalks behind the main action. Black people, Latinx, Asians, etc., have simply been erased. This troubled Loy: "I once asked, 'Why does every Negro in film have to play a servant? How about just a black person walking up the steps of a courthouse carrying a briefcase?' Well! The storm that caused. That was in the early 1930s. But later in the decade, Hollywood began to acknowledge the rest of the world, mainly through the efforts of transplanted New Yorkers."[44]

Reviewers of *The Thin Man* raved, each in their own way. *The Hollywood Reporter* called it

> [a] smart honey, a sophisticated wow. A murder story with a brilliant cast, a brilliant script, brilliant direction, and photography that tells the story in no mean terms. Don't spare the

enthusiasm on this one because if the book had thousands of readers, this picture will have millions of customers—well satisfied and with that well-fed look.[45]

New York Times film reviewer Mordaunt Hall called it

> an excellent combination of comedy and excitement. It is another of those murder mysteries wherein the astute criminologist has many opportunities to chuckle over the work of the police and, as usual, it is virtually impossible for the onlooker to pick out the murderer.[46]

Looking back 65 years after its premiere, Roger Ebert put the film in context: "For audiences in the middle of the Depression, *The Thin Man*, like the Astaire and Rogers musicals it visually resembles, was pure escapism: Beautiful people in expensive surroundings make small talk all the day long, without a care in the world, and even murder is only an amusing diversion."[47] The film garnered Oscar nominations for Best Picture, Best Director, Best Screenplay and Best Actor (Powell), but all four went instead to *It Happened One Night*, directed by Frank Capra and starring Clark Gable.

Success led to both repetition and imitation. As Samuel Marx noted that the film "had a chemistry that came out of Myrna Loy and William Powell, plus the characters of Nick and Nora Charles. It was automatic that you would now continue to put them together. The reactions are so great and it never stopped."[48] The film made national stars of Powell, Myrna Loy and even Asta. It raised Dashiell Hammett's profile and made him feel at home among the Hollywood celebrities. He wrote to Hellman: "I'm still surprised at the fuss the *The Thin Man* made out here. People bring the Joan Crawfords and Gables over to meet me instead of vice versa. Hot-cha!"[49] Hammett hit the party circuit and he drank. He woke up in mansions and, sometimes, in gutters, and drank some more. *The Thin Man* with its film sequels and later radio and TV spinoffs earned him millions. He wrote very little ever again.

In the early 1930s, an astounding 90,000,000 people a week went to the movies.[50] Tickets at America's 23,000 movie theaters cost just 25 cents in 1933.[51] MGM had budgeted *The Thin Man* as a B picture but when it returned three times its investment, Louis B. Mayer decided to take the sequel to a new level. Director Van Dyke, screenwriters Goodrich and Hackett, and actors Powell, Loy and Skippy all reenlisted for the next film and MGM put Hammett on the payroll for a new story in the emerging franchise.

The studio that produced *The Thin Man* and the franchise it spawned was Metro-Goldwyn-Mayer. But the effort required broad collaboration from politically radical writers like Hammett, Hellman and Dorothy Parker, to conservative stalwarts like Louis B. Mayer, director Van Dyke, and producer Irving Thalberg, assuring a decades-long success of ticket sales as well as a decades-long clash of politics, fortunes and egos. Founded in 1924, Metro-Goldwyn-Mayer grew into one of Hollywood's biggest studios. In 1934, the year of the first *Thin Man* release, MGM had 4000 studio employees, including 61 stars and featured players, 17 directors and 51 writers under contract.[52] Wrote Hollywood historian John Baxter: "Greatest of all the studios was Metro-Goldwyn-Mayer. It was the richest, the biggest, the most productive…. At its peak, the twenty-two stages of Metro and its hundred-acre back lot of standing sets produced forty-two feature films a year, the biggest output of any studio in the history of cinema."[53] When you sat down in a Loew's theater to see an MGM film, you knew what to expect: a quality entertainment in a clean and modern movie house, all for your 25 cent ticket. You settled into your seat with your popcorn and soda in expectation of a full afternoon or evening of entertainment. Illustrator and caricaturist Edward Sorel, born Edward Schwartz in 1929 and, happily, still with us, described what he saw when he went to the movies in the late 1930s: "Sunday matinees included a newsreel, a Bugs Bunny, a chapter of Dick Tracy, two movies, and at least one Laurel and Hardy short."[54] Hollywood churned out some 800 feature films each year in the '30s.

At Hollywood premieres, there might be dancing girls, comics and celebrities. Myrna Loy got her start dancing before shows at Grauman's Egyptian Theater. Further afield, in Minneapolis or Chicago or Tulsa, MGM stars like Harlow or Gable would come on stage for a brief appearance before one of their new films. Every MGM film started the same way: a lion would appear on screen and roar at you. Leo the Lion faced out through the MGM logo *Ars Gratis Artis,* a Latin mistranslation of the phrase "Art for Art's Sake."

Even the lion was an actor and his fierce roar a fraud, all part of Hollywood artifice. The first Leo, played by a tame African lion named Slats (1916–24), looked from side to side but, this being silent films, his roar went unheard. His best-known successor, Jackie, born wild in the Sudan and the star of 100 films including some Tarzan movies with Johnny Weissmuller, took over as Leo in 1928. With the advent of talkies, we heard him roar three times before each film. For whatever reason, Jackie looked fierce but didn't have a great roar; three different lions had to be recorded to get the famous three-part roar.[55] Though Jackie died in 1935 at age 20, his face and sound continued on MGM films through 1956. Six other lions have succeeded Jackie since then.

The motto accompanying Leo on screen, *Ars Gratis Artis,* might have more aptly, though less high-mindedly, stood for "Art for Money's Sake." Baxter calls MGM "the film-making machine par excellence."[56] In fact, the studios for all their talk of art and glamorous adornments, featuring celebrity lifestyles, made a product much like any other factory, a product like sausages or canned peas. In the case of the studios, the product was movies, and this product was sent out to the distribution points, the 18,000 Loew's theaters where the cinematic products were purchased by millions of consumers. Sometimes, almost by accident, they made art.

Each of the large studios was founded and run by Eastern European or Russian-Jewish immigrants who climbed out of poverty and became fabulously wealthy even as the country struggled through the decade of the Depression. Carl Laemmle came from Germany without family or friends and founded Universal Pictures. Adolph Zukor arrived alone and an orphan from Hungary and founded Paramount Pictures. Another Hungarian immigrant, William Fox, founded the Fox Film Corporation. Born in New York City, Harry Cohn, a child of Jewish immigrants, created Columbia Pictures. Harry, Sam, Albert and Jack, sons of a Polish peddler, founded Warner Brothers and Louis B. Mayer, born in Czarist Russia in what is now Belarus and raised in poverty in Canada, rose to helm MGM.

Their success from immigrant and ethnic beginnings is really quite extraordinary, as is their concentration in a single American industry. In his book *An Empire of Their Own*, Neal Gabler focused on this phenomenon:

> The storefront theaters of the late teens were transformed into movie palaces by Jewish exhibitors. ... Hollywood was invaded by a battalion of Jewish writers ... the most powerful talent agencies were run by Jews. Jewish lawyers transacted most of the industry's business and Jewish doctors ministered to the industry's sick. Above all, Jews produced the movies.[57]

The explanation, I believe, is twofold: Anti-Semitism kept ambitious Jews out of the best universities, the finest medical schools, the prestigious law firms, etc., so they had to create their own opportunities; and, like most immigrant groups throughout our history, Jews sought work other groups wouldn't take and then, like immigrant groups before and after them, some few worked themselves up to pinnacles of power and wealth. Blinded by the bright lights of a thousand movie sound stages, we might think the cinema attracted hordes of would-be strivers. Not in the beginning. In fact, film at its birth, like theater, vaudeville and burlesque before it, was deemed a disreputable field. Who else would work there but those who had few other choices? Gabler also points out the downside to this industry-wide success that eventually brought high salaries, mansions and political power: "Their dominance became a target for wave after wave of vicious anti-semites—from fire and brimstone evangelicals ... to Red-baiters ... for whom Judaism was really a variety of communism and the movies their chief form of propaganda."[58]

At that time, Jews were excluded from all the county clubs and gentlemen's clubs, and kept out of law firms. When they succeeded in the motion picture field, even their success was held against them. The raving anti–Semite Henry Ford took time away from his Model T assembly plants to buy and run his own newspaper, *The Dearborn Independent*. While the paper covered some world events as well as business and economic news, its *raison d'être* was to spew ethnic and religious hate. The paper attacked Jews in every walk of life as un–American, money-grubbing racial inferiors. In 1921, the paper turned its eyes on the nascent movie industry: "As soon as the Jews gained control of the movies, we had a movie problem.... It is the genius of that race to create problems of a moral character in whatever business they achieve a majority."[59]

MGM head honcho Louis B. Mayer threw a 61st birthday party for Lionel Barrymore (behind cake, flanked by Norma Shearer, left, and Rosalind Russell). Standing behind them, from left, are Mickey Rooney, Robert Montgomery, Clark Gable, Mayer, William Powell and Robert Taylor (Wikimedia Commons).

Ironically, these Jewish immigrants desperately wanted to be accepted as Americans by their Gentile peers in business and society. To do so, Jewish men (and they were overwhelmingly men) made films in Hollywood extolling American virtues for sale to Midwestern Protestant audiences. Louis B. Mayer went so far as to declare that he did not know his birthdate and adopted the birthday of his adopted country, July 4, as his own. Independence Day became a huge annual bash at MGM so studio employees could party and simultaneously honor both America and Mayer.

Not surprisingly, Mayer's favorite films were the 16 movies of the Andy Hardy series MGM produced from 1937 to 1958, all starring Mickey Rooney and sentimentalizing middle class, midwestern, rural and white American values. Who but outsiders could make such movies idealizing a heartwarming family life that existed only in nostalgic fantasy? Decades later, Loew's Corporation attorney Louis Nizer made an insightful point: "The motion picture industry grew up in the hands of unsophisticated people, untrained men who had no background as scholars or in the arts, yet they founded a new art form. That to me is the great surprise."[60]

The *Thin Man* films focus our inquiry among all the Hollywood studios on MGM and Mayer (1884–1957). Born Lazar Meir, Mayer immigrated from Russia as a child and grew up poor in St. John, New Brunswick, Canada, starting work as a junkman to support his family. At age 12 he quit school, a decision he regretted all his life, saying he should have quit at ten so that everyone would not have gotten a head start on him.[61] He was a go-getter who started from nothing. When he moved from Canada to Boston to sell scrap metal, he didn't "have the price of a sandwich"[62] and that was when a sandwich cost just five cents.[63] But somehow Mayer saw the future in film, borrowed money and converted a burlesque house in Haverhill, Massachusetts, into a movie theater.

Building on that success, he concentrated on getting films out to the smaller New England towns that other distributors had neglected. He made his first real money distributing *The Birth of a Nation* in New England. *Birth of a Nation* is one of the most racist movies ever made in America. When I showed it to my film class, these college students, mostly Mexican-Americans, were horrified at its glorification of violence against black people.

With his growing nest egg and lots of borrowed dollars, Mayer bought and refurbished several Boston theaters. To control his supply chain, he started his own film distribution company. When World War I broke out in 1914 and Europe descended into the bloody mayhem of trench warfare, the conflict had another consequence: As the European powers redirected their manufacturing efforts into war production, they had less money to invest in making movies. This interrupted the flow of the European movies American theaters had come to rely on. Mayer, like other entrepreneurs, now moved into film production to fill the void. He decamped to Los Angeles in 1918 and founded his studio, Mayer Productions, but soon got swallowed up by an even bigger fish.

That bigger fish was Marcus Loew (1870–1927), born in New York into a poor family of Jewish-Austrian immigrants. Loew quit school at age nine and went to work in a printing shop for 35 cents a day.[64] He followed the same route as Mayer but with even greater success: buying vaudeville houses and converting them to movie theaters, combining live vaudeville shows with motion pictures and undercutting the competition with an admission price of just five cents. He moved on to renovating and building huge movie temples that could seat 3500 people. His Times Square theater, Loew's State, opened in 1921 and was the jewel in the crown, featuring marble floors and walls of

Travertine stone with Sienna marble columns supporting a marble balustrade.[65] At his death, he owned 128 theaters. He too saw the need to control production, buying Metro Pictures in 1919 and Goldwyn Pictures and Mayer Productions in 1924. He merged the three into Metro-Goldwyn-Mayer. Impressed with Mayer's drive and ambition, he put Mayer in charge of the new studio, never getting involved in movie production himself. The Loews Corporation continued to grow and expand into other industries and eventually owned 124 subsidiary companies, of which MGM was merely one; "a multi-billion dollar concern with headquarters in Times Square."[66] When he died unexpectedly in 1927, his obituary on the front page of *Variety* called him "the outstanding individual figure of the amusement industries of all times—substantially, sentimentally, financially and constructively ... the multi-millionaire miracle showman."[67]

As powerful and as rich as Mayer grew through the years, we must remember that he was always an employee, a boss but a manager, not an owner. He oversaw the huge MGM lot in Culver City, 167 acres with 30 stages, phony jungles and a real zoo that housed the studio's other magnificent beast, the lion that roared before every film. There was a barbershop, a police force and a 24-hour commissary that served chicken soup. There was a house bookie, an opium den and, according to one employee, every Christmas Eve "an orgy that would have made Caligula feel at home." The studio did not employ a staff abortionist, however. For that service, its stars and contract players would travel across town to 20th Century–Fox.[68]

Mayer got involved in Republican politics: He allied himself with the fabulously wealthy and egomaniacal newspaper magnate William Randolph Hearst in supporting first Calvin Coolidge and then Herbert Hoover for the presidency. Mayer chaired the California State Republican Committee. President-elect Hoover invited him to the White House as his first overnight guest, an invitation which Mayer accepted. Then Hoover offered him the ambassadorship to Turkey, which Mayer considered and then declined.[69] Mayer earned 1.3 million dollars in 1937 (almost 20 million dollars today), as the highest paid employee in the country, "earning more in salary in 1937 than all the members of the United States Senate combined."[70] Known as "Hollywood's Rajah,"[71] he wielded unparalleled power over hundreds of actors, directors, crew, writers, etc., but he always had to answer to his New York City bosses, first Marcus Loew and then Loew's successor, Nicholas Schenck (1880–1969), known later as "The General." The studios in California sparkled in the glamour of the stars, red carpets, sensational gossip and scandal but the power was in New York. "Policy is made in New York while pictures are made in Hollywood," according to *The Journal of the Screen Producers Guild*.[72] The overall goal was to make money, and making movies was the means to this end. The General placed daily phone calls to his minions on the ground in Culver City, approving all of head producer Irving Thalberg's filming decisions. Marcus Loew had hired Mayer and, in 1951, Loew's successor, The General, fired him. Mayer spent his remaining years trying to start a new film company and feuding with Schenck. When he died in 1957, *The New York Times* called him "a Hollywood Czar," noting that he "wielded more influence than anyone else in the movie capital." He was, said the *Times*, "regarded around the world as the leading personality of Hollywood."[73] Mayer had not been widely loved. Reports of a large turnout at Mayer's funeral prompted producer Samuel Goldwyn to quip, "The reason so many people came to his funeral was because they wanted to make sure he was dead."[74]

Eight major Hollywood studios (MGM, Paramount, 20th Century–Fox, Columbia, Universal, Warner Brothers, RKO and United Artists) controlled 80 percent of the country's first-run movie theaters and "had a near monopoly over movie making in this country."[75] It was a vertical monopoly. Actors, writers and crew members signed contracts with a single studio. That's why we see so many of the same actors recycled through each studio's movies. Actors could often not choose their own roles; the studio chose the script, chose the crew and assigned the roles. Only the biggest stars had the power to negotiate which films they would appear in. The studio churned out movies which went exclusively to theaters across the country associated with that studio and no other. And, according to Andrew Sarris: "MGM was clearly the most popular (box-office grosses) and most prestigious (Oscars) of all the studios."[76] The theaters themselves have accurately been described as palaces with plush carpets, gold leaf work, sculptures collected from around the world, crystal chandeliers, Tiffany lamps and even huge pipe organs.[77] Said Marcus Loew: "We don't sell tickets to movies, we sell tickets to theaters." The Capitol Theater opened in New York in 1919 and sat 5000; the Roxy opened in 1927 with 6000 seats and three organs, with seating for a full orchestra. When Rockefeller Center Radio City Music Hall opened in 1932, it offered an orchestra, a choir and its own ballet company; it was billed as "The Showplace of the World." In the depths of the Depression, an out-of-work theatergoer could scrounge together 25 or 40 cents and watch films in a place fit for the royalty at Versailles.

The Supreme Court finally broke up the vertical monopoly of theater chains and studios as a violation of anti-trust laws in the Paramount Case of 1948 which ordered the studios to divest themselves of theater chains and free film talent from exclusive contracts. The Paramount Case ended the studio system and Loew's eventually gave up control of its shiniest creation, MGM.

MGM had been known as the "Tiffany" of studios for its high-gloss productions and famous stars. No one can dispute that Mayer stamped MGM with his taste. His films usually avoided political and social controversy and reinforced the Sunday School virtues of white, rural and middle class America with the addition of pretty girls and beautiful costumes. In MGM movies, criminals paid for their sins and the clean-cut guy got the girl. Mayer cultivated stars Greta Garbo, Clark Gable, Jean Harlow and Spencer Tracy, claiming MGM had "more stars than there are in the heavens above."[78] He also helped found the Academy of Motion Picture Arts and Sciences to present annual awards, the Oscars, not only to reward excellence in film but to show off the glitz and glamour of Hollywood and sell more movies. He saw himself in the business of creating not only stories but also stars, saying: "The idea of a star being born is bushwa. A star is created, carefully and cold-bloodily, built up from nothing, from nobody. Age, beauty, talent, least of all talent, has nothing to do with it. We could make silk purses out of sow's ears every day of the week."[79]

Said Mayer, in an interview published after his death: "We can teach anyone to act. Haven't you been to a flea circus? They can learn fleas to act. I've never met a star as stupid as a flea. Maybe almost as stupid, but not stupider. I only had three great actors: Tracy, Garbo, and Dressler.... If I give [fleas] awards they'll do anything I want. That's why I started the Academy Awards!"[80] The struggle to succeed, the fight to be a star, the quest for fame in such an atmosphere took its toll on women especially. As Karina Longworth wrote in her book *Seduction: Sex, Lies and Stardom in Howard Hughes's Hollywood*:

> In an industry run by men and fueled by male desires, most women found they could find the most success by leaving something of their "real" selves behind. In exchange for the transformative boost of stardom, they allowed—not that it was always much of a choice—their bodies,

personalities, background and/or names to be reinvented or sold. They took on personas, personas that, in some cases, so obscured who they had been that the kernel of truth behind the false front fell away.[81]

Ambition, fueled by sex, booze and money, ruled. Samuel Marx, friend to the so-called studio "Boy Genius" and "Prince of Hollywood" Irving Thalberg, described one Christmas party on the studio grounds:

> Barriers tumbled down as workers en masse paraded through stages and offices. Messenger boys linked arms with directors, stars with secretaries, janitors with executives. Kisses and embraces were exchanged in a monumental show of unrestrained joy. The resident bootleggers got so drunk they wandered the lot giving away their wares…. In the studio's projection rooms, pornographic movies enjoyed nonstop screening to the delectation of the roving celebrants. An increasing number of locked doors in the later hours indicated boys and girls were turning screen fantasies into stark realism.[82]

L.B. Mayer was "conspicuously absent" from the party, wrote Marx, but Thalberg was there and "barely made it home before he was felled by a massive heart attack."[83] He died several years later of heart disease at just 37.

The best first-hand and unvarnished account of 1930s go-go Hollywood studio life I've found is *What Makes Sammy Run* by Budd Schulberg, first published in *Liberty Magazine* in 1937 and as a standalone book in 1941. The novel traces the rise of a New York Jew from the slums to power, fame and fortune in a major Hollywood studio. Anti-hero Sammy Glick steals other writers' work, lies and manipulates people with his sole focus on personal success at the expense of just about everyone who crosses his path. Says narrator Al Mannheim, "The world was a race to Sammy. He was running against time."[84] The raw ambition, the supreme egotism and, above all, the overt Jewishness of Sammy Glick epitomized everything the outside world hated about the studio moguls and the movie industry. Sammy disclaims all artistic ambitions for his industry, saying, "After all, pictures are shipped out in cans. We're in the canning business. Our job is to make sure every shipment will make a profit."[85]

The novel hit Hollywood hard because Schulberg was not only a successful screenwriter but also the son of mogul B.P. Schulberg who partnered with Mayer in Mayer-Schulberg and, after their split, ran Paramount. This *roman à clef* in which Sammy is modeled on the writer's father caused all kinds of grief for the Hollywood inner circle. Sam Goldwyn thought the name Sammy Glick was a little too close to his own and fired author Schulberg after the novel's publication. At a meeting of Hollywood bigwigs, Mayer turned to Schulberg *père* and asked, "How could you let your own flesh and blood write such a book? You know what we should do with him? We should deport him." To which father Schulberg replied, "For Christ's sake, Louie, he's the only novelist who ever came from Hollywood. Where the hell are we going to deport him? Catalina Island."[86] Budd Schulberg, internalizing a little bit of Sammy Glick himself, went from recruiting Hollywood writers into the Communist Party as members of the Screen Writers Group to betraying them before the Red hunters of the 1950s, naming at least 15 former colleagues as dangerous Reds. He later wrote the screenplay for *On the Waterfront*, an apologia for the blacklist and the informers, with fellow rat Elia Kazan directing.[87]

Censorship has been an issue for millennia. In his utopian work *The Republic*, Plato suggested censoring artists to protect the moral development of youth. Plato thought poetry, song and theater needed to be censored for the good of society. In America, our own impulse to censor goes back to the white settlement of our shores when our Puritan forebears were described as people worried that someone, somewhere was having a good time.

Hard partying behind the cameras caused occasional scandalous headlines for the film industry but it was the movies themselves that upset the bluenoses, censors and professional Puritans. Motion pictures and movie houses threatened respectable society as they proliferated across the country. The first banned film in the U.S., *Dolorita's Passion Dance*, was shut down in Atlantic City as early as 1897.[88] The Settlement House movement, inspired by Jane Addams et al., in the 1880s, commendably sought to improve the physical lot of the newly arriving immigrant poor and waged war with the proliferating vaudeville houses of the inner cities and slums which separated the poor from their nickels and provided unwholesome entertainment to the masses. In her autobiography *Twenty Years at Hull House*, Addams recounts several tales of crimes committed by inner city children to amass nickels to get into the theaters, conjuring up the crime wave usually associated with drug addiction. She added: "The eagerness of the penniless children to get into these magic spaces is responsible for an entire crop of petty crimes."[89]

America's most famous early censor, Anthony Comstock, founded the New York Society for the Suppression of Vice. He tried closing film showings as early as 1900. In 1907, Jane Addams' hometown of Chicago, the second largest U.S. market, passed the first city ordinance censoring motion pictures. It was to be enforced, wrote Jeremy Geltzer in his book *Dirty Words and Filthy Pictures*, by "the perfect censor.... Major M.L.C. Funkhouser. He was one of the strictest censors in the country. If he saw a glimpse of ankle, the film was banned. A couple dancing closer than six inches together? That was cut."[90]

Detroit followed suit. Soon Pennsylvania, Ohio, Kansas, Maryland and New York enacted film censorship laws and created censorship boards to enforce them. By 1910, films of boxing matches were banned, right after Jack Johnson, an African American, knocked out James Jeffries, the white champion. The nascent film industry went to court to challenge the new laws, claiming free speech protection from censorship under the First Amendment to the U.S. Constitution. But in the 1915 case, *Mutual Film Corporation v. Industrial Commission of Ohio*, the Supreme Court voted 9–0 that films did not have First Amendment free speech protections because

> "the exhibition of moving pictures is a business, pure and simple, originated and conducted for profit...." Second, the Court saw motion pictures as "vivid, useful and entertaining no doubt, but ... capable of evil, having power for it, the greater because of their attractiveness and manner of exhibition."[91]

In self-defense, film producers turned to self-censorship, creating the Motion Pictures Producers and Distributors Association (MPPDA), which in 1945 became the Motion Picture Association of America (MPAA). To prove their seriousness and protect themselves from outside attacks, they tapped a well-connected Washington insider, former Republican Party chairman and Postmaster General Will Hays. Hays' office produced a 19-page list of acceptable and unacceptable topics for the motion picture industry. The so-called Hays Code was actually written by Jesuit priest F. Daniel A. Lord. Under the heading "Sex," it read in part: "[S]ex perversion or any inference to it is forbidden. White-slavery shall not be treated. Miscegenation is forbidden."[92] Miscegenation referred to sexual and marital relations between blacks and whites and was a criminal offense in many Southern states

Hays successfully defeated a Congressional resolution to investigate the film industry but enforcement was fairly lax until 1934 when Hays recruited the prominent Catholic layman Joseph Ignatius Breen (1888–1965) to be, in the words of *The New York Times*, "morals director of the Hays office."[93] For the next 20 years, Hollywood faced a new, tougher Code which, among many other rules, allowed no screen kiss to last more than three seconds. The crackdown on screen immorality came at the behest of the Legion of Decency, established by the American Bishops of the Roman Catholic Church. The studios submitted their films to Breen's office for screening in advance of release to receive a Production Code Seal which, displayed on each film, allowed them to play in American theaters.

Directors continued to test the limits as Howard Hughes did with a large-breasted Jane Russell and a specially Hughes-designed bra to reveal her bust in *The Outlaw* which, produced in 1941, went through various film cuts to satisfy the censors until its release in 1943. As late as 1947, the Our Gang film *Curley* was banned in Memphis, Tennessee, for showing black and white children in brief scenes together in the same classroom. The Supreme Court upheld the ban once again, referring back to the Mutual Film Corporation decision of 1915. With Breen at the helm, even cartoon characters had to behave: Betty Boop stopped being a flapper and started wearing a longer skirt.[94]

A 2008 NPR story noted:

> Under Breen, gangster dramas like *Scarface* were squelched and cunning sexual innuendoes from the likes of Mae West were silenced. Hollywood filmmakers were forced to convey naughty moments with elliptical references: a tight embrace, a fade to black, a train going through a tunnel.[95]

With Breen in charge of the Hays Office (with a staff of eight white men), censorship began with story development and treatments, pre-script, pre-casting, pre-filming, to "stop trouble before it begins," in the words of a staffer.[96] When studios aimed to re-release pre–Code films, they often found that movies that had run successfully just a few years before needed cuts under the new, tougher Code. John Gallagher listed the cuts made to the re-release of James Cagney's *The Public Enemy*:

> [T]he scene where Cagney is being measured for a suit by an effeminate tailor; a shot of Joan Blondell serving Eddie Woods breakfast in bed, indicating they've spent the night together; and a continuation of the scene where Cagney is hiding out in Jane's apartment, gets drunk and is unwittingly seduced by her.[97]

The whole censorship business reached dizzying heights of absurdity in RKO's *Little Men* (1940) over a planned scene of milking a cow. Breen ordered: "All its dialogue with regard to milking is highly dangerous and must be handled to avoid vulgarity and otherwise unacceptable emphasis. At no time should there be any shots of actual milking, and there cannot be any showing of the udders of the cow; they should be suggested rather than shown." All this in regard to Borden's Elsie the cow.[98]

It didn't help that Breen was also an anti–Semite working amidst the Jews of Hollywood. In a letter to the Reverend Wilfrid Parsons, S.J., editor of the Jesuit weekly *America*, Breen wrote,

> These Jews seem to think of nothing but money making and sexual indulgence.... People whose daily morals would not be tolerated in the toilet of a pest house hold the good jobs out

here and wax fat on it. Ninety-five percent of these folks are Jews of an Eastern European lineage. They are, probably, the scum of the scum of the earth.[99]

But the Code was good for business, if not for art. Movie revenues rose, Shirley Temple, not Mae West, hit the #1 spot at the box office, and state and Federal censors quieted down. After 1934, "Roman Catholics exerted a virtual veto power over the visible universe of Hollywood's Golden Age … and Hollywood came to be defined as a 'A Jewish owned business selling Roman Catholic theology in Protestant America.'"[100]

The Supreme Court revisited the matter of film censorship: In 1952, they decided that films did in fact have First Amendment rights:

> It cannot be doubted that motion pictures are a significant medium for the communication of ideas. Their importance as an organ of public opinion is not lessened by the fact that they are designated to entertain as well as inform.… That the production, distribution, and exhibition of motion pictures is a large scale business conducted for private profit does not prevent motion pictures from being a form of expression whose liberty is safeguarded by the First Amendment.[101]

But while the Hays Office had cleaned up the movies, the freshly scrubbed morals on screen did not always hold sway over either the boardrooms or the executive suites. With the power to make or break a star went temptation and abuse. Mayer, a moralist in public, was a philanderer in private.[102] Though a non-drinker, he had a cut of the studio bootlegging business. He had a deal with Western Union to read any telegrams leaving or coming into the studio that were critical of MGM. He took a cut of the profits of the commissary. He ran an antique business on Santa Monica Boulevard with antiques bought in Europe by MGM set designers: "The furniture went out the MGM back door."[103] MGM even ran its own brothel north of the Sunset Strip where "[the] girls were doubles of the stars."[104] Mayer had, said Dick Cavett, "the intellect and instincts of a shark."[105]

Mayer could and did move mountains for others when it suited him. In the midst of World War II, his brother Rudolph was interned by the Japanese in the Philippines. Mayer called New York City Archbishop Francis Joseph Spellman, the future cardinal of the Catholic Church. According to MGM publicity man Howard Strickland, Spellman "had a direct line to the pope, the pope to Hitler, Hitler to General Tojo in Tokyo. Within days Rudy was on a Swedish repatriation ship on his way to Los Angeles. To tell you this is to give you the true meaning of L.B.'s power."[106]

Sometimes Mayer just indulged personal desires and invoked his power to make and break stars on the casting couch:

> Cari Beauchamp, author of *Without Lying Down: Francis Marion and the Powerful Women of Early Hollywood*, tells a story of Jean Howard (1910–2000), a former Ziegfeld Follies dancer who had small parts in films.… Mayer chased … Howard around the room. When she said, "No way," and went off and married Charles K. Feldman, the agent, Mayer banned Charlie from the lot. For a long time after, he wouldn't allow any of Feldman's clients to work at MGM.[107]

In the same *Variety* article, Thelma Adams reported: "Mayer also allegedly groped the teenage Judy Garland, according to Gerald Clarke's book *Get Happy: The Life of Judy Garland*, and held meetings with the young woman seated on his lap, his hands on her chest."[108] In *Time* magazine, Suyin Hayes wrote:

> It was widely reported that MGM also used drugs to modulate young performers on set … plying its young actors with "pep pills," otherwise known as amphetamines, to power them

through the exhausting demands of shooting schedules, as well as "downers," or barbiturates, to force them to get enough sleep.... One biography of Garland also alleged that she was sexually harassed by Mayer, starting around the time when *The Wizard of Oz* was released, when Garland was 16. Using notes from a partial memoir written by Garland herself, former *Time* writer Gerald Clarke writes in *Get Happy: The Life of Judy Garland* that "between the ages of sixteen and twenty, Judy herself was to be approached for sex—and approached again and again," by Mayer himself and other studio executives.[109]

This was not what audiences saw on the silver screen when they went to see *The Wizard of Oz* or *The Courtship of Andy Hardy* in MGM's idealized pictures of innocent American youth.

And then came the Great Depression (1929–39). Nearly half the banks in the country closed, farmers lost their land, unemployment hit 25 percent.[110] The unemployed, the poor and the hungry stood in breadlines. So-called Hoovervilles, named for the president, were filled with the shacks of families evicted or foreclosed from their homes; they mushroomed on the edges of cities. By 1933, a million transients walked the roads and rode the rails, looking for work. There were 300,000 unemployed workers in Los Angeles County alone.[111] One contemporary reported: "One vivid, gruesome moment of those dark days we shall never forget. We saw a crowd of some fifty men fighting over a barrel

Louis B. Mayer takes a moment with young stars Mickey Rooney and Judy Garland, their innocence idealized by the presence of ice cream sodas (MovieStillsDB.com).

of garbage which had been set outside the back door of a restaurant. American citizens fighting for scrap food like animals."[112]

The Depression hit Hollywood and the movie industry as well. In 1933, a third of all movie theaters closed and ticket sales nationally fell from 110 million a week to 60 million. Columbia, Universal and Warner Brothers lost money; Fox, Paramount and RKO went into bankruptcy or receivership. MGM posted an $8 million profit.[113] MGM negotiated the Crash by temporarily cutting all salaries by 50 percent. *Thin Man* screenwriter Albert Hackett recalled that when Mayer imposed pay cuts in 1933, the studio chief "created more Communists than Karl Marx."[114]

Hollywood writers, set designers, camera operators, costumers, makeup artists, cooks and drivers were workers too and though the Hollywood life might look glamorous, "in the thirties movie people usually worked ten-hour days six days a week."[115] MGM writer Lester Cole (1904–1985) remembered fighting back, organizing the workers into a guild, not calling it a union for political purposes, and seeing it grow to 343 members in ten months. Hammett, Hellman and Dorothy Parker helped organize the Screen Writers Guild. The studios called the organizers Commies and Reds.[116] The studios were unhappy with the newly formed SWG: In an open meeting, Mayer proclaimed (sounding very Sammy Glick–ish, I might say),

> "As long as we put up the money we're entitled to final say! The only test of art is financial success! And you writers aren't like playwrights—you get paid every week whether you work or not." Every writer in the room booed him.... He left in fury; soon after, several MGM writers were fired or suffered heavy pay cuts.[117]

MGM production head Irving Thalberg attacked the writers: "They live like kings—but join a union like plumbers and miners."[118] In reality, while top writers could make $1000 a week, their juniors made do on $35. MGM dropped the idea of the 50 percent pay cut and by October 1934 the Writers Guild, under its first president John Howard Lawson (1894–1977), had enrolled 85 percent of the writers in Hollywood.[119] MGM created a separate and competing union under screenwriter James McGuinness (1894–1950), which "MGM owned lock, stock, and barrel. McGuinness was backed by ultra-rightist, anti-semitic John Lee Mahin (1902–1984) and by Howard Emmett Rogers, among others."[120] In the late 1940s and early 1950s, Cole, Lawson, Hellman, Hammett and Parker paid dearly for their Hollywood union activities when they faced HUAC investigations, blacklisting and, in some cases, prison.

A word about Dorothy Parker, one of my favorite characters of this period for her epigrams, sarcasm and biting wit. She was, as we saw in Chapter 2, an early fan of Hammett's work, which she reviewed enthusiastically in *The New Yorker*. She was, reportedly, so enamored of his work that upon first introductions, she bent to kiss his hand, discomfiting both him and Lillian Hellman, who was also present. Though Hammett never warmed to Parker, she and Hellman became lifelong friends and all three shared the trenches in the anti-capitalist, anti-fascist work of the '30s and '40s. Parker reached a large reading public through her poems, short stories and critical reviews written during stints at *Vogue*, *Vanity Fair* and especially her long career at *The New Yorker* (1926–55). Born Dorothy Rothschild, she married Edwin Pond Parker II, a well-bred alcoholic. They divorced after a short time but she kept his name. Her first book of poetry, *Enough Rope*, with a noose on the cover, was a bestseller. She followed with three more that sold well: *Sunset Gun*, *Death and Taxes* and *Not So Deep as a Well*. She is best remembered today for her clever epigrams like "Men seldom make passes / At girls who wear glasses"[121] as well as her poems, like this one which was quite ironic or, perhaps, affirmational, given that she herself attempted suicide at least three times:

> Razors pain you;
> Rivers are damp;
> Acids stain you;
> And drugs cause cramp,
> Guns aren't lawful;
> Nooses give;
> Gas smells awful;
> You might as well live.[122]

She walked from her office at *Vanity Fair* each work day to lunch at the Algonquin Hotel, joining the crew from Mencken's magazine *Smart Set*: writers Robert Benchley, Alexander Woollcott, Harold Ross, the founding editor of *The New Yorker* and an ever-changing cast of Broadway actors and writers like Ben Hecht and Ring Lardner, playwright George S. Kaufman, Donald Ogden Stewart and Arthur Kober, who would later marry Lillian Hellman.

I visited the Algonquin myself as a tourist many years later and left after drinking a martini with a napkin imprinted with my favorite Dorothy Parkerism:

> I like to have a martini,
> Two at the very most.
> After three I'm under the table,
> After four I'm under my host.

One historian called her

> a slim, pocket handkerchief–size woman ... with a wispy bob and hazel-green button eyes, fringed by long upturned lashes.... She was the embodiment of the literary flapper; flippant, flirtatious, and risqué, peppering her conversation with witty wisecracks and clever put-downs ... She was one of the few women who went toe to toe with the boys in writing, drinking. and screwing.[123]

When she was 40, Parker and husband Alan Campbell headed for Hollywood as a writing team with a salary of $5000 a week.[124] She helped write 39 screenplays for MGM, Paramount, etc.[125] Her Hollywood days became the stuff of legend. When MGM asked her what she preferred in an office, she replied, "All I need is room to lay my hat and a few friends."[126] According to Samuel Marx, "[S]he called all studio executives 'cretins' and leaned out of her office window shouting: 'Get me out of here, I'm as sane as any of you!' On hearing this, [Irving] Thalberg said, 'Oblige her.'"[127] And, on Thalberg's orders, Marx fired her.

Parker was also politically committed, involving herself in the defense of the anarchists Sacco and Vanzetti, raising money for the Scottsboro Boys and for the Spanish Republic, and helping found the Hollywood Anti-Nazi League in 1936. In 1938, she traveled to Spain, sending back reports for *The New Masses*. Hellman dedicated her 1944 play *The Searching Wind* to Parker.

When the witch hunt era dawned, the House UnAmerican Activities Committee called Parker to testify. Asked "Are you now or have you ever been a member of the Communist Party," she replied: "I was and am many things, to myself and to my friends. But I am not a traitor and I will not be involved in this obscene inquisition."[128] She invoked

Dorothy Parker in 1924 at age 31. A poet, raconteur, critic, satirist and a member of New York's Algonquin Round Table, she went west, as so many writers did, to make money in Hollywood. She shared writing credit on *A Star Is Born* (1937) and *Smash-Up: The Story of a Woman* (1947) (The New York Public Library via Wikimedia Commons).

her Fifth Amendment rights. Unlike male witnesses before the Committee, women like Hellman and Parker, who refused to name names, escaped serving time; the Southern Congressmen of HUAC did not take women seriously enough to imprison them. Upon her death, Parker left the bulk of her estate, about $20,000, and the copyrights to her work to the Reverend Martin Luther King and, upon his death, to the NAACP.

The Screen Writers Guild, with Hammett, Hellman and Parker aboard, battled with the studio bosses for years. They fought over pay but also the studio system itself, where a producer like Thalberg might have two or more writers separately working on a script, then pay them off and bring in yet another writer to reshape and rewrite their work. Often a writer who had submitted a full script was surprised to see that the final movie looked nothing like what he or she had written, whether it had their name on it or not.

On the national stage, the Depression resulted in the election of Democrat Franklin Delano Roosevelt as president in hopes that his new ideas might better reboot the economy than the mostly hands-off approach of Republican incumbent Herbert Hoover, a favorite and personal friend of Louis B. Mayer. Between the election in November 1932 and Roosevelt's inauguration in March 1933, William Randolph Hearst, in cooperation with MGM, bankrolled one of the oddest movies to ever come out of Hollywood. *Gabriel Over the White House*, directed by Gregory La Cava, has been called "the only overtly fascist movie ever made [in America]."[129]

The film begins with a fantasy of a corrupt president named Jud Hammond, played by Walter Huston, who after a near-death experience comes under the influence of the

Archangel Gabriel to save the country. Certainly the country was looking for a savior and in 1932 Hearst thought FDR fit the bill, though he later turned his bitter enemy. President Hammond's divine idea for American salvation is a dictatorship, complete with death squads. Hammond also ushers in world peace and then dies at his desk of a heart attack.[130] Political Reporter Jeff Greenfield called it "the Hollywood hit movie that urged FDR to become a fascist."[131] Mayer, a Hoover man and FDR foe, tried to get the project canned but Thalberg and Hearst overruled him.

Compare the fate of *Gabriel Over the White House* with another MGM movie, one that never got made: *It Can't Happen Here*, a warning against homegrown American fascism. Prolific novelist Sinclair Lewis, author of *Babbitt*, *Arrowsmith*, *Elmer Gantry*, *Dodsworth* and *Cass Timberlane,* decided to dramatize domestic political tensions in a time of racist extremists like Father Charles Coughlin and dictators-in-waiting like Louisiana Governor Huey Long and Fritz Kuhn of the German American Bund. The novel basically brings the Nazis to power in America with red, white and blue trimmings. Populist demagogue Senator "Buzz" Windrip wins the presidency promising to make America great again. Once in office, he boots Congress, cripples the Supreme Court and sets up concentration camps for his critics. As opposition mounts, he orders an invasion of Mexico to distract the populace.

Louis B. Mayer favored Republicans and worked to elect Herbert Hoover president in 1928. Once Hoover was elected, Mayer was his first overnight guest at the White House. Seen here posing at the White House are, from left, Edith Mayer, Louis B. and wife Margaret Shenberg, Irene Mayer and Mrs. Mabel W. Willebrandt. Edith Mayer later married William Goetz; Goetz and Darryl F. Zanuck later founded 20th Century–Fox. Her younger sister Irene married producer David O. Selznick (Library of Congress via Wikimedia Commons).

MGM purchased the rights to the novel in 1935 based on the galley proofs of the book and assigned Lucien Hubbard as producer. By early 1936, screenwriter Sidney Howard had a script and J. Walter Ruben was picked to direct with a cast including Lionel Barrymore, Walter Connolly, Virginia Bruce and Basil Rathbone. Then Mayer suddenly stepped in to shut down production, citing financial concerns. Lewis' agent produced a telegram stating that Will Hays had blocked production for "fear of international politics and fear of boycotts abroad."[132] A colleague at the Production Code Administration chimed in, calling the script "too anti-fascist."[133] Too anti-fascist? Soon after, the novel was banned in Nazi Germany.

In fact, the film industry through the 1930s routinely placed profits over their fears about what was happening to their fellow Jews in Europe, often refusing to take part in anti–Nazi protests. As late as 1939, with the outbreak of war just months away, Myrna Loy found herself under fire for her comments as she toured Norway and the Netherlands with her new husband, producer Arthur Hornblow. In Amsterdam, a film rep warned her to tone down her critique of Hitler and when she returned to L.A. to make *I Love You Again* with William Powell, she received a note from Arthur Loew, president of MGM and son of founder Marcus Loew, advising her to stay out of politics (Loew's had large investments in Germany). Loy wrote: "Oh, Lord, this still makes me so mad I could spit. Here I was [fighting] for the Jews and they're telling me to lay off because there's still money to be made in Germany. Loew and many of the company's executives were Jewish, but they condoned this horror. I know it's incredible but it happened."[134]

MGM and the other studios sold a lot of movies in Germany, and the Germans used that market share to exert their influence. A Nazi, Georg Gyssling, came to L.A. in 1933 as the German consul, in part to police the film industry. Using Article 15, a new German law, any company that distributed an anti–German film anywhere in the world could be banned in Germany. To protect their distribution market, the studios regularly shared scripts and first edits of their films with Gyssling to obtain his approval. Said screenwriter Budd Schulberg: "There were some films that Louis B. Mayer of MGM would actually run ... with the Nazi German consul and was willing to take out the things that the consul, that the Nazi, objected to."[135]

The personal was political, wrote historian Ben Urwand: "The head of MGM in Germany, Frits Strengholt, divorced his Jewish wife at the request of the Propaganda Ministry. She ended up in a concentration camp."[136]

How could American Jews collaborate with the Nazis? Wrote the BBC's Tom Brooks: "Film critic David Denby says that 'the studio bosses were all from Eastern Europe. They never lost their feeling that as outsiders and as Jews, it could all be taken away.' Consequently they may have been hesitant, in an anti–Semitic environment, of taking any action which could be construed as being favorable to Jewish interests."[137] Closer to home, however, and with their interests directly challenged, the studio moguls felt freer to act. In the 1934 California gubernatorial race, a socialist had won the Democratic party primary in a landslide and seemed destined to win power in Sacramento. The boogey man of this horror show was the mild-mannered, professorial and courtly author Upton Sinclair (1878–1968). *The New York Times* called his EPIC (End Poverty in California) campaign "the first serious movement against the profit system in the United States."[138]

Sinclair was best-known as a muckraking journalist and author of *The Jungle*, a 1906 novel which exposed the exploitation of workers in the Chicago slaughterhouses;

within months of its publication, it led to national legislation, the Meat Inspection Act and the Pure Food and Drug Act. Sinclair later dallied with Hollywood, selling his novel *The Wet Parade* to MGM for a movie in 1932. Thalberg put Sinclair under contract for future scenarios.

Things did not go well: "After meeting with Thalberg four times to discuss a project called *The Star Spangled Banner*, [Sinclair] changed the title to *The Gold-Spangled Banner* and in November 1932, MGM terminated his contract."[139] Sinclair won the Pulitzer Prize in 1943 for his novel *Dragon's Teeth* and 70 years after Thalberg fired him, another of Sinclair's novels, *Oil*, became the basis for the 2007 movie *There Shall Be Blood*, which won two Academy Awards.

In the 1934 gubernatorial campaign, *The Los Angeles Times* denounced "Uppie" Sinclair's supporters as a "maggot-like horde,"[140] arguing that EPIC represented a "threat to sovietize California…. Gentlemen—and ladies—this is not politics, it is war."[141]

The entire state establishment in government, including future governor and Supreme Court Chief Justice Earl Warren and former President Herbert Hoover, the media, including William Randolph Hearst, and the Hollywood studios, including MGM, Mayer and Thalberg, came together to deny a Sinclair victory in perhaps the first U.S. election manipulated by the media.

What caused the panic? Sinclair proposed a state income tax, a guaranteed $50 monthly pension to the elderly (this before Social Security), a 30-hour work week, public ownership of utilities and, most threatening of all to Hollywood, a tax on the film studios and higher tax rates for the studio bosses. He even threatened that California would enter the filmmaking business under his administration: "We will make our own pictures and show them in our own theaters with our own orchestras."[142] The press labeled Sinclair "a most dangerous Bolshevik beast"[143] while accusing him of being a Communist, a homosexual and an atheist.[144] To prevent a Sinclair victory, MGM first docked their studio employees, from drivers to stars, one day's pay to be funneled to the Republican candidate. Only a few writers or actors refused.

The studios threatened they'd move to Florida if Sinclair won and dispatched scouts to the Sunshine State to publicize their threat. Thalberg shot pseudo-documentary shorts to be shown in Loew's theaters in which well-dressed and barbered bit actors recited prepared scripts and pretended to be regular people afraid of a Sinclair victory, while poorly costumed people cheered a Sinclair victory. Greg Mitchell in his study of the campaign wrote: "One with a heavy accent asserted that Sinclair's plans 'worked very well in Russia' and surely would 'vork' in America. …[T]he final and most impactful Thalberg newsreel … showed boxcars filled with hobos flocking to California to take advantage of Sinclair's promised utopia."

Some of the scenes were staged or taken directly from obscure MGM movies."[145] *Thin Man* director Van Dyke, "one of the most militant anti–Sinclair directors in Hollywood … was eager to lend his talents to the big fight."[146]

Demonstrating the split within the studios, many writers, already struggling for higher pay and film credit, formed an Authors League for Sinclair. Script reader Dorothy Parker supported Sinclair, saying, "My heart and soul are with the cause of socialism."[147] The moguls closed the studios for two hours on Election Day so their workers could go to the polls. Sinclair lost, though he won almost 900,000 votes to Republican Frank Merriam's 1.1 million. Samuel Marx wrote: "There is little doubt that the doctored newsreels provided the knockout blow against Sinclair's gubernatorial aspirations."[148]

On election night, Mayer threw a victory party at the Cafe Trocadero to celebrate Sinclair's defeat. He declared, "The voters of California have made a fearless choice between radicalism and patriotism."[149] Thalberg defended his work in making the short films attacking Sinclair. At a party, actor Fredric March called the fake newsreels "a dirty trick. It was the damndest unfair thing I've ever heard of."[150] Thalberg replied in words as applicable today as in 1934: "Nothing is unfair in politics.... Fairness in an election is a contradiction in terms. It just doesn't exist."[151]

But the campaign and the Hollywood involvement made another difference as well: It spurred the rise of the SWG and technical unions upset at how the studios had manipulated them in the campaign. Screenwriter Philip Dunne said, "After 1934 we said 'Never again.' EPIC created a liberal climate in Hollywood for the first time."[152] Added author Mitchell: "Politics in Hollywood moved steadily left over the next few years. Liberals organized popular crusades against Hitler and Franco. Guild activity intensified, with many union activists claiming that the eye-opening Sinclair campaign sparked their enthusiasm. Some liberals moved far to the left and joined the Communist Party."[153]

Part of Sinclair's platform lived on. In 1938, actor Melvyn Douglas served as campaign manager in Southern California for the gubernatorial candidacy of Culbert Olson, a former EPIC leader, who beat Merriam by 200,000 votes and did get a state income tax passed.

Looking back on his campaign and the success of the studios and other employers in getting their employees to vote against their own self-interest, Sinclair said: "It is difficult to get a man to understand something when his salary depends upon his not understanding it."[154]

MGM, so successful and powerful from the 1930s through the 1950s, declined in wealth and power as television and then independent producers made inroads with their audience and the Supreme Court broke up their monopoly in 1948. The old studio, with more stars than in the heavens, was finally sold to Amazon, the online retail giant, for $8.45 billion in 2021. Amazon had previously purchased Whole Foods, Ring and Zappos.[155] Sony Pictures now owns the old studio grounds where the *Thin Man* series filmed. Warner Brothers owns many classic MGM films. MGM, producing but a few new films each year, exists today as little more than a brand name and a memory.

4

William Powell

How many people does it take to make a movie? The first Thin Man movie credits ninety-four individuals in its cast and crew, but when you add in all the people at the MGM studio who worked there each day and lent their talents to the production—the drivers, the cooks, the security personnel, the carpenters, the painters, and even the publicists, accountants and so many more—you see that it took many hundreds of people to make *The Thin Man*. Film, like theater, is a collaborative art. The writer, or writers, in this case, prepare a script; the director amends the script and chooses the cast and makes decisions about sets and schedules; the actors apply their personalities and ideas to their roles; the costume designer chooses the clothes; the cinematographer makes decisions about lighting and chooses between closeups and long shots; etc. But none makes their contribution to the film alone and all are in constant contact, adding and subtracting ideas and nuance until the film is shot, edited, cut and, finally, exhibited.

And while I will examine the efforts of director, screenwriters, and full cast in Chapter 6, I begin here with just two people, Bill and Myrna, who, for the world, became Nick and Nora. Likely neither could have done it without the other. In the insightful words of George Cukor, director of *Dinner at Eight*, *Little Women* and *My Fair Lady* (and many more),

> There had been romantic couples before, but Loy and Powell were something new and original. They actually made marital comedy palatable. I remember Bill Powell when he started out as a melodramatic actor. Then, by some alchemy, he suddenly became comic. But Myrna gave the weight to the whole thing. They hit that wonderful note because he always did a wee bit too much and she underdid it, creating a grace, a charm, a chemistry.[1]

An only child, William Horatio Powell was born in 1892 in Pittsburgh, two years before Hammett. He did well in his high school theatrical group and decided on a stage career. However, his father had little use for such frivolities and at his direction, Powell enrolled at the University of Kansas in the fall of 1911 to study law. He lasted one week.[2] Knowing he would then receive no financial assistance from his parents, Powell penned a 23-page letter to a rich aunt, begging for a loan of $1400 to go to New York to study at the American Academy of Dramatic Art. She loaned him half the money he requested which, at six percent interest, he paid back 13 years later.[3]

Upon graduation, Powell joined touring shows but also suffered weeks of unemployment before he scored a two-year run in a New York play and met his future wife, actress Eileen Wilson; they married in 1915. He acted in some 200 plays before starting his film career.[4] His first positive newspaper reviews came in a Broadway play in 1920, *Spanish Love*, which ran for 300 performances. This led a producer to approach him to appear in a silent movie, *Sherlock Holmes*, with the great star John Barrymore as Holmes and Powell as the villain Moriarty. More film roles followed, usually as the bad guy. By 1925, he had appeared in four films. Powell and Eileen's only child, William David Powell, was born in 1925. That same year, they moved west, settled in Hollywood and bought their first home after ten years of marriage. However, they separated soon after, and divorced in 1930.

Powell's biographer Charles Francisco calls him "a very private public figure."[5] and judging by the dearth of scandal or even gossip attached to his name, this seems quite accurate. His co-stars spoke highly of him and the descriptive words they most often employed were "gentleman," "debonair," "sophisticated" and "urbane." His co-star in 14 films, Myrna Loy called him "a perfect gentleman."[6] His biographer called him "a surprisingly conventional man in a highly unconventional industry."[7]

One might call Powell the opposite of Hammett. There is no record of Powell ever getting involved in politics, signing a petition or joining a political group, much less lying drunk in a gutter. Loy called him a conservative Republican. I can't find a public record of a single political word he ever uttered.

And yet his was a life marked by highs and lows. He was involved with two of the most beautiful and desirable women in Hollywood, Carole Lombard and Jean Harlow.

His relationship with his only son was at times distant and at other times quite close but ended in tragedy. In 1968, after writing for the TV shows *Bonanza* and *Rawhide*, suffering from depression and in ill health, 43-year-old William Powell, Jr., "stabbed himself to death with a paring knife."[8]

Powell's career prospered in the late 1920s and he won ever larger roles acting with such luminaries as Clara Bow (in *My Lady's Lips*), Noah Beery (in *Beau Geste*), Lillian and Dorothy Gish (*Romola*) and many who are today forgotten. In this era, Powell played a gaucho, a gangster, a cowboy, an Arab, a European playboy, a South American bandit, a con man and a Russian revolutionary in exile. In 1925, he signed a long-term contract with Famous Players–Lasky, later Paramount. At the age of 33, he had arrived as an actor. He appeared in eight films in 1926.

By 1927, Powell had acted in over 30 silent films. Then the "talkie" revolution of 1927 upended the industry. Suddenly actors with accents or speech impediments, or voices too high or too low, found themselves out of work. Powell had a nice, mellifluous midwestern baritone and experience in live stage acting and the advent of talkies boosted his career. Paramount even cast him in their very first all-talking movie, *Interference*, playing a murderer. The next year he appeared in *The Canary Murder Case* as Philo Vance, the esthete amateur detective; it was the first of his four movies as Vance. Powell found the work easy: "Mostly I creased my brows, looked to the right, looked to the left, and nodded my head profoundly—sort of hemmed and hawed, chuckling inwardly the while ... [A]t the finish.... I ended by pointing out the murderer."[9] He noted that the movie "made a mint of money for the studio and did very well for yours truly."[10] Soon he was getting star billing and taking home the highest pay of the entire cast though that might mean no more than $5000 for a film shot in a mere four weeks.[11] When Powell worked in a musical dramedy, *Pointed Heels*, his co-star Fay Wray said of him, "He had grace, style, wit, and technique. He was not absolutely handsome so that he was believable as a leading man or as a villain or whatever role. He was Olympian in the sense that he seemed to have achieved an elegant arrogance."[12]

Shortly before the actor's death in 1984, at age 91, a reporter asked the long-retired

Hollywood star if the talkies had "hurried" his stardom. He answered: "Don't be foolish. They caused it. But for talkies I would probably be a first class so-and-so in every picture. I was practically doomed by my face to play a menace."[13] When talkies came long, the well-built man with the little mustache and the seductive manner had a voice made for the eye-rolling, liquor-imbibing, sophisticated wit of *The Thin Man*.

The Stock Market Crash of 1929 ushered in the Great Depression. Stockbrokers jumped to their deaths from tall buildings and ordinary Americans, with 25 percent of the work force unemployed, queued up in breadlines or sold apples on street corners or rode the rails as hoboes searching for work.

In 1932, Powell earned $100,000 (over a million dollars today) for his starring turn in *Jewel Robbery*. His salary took up over a third of the budget for the entire film.[14] Like Hammett, Powell was raking it in but, unlike Hammett, he never seems to have let it go to his head, never blew his money, never drank to excess. "William Powell," wrote critic Roger Ebert, "is to dialogue as Fred Astaire is to dance: his delivery is so droll and insinuating, so knowing and innocent at the same time, that it hardly matters what he's saying."[15]

Powell made *For the Defense* (1930), with co-star Kay Francis (who earned just one quarter of his salary) and they began a brief off-screen romance. That relationship sputtered but their on-screen pairings continued in *Jewel Robbery* and *One Way Passage* (1932). *Jewel Robbery* has Francis as a married and bored Viennese baroness and Powell as a suave jewel thief who gets some laughs by getting his victims to smoke drugged cigarettes (marijuana, we presume, though it is never named), giggle and get the munchies. After he has several adventures escaping the bumbling police, the movie ends with Powell and Francis promising to meet again in Nice. Warners executive Darryl Zanuck had a warning for the director William Dieterle that would be repeated throughout Powell's career: "[Powell] gets almost bird-like and like a fairy, bowing and scraping too much. Keep him manly and keep him dashing and then you'll have a great romantic, adventurous story"[16] There's a droll bit of dialogue between Francis and Powell that resonates 80 years later: As they get to know each other, she asks him about himself. He answers: "I began life as a young boy." To which she responds: "It's nice to know you haven't changed sex."[17] These days, some people do. In those days, it was unthinkable and a joke.

A little later the same year, they appeared together again in director Tay Garnett's *One Way Passage*, an unapologetic tearjerker that still successfully tugs the heartstrings today. The premise of the 1932 movie is improbable enough: On a passenger ship sailing from Hong Kong to San Francisco, a dying young woman (the beautiful Francis) meets and falls in love with a man (Powell) who she does not know is being returned to the States to be executed for a murder. This is the last journey for each of them. The production heightened the film's verisimilitude by filming for six days on an ocean liner, the S.S. *Calawaii*, staffed by officers and crew from the Los Angeles Steamship Company and anchored off Long Beach.[18]

The two actors somehow make this unlikely, even unbelievable premise into a charming and touching love story. On a shore excursion in the Hawaiian Islands, Powell's character forgoes a planned escape to spend the rest of his short life back on board their ship with his newfound love. Throughout their flirtation, they habitually drink martinis together and then break the glasses, leaving the crossed stems behind on the bar. After a month-long Pacific passage, the ship docks in San Francisco and Powell and Francis disembark separately, presumably to their expected fates though promising to meet again for New Year's in Aguascalientes, Mexico. We expect each to die very shortly. The film ends in a crowded Mexican bar on New Year's Eve. Bartenders hear the sound of glasses breaking and turn to see two stems lying crossed on the bar. THE END. This film synopsis undoubtedly sounds silly but these two actors combine just the right pathos, intelligence and honest, subdued emotion to make it work. The film won an Academy Award for Best Original Story.

In 1931, Powell gave an unusually dark interview to magazine writer Gladys Hall (1891–1977), whom *The New York Times* called the "undisputed queen of the cozy confession."[19] Powell, just 39, seemed philosophical and lonely:

> Most of us are happy, I think, in our twenties, if ever. We have work to do and we are just beginning to do it. There seems to be limitless time ahead of us. The day we go through the little green door lies very far ahead…. We are enthusiastic. And enthusiasm is the blood and pulse of happiness. Before twenty we are enduring the growing pains of life. After that we are enduring the going pains of death.[20]

Working with Carole Lombard (then little-known) on *Man of the World* and *Ladies' Man* in 1931, Powell fell in love. It must have been a bit disconcerting for him to star in *Ladies' Man* with both current love Lombard and past love Francis. Powell, 38, and Lombard, 22, married in 1931. Supposedly, he wanted her to set aside her career and become a stay-at-home wife and mother.[21] When she refused, he relented and helped her acquire a top Hollywood agent and coached her in several roles.[22] They divorced two years later. And then resumed their romance. And then separated again.

Lombard, blonde, fast-talking and sexy in both a "just one of the guys" kind of way and simultaneously in an upscale glamorous way, soon came to be identified with the emerging genre of "screwball comedy." Lombard biographer Wes Gehring wrote, "Most members of the audience … equated screwballs [with Lombard].… No other actress came to be so

Carole Lombard in a Paramount glamour shot from 1932, when she was Mrs. William Powell. Making her screen debut at age 12 in 1921's *A Perfect Crime*, Lombard went on to appear in more than 50 features before her death in a plane crash in 1942. She was married to Clark Gable at the time of her death.

associated with a particular comedic form.... Audiences loved Lombard because she promised them laughs and always delivered them."[23] The elements of screwball comedy include fast-paced repartee, overlapping dialogue, farcical situations, disguises and mistaken identity. The screwball comedienne might appear ditzy and over-caffeinated but remained simultaneously funny and sexy. Plots revolved around the physical and intellectual battle of the sexes; of mismatched couples finding romance and, eventually, sharing a happy ending, usually in marriage.

In 1934, the Hays Office began enforcing movie censorship. Screwball comedies, a subgenre of romantic comedies, allowed the studios to satisfy the censors and still intrigue or titillate an audience. Well-known screwball comedies include *It Happened One Night* (1934), *My Man Godfrey* (1936) and *Bringing Up Baby* (1938). Elements of *The Thin Man* (1934) apply as well.

Lombard (1908–1942), born Jane Alice Peters, came to personify the genre. Her romance with Powell began on the set of one of the 1931 pictures in which they co-starred.[24] Though she married Powell after a whirlwind romance, just two years later she announced their marriage "a waste of time—his and mine."[25] Gossips speculated that the previously unknown Lombard had used the established star Powell for her own career advancement. Their later film *My Man Godfrey* (1936) showed there were no hard feelings as Powell insisted on the casting of ex-wife Lombard. It was a rare pairing of a real-life divorced couple playing an on-screen romantic couple.

In *My Man Godfrey* (1936), rich young people enjoy a scavenger hunt which includes finding "a forgotten man" among the down-and-out at a shanty town. Lombard drags the down-on-his-luck Powell home and in no time he is solving her family's multiple problems and winning her love. Shown, from left, are Lombard, Franklin Pangborn, and Powell.

Lombard's "anything goes" attitude may have tested Powell's reserved demeanor. He didn't like her cursing, which she sometimes did just to annoy him,[26] and she grew tired of how his buttoned-down persona transferred from the screen to their personal life. She complained, "The son of a bitch is acting even when he takes his pajamas off."[27] Lombard, who went on to marry Clark Gable, died tragically at age 33 in a plane crash while returning from a tour selling war bonds.

Powell, who broke into pictures in a silent *Sherlock Holmes*, had four outings as detective Philo Vance, whom Dashiell Hammett publicly denigrated in his book reviews of this S.S. Van Dine series. Powell starred as Vance in *The Canary Murder Case* (1929), *The Greene Murder Case* (1929), *The Benson Murder Case* (1930) and *The Kennel Murder Case* (1933).

A year before *The Thin Man*, Powell was a detective yet again. He had the three-piece suit, the charm, the quick wit and the quick action of Nick Charles but he was betrayed by a weak script and weak dialogue in the dull *Private Detective 62*. He co-starred with Margaret Lindsay (1910–1981), who is good enough to have been a Nora if she had the lines that Hammett and the Hacketts provided for Myrna Loy. The whole picture disappoints with its short scenes, quick fadeouts and truncated action in a film of less than 75 minutes. Near the beginning, one scene sparkles: Donald Free (Powell), a U.S. diplomat being shipped back to France for stealing state secrets, escapes from a French ship, swims ashore and enters a darkened house. He makes his way through empty rooms until he finds two illicit lovers in an intimate situation. Suddenly a private detective knocks down the door and threatens the woman of the couple, married to the detective's employer, with exposure. Powell, still wet from his swim, dons some dry clothing in another room and presents himself, claiming he owns the house, and says that the woman is simply meeting with the two men to discuss business. Even as he plays the detective for a sucker, he simultaneously shakes down the woman's lover for rent and the detective for a new door. He winds up with a tidy sum to begin his life on the run.

The film is also notable for the brief presence of Theresa Harris (1906–1985) as a maid. Harris, who had roles in some 95 films (including 14 in 1933 alone), was a rare talent who could act, dance and sing, but was confined to playing maids again and again due to her skin color and Hollywood's racism. In 1937, she told the newspaper *The Afro-American*:

> I never had the chance to rise about the role of maid in Hollywood movies. My color was against me any way you looked at it. The fact that I was not 'hot' stamped me either as uppity or relegated me to the small role of stooge or servant.... My ambition is to be an actress. Hollywood had no parts for me.[28]

In foreshadowings of *The Thin Man*, at one point we see an Asta lookalike among the dogs roaming Powell's office. At the end of the film, after Free has saved the damsel in distress and they appear to be going their separate ways, Free leaves Janet's apartment and walks out the building's front door. Janet calls out to him from a fourth floor window:

> **JANET:** "Don, do they let you have wives in the diplomatic service?"
> **FREE:** "Are you by any chance proposing to me?"
> **JANET:** "And you're supposed to be a detective!"[29]

Free races back into the building. Loy as Nora has much the same line ("And you call yourself a detective") at the end of *After the Thin Man*, when Nick sees Nora knitting baby socks and belatedly realizes she is pregnant. I still don't know why it's titled *Private Detective 62*. What happened to 61? The working title was *Man Killer*, which seems much better. Seven more Powell movies followed in 1933–34, including his pairing with Myrna Loy in *Manhattan Melodrama*, best remembered for being fatal for John Dillinger.

After filming *The Thin Man*, Powell made many more films, including a pairing with his lover Jean Harlow in *Reckless* (1935) and his only movie to win a Best Picture Academy Award, *The Great Ziegfeld* (1936), written by the screenwriter duo from *The Thin Man* and also co-starring Myrna Loy. Double-dating to attend the Academy Awards presentations that year were Powell with Jean Harlow and Clark Gable with Powell's ex-wife Carole Lombard.[30]

The Thin Man's success led to the sincerest form of flattery: imitation. Other studios raced to produce male-female duo detectives and to combine screwball comedy and mystery in a single new genre. RKO had a leg up because they rented out Powell from MGM and cast him with a new love interest, Ginger Rogers, in *Star of Midnight* (1935). I watched the film, curious to see how Powell would do with a female detective co-star other than Myrna Loy. The film, directed by Stephen Roberts, was released to good box office. The mystery plot is too convoluted for me to neatly summarize or, really, to even understand. It revolves around the disappearance of Mary Smith, a masked stage

William Powell and Myrna Loy first met when they co-starred in the 1934 MGM film *Manhattan Melodrama*. (Though shot prior to *The Thin Man*, it was released later.) In the film, Loy as Eleanor Packer leaves gang boss Blackie Gallagher (Clark Gable) for crime buster Jim Wade (Powell). Wade rises to the governorship as Blackie heads to the electric chair.

singer-actress who never appears in the film and the murder of a reporter trying to track her down. Powell, as the famous detective Clay "Dal" Dalzell, comes under suspicion himself but, using a ruse, flushes out the murderer at the end.

Dal seems a lot like Nick, drinking, sharing acerbic witticisms and fending off designing and beautiful women. There may be more wealthy detectives in the world than I imagined because Dal's Manhattan apartment comes complete with a garden terrace, a grand piano, a barber chair in the huge bathroom and a butler. All this without Nora's money. At one point, Dal, in a sly reference to Powell's previous film work as a detective (four movies as Philo Vance), says that people consider him "Charlie Chan, Philo Vance and the Saint all rolled into one."

The film's main interest centers on the relationship of Dal and young, beautiful, wealthy Donna Martin (Rogers), who not only aids Dal's detecting but also spends the movie trying to lure Dal into matrimony. They are quite entertaining together, though not quite at the level of Nick and Nora. At one point, this exchange precedes some physical hijinks:

> **DAL:** "Say, mind you, if I do go on and do this, I'm only doing it because of your mother. She's a nice woman. It must be terrible for a woman to have a daughter like you."
> **DONNA:** "My mother just adores me."
> **DAL:** "It would be more to the point if she spanked you. I don't mind to do it myself."

Donna turns around and bends over, puffing a cigarette, saying, "Well, this'll be new."[31] To her surprise, Dal kicks her gently in the butt. And when he turns away, she kicks him back. Contrast this to the spanking scene in *The Thin Man Goes Home* when only the man gets to do the spanking.

I only knew Ginger Rogers, born Virginia Katherine McMath (1911–1995), from her nine musical roles with Fred Astaire in which, people said, "she worked harder than Fred because she did everything he did but backwards and in high heels." She made 64 other film appearances in a wide variety of roles. *Star of Midnight*, shoehorned in between two movies with Astaire, was her only film with Powell. At film's end, Dal and Donna are wed and we are left wondering if the studio imagined more films with a witty and married couple of detectives.

Star of Midnight contains egregious racism. The only black person to appear plays, you guessed it, a maid. The script includes these nuggets: Dal to Tommy Tennant: "Now listen, Tom, you're free, white and 21. You can do as you choose."[32] When Dal tells Tommy he was right about a deduction, Tommy returns the praise saying, "You're a white man, Dalzell."[33] What higher praise could there be?

New York Times reviewer Andre Sennwald called *Star of Midnight* "sleek, witty and engaging entertainment [but it] seems like a sequel to *The Thin Man*. ...Myrna Loy, of course, will always be the perfect partner for Mr. Powell."[34]

But Loy was on strike at the time and MGM was so eager to cash in on *The Thin Man*'s success that they grasped at one female star after another to replace her. So, also in 1935, they paired Powell with Rosalind Russell (1907–76) in *Rendezvous*. It was only her ninth film in what would become a 35-year and 50-movie career; she's best-remembered for *Auntie Mame* and *Gypsy*. Set in Washington, D.C., during World War I, *Rendezvous* is a weird mashup of comedy, romance and spy thriller, none of which really work. It revolves around journalist–amateur cryptologist Bill Gordon (Powell) and Joel Carter (Russell), the niece of the Assistant Secretary of War. Cesar Romero, whom we saw in *The Thin Man*, plays Nicholas Nieterstein, a German spy. The spy plot has big holes: Why does everyone from the Assistant Secretary's niece to a German assassin have such easy access to the super-secret encryption room which has armed guards at every door, including the rest room?

What does work is the chemistry between Powell and Russell as they first meet and fall in love, all in a day. Russell later wrote,

> I felt self-conscious. Powell and Loy had been a hit in *The Thin Man*, they were an unbeatable team, so my first day on *Rendezvous*, I tried to apologize. "I know you don't want me, you'd rather have Myrna." Powell denied it: "I love Myrna, but I think this is good for you, and I'm glad we're doing it together." He was not only a dear, he was cool. If an actor thought he could get any place by having tantrums, watching Bill Powell would have altered his opinion. I remember a story conference during which he objected to a scene that he felt wasn't right for him. He was at once imperious and lucid. "It's beyond my histrionic ability to do this," he said. I thought that was delicious.[35]

She is right that she is not Myrna Loy. But who is? Russell does well but in each scene we miss the arched brow, the searching gaze, the contradiction of the commitment offered even while Loy maintains an cool distance. It doesn't help that the film's many writers have crafted Joel as a ninny. Loy could somehow play silly and yet never lose her intelligence.

Russell is also right in quoting Powell on his limited "histrionic ability." "Histrionic" usually means overly dramatic. She calls him "lucid" but we might also add the adjective "limited." In *Rendezvous*, Powell simply plays Nick Charles in a military uniform. The double takes, the sardonic smile, the pauses in his delivery, followed by rapid bursts of speech, all hark back to *The Thin Man* and every other Powell movie. He escaped these limits in a few films like *One Way Passage* and *Mister Roberts*. We cannot imagine Powell playing Hamlet or Lear, for example. These roles are beyond his limited range. Keep in mind that Stanislavsky and Method Acting, as interpreted by Lee Strasberg and others, was only then being developed and would not be seen in films until the late 1940s. The Method required actors to dig deep into their character and bring to a role their own emotional memories. The acting of the 1920s and '30s by comparison skates on the surface of a character and relies on stereotypes (e.g., the drinker, the vamp, the murderer) without examining how, for example, one criminal differs from every other criminal we've seen before.

Within his histrionic range, Powell is masterful. In the first 15 minutes of *Rendezvous*, Bill Gordon woos Russell through a panoply of charm, disdain, trickery, mockery and ardor. As Joel, Russell has the right reactions down well and when she turns from flight to her own pursuit of Bill, she clearly demonstrates the result of her character's inner struggle. But one can't help thinking that Loy, with her sardonic outer shell guarding a soft and yearning heart, would have performed even better.

Rendezvous is also a good film with which to play the game "Find the Black Actor." Or the Latino, or the Asian. Look in the Washington, D.C., street scenes, the hotel rooms and lobbies, the parties, the government offices, the train stations. Not one black actor to be found in a movie set in our capital which even in 1935 had a significant African American population.[36]

In 1935, MGM loaned Powell out to RKO and they made their own *Thin Man* knock-off, *The Ex-Mrs. Bradford*. Jean Arthur (1900–91), born Gladys Georgianna Greene, is best-known for her work with director Frank Capra in three films: *Mr. Deeds*

Goes to Town (1936), *You Can't Take It with You* (1938) and *Mr. Smith Goes to Washington* (1939). *The Ex-Mrs. Bradford*, directed by Stephen Roberts, may be the best of all the *Thin Man* imitators. Here our sleuths are, get this, not married but divorced. Powell plays Dr. "Brad" Bradford, a successful surgeon, complete with chauffeur, receptionist and a butler named Stokes, played by the hilariously droll Eric Blore. Brad's ex-wife Paula (Arthur), a writer of mysteries, wants her man back. She so complicated his life with her love of real-life murder investigations that he divorced her. Immediately upon her return to serve Brad with a suit for alimony, dead bodies start piling up.

When a jockey turns up dead mid-race, Paula pulls Brad back into sleuthing. A plethora of suspects had money riding on either the winning or losing horse and each had a motive. It all gets very complicated but Powell and Arthur keep it interesting. The dapper Powell does his well-practiced Nick Charles routine: arched right eyebrow, rolling eyes, odd little laugh and nonplussed double takes. Arthur, beautiful even in a funny hair style of the period but with some gorgeous gowns, adds a manic performance to the goings-on. Brad, like Nick, knows people in high and low places, from rich swells to ex-cons. In the final scene he brings all the suspects together for the big reveal.

But the fun is again in the relationship, not the crime, and Powell and Arthur deliver. When she catches him breaking into a suspect's apartment, she offers, "If you're gonna keep housebreaking, you better wear hair pins" as she shows him how to pick a lock. He kicks her in the shins at one point to keep her from blurting out information; a few minutes later, she kicks *him* in the shins, saying, "Now we're even."[37] At the race track trying to prevent another murder, she asks: "So did you inoculate him?" He responds, "With great difficulty." Arthur responds, "Oh, I thought you used a hypodermic."[38]

Arthur's mystery-writing avocation, for these rich people have pastimes not jobs, is never developed but one of her ideas of writing "murders for children" has the potential for macabre hilarity (but it goes unexplored). The murder weapon is also macabre: The killer places a venomous black widow spider encased in a gelatin capsule on the victim's skin. The warmth of the skin slowly melts the gelatin and the spider bites and kills the victim. How a spider hangs on to a jockey aboard a racehorse going 40 miles per hour is anybody's guess. Ignore the fact that black widow spider bites are rarely fatal and that gelatin capsules dissolve in the human stomach rather than on the skin. Ignore all that, but give the murderer points for originality and arachnophilia.

The film ends with the remarriage of Powell and Arthur's characters and paves the way for future marital sleuthing *à la* Powell and Loy but we got no sequels here. (Director Roberts dropped dead of a heart attack at the age of 40 just two months after the movie's release.[39]) This film was a one-off: Though Powell and Arthur had chemistry, Arthur's manic portrayal grates after a while, as does her voice, and we understand why Brad divorced her. Loy's secret was her underplaying of her role, both straight (wo)man to her leading comedic man, whether it be Powell, Cary Grant, Spencer Tracy, or Robert Montgomery, and yet distanced from the resulting mayhem, self-possessed and calm in the midst of tumult. Now, a movie about a divorced couple solving mysteries might have had legs in theory. This movie made money for RKO and garnered good reviews. (*The New York Times*: "In brief, list *The Ex-Mrs. Bradford* as one of the year's top-flight comedies."[40]) But though they had teamed four times previously, there were to be no further Powell-Arthur pairings. MGM finally threw in the towel, acceding to Loy's demand for the same salary paid Powell in *The Thin Man* series, and MGM reunited them in *After the Thin Man* and *The Great Ziegfeld*.

The fourth of 14 Powell-Loy pairings, *The Great Ziegfeld* is an entertaining three-hour epic. It garnered three Oscars: Best Picture, Best Actress for Luise Rainer (1910–2014) and Best Choreography. (German born Rainer scored the Best Actress Oscar again the next year for her performance as a Chinese peasant in Pearl Buck's *The Good Earth*, the first actress to win in consecutive years.) Powell was Oscar-nominated three times, for *The Thin Man*, *My Man Godfrey* (1936) and *Life with Father* (1947), but never won.

The Great Ziegfeld, the story of the theatrical wizard and Broadway entrepreneur Flo Ziegfeld, is a magical picture with its elaborate gowns and choreography, especially one theater scene with a revolving stage where the performers, numbering 180 in a single continuous scene,[41] seem to go on dancing forever atop a many-layered wedding cake–like set. The performance of Ray Bolger alone is worth the price of admission.

And then it happens: the stink in the theater, the rancid rising bile in the pit of your stomach as you watch *The Great Ziegfeld* and see Buddy Doyle impersonating Eddie Cantor in blackface, with the big lips and the white gloves of minstrelsy. Then the film dissolves into a nightmare vision of a racist America. The only actual African American performer is Libby Taylor (1902–1961), who appeared in *Star of Midnight* and played maids in at least 34 of her 49 films. Later in the film, we see an all-black band. No black people are seen on the streets of the 1893 World's Fair,

The stars of 1936's *The Great Ziegfeld*, from left, William Powell, Luise Rainer, Myrna Loy and Virginia Bruce. Rainer was the first actress to win Oscars in consecutive years, first for *The Great Ziegfeld* and then for *The Good Earth*.

aboard an ocean liner crossing the Atlantic, or on the streets of London and New York. Where'd they go?

Our favorite detective Nat Pendleton, Detective Guild in *The Thin Man*, is also in *The Great Ziegfeld*. Pendleton, who won a silver medal in wrestling at the 1920 Olympics, plays Sandow, "The World's Strongest Man," in a ridiculous blonde curly wig, that has him looking like Harpo Marx. Turns out, however, that Sandow (1867–1925), born Friedrich Wilhelm Müller in Germany, was a real bodybuilder who went to work for Ziegfeld at the 1893 World's Fair. Today, Sandow is considered the father of modern bodybuilding competitions.

Frank Morgan, later to play the title role in *The Wizard of Oz*, is here as Jack Billings, Ziegfeld's friend and rival. Billie Burke, seen as Glinda the Good Witch of the North in *The Wizard of Oz* and Ziegfeld's real-life wife, served as technical consultant. If you watch very closely, you might see chorus girl Pat Ryan, the future Pat Nixon, wife of Richard Nixon and First Lady of the United States, as an extra.

By now, Powell "had a reputation around the studios for being a 'bit of a fuss pot'.... He'd been known to lavish time on just the right arrangement of a silk square in his chest pocket.... He wouldn't dream of making an appearance without a tie, much less without a shirt."[42] Powell, this universally acclaimed "gentleman," also wooed a woman as flamboyant as he was staid, as exuberant as he was self-contained, as reckless as he was composed: "the blonde bombshell" herself, Jean Harlow. Harlow, born Harlean Carpentier in 1911, exploded on movie screens incorporating lust and recklessness in the pre–Code years. Her on-screen characters were famous for using their physical assets to manipulate men and sleeping their way to the top.

A studio scout discovered Harlow sitting in her car waiting to give a friend a lift home after an audition at Fox. "She pursued an acting career," one biographer writes, "simply to please her mother, who had decided to live out her own dreams of stardom vicariously through her daughter."[43] Like Hammett, Harlow lacked formal schooling, having dropped out of Ferry Hall School in Lake Forest, Illinois, when, in her freshman year, at the age of 16, she eloped with a man of 20. The marriage soon failed.[44]

The next year, at 17, Harlow signed a five-year contract with Hal Roach (1892–1992), who rose to prominence producing Laurel and Hardy and Our Gang comedies. You can see how Roach used her in *Double Whoopee*, one of Laurel and Hardy's last silent films: Eighteen-year-old Harlow appears as a "Swanky Blonde," according to the film credits, and is ineptly aided by Laurel as a hotel doorman. He gets her dress train caught in the closed door of a departing cab and she enters the lobby on Hardy's arm with what would be a mini-dress by modern standards but shows more of her shapely legs than the public was then used to seeing. With the sight gag over, she exits the film. But after ten previous uncredited shorts, this bit convinced MGM to show even more of her.[45]

She found her breakout role in Howard Hughes' World War I extravaganza *Hell's Angels*. Much of *Hell's Angels* was shot as a silent film when the public fell in love with talkies; a decision was made to start anew and make it a talkie. But the female lead, Greta Nissen, was a Norwegian actress with a thick accent. To replace her, Hughes plucked Harlow out of a minor role in a previously filmed party scene. In *Hell's Angels* she develops the hypersexual and amoral screen persona that followed her throughout her brief career. As Helen, she completes a love triangle with two brothers (both pilots) who are destined for combat. Drawn to Monte, the bad boy, Helen dismisses Roy, the upright brother, saying, "He'd be horrified if he knew what I was really like." She seduces Monte on the night they meet and, having invited him up to her room, purrs that famous line, "Would you be shocked if I slipped into something more comfortable?" Since the gown she has on leaves little to the imagination, we can only think she is nude beneath the robe she then dons. Her fame, and her indelible image, followed.[46]

In 1931, in less than ten minutes of screen time in Warners' big-grossing *The Public Enemy* as Gwen Allen, Harlow literally stops traffic as gangster-on-the-make Tom Powers (James Cagney) brakes his car on a busy Chicago street to look her over. Though not beautiful by today's standards, Harlow took the screen as the "It" girl of her time. Tom Powers thinks so too, and invites her into his touring car. Impressed on the set by her physical endowment, Cagney asked, "How do you keep them [her breasts] up?" "I ice 'em." said Harlow, who then returned to her dressing room to do so.[47]

Columbia changed the title of their 1931 film from *Gallagher* to *Platinum Blonde* to take advantage of Harlow's unique look.[48] According to biographer Irving Shulman, Harlow "had become the most popular, the most photographed star in movie magazines, and her fan mail increased daily by hundreds of letters."[49] *Platinum Blonde* "resulted in the founding of Platinum Blonde clubs in at least a hundred cities ... women of all ages began to imitate Jean's dress, make-up and speech mannerisms."[50]

My favorite Harlow movie is the 1932 *Red-Headed Woman*. A number of stars, including Clara Bow and Colleen Moore, had already turned down the part, not wishing to play a tart on film.[51] Harlow dyed her hair red, even for a black and white film, to play a brazen, conniving liar and home-wrecking sexual predator. She gets to show a lot of leg and a breast as well. Later she makes love to a married man in a phone booth and rises from office stenographer to French-speaking Parisian racehorse owner by film's end. In the best line of the movie, Harlow asks her gal pal, "Can you see through this [dress]?" Assured that she can, Harlow responds, "I'll wear it."[52]

Time reviewed *Red-Headed Woman* and labeled its star "Harlot Harlow."[53] The film was based on a *Saturday Evening Post* serial about which the author, Katherine Brush, a redhead herself, wrote: "It's [about] a small-town girl who sleeps her way to the top."[54] F. Scott Fitzgerald, one of the country's greatest novelists, penned the first draft of the script but Irving Thalberg rejected it and secretly gave it to Anita Loos, who later scored with *Gentlemen Prefer Blondes* as a novel, play, musical and two films. Trying to softly part ways with Fitzgerald, Thalberg and his aide Paul Bern praised his script and paid him, and everyone at the studio lined up to thank and congratulate him on his last day at the studio. Samuel Marx wrote of the charade: "All the people he met acted out the false front. He was just leaving when Director Marcel de Sano was coming in and maliciously told him he had been tricked. 'Anita Loos is starting over from the beginning.' With that Fitzgerald took off on a monumental drunk and Thalberg fired de Sano."[55]

MGM promoted *Red-Headed Woman* with advertising lines like "Take all men as you find them ... but TAKE them" and "All men go too far ... but most girls are a poor judge of distance."[56] Harlow married studio executive Paul Bern, born Paul Levy (1889–1932), in 1932 and scandal followed on their wedding night.

> If ensuing reports are to be believed, the wedding night was Kafkaesque. Mild mannered Paul Bern turned out to be a sadist, and Jean his victim. The pitiful fact of Paul's underdeveloped genitalia and impotence had driven him ... to beat his young wife.... [Harlow] was in a state of shock, with welts across her back, shoulders, and buttocks.[57]

The words of Leatrice Joy, who inadvertently saw Bern naked, may explain the fiasco: "[H]is penis was the size of a pinkie," she said.[58] Some writers attribute Harlow's later kidney problems to the beating. Bern committed suicide during the filming of MGM's *Red Dust*, two months after their wedding, precipitating a tabloid scandal enhanced by his suicide note to Jean: "Dearest Dear, Unfortunately this is the only way to make good a frightful wrong I have done you and to wipe out my abject humiliation. You understand that last night was only a comedy."[59]

The chain of events merit a Hammett detective story. The moment Bern's body was found, a call went out to L.B. Mayer. Mayer, MGM PR head Howard Strickling, David O. Selznick, Thalberg and his wife Norma Shearer arrived on the scene long before anyone bothered to call the police. Did someone move the body? Did someone else pen the suicide note? Was it *really* a suicide note? Was Bern's death suicide or murder? If murder, by whom: Harlow herself, or Dorothy Millette? It turns out Bern was already married to Millette when he wed Harlow. Samuel Marx in his book *Make Believe Saints* writes that Bern killed himself over the scandal of being a bigamist, not from the humiliation of being impotent. His "real" wife Millette committed suicide the day after Bern's death by leaping from the Delta King riverboat into the Sacramento River.

Harlow collapsed on the set of *Red Dust* when given news of Bern's death. Mayer asked Tallulah Bankhead to replace Harlow, but she refused.[60] Harlow began drinking heavily, an occupational danger in Hollywood. Patricia Highsmith, author of the Ripley series of crime novels, noted in words that might have applied equally to Hammett and other writers or to Harlow and other actors: Writers (and actors) drink 'because they must change their identities a million times in their writing. This is tiring, but drinking does it automatically for them. One moment they are a king, the next a murderer … some people actually prefer to stay the same person … all the time."[61]

Harlow was back on set four days after her husband's funeral, shooting a nude scene in a rain barrel. *Red Dust* opened six weeks later and Harlow's reputation went from "immoral siren to innocent victim."[62] *Red Dust* was the second of Harlow's six films with Clark Gable. She shows a lot of leg and thigh as the prostitute Vantine. But it was her rain barrel bath scene as Gable grabs her hair and dunks her that caused a sensation. Supposedly, after filming the scene, Harlow stood up, topless, and said, "Here's one for the boys in the lab," meaning the folks printing the "rushes," the daily film footage.[63] The director Victor Fleming snipped the footage first, knowing it would have wound up all around the country.[64] Novelist Graham Greene said of Harlow: "She toted a breast like a man totes a gun."[65]

In all, *Red Dust* is a silly story of Gable using and rejecting "bad girl" Vantine and then falling for and seducing a "decent woman," Mary Astor as Barbara, wife of the newly arrived engineer on his Indochina rubber plantation. In the end, stricken by conscience, Gable throws Astor over so she can return to her husband. Enraged by his betrayal, Astor shoots Gable; Harlow nurses him back to health. The film was shot on MGM's back lot, "on eight separate rooms but around a central compound complete with working river … with overhead piping installed to provide monsoon rain…. Live moths were released before each take to ensure authenticity, despite an alarming death toll as they constantly flew into the lights."[66]

If you want to understand the Vietnamese 100-year struggle for independence from foreign colonialists, first France, then Japan, then France again and finally the U.S., culminating in what we call the War in Vietnam, see *Red Dust* for its casual depictions of cruelty visited upon the Vietnamese, Cambodians and Laotians of "Indochina" by the white colonizers, like Gable here as a rubber plantation owner. The workers are pushed around, yelled at, demeaned, called "a bunch of monkeys," "coolies," "lazy," and addressed as "boy."[67] Though the word "coolie" originally meant simply a "hired laborer," it became a slur for Asians working in the U.S. and led to the Anti-Coolie law of 1862, a precursor to the Chinese Exclusion Act of 1882, keeping Asians out of our country after they had mined our gold, built our railroads and laundered our trousers.[68]

By the release of *Bombshell* in 1933: "Harlow was the biggest female star at MGM, if not in Hollywood on the whole."[69] Here Harlow completes the look: her eyebrows shaved off, then drawn into an extreme arch and her lips painted into a Cupid's bow. MGM publicists offered $10,000 to any hairdresser who could match the color. Naturally, no one could. Back then, there was no dye on the market that could make one's hair as white-hot as Harlow's. Her personal hairdresser, Alfred Pagano, revealed the secret decades later: "We used peroxide, ammonia, Clorox and Lux flakes."[70] The harsh chemicals caused Harlow to lose hair by the fistful and she often resorted to hats and wigs on-screen and off.

Bombshell fascinates for its knowing "inside Hollywood" look and meta-theatrical approach. Harlow plays megastar Lola Burns who is, for all intents and purposes, Harlow herself. Lola is dissatisfied with her fast-talking publicist E.J. "Space" Hanlon (Lee Tracy), a takeoff on MGM publicity head honcho Howard Strickling. The film cuts close to the bone of truth: Lola attempts to adopt a baby but "Space" thwarts her, saying: "You think I want my bombshell turned into a rubber nipple?"[71] In real life Harlow desperately wanted a child. In the film, Lola flees Hollywood only to encounter a wealthy beau, Gifford Middleton (Franchot Tone), who seems to know nothing of her Hollywood notoriety. Hanlon messes this up as well and a disillusioned Lola returns to her studio chastened and ready to work. Only back on set does Lola learn that even Middleton and his parents were only actors working for the studio. Lola then accepts her fate as a movie star and "Space" Hanlon as her man.

Directed by Victor Fleming and produced by Hunt Stromberg of *The Thin Man*, *Bombshell* is a screwball comedy meant to satirize the stardom of Clara Bow, the original "It" girl ... and beau of Victor Fleming. But if we don't know Clara Bow, we do see all the similarities to Harlow's life: an interfering father (actually her freeloading stepfather), the rain barrel made famous in *Red Dust*, the fans copying her look, a stalker, men ogling her, a star caught in the dream machine where everyone wants a piece of her. After its release Harlow was forever known by its title: the blonde bombshell. She was just 22. Harlow explained her stardom this way: "Men like me because I don't wear a brassiere. Women like me because I don't look like a girl who would steal a husband. At least not for long."[72]

There are some disconcertingly racist elements to *Bombshell*. African Americans decked out like Nubian slaves fan Lola as she lies in bed. Her maid is played by Louise Beavers at her Mammyesque best. Beavers (1900–62) appeared in dozens of films and two hit television shows from the 1920s until 1960, most often cast in the role of servant or slave. She often said she got the roles Hattie McDaniel turned down. Casting directors urged her to gain weight to keep her Mammy stature. Lola's black maid in the Arizona desert says: "I'm afraid I'm gonna get all sunburned here."[73] Such lines passed for humor then.

In 1933, Harlow married for the third time: MGM cameraman Hal Rosson had worked on several of her films. He was 38, 16 years her senior. The marriage lasted just seven months and may have been arranged by MGM to avoid a scandal of having Dorothy Baer name Harlow as the other woman in a divorce action against husband Max Baer, champion boxer turned actor.[74] We know all this is true because, in that pre–Internet age, weeklies and monthlies like *Photoplay, Picturegoer, Motion Picture, Film Pictorial, Hollywood Magazine, Modern Romances, Screen Book, Screen Guide, Screenland, Screenplay, Silver Screen* and *Motion Picture News*[75] breathlessly reported on Hollywood's foibles and scandals.

In 1934, straight off his success in *The Thin Man*, Powell met Harlow. The gossip columnists called Powell a gentleman on screen and off, "the most impeccably groomed man I ever met."[76] A former girlfriend said, "He was Nick Charles, and he was *good*."[77] Eighteen years younger than he, Harlow called Powell "Poppy," a match to her own family nickname of "Baby." To cap-

Lovers William Powell and Jean Harlow look very glamorous in an MGM publicity shot for the first of their two movies together, *Reckless* (1935). Many were puzzled by the relationship between the buttoned-down Powell and the free-wheeling, often *un*buttoned Harlow.

italize on their affair, Mayer ordered them cast together in *Reckless* (1935). The film's trailer promised "HARLOW SINGS! HARLOW DANCES!" but, since Harlow could neither sing nor dance, that was just more of Hollywood's false advertising. Virginia Verrill dubbed the singing voice for Harlow; Betty Halsey substituted for her in the dance sequences' long shots. Interestingly, Verrill (1916–1999) sang with various big bands and on the radio and regularly dubbed for stars in movies. She seemed on the verge of a breakout career herself when Sam Goldwyn cast her in *The Goldwyn Follies* and introduced her as "the second Myrna Loy." Then, irony of ironies, the studio decided she looked too much like Loy and eased her out. Thousands of women wanted to look like Loy. Verrill already did and it ruined her career. Verrill turned her back on Hollywood in 1938.[78]

Time put Harlow on its cover on August 19, 1935, looking glamorous in satin and feathers. She made *Libeled Lady* with Powell in 1936 after he had given her an engagement ring featuring a 150-carat star sapphire and costing $20,000 then[79] and worth $380,000 today. The scandal sheets informed readers that both platinum blonde Harlow and Carole Lombard dyed their pubic hair as well. Lombard once called the practice "making sure your collar and cuffs matched."[80] James Stewart made a brief appearance in *Wife vs. Secretary*, starring Gable, Loy and Harlow, and later attested to Harlow's allure and her kissing skills:

> It was then that I knew I'd never really been kissed before. There were six rehearsals, and the kissing gained each time in interest and enthusiasm. By the time we shot the scene, my psychology was all wrinkled. She was a stunning girl with a dress so low cut you had to bend down to pick it up and I was just a guy from Pennsylvania.... Her dresses were tight and she wore nothing under them.[81]

MGM's *Libeled Lady* starred Harlow, Powell, Loy and Spencer Tracy. Though Powell and Harlow were engaged, they played with different romantic partners on screen: Tracy and Harlow as one couple, Powell and Loy as the other. It has been rumored that Loy and Tracy had an affair during the shooting of the film.[82]

I wanted to see this movie because it is one of only two Powell and Harlow made together, the other being the poorly rated *Reckless*. Another screwball comedy, *Libeled Lady* is the best I've seen because the characters grow and change in the course of the film unlike *My Man Godfrey* and *Bombshell*. The premise is ridiculous as usual: You begin with a problem and then rather than seek the simplest, most direct solution, you imagine the most complicated and convoluted ploys to get what you want. In *Libeled Lady*, Tracy's character, editor at a New York City newspaper, has to stop heiress Loy from suing his paper after they accidentally libel her. Rather than apologizing publicly, or just leaving it to the lawyers, Tracy recruits ace libel expert Powell, who aims to maneuver Loy into a compromising situation so Tracy can blackmail her into dropping the case. To accomplish this, bachelor Powell must marry Tracy's fiancée Harlow, so that Loy can be presented as a homewrecker. In the end, this being a comedy, Powell and Loy marry and Tracy and Harlow marry and everyone, audience included, is happy.

Powell, self-contained, carries the film with one of his best performances, convincing us of his initial cynical, money-grubbing nature and his evolution into a man in love. Loy, as an heiress, looking more beautiful than ever, her face and body always calm and largely unreadable, can convey emotions with the tilt of her head or a look down her nose. Harlow is loud and brassy and you wonder how, this film coming just a year before her death, she might have developed as an actress if she eventually escaped the sexy persona that so often seemed to trap her. Tracy is forgettable here. The film sparkles with very "Nick and Nora"–ish dialogue:

> **Loy:** "Do you swim?"
> **Powell:** "As well as I dance."
> **Loy:** "Then you'll drown."

A bit later:

> **Powell:** "I thought I was awfully clever."
> **Loy:** "Yes, I thought you thought that."

And, as Powell removes mustard from Loy's face with his napkin, he gets even:

> **Loy:** "Am I beautiful again?"
> **Powell:** "No, just clean."[83]

The film was nominated for an Oscar for Best Picture, but lost, in an ironic twist, to *The Great Ziegfeld* which also starred Powell and Loy.

Many viewers want to see a special spark between real-life couple Powell and Harlow, but I can't detect it. Harlow supposedly wanted the part of the heiress so she could have the love scenes with Powell but MGM wanted another Powell-Loy vehicle. If anything, I saw a greater attraction between Powell and Loy but that is what the film wants us to see.

As usual, there are almost no people of color in the movie. The great actress Hattie McDaniel makes a brief appearance as a hotel maid but receives no screen credit. A 1916 fan magazine opined: "Negroes are frequently used as 'extras.' They can be attired so as to represent a variety of strange peoples."[84] Or so the studios seemed to think.

But Hollywood's willingness to appease white racism is perhaps nowhere more apparent than in the final reel of *Hold Your Man*, released in 1933. In the original print, Gable and Harlow are married by a black preacher but for prints destined for Southern theaters, a white actor was brought in to play the minister and the scene reshot.[85] In the 1940s, the president of the National Association for the Advancement of Colored People, Walter White, called for an end to the "old time mammies, slothful servants, impish toadies, and grinning hoofers" who constituted the only roles open to African Americans.[86]

Also in a bit part in *Libeled Lady*, as Tracy's butler, is Otto Yamaoka, an American of Japanese descent who plays Ching (a Chinese name) in two short scenes. Audiences could accept a Chinese character more easily than a Japanese given Japan's ongoing rampage through Manchuria, Korea and parts of mainland China. Though he was born in Seattle and quite able to speak English without an accent, Yamaoka's scripted dialogue has him speaking pidgin English. Six years after appearing in this film, he and his family were imprisoned in the Heart Mountain Center in Wyoming.[87]

During her filming of *Saratoga* for MGM, co-starring with Clark Gable in 1937, Harlow's kidney condition worsened and with filming 90 percent completed she collapsed on set. Friends took her home where she spent several days in bed under the care of her mother, a devout Christian Scientist, and without a doctor. Powell, Gable and Mayer intervened and got her to a hospital where she died on June 7, 1937. According to one report, Powell sat at her bedside and when the end came, he "sobbed and rushed from the room."[88] According to the *Los Angeles Evening Express*, Powell "went into seclusion at his home, unable to assuage his grief."[89]

Did Powell and Harlow really plan to wed? To gossip columnist extraordinaire Louella Parsons, Harlow had confided, "Poppy feels we shouldn't get married." "How do you feel?" asked Parsons. "I love him," said Harlow. "He's the only man I'd want to settle down with and raise a family. But I suppose he's right ... perhaps two movie people with careers shouldn't marry."[90] Harlow biographer David Stenn claims Harlow aborted Powell's baby because he would not marry.[91] Powell never knew, just as Hammett didn't know when Hellman had an abortion after she concluded that Hammett would never marry her.

While most biographies attribute Harlow's death at age 26 to kidney disease, Irving Shulman, in his book subtitled *An Intimate Biography*, attributes her kidney problems and death to a beating administered by her second husband Paul Bern as he flew into a self-loathing rage at his inability to consummate their marriage on their wedding night.[92] Clark Gable and Carole Lombard attended Harlow's funeral at Forest Lawn to support the grieving Powell. (Five years later, Powell returned the grim favor, attending Lombard's funeral with her widower Gable, again at Forest Lawn.) Harlow's

William Powell and Jean Harlow in a *Reckless* publicity still. Harlow reportedly wanted marriage and babies; Powell did not. Their second and last movie was *Libeled Lady* (1936) with Myrna Loy and Spencer Tracy.

obituary made the front page of *The New York Times*. "It is reported that a single white gardenia with an unsigned note was placed in her hands before she was interred, presumed to have been written by Powell. The note read, 'Good night, my dearest darling.'" Powell paid for her final resting place: a $25,000, 9×10-foot private room lined with multicolored imported marble, located in the "Sanctuary of Benediction" of the Great Mausoleum, Forest Lawn Memorial Park, Glendale.[93] Powell and Loy had to quickly go back on the set of *Double Wedding*. Said Loy: "Bill and I tried to carry on with the slapstick comedy but he collapsed and the picture kept being delayed."[94] Loy even hastened to his house one day when he intimated on the phone that he was contemplating suicide.

It is hard to watch *Saratoga* today. Though meant to be a romantic comedy, one cannot forget Harlow's physical weakness and approaching death. She finally had a role that did not require her to play a hussy, vamp or woman of the streets. Instead she is the daughter and granddaughter of horse breeders, engaged to a New York millionaire, and she gets to be a lady on-screen. The movie lets us know that her career really had no limits once she escaped the stereotypes based on her hair and physique.

MGM turned her death into box office gold. Knowing everyone would, out of grief or voyeurism, want to see Harlow's "last movie," the studio first teased the public with press releases about recasting and reshooting the movie without her. They floated the names of other actresses like Virginia Bruce and Jean Arthur as replacements. But MGM knew that fans would have nothing to do with such ideas. So the company reedited the film and used a body double, Mary Ella Dees (1911–2004) in long shots and filmed from behind while yet another actress supplied her voice. Viewers could tell the difference but at least the public got to see Harlow one last time and MGM had their biggest box office smash of 1937 when the film opened just seven weeks after Harlow's death.

By 1936, Powell had it made, professionally if not personally, standing among the top ten male box office attractions. Four of the five films in which he appeared that year received Academy Award nominations: *My Man Godfrey*, *The Great Ziegfeld*, *Libeled Lady* and *After the Thin Man*. By 1938, Powell ruled the box office at fourth place, surpassed only by Gary Cooper, Greta Garbo and Clark Gable.[95] He garnered three Best Actor nominations (for *The Thin Man*, *My Man Godfrey* and *Life with Father*), but never took home the Oscar. Perhaps most impressive was the diversity of roles and the length of his career, from his turn in *Sherlock Holmes* in 1922 to *Mister Roberts* 33 years later.

In 1940, he married a young actress, Diana Lewis, whom he christened "Mousie." When first introduced to the 5'1" actress, Powell told her, "You look just like a little mouse,"[96] and she adopted the nickname. When they married, Powell was 47 and Lewis 20. The marriage endured for 44 years, until Powell's death at age 91.

Powell *could* make a bad movie. For that, look no further than MGM's *The Hoodlum Saint*, directed by Norman Taurog. This 1946 stinker inadvertently charts Powell's decline in Hollywood fortunes as he ages ungracefully, somehow playing, at age 53, jowly and paunchy, a World War I doughboy romancing simultaneously a 22-year-old Esther Williams and 21-year-old Angela Lansbury. At one point, Lansbury's character, Dusty, asks, "Isn't it risky, playing around with religion?" The director and screenwriters answered that question at their peril as the film mixes Catholicism lite and cartoonish crooks (hardly hoodlums) who pray to St. Dismas, patron saint to penitent thieves, for help getting out of legal jams. At one point, Powell, as Terry O'Neill, enters a church and prays to Dismas; tears streak his face as his lips move but we do not hear his words. Sappiness prevails and naturally everything works out in the end. As the *Variety* reviewer wrote, "[U]nfoldment is never exciting. There's no feeling of struggle in the development of the plot, everything coming too easily to the characters—love, riches, poverty and eventual belief in St. Dismas' power for good."[97] The film was released, of course, for the Christmas season. Ernest Anderson (1915–2011), actor, college graduate and

African American, appears once in the film as Sam the elevator operator. These being semi-enlightened times, he gets several lines of dialogue.

In 1947, Powell found himself on the wrong side of the Red-hunting Senator from Wisconsin, Joe McCarthy (1908–1957)—not for taking politics seriously, as Hammett did, but rather for lampooning politicians regardless of ideological persuasion. When it came to making a film version of his successful play *The Senator Was Indiscreet*, a political satire, George S. Kaufman insisted Powell play the title role.[98] Kaufman, once lover to Mary Astor, found himself immortalized in her scandalous diary. Could this be why he was attracted to another story with a scandalous diary? Kaufman also directed the film. He won the Pulitzer Prize for Drama twice: for *Of Thee I Sing* (1932) and *You Can't Take It with You* (1938). Though he directed many Broadway stage plays and won several Tonys, this was his only venture in film direction.

In the movie, Powell plays Senator Melvin G. Ashton, a self-deluded nincompoop who aspires to the presidency. When the press gets hold of his diary detailing every other politicians' crooked dealings, they all lose their public sinecures. Well-reviewed by the critics, the film found disfavor with elected officials and its release was delayed by the House UnAmerican Activities Committee after McCarthy labeled it "un–American" and "traitorous,"[99] thereby demonstrating just how censorious and lacking in a sense of humor the Commie hunters could be. The film's producer Nunnally Johnson, who wrote, directed or produced some 80 movies, wrote a *New York Times* op-ed trying to make light of the matter:

> As for contributing to causes … the accepted view about town is that politically I am a tightwad from way back and would not give 85 cents to see Henry Wallace [once FDR's vice-president and in 1948 running for president as the Progressive Party alternative to incumbent Harry Truman] walk on water. I bat and throw right handed … Nobody [in the history of our country] had ever used politics and politicians as material for comedy. Oh, well, a few perhaps, yes, if you want to count Reds like Mark Twain, Will Rogers … we should have expected some totalitarian objections to its use in a picture.[100]

Powell himself, according to the more liberal Myrna Loy, also in *The Senator Was Indiscreet*, avoided political discussions and identified as a conservative Republican.[101] She appeared as a joke at the end of *The Senator Was Indiscreet* on a tropical island as the Senator's wife in a gray wig and a sarong. She was unpaid for her appearance; the producers gave her a new Cadillac instead.[102]

Then the dad roles were all Powell could get. He was third in the credits of *The Girl Who Had Everything* (1953), directed by Richard Thorpe, a remake of 1931's *A Free Soul* in which Lionel Barrymore won an Oscar as the dad of a gal who falls for a suave gangster hiding his true violent nature to win her love. At the end of the remake, Fernando Lamas, as gambling czar Victor Ramondi, lets slip the veil of decency and physically attacks Elizabeth Taylor and her father (Powell). For reasons of their own, his underworld cronies murder Victor; a repentant Taylor returns to her father's protective arms. The *Maclean's* magazine critic called the story "hackneyed and predictable."[103] It was Powell's last role at MGM.

In 1955, Powell, finally owning up to the vagaries and debilities of age that no longer allowed him to play a leading man, closed his film career with a marvelous turn as "Doc" in the dramedy *Mister Roberts*, based on the novel and play of the same name. The part had almost gone to Spencer Tracy.[104] The film stars Henry Fonda as Lieutenant Roberts and James Cagney as his captain and antagonist aboard the aptly named USS *Reluctant*.

Roberts wants a transfer to a fighting ship in the waning days of the War in the Pacific and Cagney thwarts him at every turn. Sadly, after the men forge the captain's signature to the transfer order Mr. Roberts wants, he is soon killed in a kamikaze attack on his new ship. Jack Lemmon won an Oscar for Best Supporting Actor as Ensign Pulver.[105]

No longer dyeing his hair nor sucking in his gut, Powell seems a natural as the avuncular "Doc." The *Variety* reviewer noted, "William Powell is just right for the role of ship's doctor, tackling it with an easy assurance that makes it stand out."[106]

My favorite snippet of dialogue:

> **Doc:** "That's mostly what makes physical heroism: opportunity. It's a reflex. I think that 75 out of a hundred young males have that reflex. You take any one of them. Say even Frank Thurlowe Pulver here. Put him into a B-29 over Japan, and you know what you'd have?"
> **Mister Roberts:** "No, I don't, doctor."
> **Doc:** "You'd have Pulver, the Congressional Medal of Honor winner. Pulver, who single-handed shot down 23 attacking Zeros. Pulver, who with his bare hands held together the severed wing struts of his plane, and with his bare feet successfully landed his mortally wounded plane on his home field. Reflex. It's like the knee jerk. Strike the patella tendon in any human being, you produce the knee jerk. Look."
> [*Doc hits Pulver in the knee and nothing happens*]
> **Ensign Pulver:** "What's the matter, Doc?"
> **Doc:** "Nothing, but stay out of B-29s, Frank, my boy."[107]

Lobby card for *Mister Roberts* (1955). The movie was based on the Thomas Heggen novel of the same name. From left are Jack Lemmon, James Cagney, Henry Fonda and William Powell. It was Powell's last movie after a long career stretching back to silent days.

Lemmon called Powell "the den mother" of the cast and crew:

> He was always tidying up, making little snacks and whatnot. If there was a flower to be had on the island [Midway Island], he'd find it and stick it in a Coke bottle. He was just marvelous—the only man I ever saw who could walk around in house slippers and shorts and retain a regal dignity like he was on his way to the coronation.[108]

James Cagney also spoke well of Powell: "What a nice man. Hell of a good actor. Just as urbane as he seemed on the screen and with a fund of theater stories that kept me hanging on his every word."[109]

This was Powell's final film. He had no plans for another film, saying, "I'm perfectly content with the lazy life unless something I just can't resist comes along. How could you resist *Mister Roberts*? But there aren't many 'Docs' coming along these days."[110] He retired to Palm Springs with his wife at age 65. He kept in touch with Loy and she visited him often. She once asked him:

> **Loy:** "What on earth do you do with yourself down here?"
> **Powell:** "I do my weeds."
> **Loy:** "For God's sake, Bill, you don't know one weed from another."
> **Powell:** "Well, it beats playing Elvis Presley's grandfather."[111]

Loy added: "Our screen partnership lasted 14 movies in 13 years, longer than any of my [four] marriages."[112]

Their films together, apart from the Thin Man pictures: *Manhattan Melodrama* (1934), *Evelyn Prentice* (1934), *The Great Ziegfeld* (1936), *Libeled Lady* (1936), *Double Wedding* (1937), *I Love You Again* (1940), *Love Crazy* (1941) and *The Senator Was Indiscreet* (1947). Loy said of Powell: "Two of the most important things about Bill Powell are his ability as an actor and his sense of humor, which are unfailing, often biting, always objective. With all the outward manifestation of a lazy, luxurious person, he is essentially a vital, supremely intelligent man."[113] Powell died in 1984 at age 91, and was buried beside his son. In its obituary, *Variety* called him "the personification of sophistication and class."[114] Loy may have summed him up best: "I never enjoyed my work more than when I worked with William Powell. He was a brilliant actor, a delightful companion, a great friend, and above all a true gentleman."[115]

5

Myrna Loy

We can accept William Powell as a WASP, soft-boiled Nick Charles, prettified for the big screen, but I think we would hardly remember him if not for the second half of this dynamic Hollywood duo, Myrna Loy. Loy became the perfect embodiment of Nora Charles: detached and cool on a rather haughty surface but simultaneously bubbling with a boundless curiosity and zest for life. Happily married, Nora doesn't just love her husband; she lusts for him. And we know just how she feels from a raised eyebrow, a tilt of her head or a cutting remark. Together Loy and Powell made Nick and Nora the most intriguing married couple in America.

Born in Helena, Montana, in 1905, Loy grew up on a ranch in Radersburg, 50 miles to the southeast, not far from the Montana mines Hammett visited as a Pinkerton detective and wrote about in *Red Harvest*. Her mother Della was a musician and sportswoman, her father David a rancher and state politician. One biographer wrote that David, on one of his frequent trips by railroad to sell livestock, took a fancy to the name "Myrna," the name of a whistle stop town his train passed through.[1] Actually, there are no towns named Myrna in the United States. We do, however, have towns named Merna in Wyoming, Nebraska, Missouri and Illinois. Since the flyspeck town of Merna, Nebraska, lies on an old railroad spur, it is likely the source of her unusual first name.[2]

Myrna changed her name from Williams to Loy in 1925, the same year she turned 20 and signed a contract with Warner Brothers for $75 a week.[3] "Williams wasn't exotic enough for an actress and a friend got the name Loy from a book of Chinese poetry."[4]

Loy spent her early years on a cattle ranch without indoor plumbing or electricity.[5] The family then moved to Helena, the state capital. She and her mother made several trips to Los Angeles, where Myrna began dance classes at age 11 and set her heart on a career in dance. When the flu pandemic of 1918 killed David Williams, Della, Myrna and Myrna's brother David moved to L.A. Myrna took both weekly ballet classes and modern dance lessons with Ruth St. Denis (1879–1968), a pioneer in modern dance in the U.S. as a performer and teacher. Loy's dance training led her, at age 16, to a larger-than-life sculpture in front of Venice High School. She posed for hours day after day as the school's art teacher, Harry Fielding Winebrenner (1885–1969) crafted a sculpture group entitled Fountain of Education. Loy, slender, with one arm lifted skyward, her full figure, barely covered in diaphanous robes, stood in the center as Aspiration, a "vision of purity, grace, youthful vigor," according to *The Los Angeles Times*. The paper included a photo and her name, in print for the first time. A few months later, the statue of Loy was removed and placed aboard the battleship *Nevada* for a Memorial Day pageant. The Fountain of Education is seen in the opening scenes of the 1978 film *Grease*.

The statue suffered from exposure to the elements and vandalism and officials removed it in 2002. Alumni raised funds to replace it with a bronze replica in 2010.[6]

Loy had to leave school at 18 without graduating. "Money was running out," she wrote in her autobiography, "and I had to work [to support herself, her mother and brother]."[7] She found work at Grauman's Egyptian Theater, a movie palace with nearly 2000 seats, on Hollywood Boulevard. She danced with a chorus twice a day for $35 a week[8] in what the movie houses called "prologues": elaborate musical performances that served to entertain the audience gathering for the feature movie. But Loy felt her career as a dancer was blocked because she lacked the sculpted legs and slender ankles expected (she had "chubby legs and thick ankles," according to one critic).

Twelve years after dancing theater prologues, Myrna Loy came to Grauman's Chinese Theater with William Powell to put her handprints and footprints in wet cement alongside so many other stars. Loy wrote there: "To Sid, who gave me my first job."[9]

While still dancing in the prologues, Loy's photo caught the eye of Rudolph Valentino, who arranged for her first screen test ... which she flunked. She tried again and won a seven-year contract at Warners. The studio fixed on her almond-shaped eyes and dancer's body and consigned her to a series of "exotic" roles as Mexican, Roma, Chinese, an Indian princess, an African spy and a Polynesian. *The L.A. Times* reported, "Myrna Loy has been signed with Warner Bros. because of her distinctly unusual and Oriental type."[10] She often played the harlot. Said Loy, looking back: "I was a dancer and could slink, so [the studios] fostered this exotic, sexy image."[11] "Wouldn't you know," said John Ford, who directed her in *The Black Watch* in 1929: "the kid they pick to play tramps is the only good girl in Hollywood."[12] Of course, Ford, a notorious womanizer, may have said so because she resisted his amorous advances. She had mostly small parts in 11 films in 1926 and 11 more in 1927.

She wore blackface in *Ham and Eggs at the Front*, a 1927 silent comedy. Ham and Eggs are two black soldiers played by white actors, Tom Wilson and Charlie Conlin respectively, who go AWOL from their black regiment. Loy plays Fifi, a black barmaid and German spy. IMDb describes the characters: "Fifi (Myrna Loy), a dusky, sultry Senegalese spy, uses her wiles to get information out of two American army soldiers, Ham and Eggs, in France during World War I."[13]

Blackface has a long and infamous American history. Those who today might say of this practice 100 years ago that it was accepted then, or that everyone did it, etc., might go back even further to the words of the abolitionist and former slave Frederick Douglass, who wrote in 1848, after having watched a blackface show, calling the performers "the filthy scum of white society. [They] have stolen from us a complexion denied to them by nature ... to make money and pander to the corrupt taste of their white fellow-citizens."[14]

It was the one role Loy apologized for in her autobiography.[15] I understand Loy had to support her family and as a small-time contract player had to take the roles Warners assigned her but her early filmography reeks of racism and sexism. Her role in *The Squall* (1929) elicited this publicity from Warners: "Meet Nubi the Gypsy Gale of Passion, an ill wind that blows no man good. Born of the storm this half clad, human hurricane takes love where she will ... from old, from young from father, from son."[16] Another site calls Nubi "a minx-like, Hungarian gypsy girl [who] seduces and holds in thrall all the male members of the family."[17]

"Gypsy," as we know, is a derogatory term for Roma people, usually described like black people in the U.S. as shiftless, thieves and oversexed. In *The Squall*, Loy's Nubi

Myrna Loy as Fifi, "a dusky Senegalese spy," in *Ham and Eggs at the Front* (1927). The all-white cast, including Tom Wilson as Ham and Charlie Conlin as Eggs, wore blackface. In her autobiography, Loy apologized.

insinuates herself into the household of a prosperous family and sleeps her way to the top, as the quintessential vamp. Our term *vamp* comes from vampire but Hollywood reserved the word for female characters, those women who sucked the life from their male victims with their sexual charms. Theda Bara starred as the original vamp, her character named "The Vampire" in the 1915 silent film *A Fool There Was*. Bara used her sensuality and body to lure and ruin a happily married man and leave him a drunken wreck. Vamps became all the rage on screen.

Loy's pay went from $75 a week in 1925, to $500 a week by 1927, and $700 a week two years later. Then things took a turn. After the stock market crash, Darryl Zanuck told her: "We can't afford you. There aren't enough wenches for you to play."[18] Without a studio contract, Loy freelanced for a bit. She got a negative review from Louella Parsons for her 1930 movie *Renegades*: "Miss Loy is one of the best looking girls on the screen, and maybe one of these days her acting will match her looks."[19] In 1928, she starred as Onoto, a Chinese slave in *The Crimson City* and in 1929 as an Indian princess, Yasmani, in *The Black Watch*.

In 1931, she signed a five-year contract with MGM and the next year she made nine films, including another risible film as a vamp, RKO's *Thirteen Women*. Loy played the chief villain, Ursula Georgi, who seeks to kill the sorority sisters who ruined her life at St. Albans Seminary for Women when they kept her out of their exclusive sorority. Loy gets to play an exotic and beautiful seductress, manipulator, murderer and attempted child killer. She put the real vampire back into vamp. Once again she plays Asian but this time she is "Hindu." I know a religion is not a nationality but tell that to the screenwriters. A police detective (Ricardo Cortez) refers to her as "a half-breed type, half–Hindu and half–Javanese, I don't know." Hatred of white people fuels her schemes, as she explains to Laura Stanhope (Irene Dunne):

> Do you know what it means to be a half-breed, a half-caste, in a world ruled by whites? If you're a male, you're a coolie, and if you're a female, you're … well…. The white half of me cried for the courtesy and protection that women like you get. The only way I could free myself was by becoming white. And it was almost in my hands when you, you and your Kappa Society, stopped me.
>
> **Laura Stanhope:** You're crazy…
>
> **Ursula Georgi:** I spent six years slaving to get money enough to put me through finishing school, to make the world accept me as white. But you and the others wouldn't let me cross the color line.
>
> **Laura Stanhope:** But we were young. Maybe we were cruel. But you can't use that to justify murder!
>
> **Ursula Georgi:** I can.[20]

The lesson from Hollywood in film after film remains: Don't turn your back on a murderous Asian. Or Chinese, or Hindu, or Javanese.

We also remember the film for another actress, Peg Entwistle, born 1908, making her one and only screen appearance as sorority sister Hazel Clay Cousins. Entwistle committed suicide just before the film's release by jumping off the "H" of the looming and iconic HOLLYWOODLAND sign on Sunday, September 18, 1932.

Loy's talent for playing "exotic women" led her in 1932 to *The Mask of Fu Manchu* and the role of Fu Manchu's daughter, the sexy and sadistic Fah Lo See. Boris Karloff (1887–1969), born William Henry Pratt, played Fu Manchu. It was based on the sixth of Sax Rohmer's popular Fu Manchu novels and filmed quickly for a December 1932 release. MGM's

Millicent Lilian "Peg" Entwistle was a British stage and screen actress. She was only 24 when she committed suicide by jumping off the HOLLYWOODLAND sign. *Thirteen Women* (1932), starring Myrna Loy, was Entwistle's sole Hollywood film.

publicity department promised: "The newest Sax Rohmer sensation! The Frankenstein of the Orient—and his devilish daughter's love drug!"[21]

In *The Insidious Dr. Fu Manchu* (1913), the first of the Fu Manchu series, Rohmer described his Asian antagonist thusly: "Imagine a person ... with a brow like Shakespeare and a face like Satan, a close shaven skull and long, magnetic eyes.... Invest him with all the cruel cunning of an entire Eastern Race ... and you have a mental picture of Dr. Fu Manchu."[22]

It took two and a half hours to apply makeup to Karloff each day of shooting[23] and the result, in the words of film historian Gregory W. Mank, presented Karloff as "[a] gassy, lisping dragon of a Fu Manchu looking like Carmen Miranda from hell in his fruit basket hat and five inch long fingernails."[24]

When Loy first read the script, she went to complain about her character, telling producer Hunt Stromberg: "I've done a lot of terrible things in films, but this girl's a sadistic nymphomaniac." Stromberg said, "What's that?" Loy replied, "Well, you better find out, because that's what she is and I won't play her that way." As a contract player, Loy didn't have a lot of choices over dialogue but Stromberg cut some of her lines. "She wasn't Rebecca of Sunnybrook Farm," said Loy, "but, as I remember, she just watched while others did the whipping."[25] The cuts didn't do her too much good. When Fu Manchu captures a handsome Englishman, Loy oversees his torture, urging muscular black slaves, bare-chested and sweaty, to whip him, yelling "Faster! Faster! Faster!" as she achieves what we can only imagine is a sexual climax.[26]

I have to admit that as a 12-year-old, I loved the Fu Manchu novels of Sax Rohmer, the *nom de plume* of Arthur Henry Ward (1883–1959), chronicling Fu Manchu's attempts at world conquest, thwarted each time by British Secret Service agent Denis Nayland Smith in a series of 13 books, many made into films. I liked the stories for the cliffhanging adventures, fiendish tortures and the overall sense, for this middle-class suburban preteen, of exoticism. I didn't realize what it really meant. This fetishism of the exotic was later named "Orientalism" by Edward Said. He saw it as the manner in which Western colonialists looked upon the East with a mixture of both fear and desire that transcended the reality of the place and its people.

The *Mask of Fu Manchu* plot is simple and quite daft. The British government dispatches an expeditionary force to the Gobi Desert to raid the tomb of Genghis Khan (1158–1227) and seize his golden sword and mask for preservation in the British Museum; never mind how the local authorities might feel about having their antiquities plundered. At the same time, Fu Manchu follows to seize the sword and mask, believing they will make him a second Genghis Khan and allow him to rule the world. Conflict ensues.

Though banal in most aspects, the film demonstrates a high level of racism and white supremacy even in the context of 1930s Hollywood. It centers on Fu Manchu, who tells his followers: "Men of Asia, may you rain down upon the white race and burn them.... Would you have maidens like this [he points to a captured young British woman paraded before them on a pallet] for your wives? Then kill the white man and take his women."[27] Poor Myrna Loy as Fu Manchu's daughter looks quite occidental even decked out in a bizarre, and therefore "exotic," three-foot-tall headdress, as the sort of "Dragon Lady" soon to be a popular stereotype in Western fiction.

We might accept all this as high camp if not for the historical context of the Yellow Peril, alternately called the Yellow Threat and the Yellow Terror, in which the "primitive" men of Asia will overrun the West. This racist trope had sufficient political sway to inspire the Chinese Exclusion Act of 1882 which not only banned immigration from China but made it impossible for Chinese immigrants already in America to ever become citizens. The Chinese were the only race of people to be singled out by the United States for special treatment through immigration legislation. The irony, of course, is that the racist tropes attached to Asians were exactly the characteristics of their Western colonizers. It was the British, French, Americans and Germans who invaded Eastern lands, colonized their people, exploited their wealth and raped their women. For all these reasons, the Chinese government objected to *The Mask of Fu Manchu* when it was originally released and the Japanese-American Citizens League objected to its re-release in 1972.

Myrna Loy as the sadistic Fah Lo See, daughter of the dastardly Dr. Fu Manchu in *The Mask of Fu Manchu* (1932). Sax Rohmer's series of Fu Manchu novels and the films that followed presented some Asians as a "Yellow Peril" that threatened Western civilization.

Today the American Alt Right and contemporary white supremacists revive the same fears with their talk of "The Great Replacement," when white people will be reduced to an oppressed minority, and the coming white genocide heralds the extinction of the White Race. One dumb movie carries all this freight. And *The Mask of Fu Manchu* drives the message home in its last scene when the victorious Brits, returning to England on a steamer, golden sword in hand, encounter a Chinese ship's steward. They question and mock him and he responds with toothless, foolish smiles, complicit to their mockery. The steward is played by Chinese actor Willie Fung (1896–1945), who played the very same stereotype of the fool, then named Hoy, in *Red Dust*, made the same year. These white people need someone to mock and lord over.

Despite the protests from the Chinese, *The Mask of Fu Manchu* went on to be a critical and financial success, many praising the performances of Karloff and Loy. In the words of one critic: "Over the decades, [Karloff] became the screen's definitive, most famous Fu Manchu, while Miss Loy's … Fah Lo See won praise as one of the most exquisite villainess of '30s melodrama…. *The Mask of Fu Manchu* became the greatest horror comic book of Hollywood's Golden Age."[28] The movie had a domestic gross of $377,000, foreign gross of $248,000 and a net profit of $62,000.[29]

Like blackface, yellowface became a staple of white entertainment. The replacement of Asian actors by white actors in Asian roles is called "whitewashing." The practice of white actors changing their appearance with makeup to play East Asian characters in films, plays. etc., is called yellowface. In her Honors Thesis at Pace University, Kelly Ng offered as examples of yellowface: Karloff in *The Mask of Fu Manchu*, Paul Muni in *The Good Earth*, Marlon Brando in *The Teahouse of the August Moon* and Mickey Rooney in *Breakfast at Tiffany's*.[30]

The Hollywood Hays office rules against "miscegenation," intimate relationships including marriage between people of different races, also complicated casting decisions. If the studio cast one well-known white actor in a film, like Muni in *The Good Earth*, all the members of his family also had to be white actors, extending the Whitewashing across the entire cast. Then throw in the so-called "Asian accent." Americans in yellowface, or Englishman like Karloff, had to speak pidgin or otherwise obscure their English behind a stereotypical Chinese or Japanese accent. Hollywood's Asian characters depended upon whitewashing and yellowface. Speaking to Elizabeth Lee on the Voice of America, Professor Nancy Wang Yuen pointed out these Hollywood stereotypes did not just adopt society's stereotypes but magnified and reinforced their racist real-world effects:

"Yellowface—meaning they actually, literally yellowed up their skin," said Nancy Wang Yuen, a sociology professor at Biola University and author of *Reel Inequality: Hollywood Actors and Racism*. "They usually slanted their eyes with prosthetics. They did it in a way that was to make fun of, that was to make Chinese and Asians look as sinister or as buffoonish as possible, and that kind of portrayal reproduced the stereotypes that were existent in society. But I would say also exacerbated the nativism and xenophobia that people had."[31]

A year after *Thirteen Women* and a year before *The Thin Man*, Loy played yet another "exotic" in the ridiculous MGM film *The Barbarian*, an execrable pre–Code supposed romance based on male dominance, rape and, once again, the liberal use of whips. Loy, slender and beautiful, plays wealthy American socialite Diana Standing, who has traveled to Cairo to marry her even wealthier British fiancé Gerald (Reginald Denny). Jamil El Shehbab (Ramon Novarro) notices Diana at the train station as he bids adieu to several of his latest foreign female admirers and pockets their gifts of jewelry. We take him, at first, for little more than a native gigolo. (*The Barbarian* was a remake of the 1924 film *The Arab*, which also starred Novarro.)

Jamil works assiduously to worm his way into Diana's retinue and eventually into her heart as he woos her with "Love Songs of the Nile" (lyrics by Arthur Freed, melody by Nacio Herb Brown). The convoluted plot has Jamil constantly appearing where Diana does not expect him, even in her boudoir. Though Gerald seems like a decent sort, we understand that his marriage to Diana will lack both love and passion. Jamil manages to separate Diana from her family as they tour the pyramids at night. He delivers her to yet another seducer, Achmed Pasha (Edward Arnold), then rescues her when Pasha begins to whip her. After killing the Pasha's men who have pursued them across the dunes, Jamil forces Diana to walk behind his horse through the burning sands. At an oasis when she rushes to the water, he tells her: "In the desert, the horses drink first." When the horse has drunk his full, Diana makes for the water again. Again Jamil restrains her: "After the horses, the men drink." When he has slaked his thirst, he allows Diana to drink. Then another whip comes out and Jamil grabs Diana by the hair, drags her across the sand and rapes her as the film goes to black. The next moment we see only Diana's dirtied and tear-stained face.

Myrna Loy luxuriates naked (or is she?) in an Egyptian pool in *The Barbarian* (1933). A whipping, a rape and a forced march through the desert are in her future before she finds happiness with her abuser.

More stuff happens, and little of it makes sense: Jamil takes Diana to his home village where we learn he is really a prince whose sojourn in Cairo as a driver, tour guide and gigolo was some sort of royal initiation. Diana and Jamil stand before the villagers to be married but she throws water in his face and he lets her go; she heads back into the desert and is met by the cavalry riding to the rescue. Back in Cairo, we find her dressing for her wedding to Gerald. But up pops Jamil again and off she goes with her lover and rapist. In the final scene, Jamil and Diana float down the Nile on a *felucca* (boat), entwined in each other's arms. As the couple cuddles, their final lines strike a particularly odious note. Diana tells Jamil that her mother was Egyptian, making Loy a "half-breed" in yet another film—I use the derogatory word only because it is ubiquitous in reviews of these films. Jamil replies: "I don't care if she was Chinese," as if that constitutes the worst case scenario.[32]

Loy does more indicating than acting, usually shot in close-up or medium shot and alternately grimacing or grinning as the scene requires. She has an erotic scene naked in a bath strewn with flowers. (In her autobiography, Loy claims to have worn a flesh-colored body suit.) The film was banned by the Hays Office the following year. Prior to the ban, producer Hunt Stromberg indelicately admitted: "Tits and sand sell tickets."[33]

Director Sam Wood (1883–1949) shot *The Barbarian* in Yuma, Arizona, for its desert scenery. After World War II, Wood emerged as one of Hollywood's fiercest anti–Communists. In 1944, he founded and served as first president of the Motion Picture Alliance for the Preservation of American Ideals, dedicated to expelling from the film industry those it identified as Communist and subversive.

Anita Loos is credited as co-screenwriter on the film with Elmer Harris. Loos (1889–1981), an actress-novelist-playwright as well as one of Hollywood's first female screenwriters, is best-known for her novel *Gentlemen Prefer Blondes*. She also wrote the scripts for the Jean Harlow vehicles *Saratoga* and *Red-Headed Woman*. The latter had fun with the idea of a smart sexy woman using credulous men on her way to the top. So how did a woman share credit for the repugnant misogynist mess of *The Barbarian*? Because the producers, director and studio execs were all men and somehow thought women would like this trash. But before Loos got the movie credit, MGM had put Frances Goodrich and Albert Hackett to work on the script. They bailed because, in the words of Goodrich, "It was all so false, all hooey."[34] Hackett and Goodrich went on to pen *The Thin Man* and two of its sequels.

In addition to Loy, *The Barbarian* stars Ramon Novarro (1899–1968), born José Ramón Gil Samaniego. Mexican-American, he began acting in silent films in 1917 became one of the top attractions of the 1920s and early 1930s. The studio promoted him as a Latin lover and sex symbol to assume the mantle of the Italian Rudolph Valentino, who died suddenly in 1926. The advent of talkies saw Novarro's film career decline precipitously as audiences found his voice a bit too high-pitched and insufficiently masculine. While playing a seducer of women on screen, he struggled to hide his own homosexuality. In 1968, two young men gained access to his home in Laurel Canyon and tortured and beat Novarro to death in an attempt to gain access to money they believed he had hidden. They left with only $20. This ghastly murder has featured in several films, TV shows and plays.[35]

Reginald Denny (1891–1967) plays Gerald, Loy's stick of an upper crust British fiancé. Born Reginald Leigh Dugmore, Denny flew with the Royal Air Force in World War I and had a fascinating off-camera second professional life in aviation, later forming a successful model plane company. During World War II, he supplied radio-controlled target drones to the U.S. Army Air Corps.[36]

C. Aubrey Smith plays a lush and a bounder as part of Diana's set. We see him again in *Bombshell* (1933) with Harlow, and as Colonel MacFay in *Another Thin Man* (1939, reunited with Myrna Loy.

We also have Akim Tamirof (1891–1972), born Hovakim Tamiryanrsin, in one of his early uncredited roles as the colonel leading the cavalry to rescue Loy. He went on to earn Academy Award nominations for *The General Died at Dawn* (1936) and *For Whom the Bell Tolls* (1943). Hedda Hopper (1885–1966) plays the aptly named Mrs. Loway, who two-times her absent husband with the rascally Jamil. While Hopper had small parts in over 100 films, mostly for MGM, we know her best as a gossip columnist which at the height, or depth, of her success had 35,000,000 readers. In the 1940s, she supported the House UnAmerican Activities Committee investigations and the Hollywood Blacklist.

Following *The Barbarian*, also in 1933, Loy starred in *The Prizefighter and the Lady* (as, of course, ...the Lady), the first of her eight outings under director W.S. Van Dyke. Opposite her and making his film debut was Max Baer (1909–59), soon to become the World Heavyweight Champion. Van Dyke got the assignment only after Howard Hawks walked off the set, upset that the film he had agreed to make for MGM with Clark Gable, *The Sailor and the Lady*, would now feature the untutored novice actor Baer and become *The Prizefighter and the Lady*.[37] MGM had always planned on Loy as the Lady but hadn't settled on the vocation or identity of her co-star. Baer had captured the world's attention by winning a June 1933 bout against the Nazi boxing hero Max Schmeling before a crowd of 60,000 in Yankee Stadium. Half-Jewish, Baer wore a Star of David on his boxing trunks. In return, the Nazi press labeled Baer "a Jewish Negroid type" and banned *The Prizefighter and the Lady* in Germany.

The film itself is pretty silly. Baer, as Steve Morgan, is a bouncer discovered by an old boxing promoter (Walter Huston). Morgan, good-looking and strong, and Loy's Belle Mercer, a club singer and gangster's girlfriend, fall in love after a single date and run off to marry. Morgan cheats on Belle continually and she keeps taking him back until she has finally had enough. They are reunited at the climactic boxing scene as Morgan rallies to win a draw against the real-life Heavyweight Champ Primo Carnera. MGM had to pay Carnera an extra $10,000 to agree to fight to a draw on film.[38]

The film wastes Loy's talents as she is called on to do little more than make anxious faces while watching Baer box. She also sings snatches of the song "Downstream Drifter" in a nightclub act. The song was written by Raymond Egan and Gus Kahn with music by David Snell. I could not determine if Loy actually sings in the film or if an uncredited singer performs in her place. The *New York Times* review, lacking anything much to say about Loy's acting, called her "attractive and efficient."[39] Baer turned out to be a halfway decent actor. He even sings and dances with a chorus line of beauties. Said the *Times* critic, "This California giant has such an ingratiating personality and an easy way of talking that one forgets signs of fistic encounters on his physiognomy. Mr. Baer is easily the outstanding thespianic graduate of the squared ring."[40]

Though attached to Myrna Loy on film, the married Baer was actually carrying on with Jean Harlow during the filming. MGM hurried Harlow into a marriage with Hal Rosson to help her escape being named a co-defendant in Dorothy Dunbar's (Mrs. Max Baer) divorce action. In addition to Harlow, Baer also had a romance with Greta Garbo. Baer's son Max Baer Jr. may be better known than his dad to those of us who grew up watching him co-star as Jethro in TV's *The Beverly Hillbillies* (1962–71). The only real surprise of the film is Otto Kruger (1885–1974) as Willie Ryan, the man we are told is a cold blooded killer and Belle's employer at his nightclub. Kruger makes Willie the most intriguing and complicated character on screen, deeply in love with Belle but unwilling to break her heart by having his rival Steve killed, as he is tempted to do. Willie loves Belle so much that in the end he brings Belle and Steve back together just to make her happy and then walks away, jilted and alone. This conflicted and sensitive killer, who wins our hearts, should be the center of the film.

But Willie's not a prizefighter and the thrills of this film reside in the boxing ring, especially the climactic championship bout between the Italian Primo Carnera, as himself, and Max Baer as Steve Morgan. MGM built a replica of the interior of Madison Square Garden on a stage on their Culver City lot. In the film, the fight ends in a draw but in real life Max Baer went on to defeat Carnera, known as "The Ambling Alp" for his height and weight, for the Championship in June 1934. Baer lost the championship to James Braddock a year later, and that shocking upset served as the focus for the 2005 movie *Cinderella Man* with Russell Crowe. The final fight scene also brings us cameos from other real fighters: Jack Dempsey referees the fight. The ring announcer introduces former champions Jess Willard and Jim Jeffries in the flesh along with the real Ed "Strangler" Lewis. A ringside broadcaster calls out the names of the celebrities in the crowd: Grover Whelan, known as "Mr. New York" and former police commissioner of the city; Bernard Gimbel, who ran the largest chain of department stores in the world; singer Kate Smith, sitting in "seats 1, 2 and 3," and Loew's chief executive Nicholas Schenck, successor to Marcus Loew and therefore owner of MGM itself, identified as "the famous movie maker."[41]

Nineteen thirty-four was Loy's breakthrough year, starring in both *Manhattan Melodrama* with Gable and Powell and *The Thin Man*. *Manhattan Melodrama* delivers what the title promises, or warns: an emotionally overwrought tearjerker with improbable occurrences, hard-to-believe characters and scenes designed to pull at your heartstrings ... in Manhattan. It's also the very first Loy-Powell movie collaboration. According to Loy:

> My first scene with Bill, a night shot on the back lot, happened before we'd even met. [Director Van Dyke] was apparently too busy for introductions. My instructions were to run out of a building, through a crowd, and into a strange car. When Woody called "Action" I opened the car door, jumped in, and landed smack on William Powell's lap. He looked up nonchalantly: "Miss Loy, I presume?" I said, "Mr. Powell?" And that's how I met the man who would be my partner in fourteen films.[42]

And in that instant a team emerged. Said Loy of Powell:

> He was so naturally witty and outrageous that I stayed somewhat detached, always a little incredulous. From that very first scene, a curious thing passed between us, a feeling of rhythm, complete understanding, an instinct for how one could bring out the best in the other. In all our work together you can see this strange ... rapport.[43]

The film's silly script has Powell and Gable's characters growing up together as orphaned friends. Gable's Blackie Gallagher, played as a child by Mickey Rooney, chooses a life of crime and Powell as Jim Wade chooses a life of rectitude and becomes a district attorney. When Blackie kills a man who would ruin Jim's chances of election as governor, Jim prosecutes Blackie and sends him to the electric chair. Loy, as Eleanor Packer, loves Blackie at first but not his evil ways and, over a long night talking at the Cotton Club, falls in love with Jim and marries him. However, Eleanor threatens to leave Jim if he doesn't commute Blackie's sentence to life imprisonment. He refuses.

At the eleventh hour, Jim goes to Sing Sing to see Blackie. Who should be there as the Death Row chaplain but Father Joe (Leo Carrillo), the man who saved their lives when their parents perished in a maritime disaster. (This was seen in opening scenes which replayed the sinking of the PS *General Slocum*, a sidewheel steamboat that really did catch fire and sink in New York's East River in 1904 at a loss of 1,000 lives.) Jim wants to save Blackie; but Blackie, who did kill someone, just not the someone he was convicted of killing, means to ride Old Sparky that very night. So the state executes Blackie.

Jim, of course, is too good to let things end there. He announces that because a murder aided his campaign and because he was ready to betray his principles to offer clemency to his childhood friend, he must resign the governor's office. As he leaves the building, Eleanor awaits, realizing what she has in a man of both compassion and principle. Someone wrote this malarkey? No matter; the public loved the film and MGM made oodles of money. The film made Gable a star and cinched the film marriage of Powell and Loy. Woody Van Dyke directed. Also in the cast is Nat Pendleton as Spud, a really dumb gangster, later to play Lieutenant Guild in the first and third Thin Man movies.

Leo Carrillo (1881–1961), playing the saintly Father Joe, worked as an early conservationist, and this prompted California to name a state park for him. At the age of 70, he rode the TV airwaves playing the sidekick Pancho on *The Cisco Kid* (1950–56). Pancho, with his (affected) mangling of English, added a comedic element to this horse opera. After the Japanese attack on Pearl Harbor, Carrillo, ironically no defender of minority rights, vehemently agitated for the removal of all Japanese and Japanese-Americans from the West Coast, a policy undertaken by the U.S. government in 1942 that forcibly and without due process removed 120,000 people, 70 percent of them U.S. citizens, from their homes.

Manhattan Melodrama earned Powell his first of three Best Actor nominations but he lost to his co-star Clark Gable, who won for *It Happened One Night*. MGM dominated the early Academy Awards presentations no doubt because studio chief Louis B. Mayer founded the awards show in 1927 to bring additional publicity and prestige to the motion picture industry. Today many remember *Manhattan Melodrama* not for the acting or the script but for what happened off-screen and outside the theater. On a tip from brothel owner Ana Cumpañaş, nicknamed "The Woman in Red" in the tabloids, the FBI staked out Chicago's Biograph Theater on a sultry night (July 22, 1934) and gunned down Public Enemy #1, John Dillinger, who had broken cover to see his favorite movie star, Myrna Loy. Dillinger and his gang had robbed more than a dozen banks throughout the Midwest. Even as moviegoers dipped their handkerchiefs in Dillinger's blood as his body lay in the street, MGM's publicity team went into overdrive, advertising the film with the caption: "Dillinger Died to See This Picture!"[44] and disseminating posters with the tag line "Dillinger risked his life to see *Manhattan Melodrama*."[45] Loy objected to the new PR campaign, saying of Dillinger's demise, "Oh, that poor man."[46] On the other hand, Hays Code chieftain Joseph Breen announced: "The government men are the heroes. It made you feel proud to be an American."[47]

Racism rears its ugly head on just a few occasions in *Manhattan Melodrama*. We have two black characters in the movie—a waiter at Blackie's gambling joint who stutters when given money and servilely asks Blackie if he can keep it, and a black prisoner in a cell near Blackie's. The latter was payed by Sam McDaniel, older brother of Hattie McDaniel, *Gone with the Wind*'s Mammy. As Blackie is led to the electric chair, he tells

McDaniel, "Don't take any wooden pork chops,"[48] because racist stereotypes are always funny, even on Death Row.

And we have a big scene at the Cotton Club in Harlem where Jim (Powell) and Eleanor (Loy) first fall in love. The Cotton Club, operated in Harlem from 1923 to 1940 by a white gangster, is the perfect metaphor for race in America in the 1930s. The club featured "all black performers, all black staff and all white customers. [It was] designed to look like a [antebellum] plantation."[49] How much worse can it get? Well, the singer at the Cotton Club is Shirley Ross (1913–1975), but she doesn't look like Ms. Ross; we know Ross was white. Oh, they put Ross in blackface. Loy thought she had escaped blackface after *Ham and Eggs at the Front* and here we go again seven years later with the same racist entertainment. Ross sings "The Bad in Every Man" which Lorenz Hart later rewrote into the hit "Blue Moon." Ross, with the burnt cork wiped off, went on to score a hit with Bob Hope on the Academy Award–winning song "Thanks for the Memory" in 1938.

MGM almost made *The Thin Man* without Loy and Powell. Mayer thought Powell too long in the tooth and that Loy lacked the necessary comedic talent. And he didn't think much of the script either. To prove Loy could take a joke, Van Dyke pushed her, fully clothed, into his Brentwood estate swimming pool. She took the fall gamely and Van Dyke made his case: She could play well-bred ladies as well as exotic vixens.[50] When Van Dyke promised to finish the movie quickly and move on to his next project three weeks later, Mayer gave in. The director finished the movie in just 16 days. When this "B" movie then made MGM lots of money, Mayer bought into the sequels and ordered production budgets usually assigned only to "A" movies.[51]

"*The Thin Man* made me [after 80 films],"[52] said Loy. "[It is] perhaps the best remembered of my hundred and forty-four features."[53] Indeed it is.

In 1936, Loy was named Queen of the Movies, and Clark Gable the King, in a national poll. Powell sent her roses upon her election; he had finished fourth to Gable in the voting. He called her "every man's dream of what a wife should be: beautiful and glamorous with a sense of humor, provocative and feminine."[54]

And while they played a married couple in 13 of their 14 films, and exhibited a preternatural on-screen chemistry, off-screen Loy and Powell were good friends over five decades though never romantic partners.

Success in *The Thin Man* meant that Myrna Loy was done playing Asian, Roman and Indian "exotics." Now she was Nora Charles and a woman of the world—and soon to be a queen of Hollywood.

Powell said that in their movie scenes together, "we forgot acting technique, camera angles, and microphones. We were just two people in perfect harmony."[55]

The romantic and sexy Nora Charles received letters each week from fans seeking relationship advice. Wrote one critic: "Theirs was a marriage that may have been made in Culver City but it played like heaven."[56] With her success came imitation: "Her profile was the most asked for in plastic surgeries in the 1930's!"[57]

Loy did something rarely seen in Hollywood in 1935: She went on strike, one of the few stars challenging MGM's power and its ability to make and break careers. She had developed a reputation at the studio for being "difficult." "Difficult" was the word attached to any actor who wanted more money or to any woman who wanted to be paid as much as her male co-star. In her case, Loy was paid half what Powell received for their roles in *The Thin Man*. Mayer dealt with difficult actors by calling them into his office and crying poor about studio profits and asking them to remember they were part of an MGM family which sometimes required personal sacrifices. MGM writer Budd Schulberg wrote about one of Mayer's successes with a disaffected star: "When Robert Taylor tried to hit him up for a raise, L.B. advised the young man to work hard, respect his elders, and in due time he'd get everything he deserved. L.B. hugged him, cried a little and walked him to the door. Asked, 'Did you get your raise?' the now tearful Taylor is said to have answered, 'No, but I found a father.'"[58]

If that didn't work, threats followed, and *in extremis* MGM simply replaced the disgruntled employee. With Loy away from Hollywood in 1935, MGM teamed Powell with Rosalind Russell in *Rendezvous*, a spy film directed by William K. Howard. In his *New York Times* review, Andre Sennwald accurately called Russell "Metro-Goldwyn-Mayer's second-string Myrna Loy." MGM announced the hunt was on for a new Nora Charles. The public protested and MGM caved. Loy only returned when she was promised an immediate bonus of $25,000 (half a million dollars today) and a raise from $3000 a week to $4000 when her contract renewed in 1937. The studio, however, trumpeted that she was returning to MGM at her current salary of $3000 a week, omitting news of its concessions. MGM had little to lose; when they loaned her out to 20th Century–Fox in 1936 for *To Mary—with Love*, Fox paid her contracted salary of $3000 while paying MGM $9000 a week for the loan.[59]

In MGM's *Petticoat Fever* (1936), Loy no longer played the exotic; others in the cast did. MGM based the film on the play of the same name by Mark Reed and it's a sort of screwball comedy with a twist: The screwball in this case is male, not female. Though shot at MGM, the story is set in Labrador. Loy recalled that the film's "snow" was actually feathers and cornstarch. In this wild northland, lonely radio operator Dascom Dinsmore (Robert Montgomery, 1904–81) pines for his absent fiancée and goes stir crazy in his icebound cabin near Eskimo Point. Then an insufferable British aristocrat Sir James Felton (Reginald Owen, 1887–72) crashes his plane, and he and his fiancée Irene Campion (Loy) seek Dinsmore's help. Dinsmore and Irene fall in love, of course, and then Dinsmore's fiancée Clara Wilson (Winifred Shotter, 1904–96) arrives to further complicate matters. Montgomery plays the screwball *à la* Carole Lombard and does it well. He bounds from chair to sofa and from emotion to emotion like an overgrown puppy. He makes his desperate need for love (or at least sex) quite funny.

In her autobiography, Loy writes that the film's fur coats were leftovers from the earlier movie *Eskimo* and smelled awful, especially on the hot stage. She wrote that between takes, "Bob would unzip his parka, squirt in some perfume, and groan, 'God Almighty, do you know how many people have lived and died in this thing?'"[60]

We no longer use the term "Eskimo" and refer to the native peoples of Labrador as Inuit. But *Petticoat Fever* features no real Labrador natives and its "Eskimos" are treated like second-class citizens. Dinsmore tells Sir James, "There isn't a woman within 500 miles" even though his "man" Kimo has recently returned with two young women. But "Eskimo" women don't count like white women.

Sir James asks Dinsmore: "How long since you've seen a woman?"

Dinsmore: "Any woman? Five months. A white woman? Seven months. A beautiful woman? Two years."[61]

Loy mixes multiple stereotypes, asking: "How do you bribe an Eskimo? With wampum or firewater?"[62] When Kimo tells Dinsmore he has brought back two "Eskimo" women, "one for you and one for me," Dinsmore tells him: "No rush. You can get 100 of them tomorrow."[63]

But the real irony and the real tragedy of *Petticoat Fever* is that its supposed "Eskimo" characters are portrayed by Japanese-Americans, professional actors, who will soon be imprisoned as members of a "dangerous" Fifth Column aiming to aid the war effort of Imperial Japan against the U.S. In Chapter 7, I trace what became of Otto and Iris Yamaoka, upon their sudden forced journey from Hollywood's palm trees to the barren plains of Wyoming.

MGM's *Libeled Lady* (1936) with Powell, Loy, Harlow and Spencer Tracy was yet another screwball comedy; I discussed the plot and the film's reception in the previous chapter. Once again, the off-screen entanglement overshadowed the on-screen acting. Powell and Harlow were a couple in real life and announced their engagement on the set.[64] Tracy, "a raging alcoholic"[65] and serial philanderer famous for affairs on shoots from "script girls to starlets," including Loretta Young, Katharine Hepburn, Joan Crawford, Ingrid Bergman, Gene Tierney, Grace Kelly and Ingrid Bergman,[66] first slept with Loy on their previous film *Whipsaw*. "[The affair] fizzled after the shooting of *Whipsaw* had ended only to be revived on the set of [*Libeled Lady*]."[67]

Over time, Loy moved from playing exotic vixens to cool customers from the upper classes. When she approached L.B. Mayer with the idea of playing a lower class woman based on a character in a book she had read, he responded, "You're a lady in my book, Myrna, and you always gotta be a lady."[68]

In 1937, Loy moved (slightly) out of that niche of sophistication with *Test Pilot* with Clark Gable and Spencer Tracy. Historians and flight buffs study the film today for its state-of-the-art military aircraft and aerial stunts rather than its forgettable plot. But the opening sequence plays well when daredevil test pilot Gable makes an emergency landing in a wheat field on the Kansas farm of Loy's parents. She pulls off the country girl role and really shines as she immediately falls for Gable; I believed that she could have milked a cow or scythed a wheat field. But then she leaves the farm and parents behind to fly to the big city and a predictable plot of boy gets girl, boy almost loses girl, boy wins girl back. The climax comes when Gable fails to save Tracy from another wreck and, sobered by his death, gives up his drinking and his stunt flying. The Gable-Tracy characters' homoerotic relationship is more convincing than the heteroerotic Gable-Loy relationship.

In all of this, one uncredited black actor appears, and I suppose the usual limit is one, as a worker pushing Gable, Loy and Tracy along in a carriage at a fairground. Needing to get his attention, Loy says: "Boy. Oh, boy."

In 1940, Loy and Powell, under the direction of Woody Van Dyke, made the comedy

I Love You Again. Its silly plot: Powell, sailing on a cruise without his wife Loy, suffers an accident at sea and returns a changed man. Loy had planned to divorce the husband she had found terminally boring but this seemingly new man excites her. A few more hits to Powell's head, a few more personality changes, and now Loy's head is spinning. Bosley Crowther loved the film and called Powell and Loy "one of our most versatile and frisky connubial comedy teams, and, given a script as daffy as the one here in evidence, they can make an hour and a half spin like a roulette wheel."[69]

Black people on screen? Any people of color? Nope. Not a one on the cruise ship, not on the dock, not in New York City and not in Habersville, Pennsylvania. Of course, Hollywood made up a city called Habersville and made sure to leave people of color out. The cast does include Carl Switzer (1927–59) as Leonard Harkspur, Jr. Switzer is best known as Alfalfa from the Our Gang comedies (1934–40). In real life, he was killed while trying to collect a $50 debt. An inquest declared the shooting self-defense but decades later a witness described it as murder.

One year after *I Love You Again*, Powell and Loy were at it again in *Love Crazy*, another screwball comedy with a convoluted plot and Powell and Loy as husband and wife. Powell carries most of the load in pratfalls and physical comedy. He also dons drag, so convincingly that even Mayer didn't recognize the new "woman" on set.[70] An added delight is Gail Patrick (1911–80) as Isobel, an old flame and a sexy bad girl who has her eye on Powell.

Particularly funny are in-jokes that recall *The Thin Man*. Patrick greets Steve for the first time with "Hello, Sugar" (as Nick greeted Nora). Powell asks her, "What happened to that wire-haired terrier I gave you?" (Asta?).[71] And who do we see in a small role as an elevator operator but Elisha Cook, Jr. (1903–95), most memorable as the "gunsel" Wilmer in *The Maltese Falcon* that same year. Cook, of the unforgettable mug, appeared in 120 movies including as a taxi driver in the movie *Hammett* (1982). His last movie role was in 1987's *The Man Who Broke 1,000 Chains*. Partly filmed in my Los Angeles home, it starred Val Kilmer and Sonia Braga.

Hammett did not frequently interact with the cast and crew of *The Thin Man*. He did develop a friendship with writers Goodrich and Hackett. According to Loy, Hammett joined her, Powell, Harlow and a few others at the home of producer Arthur Hornblow after appearing together on a radio show. Hammett got roaring drunk as usual and, while speaking favorably of Hellman, made a pass at Loy, "lunging and pawing" at her. Hornblow, Loy's first husband, intervened and sent Hammett packing.[72]

Prior to World War II, Hitler had banned Loy's films in Germany because she had criticized the Third Reich.[73] With the Japanese attack on Pearl Harbor and Hitler's declaration of war on the United States, Hollywood stars had to make career-challenging decisions. Some enlisted and some shirked service. Loy, in her own way, enlisted: As actress Kathleen Turner recalled years later: "No Hollywood star made more financial and career sacrifices for her war work than Loy."[74] From 1942 to 1945, Loy put her film work on hold. She led bond sales, worked with the Red Cross, entertained the troops and visited military hospitals, meeting with the severely wounded, amputees, burn victims and soldiers in wheelchairs. Loy wrote in her autobiography, "I would have fun with them and then go to the ladies' room and cry."[75] She organized USO canteens and said, "I received more than fifty thousand letters from lonely soldiers overseas asking me to marry them. Each one declared he knew I'd make the perfect wife."[76]

Loy befriended First Lady Eleanor Roosevelt, with whom she later worked on many postwar political campaigns and a U.N. Commission. She never met FDR despite several trips to the White House. But Grace Tully, aide to FDR, announced, "Though the fact may disappoint members of other fan clubs, the President's favorite actress was Myrna Loy. He plied Hollywood visitors with questions about her, wanted very much to meet her."[77]

Years later, Loy turned against the U.S. War in Vietnam, saying, when shown a photo of herself in her World War II USO uniform: "Those times were different from today. I would never don such an outfit in support for the current conflict in Vietnam."[78]

Loy's two best-remembered films after *The Thin Man* are the magnificent *The Best Years of Our Lives* and *Mr. Blandings Builds His Dream House*. *Best Years* follows the challenges faced by returning World War II servicemen. It had a prestigious pedigree: Samuel Goldwyn hired MacKinlay Kantor (1904–1977) to write a novel based on the theme of war vets, which was published in 1945 as *Glory for Me*. Like Hammett, Kantor had begun his career writing for the pulp magazines and then graduated to the "slicks"; in 1956 he won a Pulitzer in fiction for his novel *Andersonville*. Goldwyn hired the Pulitzer Prize–winning playwright Robert Sherwood to turn the novel into a screenplay. Goldwyn offered Loy the role of Milly. She hesitated, fearing the reputation of the director William Wyler, confiding to Goldwyn that she had heard he was a sadist. "That's not true," Goldwyn assured her. "He's just a very mean fellow."[79]

The cast of *The Best Years of Our Lives* (1946). Shown from left are Harold Russell, Teresa Wright, Dana Andrews, Myrna Loy, Hoagy Carmichael (standing) and Fredric March. The film presented a realistic take on World War II veterans returning to civilian life. Loy was once again the perfect wife.

The movie took four months to shoot.⁸⁰ But Goldwyn knew he had a winner and rushed the opening to November 22, 1946, to qualify for Academy Award consideration. One reviewer called it "as near perfection as popular art aspires to be."⁸¹ The film won seven Oscars including Best Picture, Best Actor for Fredric March, and Best Supporting Actor for Harold Russell. Goldwyn charged the then unheard-of admission price of $1.40 a ticket and the movie broke attendance records everywhere it played.⁸²

In the film, three servicemen return after the war. Al (March), married to Milly (Loy), comes back a semi-alcoholic. Fred (Dana Andrews) learns that the woman (Virginia Mayo) he married just before shipping out has cheated on him; Fred is unskilled and nearly unemployable. Homer (Russell), who lost both hands in the military in real life and who had never acted in a film before, fears that people will reject or pity him for the steel prosthetics that now replace his hands.

Loy received top billing and you can see why. Once again she plays the nearly perfect film wife, a title she hated: "Some perfect wife I am. I've been married four times [to producer Arthur Hornblow Jr., advertising executive and rental car heir John Hertz Jr., producer-screenwriter Gene Markey and producer Howland Sargent], divorced four times, have no children, and can't boil an egg."⁸³

Low-key and quietly assertive, Loy does her most effective acting with her face and voice. When she tells her husband, "Al, shut up," she conveys both strength and deep caring and makes us each wish our name was Al. One critic called Loy "cool, and detached on the surface, vulnerable and romantic underneath."⁸⁴

Find the black, Latinx or Asian actors in *The Best Years of Our Lives*? Yes, five black actors: the powder room attendant, the airport porter, a club musician—all as usual—but also a man in an unemployment line surrounded by many other veterans and, near the beginning, a black man in military uniform. Not one, however, gets a single line of dialogue.

People tend to like RKO's *Mr. Blandings Builds His Dream House* (1948) which teamed Loy with Cary Grant for the third and last time (after *Wings in the Dark*, 1935, and *The Bachelor and the Bobbysoxer*, 1947). But the laughs are few, in my opinion, and the characters with whom we are meant to empathize have way too much money to be considered middle class as the film would have us believe. Finances are the main theme of the movie and dollar figures earn more screen time than family friend Melvyn Douglas. We learn that Mr. Blandings (Grant), an ad executive, earns $15,000 a year, the equivalent of $170,000 today. Back then the average family income was just $3200. Middle class, my two eyes. The country home he builds on 35 acres in Connecticut winds up over budget at $30,000 which seems a steal at just twice his annual salary. My folks bought their first home in the suburbs in 1952 for $8000.

My other problem lies with the subplot: Grant's inability to come up with a catchy advertising slogan for his client "WHAM Hams." His job is saved by their live-in maid (a maid for a middle-class family?). Gussie (Louise Beavers, of course), while serving breakfast, speaks these immortal words: "If you ain't eating WHAM, you ain't eating ham."⁸⁵ Grant plagiarizes her words, saves his job and his new home and rewards Gussie with a $10-a-week raise. Time to go on strike, Gussie.

The film was directed by H.C. Potter (1904–77), father of Dr. Robert Potter, my dissertation chair at the University of California Santa Barbara in 2003. I wish I'd asked Bob for his Myrna Loy stories. The cinematographer, James Wong Howe, worked the cameras on *The Thin Man*.

After World War II, Loy worked for liberal causes. *The Hollywood Reporter* attacked her as a Communist for reading the preamble to the U.N. Charter at a meeting of the American Slav Congress, listed as a subversive organization by the Justice Department. She filed a million dollar suit against the paper and averred, "I am not a Communist, I do not belong to the Communist Party.... I am not disloyal."[86] *Hollywood Reporter* printed a front page retraction.

Loy campaigned for Democrat presidential candidates Adlai Stevenson and John F. Kennedy and later for Senator Eugene McCarthy's insurgent primary campaign against incumbent President Lyndon Johnson to end the war in Vietnam.[87] In 1950, she accepted an appointment to the National Commission for UNESCO, the United Nations Educational, Scientific and Cultural Organization, working for world peace through education, art, science and culture, and continued working with the U.N. throughout the 1950s. In the 1960s, her focus shifted to civil rights and she served on the National Committees Against Discrimination in Housing. She spoke forcefully at a public meeting for an anti-discrimination clause in New York City housing. When her amendment passed, she wrote, "Because of this other image of me, the newspapers, which might have buried the hearings, gave them headline coverage. We even made the *Daily News*! The amendments passed unanimously. All I can say is, thank God for *The Thin Man*!"[88]

Singer-actress-civil rights activist Lena Horne called Loy "a great star and a woman of accomplishment who is angry about all the right things."[89] Said actor Tony Randall, who appeared with her in the TV series *Love, Sidney*: "She had an intellect. She never cared very much about clothes or anything like that. She cared about causes."[90]

Loy developed a late-in-life taste for live theater and toured the country with several shows. In 1964, she appeared in Neil Simon's *Barefoot in the Park*. Co-star Richard Benjamin recalled that wherever they were touring, one scene would repeat: The company would go out to dinner together and "inevitably a distinguished looking gentlemen—a different one in every town, but always with gray hair—would approach Myrna politely." He would apologize for intruding and then tell her, "I had to tell you that I have always loved you."[91]

Although Loy was never an Oscar winner, the Academy made amends by presenting her with a Lifetime Honorary Award "in recognition of her extraordinary qualities both on screen and off" in 1990. She died three years later at 88.

6

The Rest of the Cast and Crew

It took just one man, Dashiell Hammett, to write the novel *The Thin Man*. Though Powell and Loy became the face of the franchise in movie after movie, it took a village, an MGM studio village, to make *The Thin Man* movie. Louis B. Mayer ran MGM, but New York kept him on a short leash and he had to report constantly to first Marcus Loew and later Nicholas Schenck. Irving Thalberg (1899–1936), the ill "boy wonder" and head of production at MGM, kept the movie factory running on the mass production model he learned from Henry Ford, overseeing the work of writers, other producers, directors and actors. Mayer, twice Thalberg's age, and Thalberg originally enjoyed a father-and-son–type relationship but as time passed, they regularly feuded over business decisions and creative choices and sent their individual private reports back to Schenck. Mayer took advantage of Thalberg's death at age 37 to secure his personal grip on the MGM studio. F. Scott Fitzgerald made a Thalberg-like character, Monroe Stahr, the protagonist of his 1941 novel *The Last Tycoon*.

When it came to creative choices, Thalberg usually sided with his veteran producers and he supported Woodbridge Strong Van Dyke II (1889–1943) in his plan to buy the *Thin Man* novel and cast Powell and Loy. In many ways, Van Dyke was an odd choice to direct an urban and urbane detective film. He had cut his teeth as a do-anything assistant to D.W. Griffith on his film *Intolerance* in 1915. Previously "a miner, logger, stage driver, expressman, grocery clerk, and laborer,"[1] Van Dyke earned Griffith's confidence because, Griffith said, "When I told Van Dyke to do something, he did it with a maximum of speed and a minimum of fuss."[2] In the nickelodeon era, Van Dyke cranked out serials in nine days and Westerns in three. Sometimes he wrote his own scripts; sometimes he filled in on screen when an actor went missing. He took a crew to Polynesia for *White Shadows in the South Seas* (1928) and into four African countries in seven months for *Trader Horn* (1931). One crew member fell into a river and was eaten by a crocodile, and "a Native boy ... was killed by a charging rhino (a catastrophe that was captured on film and used in the movie)."[3]

The New York Times quoted Van Dyke speaking of his work on *Marie Antoinette* in 1938:

> All my life I have been studying people; it is part of a director's job. I have met and enjoyed all kinds, the good and the bad. White, black, yellow, or brown, human beings are fundamentally the same no matter where you find them. I kept only one purpose in mind; that was to make my characters as little like kings and queens, and princes, and as much like ordinary human beings as possible.[4]

Just before Van Dyke was born his father, a Superior Court judge, died suddenly:

There was no insurance. My mother, Laura Winston, with a baby to support, went back to the calling she had followed before her marriage—the stage. I was raised in a theater trunk. We went on the road, up and down the coast, into the Middle West, all over the U.S. When I was 5 years old they starred at the old San Francisco Grand Opera House in *Blind Girl*. Much to my disgust, I played the little blind girl in wig and pinafore. I think I've been to school in every state in the Union. Whenever the company stopped off long enough in any city I went back behind a school desk. The rest of the time my mother taught me.[5]

He helmed some 80 movies in his relatively short career (1917–42), many of them part of this book's focus: *The Thin Man, After the Thin Man, Another Thin Man* and *Shadow of the Thin Man*, as well as films Powell and Loy did outside the Thin Man series. He worked fast and brought his films in under budget. Some critics felt that his fast camerawork and improvisational dialogue lent his films an air of intimacy and verisimilitude while others called him just plain rushed and sloppy.

I watched *Eskimo* because it offered the rare chance to see Van Dyke as both director and actor. The 1933 MGM film, produced by Hunt Stromberg, combines both realistic nature scenes and racial fantasy. Filmed above the Arctic Circle in Alaska, in difficult circumstances, the scenery of frozen tundra, migrating reindeer herds and ships stuck in ice nicely sets the stage as Indigenous people go about their lives hunting, racing their dog sleds and building igloos.

The exotic locale serves as an excuse for a lot of *National Geographic*–style highbrow eroticism. An Inupiaq woman pulls her breast out of her blouse and the camera hungrily closes in as she offers it to her infant. For the plot, much is made of the supposed native tradition of one man offering his wife, or wives, to a man who has been too long without a woman. All in all, the movie Eskimos are rather free in their sexual relations. In fact, when box office sagged for *Eskimo*, MGM changed the film's title to *Eskimo Wife-Traders*. To further sales in the European market, the company added "some steamy sex scenes and renamed it *Mala the Magnificent*...."[6] The film does contain exciting action footage of a walrus hunt, a caribou hunt and a whaling expedition in boats dwarfed by the whales. Greedy and lascivious white men intrude on this romantic natural paradise and our protagonist Mala kills the ship captain who has raped his wife. Mala escapes to care for his two new wives. As Mounties pursue him for murder, he and wife Iva choose death in each other's arms on an ice floe in the open sea. Van Dyke plays the Royal Canadian Mounted Police inspector and we get to see the director in a rare screen role in all his ramrod-straight, square-jawed, crewcut authoritarian manner. For a director, he wasn't a bad actor.

Today "Eskimo" constitutes a racial slur formerly applied to these arctic people by their colonizers. Collectively we know them today as Inupiat and individually as Inupiaq. The film opens without credits but with the statement that these are really natives, "primitive Eskimos," not actors, and that the movie will offer a look at "their primeval creed." While the Indigenous speak in their own language (Inupiat, translated into English on intertitle cards like silent films) a little research shows us that while some of the actors are in fact indigenous, the leads have been imported from Hollywood because, said Van Dyke "everyone knew Eskimo women couldn't act."[7]

Lotus Long, born Lotus Pearl Shibata (1909–90), appears as Iva, Mala's second wife. Long, born in New Jersey and the daughter of a Japanese father and a Hawaiian mother, had no previous acting experience but went on to appear in nearly 20 movies. Having played many roles on screen as a Chinese woman, she was able to avoid internment with other Japanese in Los Angeles in 1942 and rode out World War II in her Beverly Hills home. After the war, she undertook the infamous role of the traitor Tokyo Rose in the 1946 film *Tokyo Rose*.

Lulu Wong Wing (1902–95) was the older sister of Anna May Wong, the first Chinese-American Hollywood movie star. Lulu appears as Abu, Mala's first wife. Reviewers later dubbed her "the Eskimo Greta Garbo."[8] Iris Yamaoka, Japanese-American, also appears as one of Mala's "more amusing if slightly dim wives."[9] She plays an Inuit again in *Petticoat Fever*. So we have two Japanese-Americans and one Chinese-American as Inupiat in a movie heralding its authenticity. Van Dyke brought in real Inupiat to teach these three the rudiments of the language.

Poster for director W.S. Van Dyke's *Eskimo* (1933) with Ray Mala, Peter Fruechen and some very non-native Alaskans: Chinese Lotus Long and Lulu Wong Wing and Japanese Iris Yamaoka. Ten years later, the latter was imprisoned at the Heart Mountain internment camp in Wyoming.

MGM based the movie on two books by the Danish arctic explorer Peter Freuchen (1886–1957), but Freuchen had written about the Inuit in Greenland. The Inupiat of Alaska neither built igloos nor sewed animal skin tents like their Greenland relations. The film crew soon discovered why: the snow-block igloos quickly melted or blew away and had to be constantly rebuilt, a job Freuchen claims to have taken on himself. For his part, Van Dyke warned his male crew members not to dally with native women and added: "As a rule [the women] are indescribably homely and utterly filthy."[10] According to Freuchen, Van Dyke brought along Emil, a Swiss chef from the Hotel Roosevelt in Hollywood and plenty of liquor to keep the white cast members well fed and watered.[11] Freuchen also said that the day the kitchen ran out of fresh grapefruit, the three lead actresses refused to work until "a plane was sent to Seattle for a supply of fresh fruit."[12]

But it is in racial matters that things get really confusing. The planned male lead, incensed that crew members had made a pass at his wife, walked off the set and could not be enticed to return. Van Dyke turned to Hollywood cameraman–bit actor Ray Wise (1906–52), whom he had earlier rejected for the role of Mala. Fathered by a Russian Jew, William Weisbleeth, who had abandoned his teenaged Eskimo mother, Wise "was a mixed breed love child,"[13] born in Candle, Alaska. Van Dyke had earlier "turned Wise down fast ... on the grounds that he was part Jewish.... Van Dyke refused to consider a leading man who was a half-breed."[14] The word *half-breed* is another racist term which harkens back to miscegenation laws when people were forbidden to marry out of their racial caste. In desperate need of a leading man, Van Dyke had a change of heart and sent back to Hollywood for Wise. Following the release of the movie, Wise changed his name to that of his *Eskimo* character: He became Ray Mala. Mala was the first non-white actor to play a leading role in a Hollywood movie.[15]

So Hollywood had, intentionally or not, imported an Alaskan native thousands of miles from Hollywood and then shipped him back to Alaska to play an Alaskan native. Universal's press machine dubbed him "The Eskimo Clark Gable" when distributing his early film *Igloo*, also distributed under the title *Manna*. Regarding the film's premiere: "All day a team of reindeer had been driven around the streets of New York advertising the show and there was not one empty seat."[16] The film had taken 17 months to film and MGM lost about a half million dollars on the venture.

Tinseltown then relegated Mala to roles as Japanese, Hawaiian, Native American and Mexican characters in films like *Last of the Pagans* (1935), a take on Herman Melville's *Typee*. One reviewer called it "a relentless parade of cultural imperialism and cliches about primitive people and noble savages."[17] In 1936, Mala was featured in *The Jungle Princess* starring Dorothy Lamour and Ray Milland; he was an American Indian in the 1938 serial *The Great Adventures of Wild Bill Hickok*, and an Indian again in 1939's *Union Pacific*. Mala was often cast as Native American alongside his friend, the Italian-American actor Iron Eyes Cody (1904–99).[18] Cody, a Sicilian, born Espera Oscar de Corti, worked regularly in movies and later became well known for his anti-littering TV spots. His true name and Italian birth, which he had denied all his life, became public after his death.

Mala found more success and steady work as a cinematographer, working with directors Howard Hawks, Otto Preminger and Alfred Hitchcock, among others. In a *Los Angeles Times* interview after the release of *Eskimo*, Mala said: "People down here ask me all sorts of questions about my life as an Eskimo. They think it is very funny. When I give them my answers to anything they say: 'What a terrible way to live. What strange people.' It never occurs to them that I, in turn, think their existence equally incredible."[19] Mala died at just 45 years of age.

"One-Take" Woody also died young. Suffering from a heart condition and cancer and having foresworn medical treatment as a Christian Scientist, he put a bullet in his brain at the age of 53, leaving a wife and three young children. MGM kept the actual cause of death out of the newspapers. Film critic Andrew Sarris proffered his judgment on Van Dyke in *American Cinema: Directors and Directions (1929–1968)*, relegating him to the lower tier of American film directors but adding: "Woody Van Dyke made more good movies than his reputation for carelessness and haste would indicate." Perhaps carelessness and haste are precisely the qualities responsible for the breezy charm of *Trader Horn, The Thin Man* and *After the Thin Man*.[20] Myrna Loy stated, "He wanted spontaneity and speed assured it. Woody demanded extraordinary deeds and you needed the discipline to go along with it or you couldn't work with him. He ultimately became too fast; it became an obsession. But his pacing and spontaneity made *The Thin Man*."[21]

Hunt Stromberg (1894–1968) produced *Eskimo* and the first three Thin Man movies. A producer gets his name in the film's credits but their role can be a little hard to pin down. While a film is a collaborative process of many talents, the producer, like a circus ringmaster, is in overall charge of the filmmaking process, planning and coordinating all aspects of the project: selecting the script, arranging financing, choosing the director, overseeing editing. In the 1920s and '30s, Stromberg served as one of the Big Four at MGM (with Mayer, Thalberg and Harry Rapf) and later led his own independent production unit within the studio, earning a guaranteed salary of $8000 a week and a percentage of Loew's profits as well.[22] He produced more than a hundred MGM films and worked with Van Dyke as director on 12 of them. After Thalberg's death, Stromberg rose in prominence and became one of the ten highest-paid executives in the U.S. He became addicted to pain killers after rupturing a disc in his back.[23] Forced out of MGM by Mayer in 1942, Stromberg struck out on his own but had hits and misses in equal measure. He retired from the industry after the death of his wife in 1951. He was wealthy not only from his film career but through investments in several racetracks, including Hollywood Park and Santa Anita.

Studios usually maintained a story editor and a pool of readers and writers. The readers pored over newly released books and articles looking for movie material. The method mixed madness and invention. As John Baxter noted, "Plays and novels were usually bought on the basis of a synopsis prepared by a Screen Story Analyst or 'reader' and retold verbally to a producer.... Most Hollywood films used only a book's title and skeleton plot, discarding the substance of the plot or replacing it with material from other sources. Plagiarism, intended or accidental, became widespread."[24] Lillian Hellman, and many others with writing aspirations, began their Hollywood careers as readers. But when readers graduated to writers, challenges mounted. One writer might submit a draft only to have a producer ask another to rewrite it and then repeat the process until some kind of filmable plot emerged. Writers watched movies on opening day to read the film credits just to see who the studio would surprise with the honor of authorship.

The Thin Man was scripted by a married couple, Frances Goodrich and Albert Hackett. With a bit of exaggerated family pride, Frances' nephew and biographer called the writing duo "the real Nick and Nora [Charles]."[25] Both Goodrich and Hackett began their careers as actors and segued into writing. Goodrich (1890–1984), a Vassar College graduate, began acting in stock companies and moved on to Broadway. She married and divorced actor Robert Ames and then renowned historian Hendrik Willem van Loon, best known for his book *The Story of Mankind*. In 1928, she met Albert Hackett (1900–1995), nine years her junior, son of an actress; he had been a child actor on Broadway and in films. So began a writing and romantic partnership that lasted 34 years. Their success on Broadway led to signing with MGM, which was always on the lookout for new talent. In Hollywood, they proved particularly adept at rewriting previously published properties, like *The Thin Man*, for the screen. They adapted Owen Wister's *The Virginian*, S.N. Behrman's *The Pirate* and Edward Streeter's *Father of the Bride*. They achieved their greatest success with *The Diary of Anne Frank*: Their original Broadway adaptation won the Tony in 1956 for Best Play, and its script received the 1956 Pulitzer Prize for Drama. The 1959 screen version garnered three Oscars.

David Goodrich, nephew to Frances, and loyal to his aunt, wrote in his book *The Real Nick and Nora*, "The bond between the Hacketts was much more Charles like than that between Hammett and Hellman."[26] This, of course, contradicts Hammett himself, who credited his lover Lillian Hellman as his inspiration for the character Nora, and also Hellman, who remembered that some of the dialogue in the novel came directly from her own chats with Hammett. Writer Ian Hamilton probably got it right when he

Irish-born Maureen O'Sullivan, *The Thin Man*'s Dorothy Wynant, had a 10-year career as Jane in six Tarzan movies, beginning with *Tarzan the Ape Man* in 1932. She is shown here with Johnny "Tarzan" Weissmuller.

said: "The Nick and Nora Charles partnership was Dashiell Hammett's invention but Albert and Frances Hackett knew it from within and added much that was their own."[27] And we must credit Stromberg and Van Dyke with choosing a husband-and-wife writing team to bring a husband-and-wife detecting team to the screen. Goodrich and Hackett became personal friends with Hammett and Hellman. According to Hackett, "Dash and Lilly were very satisfied with what we had done [on the script] and that's how we got to know them."[28]

After Powell and Loy, a stable of MGM contract players rounded out the cast. Maureen O'Sullivan (1911–1998), mother of Mia Farrow, appeared as Dorothy Wynant. O'Sullivan was best known for her role as Jane in six Tarzan movies with Johnny Weissmuller, first in *Tarzan the Ape Man*, directed by Woody Van Dyke in 1932. She joined Powell again after *The Thin Man* in *The Emperor's Candlesticks* (1937).

Cesar Romero (1907–94), seen in *The Thin Man* as bigamist Chris Jorgensen, began his career as a nightclub dancer and appeared in over 120 films (six as The Cisco Kid), often in the stereotypical role of the Latin Lover—though he never married in real life. *The Thin Man* was his second film role. Son of Cuban immigrants, Romero claimed to be a grandson of Jose Marti, the renowned poet, called the Liberator of Cuba.

Skippy, born 1931, date of death unknown, played Asta. He was discovered in a pet store window by animal trainer Henry East. East knew he had the makings of a film star when he noted Skippy's singular alertness. As James Lileks wrote in *The Star Tribune*, "All the other pups were sleeping, but Skippy was pressed up against the glass, eager to see everything. East took him home and put a bone in an unused movie camera. For the rest of his career, Skippy looked into the camera to see if it might contain a treat. It didn't, but what the camera saw was a treat for the audience."[29] Skippy played Asta in the first three Thin Man films, earning $200 a week by the second film while his trainer earned $60 a week. With his roles in the *Thin Man* series, Skippy became "the best known dog in the country with Franklin Roosevelt's Fala a close second."[30] Skippy's film biography states: "Asta's popularity led to a massive increase in the breeding of wire-haired terriers. Everybody wanted to own one, or, at least, have a dog by that name. William Powell wanted to buy Asta himself but the Easts refused."[31]

MGM added a secretary to answer Asta's fan mail. After his Thin Man outings, Skippy appeared in *Bringing Up Baby*, *Topper Takes a Trip* and *The Awful Truth*. At some point, the first Skippy died and another Skippy took over his chores. Myrna Loy remembered her various doggie co-stars: "Several wire haired terriers played our scene stealing pet over the years, but we weren't allowed to make friends with any of them. The trainer feared it would break the dogs' concentration. The first one, Skippy, bit me once, so our relationship was hardly idyllic."[32]

Minna Gombell (1893–1973), as Mimi, made over 50 films between 1929 and 1951. She played a number of strong women including Mrs. Oliver Hardy in *Blockheads* (1938). Her third husband Myron C. Fagan (1887–1972), a playwright and later an anti–Communist conspiracy theorist, authored 83 booklets with titles like *Moscow Over Hollywood*, *How the Great White Nations Were Mongrelized* and *Why Kennedy Must Be Impeached*.[33] Fagan defamed his wife's former *Thin Man* co-star Myrna Loy in a speech at El Patio Theater in Los Angeles on April 12, 1948, calling her "a young woman who thinks nothing of giving her name and her moral and financial support to the enemies of the America which has made her popular and wealthy."[34]

Edward Elis Tanner (1870–1952) played the murder victim, Clyde Wynant, the real

Thin Man of the film title. He played supporting roles in more than 30 films and 20 Broadway shows. The script calls for him to grimace threateningly when leaving Julia Wolf's apartment: "Wynant turns at the door and smiles—a terrifying smile—and walks out. The CAMERA SWINGS QUICKLY BACK TO JULIA. She looks after him terrified."[35] But on the screen Tanner's melodramatic grimace comes across as laughable rather than scary.

Cyril Thornton (1905–1990), in one of his first of 56 movie roles, plays Tanner, the ex-con bookkeeper. He reunited with co-stars Powell and O'Sullivan in *The Emperor's Candlesticks* in another small part three years later.

Nat Pendleton (1895–1967), an Olympic wrestler who won a silver medal for the U.S. in 1920, is seen here as detective John Guild. He made some 114 films, usually in supporting roles. He appeared in nine Dr. Kildare movies and two Abbott and Costello comedies. He returned in *Another Thin Man*.

Henry Wadsworth (1903–74), who played Dorothy's boyfriend, made 21 films from 1929 to 1945.

William Henry (1914–82), just 20 years old in *The Thin Man*, plays the odd and precocious Gilbert Wynant. He began his career as a child actor and worked on over 120 films, 12 of them with John Ford. He ended his career as a character actor.

Harold Huber, born Harold Joseph Huberman (1909–59), played murder victim Nunheim. He acted on stage and in over 90 movies.

Natalie Moorhead (1901–92), as blackmailer, thief and murder victim Julia Wolf, appeared in some 60 movies from 1929 to 1940. She also appeared with William Powell in *The Benson Murder Case* and *Shadow of the Law*. *The Kenosha News* called her "fascinating"[36] and *The Richmond Times Dispatch* tagged her as "the best dressed girl in pictures."[37]

Edward Brophy (1895–1960) appeared in some 100 films, often as a gangster, as he is here as Morelli. He often got to play comic characters. He returns as Brogan in *The Thin Man Goes Home*. Perhaps most famously, he voiced Dumbo's friend Timothy Q. Mouse in Disney's *Dumbo* (1941).

Porter Hall (1888–1953) had his first major film role here at age 45 as the murderer Macaulay, but went on to make 75 more films, often as the villain. He appeared in the second film version of Hammett's *The Maltese Falcon*, retitled as *Satan Met a Lady*, with Bette Davis in 1936.

In minor roles we have Will Aubrey, William Augustin, Polly Bailey, Arthur Belasco, Brooks Benedict, Tui Bow, Raymond Brown, Ruth Channing, Jack Cheatham, Clay Clement, Nick Copeland, John Dunsmuir, Pat Flaherty, Douglas Fowley, Christian Frank, Kay Garrett, Kenneth Gibson, Dick Gordon, Creighton Hale, Sherry Hall, Edward Hearn, Robert Homans, John Irwin, Thomas Jackson, Sydney Jarvis, Tiny Jones, Kenner Kemp, Dixie Laughton, Walter Long, Fred Malatesta, Hans Moebus, William O'Brien, Frank O'Connor, Henry Otho, Garry Owen, Lee Phelps, Alexander Pollard, Albert Pollet, Bob Reeves, Bert Roach, Rolfe Sedan, Gertrude Short, Lee Shumway, Pietro Sosso, Ben Taggert, Phil Tead, George Templeton, Harry Tenbrook, Huey White and Charles Williams as uncredited cops, reporters, party goers, etc.[38]

And among these 54 uncredited bit actors is the only black actor: John Larkin (1877–1936). Larkin plays one of the few film roles open to a black man in white-produced films, a railroad porter. So segregated and exploited were railroad porters that famed civil rights leader A. Philip Randolph established the nation's first majority-black labor union, the Brotherhood of Sleeping Car Porters. At his death, *The Washington Post* wrote of Randolph

> At a time when American society was almost entirely segregated, he was the first to use economic power to better the lot of blacks. He began in one of the few industries to which blacks were relegated—and in which they could make their economic power felt.
>
> In 1925, he organized the Brotherhood of Sleeping Car Porters. It was the first black union granted a charter by the American Federation of Labor. In 1955, when the AFL merged with the Congress of Industrial Organizations to form the AFL-CIO, Mr. Randolph was instrumental in persuading it to ban discrimination in unions.[39]

Randolph and his union, in collaboration with Bayard Rustin, planned the first civil rights march on Washington during World War II, threatening to publicly undercut U.S. claims to be defending American democracy against Nazi racism when, in fact, African Americans faced discrimination in all avenues of American life from the crucial defense industry to Hollywood. In 1941, President Roosevelt issued the first federal mandate, Executive Order 8802, barring discrimination in the defense industry that received government contracts. Randolph called off the march but the idea of calling for a national march on Washington was taken up again by the Rev. M.L. King, Jr., in 1963.

In *The Thin Man*, of course, the porter is just another happy black worker, played by a presumably equally happy actor, John Larkin.

We should also single out the film's photography, the shots composed by the renowned James Wong Howe. Born Wong Tung Jim in China, Howe (1899–1976) worked on over 130 films. He pioneered the use of shadow in black and white film, seen in this film in his memorable elongated shadow of the Thin Man beneath a city street light at night in the opening minutes. A *New York Times* critic noted, "[Howe's] work—particularly his penchant for dramatic high contrast lighting ... earned him the nickname Low-key Howe."[40]

Howe was also a master of deep focus photography in which near and distant objects remain simultaneously in focus. Professional success led to wealth and acclaim for Howe. He went on to win Oscars for *The Rose Tattoo* (1955) and *Hud* (1963). He also directed a feature, *Go, Man, Go* (1954) with Sidney Poitier and Ruby Dee. Off-screen, Howe contended with the general anti–Asian bias of the country. He could not become a citizen until the repeal of the Chinese Exclusion Act in 1943 and his marriage to Sanora Babb, a white woman, was not legally recognized until 1948 due to racist anti-miscegenation laws. According to Jon C. Hopwood: "During World War II anti–Asian bigotry intensified, despite the fact that China was an ally of the United States in its war with Japan. Mistaken for a Japanese (despite their having been relocated to concentration camps away from the Pacific Coast), [Howe] wore a button that declared 'I am Chinese.' His close friend James Cagney also wore the same button, out of solidarity with his friend."[41]

7

The Thin Man and Race

I don't really believe in race. The Swedish naturalist Carl Linnaeus (1707–1778) divided humans into four races: European, American, African and Asian. Imperialists, slavers and eugenicists quickly put his divisions of humanity to work to justify racial hierarchies, usually with white people at the top. I'll use the term *race* here as we commonly use it though I find the very concept absurd. We usually base our ideas of race on skin color as a marker of classification and division. In the U.S., historically, the white (European) race enslaved the black race (African), killed off the red race (American) and exploited the yellow race (Asian).

Applying these historical norms, I noticed the absence of black people in the novel *The Thin Man* and the subsequent films. We call that "whitewashing." Then I noticed how they used white actors to portray black people by corking their faces. We call this "blackface." And there is "redface." Think of all the Caucasian actors who masqueraded as Indigenous people in the Westerns, full of stereotypes of "Indians" as cruel and savage, or even impossibly noble. Hollywood stars of the 1930s masquerading as Indigenous in film versions of James Fenimore Cooper's *The Last of the Mohicans* include such odd fellows as Wallace Beery, Bela Lugosi, Bruce Cabot and Buster Crabbe. Then I noticed the prosthetics: the buck teeth, drooping mustaches and elongated eyes used to have white actors play Asians. We call this "yellowface." Then I realized how the few Chinese, Japanese and Inuit actors on 1930s film screens played whatever "exotic" character the script called for: Japanese actors portrayed Chinese, Chinese actors portrayed Pacific Islanders, etc., as if they were interchangeable and all looked alike. Then I noticed no two people of different races ever kissed on screen or got married at the end of the film. I realized that you cannot look at these Hollywood movies without thinking about race because the studios, producers, directors and actors spent a lot of time thinking about race for you.

Looking at Myrna Loy's roles before her success in *The Thin Man* introduced me to the weird world of Hollywood stereotypes. In 1926, Loy was cast as an Italian in *Don Juan*; in 1927 as Roma in *Across the Pacific*; again in 1927 as Mulatta, in *The Heart of Maryland*; in 1930 as a Mexican in *Rogue of the Rio Grande*. In *Ham and Eggs at the Front*, the absurd casting had all three leads, Tom Wilson, Heinie Conklin and Loy, in blackface. Wilson (Ham) and Conklin (Eggs) portray African American doughboys. Loy is Fifi, "a dusky, sultry Senegalese spy."[1]

In 1928, Loy played Azuri, a Moroccan native dancing girl, in *The Desert Song*. This film, she said, "kind of solidified my exotic ... image."[2] In the 1929 film *The Black Watch*, she plays Yasmani, an Indian princess. Also in 1929, she played a Mexican-American in *The Great Divide*; "a native girl" in *Evidence*; "a South Sea native girl" in *Isle of Escape*;

7. The Thin Man *and Race*

an Argentinian in *Cock o' the Walk*. She garners near top billing in 1932 as a half–Javanese Eurasian in *Thirteen Women* and Fu Manchu's sadistic Chinese daughter in *The Mask of Fu Manchu*. Then she hits it big in 1934 in *Manhattan Melodrama* and *The Thin Man* and escapes the dual stereotypes of vamp and racial exotic for the rest of her long career.

Odd casting indeed for an actor of Welsh parentage who grew up on a Montana ranch. In her autobiography, Loy wrote:

> My bit as a mulatto in *The Heart of Maryland* led to a role that I'm very much ashamed of. Zanuck wrote *Ham and Eggs at the Front*, a blackface parody of *What Price Glory* casting me as a spy. How could I ever have put on blackface? When I think of it now, it horrifies me. Well, our awareness broadens, thank God! It was a tasteless slapstick comedy that I mercifully recall very little about.[3]

Hammett set the *Thin Man* novel in New York City. African Americans, some 200,000 people who had moved up from the South between 1917 and 1925, settled in New York as part of the Great Migration.[4] You could not walk the streets of Manhattan in 1933 without seeing a black person. But we must presume Hammett saw none, since none of the novel's characters are black. The producer and director who placed the first Thin Man movie in New York saw none, since no black actor appears in the film. We don't see any black people walking in the streets, entering the stores, or sitting in a park reading a newspaper. They are unseen. They are "whitewashed" away, removed from the picture.

If you played a drinking game where you drank only when you saw a black actor in any of the six Thin Man movies, you would remain stone cold sober to the end. Why whitewash the world? Because white people felt more comfortable in a monochromatic world. The Golden Age of Hollywood (1929–41) could also be called the White Age of Hollywood.

But where did that leave black people who went to the movies? George Gerbner, a professor of communication, wrote: "Representation in the fictional world signifies social existence. Absence means symbolic annihilation." In his book *Moving Pictures: An Introduction to Cinema*, Russell Sharman enlarges this concept:

> The idea here is that when you see yourself in cinema, that is, when you see characters in film and television that look like you, talk like you, live like you, it affirms your place in the world. It assures you that you do, in fact, exist and have a role to play in society. And that starts at a *very* young age, often before you've formed clear ideas about the world outside your own home and family. Seeing yourself represented in the fictional world of cinema points to (signifies) your social existence long before you have the opportunity to put that knowledge into practice.... Now imagine you never see anyone on screen in film or television that looks like you, talks like you or lives like you.... It can begin to feel as though you've been erased. That you have no place in society.[5]

And when you wanted a laugh, when you wanted a song, when you wanted a dance, you always had blackface. But blackface could not be separated from white racism. Al Jolson built his career on blackface.

Al Jolson also "was active in the late 1930's advocating a physical wall be built around portions of the San Fernando Valley [where he lived] in order to keep African Americans out."[6]

For those who might argue that blackface constituted an acceptable amusement of the time, like the TV host Alicia Malone on Turner Classic Movies introducing the film

Princess Tam Tam on May 12, 2021: "You will see some white actors in dark makeup [which was] the practice at the time." I would ask what practice? By whom? Why? People often defended white performers who darkened their skin with burnt cork and performed minstrel shows as something socially accepted at the end of the 20th century, ignoring the fact that it was understood as racist from the beginning by many like abolitionist Frederick Douglass as early as 1848.

When a daring film producer did include a black actor and they were not singing or dancing, they were cast as servants, maids and butlers, or figures at the edges of the action like the railroad porters who carry the Charleses' luggage or take their tickets in later Thin Man films. Writes Miriam Petty in *Stealing the Show: African American Performers and Audiences in 1930s Hollywood*: "The thirties were an era of normative Jim Crow segregation throughout America [and] found America less than a century removed from the endowed formal and legal slavery and somewhat enamored of an idealized slave-owning past as manifest in the popularity of the plantation setting in period films."[7]

One recurrent trope of this nostalgia for the antebellum South was the Mammy figure, best known from the film *Gone with the Wind*

Al Jolson (1886–1950) was born in Lithuania, the son of a cantor who moved the family to the United States. He became a worldwide sensation singing African American blues and jazz songs, often in grotesque blackface makeup with its origins in minstrel shows and racist tropes.

but also common in several of the Thin Man movies and in other films starring Powell and/or Loy. To play Mammy on screen, MGM turned to either Hattie McDaniel or Louise Beavers, almost interchangeably where the role called for an overweight, seemingly asexual, middle-aged black woman who dispensed folk wisdom while always smiling and serving the needs of her white employers. This servant had no last name, no husband, no children of her own.

Both of Hattie McDaniel's parents were born into slavery. Her father served in the Union Army and was wounded in the Civil War.[8] You can see McDaniel (1893–52) in

Libeled Lady (1936), with Powell and Loy, as an unnamed and uncredited hotel maid, and in *Saratoga* (1937) as Rosetta, Jean Harlow's maid. Her film career had her playing servants again and again. She had, in fact, worked as a maid in real life and spoke pragmatically about the on-screen typecasting: "I can be a maid for $7 a week. Or I can play a maid [on film] for $700 a week."⁹ She most famously played house servant Mammy in *Gone with the Wind* and won the Academy Award for Best Supporting Actress, becoming the first African American Oscar winner. She was, however, barred from attending that movie's premiere in Atlanta at the segregated Loew's Grand Theater.

Louise Beavers (1902–62) acted in some 100 movies including *Bombshell* (1933), as Jean Harlow's maid, and with Loy and Powell in *Shadow of The Thin Man* as their maid. In that film, and so many others, Beavers went on force feed diets, "compelling herself to eat beyond her normal appetite ... [I]t was a steady battle for her to stay overweight ... [H]er voice had no trace of dialect or Southern patois. When the talkies came in, she schooled herself in the slow-and-easy backwoods accent compulsory for every black servant ... [S]he was always happy, always kind...[and] usually lacked a private life of her own."¹⁰

The Mammy stereotype assuaged white fears of blacks, fears that black people might hate us for our racism. It froze nostalgia for the plantation South in a rosy glow that helped undermine political efforts to end racial segregation and racial violence. In fact, the United Daughters of the Confederacy, Jefferson Davis Chapter, wanted the U.S. government to erect a monument "in memory of the faithful colored mammies." They hoped this monument might be built on the Washington, D.C., Mall, not far from the Lincoln and Washington Memorials. This absurd plan actually passed the Senate in 1923.¹¹ The goal, according to *The Atlantic,* was "a massive slave woman, hewn from stone, cradling a white child atop a plinth." The magazine quoted a Southern Congressman on the intention: "The traveler, as he passes by, will recall that epoch of southern civilization [when] fidelity and loyalty [prevailed]. No class

Actress Louise Beavers (seen here in 1936's *Rainbow on the River*) appeared in several Thin Man films and 100 other movies, often as a nanny or maid. MGM enforced a diet regimen to make her meet the overweight appearance of the stereotypical "Mammy," a desexualized and happy servant of white people.

of any race of people held in bondage could be found anywhere who lived more free from care or distress."[12] Just weeks before, the Senate let a Southern filibuster defeat an anti-lynching bill. One Southern Senator called it "a bill to encourage rape" by blacks. This at a time when whites were lynching an average of one black person every week.[13] African Americans and descendants of Union soldiers mounted a political counterattack and the "Mammy Bill" died in a House Committee as Congress adjourned without taking action.

Hollywood also made avowedly racist movies like *The Birth of a Nation* (1915), D.W. Griffith's three-hour extravaganza which was the first movie ever shown in the White House, for President Woodrow Wilson, a Southerner who worked to resegregate the U.S. federal civil service. The most racist American film I have ever seen, *The Birth of A Nation* with its scenes of Southern womanhood at the mercy of drunken, ape-like, marauding blacks developed sympathy for the newly reorganized Ku Klux Klan and served as their most effective recruiting tool. Historian John Hope Franklin called *Birth of a Nation* "the midwife in the rebirth of the most vicious terrorist organization in the history of the United States."[14] Walter White (1893–1955), leader of the National Association for the Advancement of Colored People, reflected on the power of film: "The most widely circulated medium yet devised to reach the minds and emotions of people all over America was perpetuating and spreading dangerous and harmful stereotypes of the Negro."[15]

Some filmmakers made films specifically for black audiences. Such movies, called "race films" and numbering some 500, were made outside the Hollywood studio system and were most often financed and directed by white people, with small budgets and all-black casts, to be shown in segregated black theaters in the South and in black neighborhoods in the North. The most successful black filmmaker, Oscar Micheaux (1884–1951), had previously worked as a Pullman porter and then a South Dakota homesteader. After he turned his hand to writing novels, he traveled east to sell them himself. When he saw the burgeoning interest in film, he turned his novels into screenplays, raised his own money and directed 44 race films, some of them explicitly anti-racist. In *The Washington Times* years later, Cheryl Wetzstein wrote of his work:

> In contrast to Hollywood's mainstream movies that limited blacks to roles as buffoons or menial workers, Micheaux's all-black casts showed complex men and women with dignity, intelligence, economic solidarity and racial pride. His films didn't shy away from racial issues, including mixed-race romances, even though some theaters banned his daring work. His second film, the 1920 silent *Within Our Gates*, was widely seen as a direct response to the racist arguments put forward in D.W. Griffith's classic *Birth of a Nation*. He once remarked, "I have always tried to lay before the colored race a cross-section of its own life, to view the colored heart from close range."[16]

Within Our Gates has been called "the biggest protest against Race prejudice, lynching, and 'concubinage' that was ever written or filmed."[17] Micheaux was forgotten after his death in 1951; his life and films are being rediscovered today. In the 2021 documentary *Oscar Micheaux: The Superhero of Black Film,* one director calls him "the most important black filmmaker who ever lived" and another says: "He was Spike Lee before there was a Spike Lee."[18]

Race films constituted a world separate from the majority of film, whose imagery conjured an idealized white world devoid of people of color. In race films, on the other hand, black audiences could have their own stars who reflected not only their skin color but the lived experiences of their race creating an alternate universe rarely seen by white audiences. In his book *Reel Black Talk: A Sourcebook of 50 American Filmmakers*, Spencer Moon wrote that Micheaux "knew how to market his talent. He created Black counterparts to the Hollywood legends. He had the Black Valentino—Lorenzo Tucker; the sepia Mae West—Bee Freeman; the Negro Harlow—Ethel Moses; the Colored Cagney—Alfred 'Slick' Chester."[19] Tucker (1907–86), who appeared in Micheaux's *When Men Betray* (1928), *Wages of Sin* (1929) and *Veiled Aristocrats* (1932), was also referred to as the colored William Powell. His agent pressured the light-skinned Tucker to pass as white to further his career, but he refused.

White filmmakers occasionally swam against the racial currents of their time. In all my reading about race and racism in 1930s Hollywood, I have repeatedly seen the 1934 Universal film *Imitation of Life* held up as an exemplar of racial progress and in advance of its time. I knew I had to see it. It was released the same month as *The Thin Man*. I found *Imitation of Life* an ambivalent, ambiguous, provocative, conflicted and ultimately unsettling picture of Hollywood's take on race relations in America. While films do reflect the mores and movement of society at large in the moment of their release, we also know that films change a society at the same time. They leave their mark for good or ill on their viewers. And I found more to think about in this film than in any other I viewed.

Directed by John Stahl and starring Claudette Colbert (1903–96) and Louise Beavers, *Imitation of Life*, based on Fannie Hurst's best-selling novel, tackles social issues of single parenting, sexism and racism within a conventional melodrama. It is simultaneously racist and anti-racist; about as good as white Hollywood got on race. The story follows two single parents of young girls who combine their talents to succeed in business even while they sacrifice romantic relationships and, eventually, estrange the daughters for whom they have sacrificed so much. Clearly a conventional tearjerker. Unconventionally, one parent is white and one is black, and they work together and live under the same roof for over ten years. The relationship is often respectful (anti-racist) but often unequal (racist). Colbert's character, Bea Pullman, is struggling to continue her deceased husband's maple syrup business when she meets Beavers' Delilah Johnson, who makes delicious pancakes from a secret family recipe: a match made in Heaven. They open a storefront pancake house at the Jersey Shore and make a nice living. Then a customer suggests they box and sell the pancake batter. They do and become wealthy.

Complications arise: Delilah, though now rich, decides to continue living with best friend Bea, an odd note of dependency, and things are never quite equal. Bea lives upstairs and Delilah downstairs in their new mansion. Bea calls her friend Delilah but Delilah calls Bea, Miss Bea. Delilah has several scenes in which she massages Bea's tired feet. Bea never massages Delilah's equally tired feet. Bea hosts a big party to celebrate ten years of success of Aunt Delilah's Pancake Flour; we see no black guests, and even Delilah stays out of sight in the basement. Delilah gets no romantic interest but Bea falls in love with Stephen Archer (Warren William), an ichthyologist; much fun is had by white people at Delilah's lack of knowledge of the word and its correct pronunciation.

Bea's daughter Jessie, now 18, also falls for Stephen. Bea decides to postpone her wedding, perhaps forever, to avoid crushing Jessie. Delilah's daughter Peola (played by the beautiful Fredi Washington) rejects her race and her mother and commits herself to passing as white. As often in Hollywood stories, wealth brings problems rather than happiness. Delilah's funeral (from a broken heart at her daughter's estrangement) makes up the film's grand finale. Marching bands from black lodges, a horse-drawn white hearse and an honor guard of raised swords stop traffic on the city streets in Delilah's honor as Peola rushes in sobbing to beg her mother's forgiveness.

Writer Langston Hughes (1902–1967) burlesqued the plot soon after the film's release in his play *Limitations of Life* by reversing the races so that Audette Aubert is a white maid who speaks with a Southern drawl and Mammy Weaver, in evening gown after a night at the opera, speaks "perfect English with an Oxford accent."[20] The beautiful, blonde Audette rubs Mammy's feet while complaining that her daughter Riola wants to be black: "She's lyin' out in the backyard in de sun all day long tannin' herself everyday tryin' hard to be colored."[21]

The film's hokey, easy-to-spoof plot and stereotyped characters (the mammy-like nurturing Delilah and the tragic mulatto Peola) might blind us to what makes the film unique given its studio origins: its willingness to empower black characters to make life choices and to show the complexity of their inner emotional lives. Having made *Imitation of Life,* Hollywood then eschewed any more such moderately integrated racial plots until after World War II, 11 years later. We might (not) be surprised that "the commissars at the Production Code deemed the film, with its overt intimations of race mixing, fraught with grave danger to the industry."[22]

Another "danger" to the industry: Josephine Baker (1906–75), born Freda Josephine McDonald. Her path intersected film, race and, in a way, Dashiell Hammett. Born to a poor family in Missouri, Baker went to work for a white family at the age of seven. At 11, she fled from a race riot in East St. Louis where "mobs of armed whites invaded black districts.... Fleeing blacks were not only savagely beaten but were in many cases shot or lynched. Baker ran for her life and said, 'I have been running ever since.'"[23] She married and divorced at 13, danced in vaudeville at 14 and went on the road. At 15, she left her husband Willie Baker but kept his name. A Paris revue hired her out of New York's Plantation Club and she conquered Paris in her "danse sauvage," a white dream of an erotic and comic African dance. Shimmying with little more than a belt of bananas at her waist, Baker toured Berlin and Moscow in 1926. She subverted the reductive sexy image of animalistic abandon with a knowing look and a self-mocking goofiness. In 1927, she became the first black woman to star in a major motion picture, the silent *Siren of the Tropics*. In 1935, she starred in *Princess Tam Tam*, a sort of updated Pygmalion story shot on location in Tunisia; in it, Baker, as the poor Alwina, begs and steals to survive. A French writer discovers her, teaches her manners, arranges math, art, dance and piano lessons and takes her back to France to charm the locals as a purported princess. The screwball comedy ends with Alwina ensconced in a Tunisian villa with a male actor whose skin has been darkened to make him an appropriate match for her.

That same year, she returned to New York to appear in the Ziegfeld Follies, the first and last black woman to perform there, in a show with the likes of Fanny Brice, Bob Hope, Eve Arden and Edgar Bergen. According to a recent documentary, because she was black, she had to use the apartment building service entrance to access her luxury suite. The next year, she fled again to Paris. In Chapter 11, we shall see Baker and Hammett in New York.[24]

As I said, Myrna Loy induced me into meditations on race in Hollywood in the 1930s. *The Thin Man* whitewashed the city of New York. Loy wore blackface in *Ham and Eggs at the Front* and a lighter brownface in *The Squall* and *Thirteen Women*. She went all-out yellowface in *The Mask of Fu Manchu*. I know Sax Rohmer's Fu Manchu novels

7. The Thin Man *and Race* 117

Singer-dancer-actress Josephine Baker fled racism in the United States for stardom in France. During World War II, she served in the French Resistance and in 2021 her body was interred in the Pantheon in Paris with full military honors. This publicity photograph dates from 1927 when she appeared in the *Folies Bergère*.

well as I devoured them as a boy just entering puberty. I reveled in the the scenes set in opium dens and the Chinese villains scheming to rule the world. But my 12-year-old enthusiasms turned to adult disgust.

Rohmer began writing serialized stories for pulp magazines. Like Hammett, he grew popular and rich on his stories. While Hammett created hard-boiled detectives, Rohmer, who never set foot in China, mined the contemporary public discourse of a Yellow Peril epitomized by his own creation, the villain Fu Manchu, whose plots are foiled by the brave and intelligent English officer Denis Nayland Smith over some 13 Fu Manchu novels. Rohmer became "one of the most highly paid and widely read authors in the English language."[25] His novels reached more readers and did more for anti–Asian racism than all the learned works of Social Darwinists like Herbert Spencer and Thomas Malthus, who believed that Darwin's evolutionary theory applied to politics; that the survival of the fittest supported eugenics and racism and whose adherents often supported imperialism and fascism. Hollywood came calling.

The Yellow Peril was one of those fever dreams of the white imagination. All of the usual tropes applied to black people (sexual depravity, hatred of whites, primitive ape-like men and women, exotics and unknown "others" who posed a racial threat to white Christian civilization) were repurposed against Asians. Such ideas could be found in popular books of the day like *The Rising Tide of Color Against White World-Supremacy* (1920) by Lothrop Stoddard, which warned against miscegenation and trumpeted: "Colored migration is a universal peril, menacing every part of the white world."[26] Occidental imperialists in Russia, Germany, England and the U.S. used the fear of the Yellow Peril to justify their own projects to invade, subjugate and colonize China. They passed laws to limit Asian immigration to the West. The movies picked up the prejudices of their time, amplified them on film and sent them back out into the world.

When the U.S. conducted its decennial census in 1840, it found just four Chinese people within a population of 17,000,000. The first female Chinese immigrant to the U.S. may have been Afong Moy in 1834. Two American traders seem to have purchased her in China when she was 14 and brought her to the U.S. to help sell their wares. Her bound feet, use of chopsticks and her Asian clothing titillated the public. As a Chinese woman, she was an object both exotic and erotic. She wound up in P.T. Barnum's Museum.[27] The journey from Afong Moy to Hammett's Hsiu Hsiu to Myrna Loy's Fah Lo See was not a long one in time or temperament.

The California gold strike of 1848 brought an influx of treasure seekers from around the globe, including China. The U.S. War Department began studying an east-west railroad to tie California to the Union in 1853 and actual work on what became the Transcontinental Railroad began in 1863. The Union Pacific hired thousands of Irish immigrants to build the line heading west, and the Central Pacific hired thousands of Chinese immigrants to build the tracks heading east, the most dangerous line as digging through the mountains required dynamite and caused avalanches. Some 1200 Chinese workers died in the effort, which was completed in 1869.

By 1880, the Chinese population in the U.S. numbered 105,000.[28] As the number of Chinese immigrants grew, so did nativist sentiment against them; labeling them dirty, uneducated, "coolies," rapists and criminals. Writing in the *New York Daily Tribune*, Horace Greeley, an abolitionist of all things, offered his editorial opinion of the Chinese in 1854: "They are uncivilized, unclean, and filthy beyond all conception, without any of the higher domestic or social relations; lustful and sensual in their dispositions; every female is a prostitute of the basest order; the first words of English that they learn are terms of obscenity or profanity, and beyond this they care to learn no more."[29]

Anti-Chinese violence flared in the late 19th century with Chinese communities burned and looted in the Western U.S.; in white riots in Los Angeles in 1871, in San Francisco in 1877, Wyoming in 1885 and Oregon in 1887. In 1885, Tacoma, Washington, expelled all Chinese. Two hundred other cities followed suit.[30]

In 1882, Congress passed the Chinese Exclusion Act, which not only closed immigration to Chinese but also barred Chinese already here from naturalization: They could never become citizens, own property, testify in court cases involving whites or vote. U.S. Senator James Phelan (1861–1930) ran for reelection in 1920 under the slogan "Keep California White."[31] In 2022, a pair of Levi's jeans from the 1880s, discovered in an abandoned mine, sold at auction for $76,000. They had a distinctive label inside, advertising "Levi Strauss & Co.," and affirming it as "the only kind made by White Labor."[32]

Against the background of this racist history,[33] Dashiell Hammett wrote the short story "Dead Yellow Women." Originally published in *Black Mask* in November 1925, it features his serial protagonist, the Continental Op, agent for the Continental detective Agency. The Op investigates the abduction of a wealthy Chinese woman, Lillian, and the murder of her father and two of her Chinese house servants. The title alone reeks of racism and the story only supports it. Involved in this nefarious business is Chang Li Ching, who sits in San Francisco's Chinatown like a local Fu Manchu. Ching, we are told, has a "round, shrewd yellow mask of a face."[34] Naturally his underlings speak only pidgin English as in this exchange:

Servant: "What wan?"
The Op: "I want to see Chang Li Ching."
Servant: "No savvy. Maybe closs stleet [sic].... No savvy Chang."[35]

The Chinese also smell funny; as the Op says, "An odor came to me—an unmistakable odor—the smell of unwashed Chinese."[36]

But in describing a slave girl found by the Op, Hammett channels the erotic exoticism of Afong Moy: "She wasn't four and a half feet high—a living ornament.... Her face was a tiny oval of painted beauty, its perfection emphasized by tiger lacquer black hair.... Gold earrings swung beside her smooth cheeks, a jade butterfly was in her hair.... Lavender stockings showed under her short lavender trousers, and her bound-small feet were in slippers of the same color ... she was impossibly dainty."[37] The story concludes with the Op avowing: "I've stopped eating in Chinese restaurants ... if I never have to visit Chinatown again it'll be soon enough."[38] Sax Rohmer had reached for the same tropes when his *Mask of Fu Manchu* narrator described Fah Lo Suee: "[T]he woman who wore a green, sheath-like dress and gold shoes, had a delicate indolence of carriage, wholly Oriental. About one bare ivory arm ... she wore a massive jade bangle in six or seven loops. A golden girdle not unlike a sword belt was about her waist, and a tight green turban on her head."[39]

Hollywood resorted to yellowface to film *The Mask of Fu Manchu*, just as they would again and again: with Paul Muni and Luise Rainer in *The Good Earth*, with Katharine Hepburn, absurdly, in *Dragon Seed*, and most grotesquely, Mickey Rooney in *Breakfast at Tiffany's*. The list also includes Lon Chaney (*Shadows*), Edward G. Robinson (*The Hatchet Man*), Peter Lorre (his Mr. Moto movies), Anthony Quinn (*China Sky*), Shirley MacLaine (*Gambit*), Rita Moreno and Rex Harrison (*Anna and the King of*

Siam), John Wayne (*The Conqueror*), Marlon Brando (*The Teahouse of the August Moon*), Lupe Velez (*East Is West*), Alec Guinness (*A Majority of One*), Tony Randall (*7 Faces of Dr. Lao*), John Gielgud (*Lost Horizon*), Max von Sydow (*Flash Gordon*), Linda Hunt (*The Year of Living Dangerously*), Eddie Murphy (*Norbit*), David Carradine (*Kung Fu*), Joel Grey (*Remo Williams: The Adventure Begins*), Peter Sellers (*The Fiendish Plot of Dr. Fu Manchu*), Yul Brynner (*The King and I*) and many others. For *The Mask of Fu Manchu*, it took some two hours to have various prosthetics applied to make Boris Karloff appear Chinese. And when, as Fu Manchu, he utters the lines "Rise up, men of Asia! Kill the white man and steal his women!"[40] we have the Yellow Peril personified.

Yes, Karloff was only an actor playing a role. And actors are not their characters. The actor who plays a serial killer on TV is not a serial killer in real life. We reward actors for their versatility as they take on a wide range of roles; and for a white actor to play an Asian character is still just acting. But the reality is that the Asian roles have historically been no more than stereotypes in which white people's basest xenophobic and racist fears have created characters that debase their race. Anna May Wong (1905–61), born Wong Liu Tsong, the first Chinese-American movie star, explained why she left Hollywood: "I was tired of the parts I had to play. Why is it that on the screen the Chinese are nearly always the villain of the piece, and so cruel a villain—murderous, treacherous, a snake in the grass. We are not like that."[41]

Rohmer's Fu Manchu novels traded in the ugliest stereotypes. When they were banned in Germany in 1936, perhaps because the Nazis mistakenly thought him Jewish, he protested that he could not understand this censorship: "My stories are not inimical to Nazi ideals."[42] How right he was. Ironically, Rohmer died on a visit to New York from the Asian flu, as it was then called.

Soon there were new Asians to vilify as the Japanese rose to power in Asia, defeating the Russians in war in 1905; the first modern example of an Asian nation defeating a European power, and then invading Manchuria in 1931. Here was a new Yellow Peril. The U.S. amended the Chinese Exclusion Act in 1924 to add the Japanese to its list of unwanted Asian immigrants, and Hollywood turned its antipathy from China to the Imperial Japanese aggressors. The Yellow Peril that Sax Rohmer wrote about, that Hollywood filmed in *Broken Blossoms* (1919), *Chinatown After Dark* (1931), *Thirteen Women* (1932), *Red Dust* (1932), *The Painted Veil* (1934) and *San Francisco* (1936), led to a racial hysteria following Pearl Harbor. Within months of the Japanese attack, the U.S. government forced 120,000 Japanese and Japanese-Americans from their homes and imprisoned them for years without warrants, charges, trials or appeals. This mass incarceration included Hollywood actors of Japanese descent.

Throughout these pages, I have written about a film's cast members beyond the well-known leads. Their biographies and filmographies often illuminate both U.S. and film history. In looking at the cast of *Libeled Lady* (1936), I found low on the list of actors one Otto Yamaoka (1904–67). In the film he plays Spencer Tracy's servant, Ching, and as he helps Tracy get dressed in formal wear he shares a few lines of dialogue with the star. Otto was born in Seattle of Japanese immigrant parents. The family moved to Los Angeles in the 1920s, after the death of their father, and Otto developed an interest in acting and tried to break into the movie business even as he worked at a Hollywood costume shop. He had small parts in some 31 movies from 1930 to 1940, including another film with Powell, *The Benson Murder Case* (1930). In that and other films, he went uncredited. He usually portrayed servants and, though Japanese, usually played Chinese men on film with names like Chung, Chung Ho, Fugi, Kito, Kono, and Togo. One exception was his credited role as Kimo, an Inuit, in *Petticoat Fever* with Myrna Loy. His other larger role came in *The Black Camel* (1931), as Kashimo. This detective movie starred the Swedish-American Warner Oland (1879–1938) in Yellowface in one of his 16 turns as Charlie Chan. Oland also portrayed Fu Manchu in three films.

Otto Yamaoka had five siblings, including a sister, Iris, six years his junior, and she also showed an interest in acting and broke into the movie business in 1929 in *China Slaver*. She earned spots in seven films including *Eskimo* in 1933 and *Waikiki Wedding* in 1937. She and Otto both appeared in *Petticoat Fever*. There were few Asian actors in Hollywood in the 1920s and '30s; one book counted five Japanese female actors besides Iris and three Japanese male actors besides Otto.[43] Japan was out of favor and film producers asked Japanese actors like the Yamaokas to play Chinese, Polynesian and Inuit characters. In *Eskimo*, according to Ray Mala biographer Lael Morgan, Iris "played one of Mala's more amusing if slightly dim wives. Unfortunately the girl fainted the first time the cast killed a walrus and despite [author] Freuchen's ridicule, made no secret of her squeamishness. She was, however, being courted by cameramen Clyde De Vinna and Josiah 'Bob' Roberts, assuring her some excellent footage."[44]

Presumably the Yamaokas would have continued seeking roles in film while working in their costume shop. Neither had ever been to Japan and both were American citizens by birth. Perhaps they were happy with their acting roles, the stars they got to know, seeing themselves on the screen. At some point, Otto married. Iris never did. Undoubtedly they both made plans for their future. Then the police rounded them up and took them far from Hollywood, never to return.

Racism made it possible: the Chinese Exclusion Law, the Sax Rohmer novels, Hollywood's movies like *The Mask of Fu Manchu* and 60 years of stoking fears of a Yellow Peril made it possible. From the trafficking and exhibition of Afong Moy to 1905 headlines from *The San Francisco Chronicle*—"Crime and Poverty Go Hand in Hand with Asiatic Labor," "Brown Men are Evil in the Public Schools," "Japanese a Menace to American Women," and "Brown Asiatics Steal Brains of Whites," among others[45]—to *The Los Angeles Times* on December 8, 1941, the day after Japan's attack on Pearl Harbor, writing, "We have thousands of Japanese here…. Some, perhaps many … are good Americans. What the rest may be we do not know, nor can we take a chance in the light of yesterday's demonstration that treachery and double dealing are major Japanese weapons."[46]

Lieutenant General John L. Dewitt, head of the Western Defense Command, told newspapers: "A Jap's a Jap." He expanded on that sentiment before Congress: "I don't want any [people of Japanese ancestry] here. They're a dangerous element…. There is no way to determine their loyalty. It makes no difference whether he is an American citizen, he is still Japanese … we must worry about the Japanese all the time until he is wiped off the map."[47] In Los Angeles, home to a third of the Japanese and Japanese-Americans in the country, the County Board of Supervisors fired all Japanese-American employees. L.A. Mayor Fletcher Bowron put all city employees of Japanese descent on an indefinite leave of absence.[48] Japanese and Japanese-Americans faced a statewide 8 p.m. curfew when they had to be off the streets. Their savings and checking accounts were frozen.[49]

And then the Army rounded them up. While our government arrested German American Bund members and homegrown Italian Fascists, they dealt with these individuals on a case-by-case basis and did not imprison other descendants of Axis Powers nations solely on the basis of national origin. About 3,000 Italians and nearly 11,000

Germans were detained.[50] Most of them, unlike the Japanese, had individual, though legally flawed, hearings. Their numbers represented a tiny percentage of the more than 1.2 million people of German birth living in the United States in 1940 and some three million Italian immigrants.[51] U.S. Congressman John E. Rankin (1882–1960), Democrat of Mississippi and a proud segregationist, said: "This is a race war.... The White man's civilization has come into conflict with Japanese Barbarism.... One of them must be destroyed."[52] Rankin, anti–Japanese, anti-black, anti–Semitic, later helped establish the House UnAmerican Activities Committee which so bedeviled Hollywood, unions and universities after World War II and negatively impacted the careers of Dashiell Hammett, Lillian Hellman, Myrna Loy and many others.

To protect the California, Oregon and Washington coasts from Japanese invasion, the government declared a Japanese exclusion zone from the Pacific Ocean 100 miles east. 120,000 Japanese-Americans were forced from their homes and incarcerated without charges, trials or convictions when President Roosevelt issued Executive Order 9066. Seventy percent of them were American citizens. It didn't matter that these men and women of Japanese ancestry had undertaken no act of disloyalty. For General DeWitt, their inaction proved their evil intent. He said: "The very fact that no sabotage has taken place to date is a disturbing and confirming indication that such action will be taken."[53] But no such disloyal acts ever occurred. Most of these people were fiercely patriotic. In fact: "not a single American of Japanese descent, alien or citizen, [was] charged with espionage or sabotage during the war."[54]

But they were all locked up. For an instant, Otto and Iris Yamaoka might have hoped their innocence of any crime, having had their faces on film screens from coast to coast, or their highly placed and well-known friends, like Myrna Loy, Spencer Tracy and Louis B. Mayer, might save them. They didn't. As one Japanese, Paul Tanito, said: "Nobody stood up for us. People just looked away."[55]

In March 1942, the government ordered Iris and Otto Yamaoka and their mother, Jha, and Otto's wife Mizuye "Mia" Ichioka and their son Tod, to report to the so-called Assembly Center at the Santa Anita Race Track, one of 15 temporary prisons in converted fairgrounds, racetracks and livestock auction grounds.[56] Mia had also struggled to build a Hollywood career with parts in *Streets of Shanghai* (1927), *Love Before Breakfast* (1936, as Carole Lombard's maid) and in *West of Shanghai* (1937), with Boris Karloff wearing yellowface yet again.[57]

Santa Anita, just 20 miles from Hollywood Boulevard, opened in 1934 and had regularly attracted stars like Oliver Hardy, Will Rogers, Cary Grant and Jane Russell. That all changed in March 1942 when it became home to 19,000 prisoners. *The Los Angeles Examiner* gave the track its new name: "Japanita."[58] Evacuees had been given 24 to 48 hours to pack, sell their possessions, homes, businesses or farms for a fraction of their worth or simply abandon them. According to Bradford Pearson's excellent book *The Eagles of Heart Mountain*, "Issei veterans of World War I wore their US Navy uniforms and decorations on the day of removal."[59] Like thousands of others, Otto and Iris were assigned to a former horse stall, still reeking of eight years' worth of manure and urine, handed a sheet and told to stuff it with straw for their bed. The prisoners had only 150 showers but "the showers were intended for horses—communal, partitionless."[60] So they remained for the next months while the Army built ten more durable camps east of the Sierras and west of the Mississippi in California, Arizona, Idaho, Wyoming, Colorado, Utah and Arkansas. By October, prisoners were shipped east.

In her book *Desert Exile*, Yoshiko Uchida provided a first-person account of what her family encountered when bussed to the temporary Assembly Center at the Tanforan Racetrack where she, her sister and mother were assigned to Barrack 16:

> Barrack 16 was not a barrack at all but a long stable raised off the ground with a broad ramp the horses had used to reach their stalls. Each stall was now numbered and ours was number 40. That the stalls should have been called "apartments" was a euphemism so ludicrous it was comical. When we reached stall number 40, we pushed open the narrow door and looked uneasily into the vacant darkness. The stalls were about ten by twenty feet and empty except for three folded army cots lying on the floor. Dust, dirt and wood shavings covered the linoleum that had been laid over manure-covered boards. The smell of horses hung in the air, and the whitened corpses of many insects still clung to the hastily white-washed walls. …a single electric light bulb dangled from the ceiling and a one-inch crevice at the top of the north wall admitted a steady draft of the cold night air. We sat huddled on our cots, bundled in our coats, too cold and miserable even to talk.[61]

This would be the family's home for the next five months until they were shipped off to Camp Topaz in the Utah desert.

Also at Santa Anita was five-year-old future actor George Takei, who described his family's experience: "Suddenly we saw two soldiers marching up our driveway. They carried rifles with bayonets on them. My father answered the door and they pointed their bayonets at him…. [At Santa Anita] each family was assigned a horse stall to sleep in temporarily while barbed wire camps were being built in some of the most desolate, godforsaken places in the United States."[62] The government sent Takei and his family on a sealed train, shades drawn, to Camp Rohwer in Arkansas, the easternmost camp. They sent Iris and Otto Yamaoka to Heart Mountain, Wyoming, 1122 miles from their former life, friends and home in Los Angeles. Pearson describes the transit east:

> Sometimes the route took three days, sometimes a week. Some trains sped through the desert in pitch darkness, curtains drawn tight, while others leaked light, allowing children to peak through, hoping to spot a cowboy. There were no beds, no pillows … a train with few bathrooms. Pregnant women sat on the unforgiving wooden seats, praying that their child wouldn't arrive before their final destination, wherever that was.[63]

Wrote Buddhist priest Nyogen Senzaki, in his poem "Leaving Santa Anita," "This morning, the winding train, like a big black snake, takes us as far as Wyoming."[64]

The geological anomaly called Heart Mountain towers 8000 feet over a prairie wasteland. This formerly empty space, down the road from Cody, had a population of 10,000 prisoners, mostly relocated from the Los Angeles area, making it for several years the third largest population center in Wyoming. Prisoner Frank Emi described conditions awaiting them: "It was in the middle of a dusty prairie. You could hardly see 10 or 25 feet ahead of you … [T]he winter was the coldest in Wyoming history, it was 30 below zero. If you went to the restroom, which was located outside and wet your hands or took a shower your head would be in icicles and if your hand was still wet it froze to the metal doorknobs…. We didn't even have topcoats when we arrived. We were California boys."[65]

The Army had little experience building family housing units but lots of experience building barracks so they built ten camps filled with row after row of military barracks. At Heart Mountain, they built 450 barracks, each containing six apartments. They assigned several families, who may or may not have known each other previously, to an apartment which contained a stove for heat and a single bulb for light, but no kitchen or bathroom. Everyone ate at the multiple camp mess halls and visited latrines and showers with no stalls or other form of privacy. The barracks had tarpaper exteriors and no insulation; summer days topped 100 degrees and winter nights fell below -30 degrees. A high barbed wire fence and soldiers armed with machine guns in nine high watchtowers guarded the camp.[66] Also imprisoned at Heart Mountain was ten-year-old Norman Yoshio Mineta, and his family from San Jose, California. As an adult, Mineta served ten terms as a California Congressman and in the cabinets of Presidents Bill Clinton and George W. Bush. Looking back at his internment, he wrote, "My family was told by the military authorities that internment was for our own protection, but the machine guns and searchlights in the guard towers ... faced inward ... [W]e were incarcerated solely because of our ethnic background."[67] At the camp, Mineta, a Boy Scout, befriended a local Boy Scout, Alan K. Simpson, who visited the camp with his Troop. Simpson grew up to serve as a Republican Senator from Wyoming. Based on that shared experience, Mineta and Simpson co-sponsored the Civil Liberties Act of 1988, which paid reparations to internment survivors 40 years after their imprisonment.

I have quoted other prisoners because the written record on Otto, Iris, Jha, Mia and Tod in the camp is slim to non-existent: no letters, no memoir. The inmate newspaper *The Heart Mountain Sentinel* reported that in November 1942, Otto stood for election to represent Block 29 in the committee that would write the camp charter. (He didn't win.) Did anyone from home care about Otto and Iris and their mother? Did anyone from Hollywood send even a care package, let alone visit? Did Otto and Iris sit in the dark of

This photograph of Heart Mountain was taken by Yoshio Okumoto, circa 1943–45. It is a gift of Grace Kawakami and is owned by the Yoshio Okumoto Collection of the Heart Mountain Wyoming Foundation and used with permission. Actors Otto and Iris Yamaoka were imprisoned here.

a barracks on movie night and see themselves on screen as they sat among hundreds of their fellow prisoners?

In 1943, the government allowed Heart Mountain prisoners to leave as long as they did not return to the West Coast. California Governor Earl Warren, he of the earlier anti-EPIC campaign, wanted no prisoners returned to his state, calling them "all potential saboteurs."[68] At the same time, Wyoming passed laws that prevented the Japanese-Americans who had been interned at Heart Mountain from remaining in the state.[69] Those ready to try to begin a new life in the east received $25 and a one-way train ticket. Iris and Otto Yamaoka and their family headed for New York, the city where their older brother George (1903–1981) lived. George had a law degree from Georgetown University. Ironically, General Douglas A. MacArthur, the Supreme Allied Commander in the Far East, appointed George counsel general to Japanese military officers and civilian leaders accused of war crimes, several of whom were tried and executed for their part in the war.[70]

In New York, Iris became a bookkeeper for the Methodist Committee for Overseas Relief where she worked for the last 17 years of her life. She died in 1960 at age 49.[71] Otto rented offices on Wall Street and imported Japanese films for the American market.[72] He died in 1967 at age 63. I thought: why didn't they return to Hollywood when the war was over? Why didn't they try to restart their acting careers?

Possible answers come from other survivors. In the documentary *Betrayal: Surviving an American Concentration Camp,* one survivor said, "[The Army] took us there where we didn't want to go. And then they let us go when we had nowhere to go."[73] Many were afraid of returning to the West Coast where nativist sentiment ran strong and residents made it clear they wanted no Japanese in their communities. In her memoir of her childhood imprisoned with her family at the Manzanar camp, Jean Wakatsuki Houston wrote, "[T]he very thought of going back to the west coast filled us with dread.... It was the humiliation. That continuous, unnamed ache I had been living with.... I knew ... that if someone looked at me with hate, I would have to ... swallow it, because something in me, something about me deserved it."[74]

Wakatsuki's older siblings headed for the East Coast upon release, just as the Yamaokas did. She wrote: "It was 3,000 miles away, with no history of anti-orientalism, in fact no Oriental history at all. So few people of Asian ancestry settled there, it was like heading for a neutral country."[75]

Perhaps the Yamaokas felt ashamed; ashamed of how their friends had abandoned them, ashamed of what had been done to them, as if they deserved it. And Iris' death at just 49? Otto's at 63? I think their imprisonment played a part here also. Said another survivor in words that resonated with me: "Many [survivors] died early from suppressed rage."[76]

In 1980, the U.S. Congress, after years of agitation from camp survivors and civil libertarians, set up a commission to investigate the legacy of the Japanese internment camps, interviewing and taking testimonies from its victims. In its final report, the commission called the lockup a "grave injustice" motivated by "racial prejudice, war hysteria and the failure of political leadership."[77]

The Civil Liberties Act of 1988, co-sponsored by Congressman and former prisoner Norman Mineta and Wyoming Senator Alan Simpson, and signed by President Reagan, officially apologized for the internment on behalf of the U.S. government and authorized a payment of $20,000, equivalent to $48,000 in 2022, to each former internee still alive when the act was passed. By then, Otto and Iris, their mother Jho, who had all been imprisoned together at Heart Mountain, had died, along with thousands of other internees.

Lobby card for the 1942 film *Little Tokyo U.S.A.* Complete with white actors in yellowface, it imagines Japanese Americans plotting sabotage in the days after the Pearl Harbor attack, though no such acts of disloyalty ever occurred. The film closes with images of Japanese and Japanese Americans being forced out of their homes to be shipped to internment camps. Shown here, from left, are George E. Stone, Harold Huber, Abner Biberman.

Hollywood did do something about the internment. They made a movie. 20th Century–Fox's *Little Tokyo, U.S.A.* (1942) is a hysterical racist detective film. After a prologue warning of a vast Japanese espionage apparatus within the U.S., the film, set in 1941 just prior to the Pearl Harbor attack, follows a police detective (Preston Foster) investigating a Japanese-German spy ring in Los Angeles' Little Tokyo. These Japanese spies, played by various white actors wearing yellowface (Harold Huber, June Duprez, Abner Biberman), succeed in getting the detective jailed for murder. The detective gets out of jail, tricks the ringleader into confessing as police listen, and busts the spy ring.

The worst is saved for last: We see real-life documentary footage of the government rounding up Japanese for transport first to the assembly centers and then to the internment camps. Families stand forlornly on street corners. Soon the streets are deserted. The internment, the movie assures us, was a necessity. The final words emblazoned on the screen warn of future disloyalty: "Be vigilant, America."[78]

It was 13 years before Hollywood made a film sympathetic to Japanese-Americans, *Bad Day at Black Rock* (1955). It was followed by, among others, *Farewell to Manzanar* (1976), *Come See the Paradise* (1990) and *Snow Falling on Cedars* (1999).

8

After the Thin Man and *Another Thin Man*

The surprising success of *The Thin Man* impelled MGM to reunite all involved in a 1936 sequel, a bigger and better movie meant to make a bigger and better profit. Mayer gave the team a bigger budget and a longer schedule. This allowed them to quit Culver City stages for on-location shooting in San Francisco. It meant bringing back the whole team: Powell, Loy and Asta on the set and director Van Dyke behind the cameras; Hunt Stromberg as producer and Goodrich and Hackett working from a new original treatment by Dashiell Hammett.

They couldn't change the title even though the Thin Man of the original, Clyde Wynant, had died in the first movie. But who did the public think was the Thin Man anyway? Was it Hammett, lean and dashing on the cover of the novel, or William Powell, martini in hand, on film?

As *The Thin Man* ticket sales rolled in, MGM signed Hammett to write a screenplay for $2000 per week, not to exceed ten weeks.[1] Working out of the comfort of the Beverly Wilshire Hotel, Hammett produced a story of 112 pages. He wrote most days, and drank and partied each night. Having completed this treatment, he signed an additional contract as editorial consultant to the movie at $1750 per week. But the drinking caught up to him once again and he fell ill, had to be hospitalized, and was a no-show at story conferences with Hackett and Goodrich.[2] It needs to be said, however, that Hammett's foundational stories for *After the Thin Man* and *Another Thin Man* give the lie to the common wisdom that he wrote nothing of value after his fifth and final novel.

Director Van Dyke was nervous about a sequel: "The word 'sequel' is a bugaboo that frightened most directors, and I am no exception, for if the sequel fails to approach the parent film in public favor or financial returns, it is the director who is left holding the bag."[3] He need not have worried. Louis Mayer had his hands full with Myrna Loy and the reason was, as always, not the euphemistic "creative differences" but cold, hard cash. Loy, knowing a good thing when she saw it and an unfair situation when she felt it, agitated to renegotiate her contract for more than $1500 a week, just half of what MGM paid Powell. Mayer finally gave in.

The use of time in *The Thin Man* and its sequel is striking and amusing: *The Thin Man* is set in New York over the Christmas holiday. The sequel begins just a few days later: It is New Year's Eve in San Francisco, the Charleses' hometown. *The Thin Man* ended with Nick and Nora beginning a train trip west and *After the Thin Man* begins with the train's arrival in San Francisco. It's as if we, the audience, never left Nick and

Nora at all, though the first movie premiered two years earlier. And Nick and Nora certainly haven't changed. The movie opens in their sleeping car:

> **NORA:** "How they can expect a woman to still have any mystery left for a man … after living in a place like this for three days, I don't know."
> **NICK:** "You don't need mystery. You've got something better and more alluring."
> **NORA:** "What?"
> **NICK:** "Me."[4]

This exchange was not in Hammett's treatment; it came direct from Goodrich and Hackett. Though the couple did base much of their script on Hammett's original story, perhaps 90 percent, with the same plot and the same characters, they once again added much of the witty dialogue between Nick and Nora. The first 20 minutes may be the film's best. The Charleses' sleeping car is filled with drinking paraphernalia. Nick is trying to shave when Nora bursts in, inadvertently throwing him against a wall with the razor at his throat. He says "Hello, darling." Nora finds Asta in her hat box. Nick is already imbibing:

> **NORA:** "I thought you were going to pack."
> **NICK:** "I *am*. I've been putting away this liquor."

He wraps his cocktail shaker in one of her dresses and puts it back in her luggage.[5]

A lobby card from *After the Thin Man* (1936), the first Thin Man sequel, is all bright colors and smiling actors although the film contains three murders. But audiences turned out not for the violence or even the mystery but for the smart repartee guaranteed by the casting of Myrna Loy and William Powell.

Joseph Breen of the Production Code Administration raised issues: "It will be necessary to limit all unnecessary drinking to an absolute minimum."[6] But the Charleses still drink plenty on-screen, and Nick often seems tipsy. Their alcohol consumption does decline in later films, but not here. Breen was also uncomfortable with Nick's handling of Nora's underwear in the train scene and so it seems dresses were substituted.

Reporters meet the train, asking Nick about the Wynant case and if he is back in the detecting business. "No," says Nick, "I've retired. Just going to take care of my wife's money so I'll have something in my old age"—a repeat of one of the best jokes from the novel and first movie.[7]

Nick and Nora struggle through the scrum. Nora announces she has lost her purse and Nick identifies his old pal and pickpocket "Fingers" in the crowd. He introduces him to Nora and without a nod of reprimand or exposure, Nora gets her purse back. She tells Nick, "You do know the nicest people."[8]

The movie plays with the discrepancy between high (Nora) and low (Nick) society. In the movie, in a scene not in Hammett's story, their car drives through San Francisco and Nora says hello to a well-dressed couple in another car. Nick asks, "Who is that?" and Nora replies: "You wouldn't know them, darling, they're respectable."[9]

Van Dyke liked filming exteriors in San Francisco but complained of the fog ruining his shots and how the filming drew crowds of distracting spectators. Loy remembered: "We shot all over town."[10] But Van Dyke played fast and loose with Frisco landmarks. When Nick and Nora drive from the train station to their home, we see the exterior of Coit Tower, not a private residence at all. Two hundred ten feet tall, the Art Deco tower on Telegraph Hill was built in 1933, with funds from the will of Lillie Hitchcock Coit (1843–1929), to beautify San Francisco. It's a popular tourist destination to this day and has appeared in over 20 films, including Hitchcock's *Vertigo*.[11] It makes an impressive front door for Nick and Nora.

Powell's fiancée, Jean Harlow, tagged along for the filming. But when the stars checked in at the St. Francis Hotel, the management, believing like most of America that Powell and Loy were a couple, had booked them into a bridal suite while relegating Harlow to a single room downstairs. Powell wound up in the downstairs single; Loy and Harlow shared the suite and stayed up talking all night.[12]

When Nick and Nora arrive at their "home," they find a New Year's Eve Party in full swing though none of the many guests recognize their supposed "hosts." Nick and Nora start dancing. Asta runs around back to reunite with "Mrs. Asta," only to discover that she has had a litter of pups in his absence. They all look like Asta until one black pup wanders out of the doghouse. Asta spots a black Scotty squeezing under a fence into the yard. The scene aims for the funny bone as Asta is cuckolded but one has to wonder about its possible comments upon human race relations and miscegenation. Van Dyke had to fight with Breen to keep the scene in the movie since it touched upon sex and race—though of the canine persuasion.

And where are the Black people? Latinos? Asians? This is, after all, the urban metropolis of San Francisco. Yet we see but three black actors in the movie: two train porters and one street urchin among a group gathered around Nick's car.

As the Charleses join the festivities at their mansion, they receive an urgent phone call from Nora's cousin Selma (Elissa Landi): Her husband Robert Landis has disappeared. Nick and Nora rush to a dinner party at Nora's upper crust Aunt Katherine's home. The mystery part of the film, a bit less interesting than the whirlwind opening, begins.

Nora's family has never approved of her marriage to Nick. Aunt Katherine tries to prepare her guests for Nick's arrival by reminding them to be sympathetic to "poor Nora," who married a wastrel. Meanwhile, Nora is also preparing Nick for what he will encounter, telling him: "You'd better pull yourself together."

"Don't worry," replies Nick. "One squint at Aunt Katherine would sober anyone."

As the Charleses step into Aunt Katherine's home, the elderly butler, bent over with rheumatism, says to Nick: "Will you walk this way, sir?" Nick replies: "I'll try" and follows him while imitating his walk. The butler remains the butt of continued sight gags in the movie: collapsing under the weight when a coat is thrown over his arm or lurching precipitously when someone so much as touches him. In the drawing room, various guest refer to Nora as "poor Nora." Nick asks her why and she replies: "That's because I'm married to you."[13]

The play of high and low class continues. Hoity-toity Aunt Katherine, played by Jessie Ralph, refers to Nick throughout as Nick-o-las, drawn out like today's commercial for Ri-co-la. At the boring dinner, as the elderly guests doze off, Nick has an imaginary conversation with his sleeping dinner companions. This class inversion proved popular during the Depression, showing you didn't need wealth to be happy and that one could, like Nick, rise and fall between social classes. Nick's lowlife friends find a lot more fun in life than Nora's somnolent relatives.

The plot thickens as Cousin Selma informs Nora that her husband Robert has disappeared and then admits she doesn't love him because he has been cheating on her. Our Inciting Incident, occurring before the movie begins, is the three-day disappearance of Robert. The Point of Attack, which gets things rolling, occurs when Selma begs Nick for help and Nora pushes him to accept.

David, a friend of the family and obviously in love with Selma, arrives to comfort her. The quest to find Robert seems rather specious since Selma has announced she no longer loves him, and Nora has counseled her cousin to divorce him. Our plot might have sputtered to an end right there if Selma had taken this good advice.

Nick and Nora go to the Lichee Club, a Chinese-themed night club, and encounter Robert there with his newest flame, Polly. Also at Li-Chee is Polly's brother Phil and gangster Dancer (Joseph Calleia), co-owner of the club. Seated at a table, Nick orders two Scotch highballs "quick." As the waiter starts to leave, he adds: "No. Better make it three. One for the wife." At the club is Dancer's partner, Lum Kee, the brother of a man Nick sent up the river. Lum Kee speaks pidgin English, quite like the "comic" Asian character in *Red Dust*.

> **KIM LEE:** "You bet you. You catch my brother. You play trick on him."
> **NICK:** "No play trick on him, no catch him. You bet you. Is he still in?"
> **KIM LEE:** "You bet you. For five years more."

We learn from Polly's conversation with Dancer that she is only leading Robert on, her real affections lie elsewhere. Robert phones David and shakes him down for money to leave town. David tells Robert he'll meet him with negotiable bonds on a certain street corner in ten minutes. Robert leaves. Dancer sends Nick and Nora drinks on the house. Says Nick, in words from the Hammett story repeated in the Goodrich-Hackett screenplay, "That's mighty white of you."[14]

A bunch of thugs, old acquaintances from Nick's detecting days, join Nick and Nora at their table. They constitute an alternate universe from Nora's "respectable" but boring family. These bad boys admire Nora and one of them, not knowing they are married, tells Nora, "When [Nick] gives you the sack, let me know, will ya?" Nora, smiling, responds: "I certainly will."[15] But Nick can play that game too. When the lights go out at the Lichee at midnight and then snap back on a minute later, we see Nick kissing a cute blonde. Nick apologizes: "I thought you were my wife." The blonde, however, has no complaints.

While Hammett puts most of the details into his story, he also knows when to take short cuts, writing on page 57, "[Here we have] a long description of a dress that can be written much more accurately by Miss Goodrich than by Mr. Hammett."[16]

Robert is found shot to death on the street and we have a collection of suspects: Selma, because she hated Robert for cheating; Dancer, who wanted Polly and the money, with Robert out of the way; Polly because she wanted the money and maybe Dancer but not Robert; Phil, introduced as Polly's brother but actually her ex-husband, who wants in on the extortion racket; Lum Kee, because he is Dancer's partner; Aunt Katherine, because she does not want Robert to desert Selma and bring scandal to the family; David, who hates his rival Robert, and Selma's physician Dr. Kammer, who looks guilty and speaks with an accent.

Two more murders follow: Phil and then Pedro, janitor of the building where Polly entertained Robert. Now we have three murders here just as we did in *The Thin Man*. The killings lead to some madcap slapstick as when Asta steals a note thrown through Nick's window and Nick and Nora chase him around the apartment to retrieve it. And Nick always has a thoroughly in-character wisecrack, as when he says to Nora, "Let's get something to eat. I'm thirsty."

There are gorgeous gowns worn by various female supporting characters but none as stunning as those Nora slips in and out of from scene to scene. The women are not solely window dressing for the story: though Selma simpers and Polly weasels, Nora, as usual, and also Aunt Katherine prove to be formidable characters. However, women do not hold power: once again the reporters, police, all people of authority outside the home are men.

Lieutenant Abrams brings Polly, Selma, Dancer, Lum Kee and David into the presumed killer's apartment for the final reveal. Who is the killer? More importantly where did Hammett get that name Lum Kee for our sole Asian character? Perhaps from the supermarket. Turns out Lee Kum Kee is a brand of Chinese sauces—oyster sauce, soy sauce, Hoisin sauce, etc., made for 130 years by a Hong Kong–based company. Maybe Hammett liked Chinese food. In any case, Lum Kee, inscrutable until now, plays the hero at the end when the real killer, David, informs the others: "I've got six bullets in this gun. …One for myself, and the rest for anyone who tries to stop me." Kee throws his hat at David to distract him as Nick and others disarm and overpower him. Nick explains that David not only killed Robert, his rival for Selma's affections, but framed her for the murder as revenge for throwing him over for Robert in the first place. Someone should have just counseled David to walk away from such feckless people, but then we wouldn't have a movie.

All ends well. Once again ensconced in a railroad sleeping compartment headed east, we find Nick in bathrobe, Nora in nightgown. Nick holds a drink. Nora knits. He sees what she's knitting and asks her, "What's that?" She smiles. He drinks and says, "Looks like a baby sock." His jaw drops as he realizes what is happening. Nora says: "And you call yourself a detective." In fact, the Hacketts, tired of Nick and Nora by this time, hoped giving the couple a baby would end the franchise. Goodrich had wanted greater finality, writing, "We wanted to kill them both at the end [of the second film] just to be sure, but Hunt [Stromberg] wouldn't let us."[17]

Van Dyke and Stromberg surrounded Powell and Loy with a strong supporting cast. And no one made it bigger after this film than James Stewart (1908–97), here as David in an early movie role. Stewart graduated from Princeton with a degree in architecture but got hooked on theater and played small parts in summer stock. He made his first movie in 1935 and, as his movie career took off, he appeared in nine films in 1936 alone. Director Van Dyke first worked with him that year in *Rose-Marie*, a Jeanette MacDonald-Nelson Eddy vehicle; Stewart was a criminal in that one also. He became a break-out star in 1938 in Frank Capra's *You Can't Take It with You* and confirmed that status in Capra's 1939 classic *Mr. Smith Goes to Washington*. The first major Hollywood star to enlist following the Pearl Harbor attack, Stewart flew 25 combat missions, won decorations for valor and left active duty as a colonel; continuing his service in the reserves where he reached the rank of brigadier general. He made another classic, *It's a Wonderful Life* (1946) as his first film upon returning to civilian life. In all, he appeared in some 80 films, most memorably in Westerns and three Hitchcock thrillers. He received five Oscar nominations over the course of his career, winning one for *The Philadelphia Story*. He is the best known of all those who acted in *Thin Man* movies and was truly a Hollywood icon. Years later, screenwriter Hackett said: "We helped start Jimmy Stewart's career."[18] And Myrna Loy remembered their time together on the *After the Thin Man* set: "Jimmy Stewart ... was very excited and enthusiastic about it all, rushing around with his camera taking pictures of everybody on the set, declaring 'I'm going to marry Myrna Loy.'"[19]

Ellissa Landi (1904–48), born Elisabeth Marie Christine Kühnelt, played Nora's cousin Selma. She was born in Venice and toured Europe with an acting troupe. She came to the U.S. in 1931 and landed several movie parts, then retired from films in 1937. Turning to writing, she published six novels and a book of poetry, all out of print today. An accomplished pianist, she played the piano as Selma in Aunt Katherine's home. She developed cancer and died at age 43.

In 1937, Landi was featured in MGM's *Hollywood Tea Party* (one of her last film roles and one that contrasts markedly with an actual and unfilmed MGM party of the same year. The 20-minute *Hollywood Tea Party*, an MGM puff piece, was directed by newcomer Roy Rowlan (1910–95), 26 at the time. Rowland had married the niece of Louis B. Mayer. This was the first of 26 shorts that Rowland directed before getting a shot at a full-length feature, *A Stranger in Town* (1943). His youth and inexperience alone cannot explain the rancid racism of *Hollywood Tea Party*. The concept is simple enough: Viewers are invited to a beachside party of MGM stars who sit among various well-dressed white people as they are served drinks by young, scantily dressed Asian women.

Co-hosting the party with Landi is Charlie Chase (1893–1940), born Charles Joseph Parrott, introduced here as Charlie "Chan" Chase and sporting a pasted-on Fu Manchu mustache and a "coolie hat." He speaks not his native English which we might believe he has mastered but "Chinese-accented" pidgin. Chase worked on short comedies for Hal Roach and once was as popular as Laurel and Hardy. But he drank himself to death at age 46. The public forgot his comedic skills until rediscovering his work more than 50 years after his death.

The whole affair is insulting. The wonderful actress Anna May Wong, with great poise, makes a brief cameo appearance, showing off various Chinese dresses. However, elsewhere, bikini-clad girls prance before a statue of the Buddha. Five black men in chauffeur uniforms sing. Chase and Landi force tenuous and stifled repartee but come up with a singularly hilarious bit:

> CHASE: "Charlie bring from Orient very pretty present for charming hostess, Missy Lissy Land."
> LANDI: "Thank you very much."
> CHASE: "Attention. Eeny, meeny, many mo, I bring token from Tokyo." [He lifts a scarf to reveal two love birds.]"
> LANDI: "Oh, how sweet."
> CHASE: "Old Chinese proverb say: When on visit, always give hostess the bird."[20]

Landi, whom MGM had publicized as the next big star, found her roles getting smaller and smaller. She later told a reporter: "Look at that awful part in *After the Thin Man* [1936].... They said it was a big picture—well, what of it? My part wasn't big. But I've decided I'll not let the studio say I'm difficult, so I do every role they give me and say nothing." She later fled Hollywood, saying: "I wasted seven good years of my life there."[21]

That other 1937 MGM party I mentioned was no tea party. As told in a *Hollywood Reporter* review of the 2007 documentary *Girl 27*, Patricia Douglas, a 17-year-old virgin and wannabe actress, was raped at a convention party thrown by MGM for hundreds of its movie salesman at the Hal Roach Studio's 500-acre ranch, celebrating a profitable year for the studio in the midst of the Depression. Louis B. Mayer greeted the salesmen with a welcoming speech, as quoted by *Girl 27* director David Stenn: "Our fine Chief of Police [James] Davis remarked to me a moment ago [that I] must think a lot of these men to have sent the beauty that he sees before him." The allusion was not to local sunshine or orange groves. "These lovely girls—and you have the finest of them—greet you ... and that's to show you how we feel about you, and the kind of a good time that's ahead of you.... Anything you want."[22] In the words of *The Reporter*:

> Cigar smoke swirled, champagne bottles were popped, and by the end of the evening, [Patricia] Douglas, then a 20-year-old virgin ... was the victim of rape. ... Even though she pressed charges against salesman David Ross, powerful men conspired against her, and the case was dismissed. Douglas was shattered. She became a recluse and refused to talk about the incident for decades."[23]

According to Stenn, Douglas had already appeared as a dancer in *This Is Africa* and *Gold Diggers of 1933*. But in May 1937, Douglas was just one of some 120 female dancers who answered an MGM casting call, got costumed in skimpy get-ups and were bussed after dark to the remote ranch, having been told they would be in a film. But they found no cameras, no studio crew. They were met by 280 celebrating salesmen, to whom MGM had provided 500 cases of champagne and Scotch. Ross raped her in the parking lot. The MGM parking attendant witnessed the rape but, after being promised an MGM job for life, denied he had seen anything.[24] Stenn charges that MGM and the courts colluded to protect Douglas' rapist, having discovered a three-page letter from William Randolph Hearst to Louis B. Mayer saying in part: "Shut this down, make her stop. Do you realize how damaging this is to the whole movie picture industry?"[25] Patricia Douglas never danced again, never acted again and stated that for the rest of her life, "I never had an orgasm. I was a frigid woman."[26] But, back to the show....

Joseph Calleia, born Giuseppe Maria Spurrin-Calleja (1897–1975), played Dancer. Calleia acted on Broadway and appeared in movies, often as the swarthy villain. In 1942 he played Nick Varna in *The Glass Key*, also based on a Dashiell Hammett novel. Malta, his nation of birth, later issued a stamp in honor of his Hollywood success. He retired to that island after concluding his acting career.

Jessie Ralph (1864–1944), who assayed the aristocratic but tough-as-nails Aunt Katherine, made some 60 other films. She appeared with William Powell and Myrna Loy again in *Double Wedding* (1937).

Reminiscent, in looks and manner, of Errol Flynn, Alan Marshal (1909–61) played Selma's cheating husband, Robert. Born in Australia, like Flynn, Marshal acted on the stage and in many movies. In 1961, he suffered a heart attack performing onstage with Mae West in her play *Sextette*. Though he finished that evening's performance, he died later that night at the age of 52.[27]

The obnoxious, fast-talking lawyer Casper was played by Teddy Hart (1897–1971), brother of Lorenz Hart, half of the Rodgers and Hart musical powerhouse. Teddy later appeared in four Ma and Pa Kettle films.

Sam Levene (1905–1980), born Scholem Lewin in Russia, played Lieutenant Abrams. He had a long career on stage and film. *After the Thin Man* was his third film role. He appeared in many movies as either a cop or a gangster. He reappears as Abrams in *Shadow of the Thin Man*. He much preferred stage work, saying: "Being in the presence of an audience and hearing their applause is what keeps an actor going much more than appearing on some cold ... soundstage in Hollywood."[28]

Dorothy McNulty (1908–2003), a singer-dancer later known as Penny Singleton, played Polly. She sang two songs in *After the Thin Man*. She is best-known for portraying Blondie Bumstead in 28 films (1938–50). She later voiced Jane Jetson on the cartoon TV series *The Jetsons*.

William Law (1896–1940), played Lum Kee and appeared the next year in *The Good Earth*. According to the March 10, 1937, issue of *The Saratogian*, Law was actually a millionaire importer in San Francisco who would travel down to Hollywood to act in movies for fun, spending more on transportation and lodging than his acting roles paid.[29]

George Zucco (1886–1960), born in England and wounded fighting in World War I, played the menacing Dr. Kammer. He appeared in some 90 films as a character actor, often as a doctor or villain or both.

Paul Fix (1901–1983) played Phil, the second victim; *After the Thin Man* was one of 17 movies in which he acted in 1936. He appeared in a vast number of movies, including 27 John Wayne Westerns, and may be best remembered for his recurring role as the marshal on the TV show *The Rifleman*. Fix had to overcome a fear of guns to be able to act in Westerns and gangster films after being shot in the face as a child while playing around with a gun with his brother. "There are pictures taken of me a few years after the accident and I'm always running away from the camera," Fix told *The Daily Item* in 1960. "I couldn't stand to have anything pointed at me, thinking it might shoot."[30]

Hunt Stromberg (1894–1968) produced all of *The Thin Man* movies and many Jean Harlow films. According to his *New York Times* obituary, he was "known as Hollywood's No. 1 producer in the mid-1930's and for a decade was among the ten Americans listed by the Treasury Department as having the highest income."[31]

Francis Goodrich and Albert Hackett wrote this second Thin Man script, based on a story by Dashiell Hammett. Returning director W.S. Van Dyke said of their efforts: "It was not an easy task for the Hacketts to grope back through three years of time to catch the same characteristic idioms, voiced by Bill and Myrna in the first story."[32] But their snappy Nick and Nora dialogue shows that they did. For example, after Nick proves Selma not guilty of murder, we get this exchange:

> **NICK:** "Did I ever tell you that you're the most fascinating woman this side of the Rockies?"
> **NORA:** "Wait 'til you see me on the other side."[33]

Goodrich and Hackett were nominated once again for an Oscar for Best Adapted Screenplay, but lost to the writers of *The Story of Louis Pasteur*.

MGM released *After the Thin Man* on Christmas Day 1936 and it went on to become the sixth highest grossing film of 1937[34] and the most successful of the series at the box office. Critics had as good a time as paying customers. Frank Nugent wrote in *The New York Times*:

> If *After the Thin Man* is not quite the delight *The Thin Man* was, it is, at the very least, one of the most urbane comedies of the season. …Sequels commonly are disappointing and Metro-Goldwyn-Mayer was borrowing trouble when it dared advance a companion piece to one of the best pictures of 1934. But Dashiell Hammett's sense of humor has endured, W.S. Van Dyke retains his directorial facility and William Powell and Myrna Loy still persuade us that Mr. and Mrs. Nick Charles are exactly the sort of people we should like to have on our calling list on New Year's Day and for all the rest of the year.[35]

Variety had its say from Hollywood:

> First thing everyone will want to know about this one is whether it is as good as *The Thin Man*, and the answer is that it is—and it isn't. It has the same stars, William Powell and Myrna Loy; the same style of breezy direction by W.S. Van Dyke; almost as many sparkling lines of dialog and amusing situations; but it hasn't, and probably couldn't have, the same freshness and originality of its predecessor.… It's the "same" all the way through, and while that's a guarantee of a certain general excellence, it's the reason why it does not shine so brightly.[36]

The Times of London review put its finger on the human heart of the film:

> The air of married happiness which Mr. William Powell and Miss Myrna Loy contrive to convey … is of far more interest than the tracking down of the murderer … [H]ere is the genuine material of marriage—the private jokes … the routine of daily life, the amused and affectionate tolerance each shows … the other … [I]t is the gaiety, the proper but never exaggerated sophistication, the charm, and the irresponsibility, within limits, they bring to their lives which more than justify this sequel.[37]

But the best reviews arrived at the ticket offices where *After the Thin Man* raked in a profit of $1.5 million, "doubling the grosses *The Thin Man* achieved on its first run."[38] Soon after, Hammett sold all the rights to *The Thin Man* to MGM.

In Hollywood when a movie makes a lot of money, a studio knows only one thing to do: repeat. So MGM gathered the old gang together and filmed sequel number two, the third film in the franchise. Producer Stromberg and director Van Dyke reported for duty as did Powell, Loy and Skippy and screenwriters Hackett and Goodrich.

Sort of present and sort of absent was Dashiell Hammett. He had sold his rights to Nick and Nora but MGM paid him a hefty $35,000 fee for a new story on which to base a screenplay. For the story, Hammett drew on one of his earlier short stories, "The Farewell Murder," published in *Black Mask* in 1930, for some dialogue, plot points and several characters. And then with the money in his pocket, Hammett fell off the wagon once again.[39] Goodrich and Hackett spoke about their work with Hammett this third and last time: Goodrich said, "[He] was reclusive and often drunk in his ridiculous hotel suite, and working with him was no pleasure."[40] Unhappy with what Louis B. Mayer called Hammett's "irregular habits"[41] and even more perturbed by his rabble-rousing with the Screen Writers Guild, MGM cancelled his contract. Hammett was now done with the franchise, Hollywood and, it seemed, writing.

Powell returned to MGM after cancer surgery. Loy remembered: "He still seemed a bit frail."[42] Van Dyke limited Powell's work to six hours a day. After three surgeries and radiation treatment over two years away from the studio, Powell now used a colostomy bag. No one used the words rectal cancer or breathed such a diagnosis to the press until years later. Many didn't believe the dignified Powell had a rectum.[43] During his illness and convalescence, MGM had played with the idea of signing a new actor, considering Melvyn Douglas and Reginald Gardiner for the role.[44] But Loy refused to return without Powell.

When Powell returned, he said that it felt "like coming home again. Myrna and Woody were wonderful. If they had been sentimental or emotional about it—I don't think I could have stood it, I was so choked up. But those two knew. All they said was, 'Well, Powell at last—and late again.'"[45]

MGM made Powell's return big news in advertising. The trailer proclaimed, "He's back! And William Powell's return to the screen is the best movie news in two years!" (with "Happy Days Are Here Again" on the soundtrack).[46] The film's working title was *The Thin Man Returns*, seemingly in Powell's honor, but it was later retitled to *Another Thin Man*.

The film opens with the peripatetic Nick and Nora returning to New York with their one-year-old Nick Jr. The baby was played by eight-month-old William Anthony Poulson, who was chosen from several hundred candidates. This would be his only acting gig. Powell expressed to Myrna Loy his dismay at having an on-screen child: "Why do we want this kid? First thing you'll know, he'll be in kindergarten, then prep school, then college. How old will that make us?"[47] Hammett didn't like the idea of Nick Jr. either. According to his daughter Jo:

> He particularly loathed child actors—mostly for what their mothers had made them into. After a morning watching children being interviewed for a part, he said he felt like going out and burning down an orphanage. He told us about a casting interview for the baby in a Thin Man sequel. The interviewer told the child's mother that he would have to work with Asta, who didn't like children, so it might be dangerous. "No problem," she answered; that didn't worry her at all.[48]

As their train enters Manhattan, we see all the frenetic activity of trunk after trunk being unloaded and wheeled up to Nick and Nora's hotel room; there's even a life size toy fire hydrant for Asta. Room service enters with whiskey and soda and a nurse for Nickie Jr., Dorothy Waters, played by the redoubtable Ruth Hussey. Her furtive behavior alerts us that we'll have to keep an eye on her and our suspicions are confirmed when we later see her take to her heels when a murder is committed. Nora speaks with a friend on the phone: "We had a lovely trip. Nick was sober in Kansas City.... I'm dying to have you see the baby.... We kind of like him."[49]

We see the new baby upsetting Asta by chewing on his bone. Nickie is a fat baby interested mainly in "eating and sleeping." He knows two words, "drunk" and "gimme."⁵⁰

Now Nick calls Nora "Mommy" and continues this inane form of endearment throughout the movie. Gone is "sugar" and "beautiful"; now it's always "Mommy" or "Mama." (I am reminded that President Reagan called wife Nancy "Mommy.") The movie plot closely follows Hammett's story. What Hackett and Goodrich do so well is to think visually and let pictures take the place of dialogue, as when Nora stuffs Nickie Jr. in a dresser drawer to sleep and Asta seeks a dresser drawer of his own to sleep in. And when Nora, in the middle of the night, places an awakened Nickie Jr. on a sleeping Nick's face and encourages Nickie Jr. to pull his dad's mustache. I especially like this sequel for all its dark atmospherics, often filmed at night and with lots of action. There's still sharp repartee:

The second Thin Man sequel, *Another Thin Man* (1939), introduces Nicky Jr. Although the copy chortles "Mr. & Mrs. Thin Man have a b-a-b-y!" Powell and Loy look none too thrilled about this newest addition.

> NORA: "I got rid of all those reporters."
> NICK: "What did you tell them?"
> NORA: "That we were out of Scotch."
> NICK: "What a gruesome thought."⁵¹

But the plot soon spirals out of control with complication heaped upon complication. It goes something like this: As they settle into their hotel room, Nora gets a call from Colonel Burr MacFay (C. Audrey Smith), a business partner of Nora's father. He fears he will soon be murdered. He dispatches a car and driver to bring Nick, Nora, Nickie Jr. and the new nanny to his Long Island estate. As the car enters the estate grounds in the dark of night, the headlamps pick up the body of a man on the ground. Nick insists the car stop. The chauffeur stops and runs away. When Nick searches, he finds no body in the road. What's going on?

The colonel, who has amassed a fortune by means fair or foul, suspects a former convict lurking in the vicinity will soon kill him. The house is filled with people, all of whom become suspects when the colonel is found with his throat slashed. The murderer might be the housekeeper Mrs. Bellam (Phyllis Gordon), once romantically involved with the colonel; ex-con Phil Church (Sheldon Leonard); his gun moll Smitty (Muriel Hutchison); his criminal colleague Dum-Dum (Abner Biberman); the colonel's adopted daughter Lois (Virginia Grey); her fiancé Dudley Horn (Patric Knowles) or MacFay's secretary Freddie Coleman (Tom Neal), who's in love with Lois. Then there's the new nanny who has gone missing.

Things seem strangely similar to the earlier two movies: The Dudley-Lois-Freddie triangle is reminiscent of both *After the Thin Man*, with Selma in the middle, and *The Thin Man*, with Dorothy pursued by two men. This time Hackett and Goodrich treat us to a scene of Asta running around with a knife, possibly the murder weapon, while people try to get it away from him; quite like Nick and Nora's pursuit of Asta when the dog stole a note in *After the Thin Man*. And just as in the two previous films, there are three murders. Killers seem to be trinitarians and writers seem to repeat themselves.

Two extended scenes work well. When Nick finds a matchbook in Church's coat with an ad for Harlem's West Indies Club, he heads there. This is reminiscent of Powell and Loy at the Cotton Club in an earlier film. At the West Indies Club, a maître d' (Nestor Paiva) meets Nick at the entrance. He asks:

Maître d': "You are alone?"
Nick: "The good are often alone."
Maître d': "I will fix it so you will not be good long."[52]

Nick spots someone at a corner table surrounded by male admirers. Of course, when he goes to the table, he finds it's Nora doing a bit of detecting on her own. Nora asks, "How did you know I was here?"

Nick: "I saw a great group of men standing around a table. I knew there was only one woman in the world who could attract men like that." Nora smiles until Nick adds: "A woman with a lot of money."[53]

The other excellent scene is Nickie's first-year birthday party organized by a slew of ex-cons, all sent up the river by Nick but happy to celebrate his son's birthday (and guzzle Nick's booze). But the ticket of entry is to bring an infant. Worried that his miscreant peers might have kidnapped babies to attend, "Creeps" guards the door and warns them, in one of the best lines in the movie, "We don't want no hot tots."[54] However, Hammett's story had the crooks passing babies in and out of the hotel windows, rented at a buck a head, to provide each new guest with the required infant accompaniment. Goodrich and Hackett have everyone enter by the door and only mention, but don't show, the baby rental. Nickie Jr.'s birthday gifts include several blackjacks.

This birthday party, so reminiscent of the Christmas Eve party in *The Thin Man*, is both the highpoint of this sequel and a sad example of how the best ideas get repeated throughout the series. A hood named "Wacky" is played by an uncredited Shemp Howard. Howard earlier appeared in blackface in vaudeville shows with brother Moe and later replaced an ill brother, Curly, to become one-third of the Three Stooges with Moe and Larry Fine.

Once again Nick reveals the killer as the last person we suspected: Lois, the adopted daughter of the slain Colonel MacFay. To do so, he has to reconstruct a convoluted murder scheme involving a pistol, electrical current and wet paper. It's a sequence any amateur criminologist in the audience would have difficulty following. The big clue this time is that Nick has noticed that Lois and her party girl alter ego Linda Mills are one and the same because both sleep without pillows, a bit of Sherlock Holmes–like deduction. When Linda claims to have kidnapped Nickie Jr. and bargains for her freedom, a woman enters carrying little Nickie; Linda kidnapped the wrong infant. In Hammett's story, Linda explains her error: "Kids are like Chinamen—how can you tell 'em apart?"[55] a bit of anti–Asian racism played for laughs.

By this third Thin Man, you can see the formula: Nick is asked into a case at a time of crisis, he demurs but Nora insists, a body turns up, there is a party that showcases all of Nick's underworld pals (Christmas, New Year's Eve, Nickie Jr.'s birthday party), all the suspects are gathered at the end, and the murderer is revealed. The audience knows just what to expect and buys tickets anyway.

Another Thin Man was Hammett's last piece of long fiction. He wrote an eight-page treatment for a *Sequel to "The Thin Man"* that was never produced as he must have known it would not be. In it, he brings back characters from his earlier Thin Man stories: Mimi, Christian, Dorothy, Gilbert, Morelli, Dancer and Macaulay, who has escaped from prison dressed as a woman; events of earlier movies are repeated; and it is heavy on a convoluted plot. In the end, we learn that Nick is the murderer who has paid off witnesses to finger Dancer for the killing. MGM told Hammett "thanks but no thanks." He had nothing to do with the next three sequels.

Once *Another Thin Man* was in the can, Powell, who had begun dyeing his hair in his forties, said, "By the time I'm ready for another Thin Man, Myrna and I will be too old to play anything but character parts."[56]

Soon after the film opened, Powell met Diana Lewis while MGM was shooting publicity stills for her at his estate in Beverly Hills. He asked her out that very night. He was 47 and she was 21. They married in 1940 after knowing each other less than a month.[57] The marriage lasted until his death 44 years later.

Another Thin Man offers an odd convergence of race and place. There are no black people on New York streets but when Nick and Nora head up to the West Indies Club, there are of course Cubans, Afro-Cubans among them. The couple performing a highly choreographed and very beautiful dance are the darkest people in the movie. The dancing couple was known as Rene and Estela, who were real-life headliners at New York's Havana-Madrid Club. René Rivero Guillén and Ramona Ajón, stage names René and Estela, were an Afro-Cuban dance team from Matanzas, Cuba, famous for their mastery of the Rhumba, Mambo, Son and Danzon. They go uncredited in this movie.

We have a supposedly Cuban character in the role of Phil Church's servant and accomplice "Dum-Dum" (Abner Biberman). Do we think, when we hear that name, of a dum-dum bullet, a hollow-nosed cartridge? Or is this just colloquial for dumb? Biberman, who had a long acting career and roles in *His Girl Friday* and *Gunga Din* (and later directed for movies and TV), was not Cuban. Born in Wisconsin, his "exotic" looks landed him parts as a Japanese Army officer, a South Seas islander, and an Indian bandit. Gender roles are fixed: Women are never police officers, never reporters, never a DA, never a lawyer, a doctor or a judge. In this area, Hollywood generally reflected a sexist society at large. There are strong and powerful female characters, good or bad (Nora, Smitty and Lois) just as we had Aunt Katherine in *After the Thin Man*.

Sheldon Leonard, born Sheldon Leonard Bershad (1907–97), one of my favorite actors in his rare appearances on TV comedies like *The Dick Van Dyke Show*, plays chief hoodlum Phil Church. Leonard lost his job on Wall Street with the stock market crash of 1929 and turned to acting. *Another Thin Man* was an early film role in a decades-long career as actor, writer, director and producer. He reported that he moved behind the camera when somebody said, "If you don't like the way we're doing it—why don't you do it yourself?," "and the next thing I knew I was a director and then I became a producer from being chronically dissatisfied with directors."[58]

Ruth Hussey (1911–2005), seen as the beautiful nanny with a shady past, was at the start of a 40-year career, often in starring roles. She was Oscar-nominated for Best Supporting Actress for her work in *The Philadelphia Story*.

Virginia Grey (1917–2004), plays Lois MacFay aka Linda Mills. Her career illustrates the nonstop work of successful actors at that time. She first appeared in films in 1927 at the age of ten and already had 32 movie credits by the time of *Another Thin Man*. In all, she made over 100 movies. Grey tested to fill in and finish *Saratoga* after Jean Harlow's death. While she didn't get the part, her encounter on that set with Clark Gable led to an affair of several years.[59] She later transitioned to TV work.

C. Aubrey Smith (1863–1948) is Colonel Burr MacFay, the first murder victim. He moved from a successful career in British and South African cricket to acting, appearing in 65 films. He founded the Hollywood Cricket Club with a field at Griffith Park.

Patric Knowles (1911–95) plays Dudley Horn, Lois's fiancé and the second to die. Another Englishman, he appeared in over 100 movies in England and the U.S. and moved into U.S. TV in the 1950s.

Tom Neal (1914–72) appears as Freddie Coleman, MacFay's secretary, who is in love with Lois. Neal presents a sad personal story. He had a career as a successful amateur boxer and segued into acting but Hollywood dropped him when in 1951 he severely beat actor Franchot Tone in a fistfight over actress Barbara Payton. Years later, a jury convicted him in the murder of his estranged wife and he spent six years in prison.

Phyllis Gordon (1889–1964) plays Mrs. Isabella Bellam, MacFay's housekeeper and, possibly, Lois' mother. Gordon herded cattle as a teenager in Oklahoma, before beginning her long career in movies.

For my money, Don Costello (1901–45) as "Diamond Back" Vogel probably does the best acting job in the film as a shifty ex-con. He appeared in over 30 movies in his short life.

Muriel Hutchinson (1915–75) plays the intriguing Smitty, who stands up for her right to date Phil Church while her husband languishes in jail. Smitty, it seems, likes them both. Hutchinson acted on the Broadway stage and made several movies. She retired from acting in 1953 when she married; she and her husband ran a New York City art gallery until her death.

Marjorie Main (1890–1975), born Mary Tomlinson, plays a wisecracking Mrs. Dolley, who rents out rooms to young women like Linda Mills, and here gets handsy in a flirtatious scene with Nick Charles. Main is best known for her role of Ma Kettle in all nine Ma and Pa Kettle movies, a sort of precursor to the *Beverly Hillbillies* TV comedy.

In his only film, William Anthony Poulson appears as Nickie Jr. He never acted again. His death has been listed as 2017[60] but also as 1973, in the book *Thoughts on the Thin Man*.[61] Now there's a mystery.

Harry Bellaver (1905–93), born Enricho Bellaver, plays "Creeps." Bellaver, the son of Italian immigrant laborers working in the coal mining camps of Hillsboro, Illinois, had a difficult early life. He got no further than the sixth grade and found employment as a teamster, farm hand and coal miner. Then he won a scholarship to Brookwood Labor College, founded by the great pacifist and Quaker, A.J. Muste, with a Board of Directors drawn from unions in the American Federation of Labor. Bellaver began acting at Brookwood in student productions and then worked on the professional stage. *Another Thin Man* was his first film role. He is probably best-known for his continuing role as Sgt. Frank Arcaro in all but two episodes of the long-running television series *Naked City*.

MGM released *Another Thin Man* on November 17, 1939. Reviews were only so-so compared to the two earlier Thin Man films. *The New York Times* critic wrote:

> In the gay tradition of its predecessors, howbeit a trifle more forced in its gayety, is *Another Thin Man*.... With William Powell back in domestic harness as Nick Charles, with Myrna Loy as the almost too-perfect helpmeet, and with—of all people—a Nick Jr. to guarantee the continuance of the series, this third of the trademarked Thin Men takes its murders as jauntily as ever, confirms our impression that matrimony need not be too serious a business and provides as light an entertainment as any holiday-amusement seeker is likely to find. This still does not mean that we are willing to comply completely. Some of the bloom is off the rose. A few of the running gags are beginning to show signs of pulling up lame.[62]

The Hollywood Reporter noted a "sparkling script, splendid performances in every role under the most facile and deft direction [of Van Dyke] ... [A]udiences are going to have a swell time."[63]

Goodrich and Hackett wrote seven films for the duo of Van Dyke and Stromberg, and they received Oscar nominations for their first two Thin Man scripts. But the third time was not the charm. Neither they nor anyone else involved on *Another Thin Man* received Oscar nominations. Goodrich and Hackett did, however, later win the Pulitzer Prize for their stage adaptation of *The Diary of Anne Frank*, and then adapted that for the movies. Said Goodrich: "We do everything together. Poor Hackett. He never gets away from me. He never gets to take advantage of all the opportunities in Hollywood—and there are so many."[64]

After *Another Thin Man*, Goodrich and Hackett fled Hollywood. *Another Thin Man* netted more than $2 million[65] and that guaranteed another sequel.

9

Hammett, Act III

Hollywood, its venality and crassness, its extravagance and temptation, didn't destroy Dashiell Hammett but it certainly provided the money and fame to super-charge his self-destruction. Hammett drank and got mean. Hammett drank and got sick. Hammett drank and stopped writing. Hammett drank and stopped drinking. And then he went back to drinking again. Friends rushed him to hospitals to dry out. Friends picked him up out of the gutter. His daughter Jo never stopped loving him, not even after he had abandoned the family in Los Angeles. She told one writer:

> Papa was lots of people.... He's there when Spade tells Brigid O'Shaughnessy that he doesn't mind a reasonable amount of trouble.... He'd do the job, take the risks, but ... he wouldn't "play the sap for her." That was pretty much how my father met his obligations in life—personal and otherwise. He did what he thought he had to do; then he was history.[1]

She added: "I could never understand his drinking because it seemed to make him miserable."[2]

Hammett's daughter Mary also became an alcoholic and a drug abuser. Sometimes father and daughter got drunk together and created nasty rows. Mary also suffered from mental illness and attempted suicide. Lillian Hellman later claimed Mary was not Hammett's biological daughter and that he had married her mother, a nurse he had met while convalescing during World War I military service, only to spare her the shame of being an unwed mother. If true, that might bolster Jo's claim that Hammett could step up to meet commitments when necessary.

Sometimes Hammett's drinking and libido led him into the realm of somewhat comedic debauchery matched with a casual adultery. The humorist S.J. Perelman (1904–79) wrote for the Marx Brothers films *Monkey Business* and *Horse Feathers* and won an Academy Award for his *Around the World in 80 Days* (1956) screenplay, all the while writing funny pieces for *The New Yorker*. Perelman reportedly had an open and unhappy marriage with his wife Laura.[3] Hammett tested their arrangement when he developed an interest in the "tall and gorgeous" Laura,[4] sister of Nathaniel West, his sometime indulgent landlord in New York. Hammett hired a prostitute to join a party at the Perelman residence in L.A. and directed her upstairs when Perelman entered the bathroom. Some minutes later, Hammett somehow maneuvered Laura upstairs to be sure she discovered S.J. *en flagrante*. Hammett, sympathizing with Mrs. Perelman's dismay, whisked her off to a consolation weekend in San Francisco.[5] Friends saw something of Laura in Nora Charles. Laura's dog's name, Asta, made it into Hammett's *The Thin Man* and canine history.[6]

On January 15, 1938, Hammett wrote Lillian Hellman from L.A., "For the record this is my tenth month without drink."[7] But there were often letters like this and then long periods when he could not make that claim. Said Hellman: "I always thought that the reason Hammett drank so much was that he was basically a shy man and the drinking made him less shy. But I don't know whether it's true or not."[8]

The long Hammett-Hellman relationship featured all the dizzying ups and downs of a roller coaster. One biographer noted that in the mid–1930s, Hellman "drank, smoked, and partied nonstop…. One observer called Hellman 'a tough broad … the kind of girl who can take the tops off bottles with her teeth.'"[9] She sometimes rescued Hammett when he was drunk or ill. "Once, when she received a letter to join him on the west coast, she arrived: only to find him drunk and in bed with a prostitute. In a rage she smashed up furniture and returned immediately to New York."[10]

From 1927 to 1934, Hammett wrote fifty-two short stories[11] and 5 novels. As I worked on this book,

Lillian Hellman, one of America's greatest playwrights. She moved to Hollywood in 1930 and read scripts at MGM for $50 a week. There she met Dashiell Hammett and they began their tempestuous, decades-long relationship. This picture is from 1935, the year when she, Hammett, Dorothy Parker and other writers founded the Screen Writers Guild (March 1935 issue of *The Stage* via Wikimedia Commons).

people contacted me to say a sixth Hammett novel had been published posthumously. I wondered why none of his biographers mentioned this. The work in question was first published while Hammett lived. At 72 pages, "Woman in the Dark" isn't even a novella. It originally ran in three consecutive issues of *Liberty Magazine* in 1933. With permission of the Trustees of Hellman's will, Doubleday reprinted it in 1988. It's a page-turner but does not demonstrate near the literary merit of Hammett's novels. The 1934 film *Woman in the Dark* starring Fay Wray, Ralph Bellamy and Melvyn Douglas was based on Hammett's longish short story. After *The Thin Man* in 1933, he stopped writing almost entirely. Sixteen movies were made from his works[12] so he no longer needed to write to earn his daily bread. Did he find himself as an author unable to strike out in a new direction? He wrote to his publisher, Alfred Knopf, in 1932: "I think the Thin Man [a first draft later abandoned] will be my last detective novel: we'll try our luck in another genre."[13]

But maybe detective fiction was all he knew. His daughter Josephine said after his death:

[P]eople ask when the ice is broken, and they get to the thing they really want to know, the important thing: "Why did your father stop writing?"… "Well, he drank, you know" I begin.

"And for a long time he had enough money so he didn't have to write. He could do other things like politics and fishing. He wanted to go mainstream, but that was scary, because he'd been so successful with mysteries. Then there was the Army. And his health was bad." ...The answers are okay; it's the question that's wrong. He didn't stop writing. Not until the very last. What he stopped was finishing.[14]

Hammett later began three novels, evinced enthusiasm for each in turn but never finished any, including 25,000 words committed to one entitled *Tulip*, often accepted as his own requiem as a writer. He gives "Pop," a central character in *Tulip* (and the nickname given to Hammett himself during his World War II service by his Army mates) some final thoughts on life and writing: "If you are tired you ought to rest and not try to fool yourself and your customers with colored bubbles."[15] Here most biographers pause and then end their tales of Hammett. But the story I have pieced together is much more interesting: Hammett did keep writing and he found a more important arena for his commitment: political activism.

Even so, a good deal of that writing occurred with Hellman, within their on-again, off-again tempestuous personal and professional 30-year relationship. Hellman, who started as a $50-a-week "reader" at MGM, became one of the four greatest American playwrights of the 20th century along with Eugene O'Neill, Tennessee Williams and Arthur Miller. One lover and biographer called her "bombastic, opinionated, dazzling, enraging, funny, peevish, bawdy."[16] But she didn't succeed alone. Hellman spoke of her debt to Hammett in 1979: "His effect on me was enormous. I've long had the belief ... that without Hammett I wouldn't have written.... He taught me, in a sense, to write."[17] In 1934, Hammett pointed Hellman to the source material for her play *The Children's Hour* (a dramatic writeup of *The Great Drumsheugh Case* in William Roughhead's 1930 book *Bad Companions*) and, according to Hammett biographer Vince Emery, might have claimed co-authorship. The original 1810 court case involved lesbian schoolteachers in Scotland. Hellman dedicated the script to Hammett.[18] The play opened on Broadway in November 1934 and was a great success.[19] Samuel Goldwyn (1882–1974) bought the film rights to *The Children's Hour* even as it ran on Broadway. But having lesbians in a movie violated the Code against sexual perversions. When Code enforcers would not give their permission for Goldwyn to use the script for the film version because the main characters were lesbians, he announced, in what is likely an apocryphal anecdote: "That's all right, we'll make them Armenians." The play was filmed in 1936 as *These Three* and their sin became heterosexual adultery, not gay love.

One day in 1938, Thin Man screenwriters Goodrich and Hackett found Hammett half dead in a rented room. The hotel refused to check him out without payment of his $8000 bill. Lacking the cash, the couple snuck him out the back exit and put him on a plane heading east ... to Hellman.[20] After hospitalization and recovery, he helped her write *The Little Foxes*, another American classic. Hellman said that this play "was the one that was most dependent [on Hammett.]"[21] It also scored a success on Broadway in 1939, running for 410 performances.

At her Westchester County (New York) rural estate, Hardscrabble Farm, Hellman and Hammett set to work together on *Watch on the Rhine*. Hellman saw Hammett in the play's anti-fascist protagonist Kurt Muller. She wrote: "I suppose there's some of Hammett in almost every character I ever wrote. In everything I've written, Hammett has been somewhere, some form of him."[22] *Watch on the Rhine* opened on Broadway in April 1941 and ran for 378 performances. Hammett wrote the 1943 screenplay for

Warner Brothers for $30,000 and the picture garnered a Best Picture Oscar nomination; it lost to *Casablanca*. The Academy also honored Hammett with a screenwriting nomination; he also lost out to *Casablanca*'s three writers. *Variety* called the film *Watch on the Rhine* "better than its original stage version."[23]

Hellman and Hammett collaborated again on the lesser-known play *The Autumn Garden*, with Hellman's name as author and the play dedicated to Hammett.[24] She gave him 15 percent of her royalties. The play concerns four couples breaking apart in a summer resort near New Orleans. The alcoholic artist at the play's center, Nick Denery, has Nick Charles' first name and all of Hammett's bad habits. Fredric March originated the role on Broadway opposite Jane Wyatt as his wife Nina. (Why Nina and not Nora, I wonder.) *The Autumn Garden* cuts close to the bone for Hammett, presenting Nick as a failed artist and a failed human being: drunk, self-pitying and a philanderer. Once talented, he has been unable to finish a painting in 12 years. Do the math: The play is set in 1949; Hammett last completed a novel in 1933. Nick tells Nina, rather unconvincingly: "If I haven't finished every picture I started it's because I'm good enough to know they weren't good enough." Retorts Nina: "You have very handsome reasons for what you do not finish."[25] Nick hits on each woman who enters his orbit and seems surprised that Nina minds. "Don't you have fun any more?" he asks her. "I don't think so," she replies.[26] One wonders how Hammett stomached it.

Nick concludes Act II trying to seduce Sophie, who is engaged to another man, with the wrenching confession: "Don't be so young. Have a little pity. I am old and sick."[27] In the end, Nick and Nina leave the guest house and its occupants in a shambles but remain themselves emotionally locked together. The play, though well enough reviewed, ran for just 100 performances. The Hammett-Hellman relationship continued for some 31 years. One biographer noted: "Their destructive, symbiotic, love-hate relationship, fueled by contrary egos, vile tempers, much alcohol, and gross infidelities, continued until Hammett's death."[28] It went so far that Hellman, when she learned she was pregnant by Hammett, aborted the fetus. In 1937, he proposed marriage even as he dallied with other women.[29] She declined, twice, later explaining: "We did have two periods of planning to be married. The first time, he disappeared with another lady. That's not really fair—I was disappearing too.... We were both of that nutty time that believed that alliances could stand up against other people. I should have known better, because I had a jealous nature."[30] Regarding their last years together, Hellman said: "It was an unspoken pleasure, that having come together so many years, ruined so much and repaired a little, we had endured."[31]

After 1933, Hammett's writing took in new genres: playwriting and screenwriting in collaboration with Hellman. He didn't stop writing; he stopped writing detective fiction. But he stopped a number of things including drinking and racism as he got more deeply involved in political activism. Working to form a Screen Writers Guild in opposition to studio management and his work against fascism at home and abroad led him to the Communist Party.

Hollywood writers of all salary levels banded together and formed the Screen Writers Guild in March 1933, when Louis Mayer announced that MGM was cutting the wages of all studio employees by 50 percent. Hammett and Hellman joined the organizing effort along with Hackett and Goodrich, Dorothy Parker and Donald Ogden Stewart *et al.* As a union, these writers demanded credit for their work and fair wages.

To fight the new union, the studios created their own in-house organization, the

Screen Playwrights (owned by MGM lock stock and barrel[32]) and blacklisted writers belonging to the new SWG. Over at Warner Brothers, Harry Warner spoke at a meeting where the SWG asked for a minimum wage:

> Is that all they want? That's all they want.... Those dirty communist sons of bitches ... they want to take my goddam studio, my brothers built this studio ... they want to take my goddam studio. I came from Europe ... my father was a butcher ... you dirty communists.[33]

Harry's brother Jack Warner called screenwriters "schmucks with Underwoods."[34] After much shouting, picketing, name-calling and threats, the National Labor Relations Board named the Screen Writers Guild the sole organizing body for Hollywood screenwriters and the studios seemingly acquiesced.

The end of World War II meant lots of labor strife as wartime wage and price controls ended and the Democrats' control on power slipped after FDR's death. Republicans seized the opening to reject New Deal reforms and contest for national power. With a finger to the political winds, Harry Truman, newly elevated to the White House, sought to outflank Republicans with his own government's Loyalty Program, insuring his 1948 election but ushering in McCarthyism and the witch hunters. Suddenly the Socialist and Communist affiliations of hundreds of thousands of Americans meant treason rather than dissent.

The Depression, the war against Nazi Germany and its allies and the rather liberal 13-year presidency of Franklin Delano Roosevelt, uncorked the pent-up power of reformers and revolutionaries. Though they had failed to elect Upton Sinclair and secure victory for the EPIC campaign, various factions worked, sometimes cooperatively and sometimes antagonistically, to fight racism and union-busting at home and fascism abroad.

We can see Hammett, born below the Mason-Dixon line, develop from racist to anti-racist. His daughter Jo tracked the evolution of his racial thinking:

> He had begun life with the usual racial biases.... His Maryland ancestors had been slave owners, and his early stories are full of the usual stereotypes—comic Negroes, sinister Orientals, and the rest.... Papa had begun by accepting this attitude but he grew out of it. In the early forties he belonged to an organization called something like "Negroes and Allies" and showed me his membership card with pride.[35]

We saw Hammett's early racism in short stories like "Dead Yellow Women" and in *The Thin Man* when he dismisses one unseen and extraneous character with the N-word.[36] (The slur is uttered by detective Guild and not Nick Charles, a comment more upon the cop's character than the detective who is Hammett's alter ego.) Closer to home and more disturbing is this story told in Richard Layman's *Shadow Man: The Life of Dashiell Hammett*: Hammett, short on cash as usual, sent his black chauffeur to collect a loan with a note reading, "Give the jig the bundle. Dashiell Hammett."[37] "Jig," short for jigaboo, is a racist slur, supposedly from the Bantu language and used to describe servile individuals. Hammett places additional slurs of African Americans in the mouths of detectives in his second novel *The Dain Curse*: "shine," "dark meat," "dinge," "big smoke," etc.[38]

But as Jo said, her father traveled far from his early casual racism into active anti-racist activity in conjunction with his work as a member of the Communist Party, USA. He probably joined the CPUSA in the '30s (no membership card has surfaced). His membership was no secret. In addition to helping found the Screen Writers Guild, he joined Hellman, Louis Untermeyer, I.F. Stone, Arthur Miller and others in creating the League of American Writers in 1935, with membership limited to published writers, and with the goal of fighting racism and fascism. The League of American Writers elected Hammett president in 1941 and *The New York Times* noted that the resolutions passed at the group's annual convention "generally followed the Communist Party's line."[39]

From 1939 to 1940, Hammett helped publish *Equality*, "A Monthly Journal to Defend Democratic Rights and Combat Anti-Semitism and Racism." He joined the Civil Rights Congress. He evolved from a strike-breaking Pinkerton to a civil rights activist and Communist. The galvanizing racial event of the 1930s in the South was the conviction of "The Scottsboro Boys": Nine young blacks, aged 13 to 19, traveling from Chattanooga to Memphis, were taken off a freight train in Alabama in March 1931, along with Ruby Bates and Victoria Price, two white women who may have been prostitutes. When confronted by police, Ruby and Victoria cried rape. A white posse took the nine to the Scottsboro, Alabama, jail and a lynch mob gathered outside. A local newspaper headline called them "9 Negro Brutes."[40] When the trial got underway a month later, a mob once again formed around the courthouse and the governor called 200 National Guardsmen into service. The town pressed a local lawyer specializing in real estate law into service as the defense attorney. The nine teens were quickly convicted in one trial by an all-white jury, yielding eight death sentences and life imprisonment for the 13-year-old.

The CPUSA took up the Scottsboro case and made it a national and international *cause célèbre*. Hammett lent his name and voice to the outcry. On appeal, the Supreme Court ruled for a new trial. For the second trial, the Alabama State Attorney General stepped in to prosecute. This time the men got separate trials but again each jury was all-male and all-white. At the first retrial, the defense called Ruby Bates, who had disappeared for months. She dramatically reappeared and admitted lying in her earlier testimony. But one prosecutor told the jury, "Show the world that Alabama justice cannot be bought by Jew money from New York." The jury found the defendant guilty again. The presiding judge, an Alabama native, at the risk of his own political career, set aside the guilty verdict and ordered yet a third trial. Demonstrations continued worldwide: "Whites and Blacks marched side by side for the first time since Reconstruction,"[41] cognizant that between 1880 and 1940, white mobs had lynched 5000 black men and women mostly in the Southern states.[42]

At a third trial, a white jury convicted Haywood Patterson yet again. But on appeal, the U.S. Supreme Court ordered a new trial in which blacks could not be excluded from the jury. In response, Alabama dropped all charges against four of the men and in 1937 freed them after six years in jail. In 1943, Alabama pardoned and released two more men. In 1948, the last remaining man in custody, Haywood Patterson, after spending 17 years in prison, escaped and fled north. When he was recaptured, the governor of Michigan denied his extradition back to Alabama.

Hammett also campaigned, through speeches, writing and fundraising, to support the Abraham Lincoln Brigade, to oppose Mississippi's arch segregationist, populist and Ku Klux Klan member, U.S. Senator Theodore Bilbo. He joined a committee to raise funds for Jewish war refugees. He joined Paul Robeson in publicly opposing police violence against black people and, when elected president of the New York Civil Rights Congress, asked that the New York City mayor "stop police brutalities toward blacks."[43]

In July 1936, General Francisco Franco, supported by the *falangists* (the Spanish aristocracy) and the Catholic Church, launched a military coup from his base in

Morocco against a freely and legally elected Republican government in Madrid. This ushered in four years of vicious civil war that may have killed as many as one million Spaniards and resulted in untold bloody atrocities. Spain constituted one of the last free countries in Europe after Germany, Austria, Hungary, Italy, Portugal, Romania, Slovakia, Estonia and Latvia had turned fascist. Hitler and Mussolini quickly moved to support Franco in Spain with troops and weapons. France and the Soviet Union supported the legitimate Spanish government but this proved no match for advanced German weapons, Italian planes and elite fighters.

In 1937, the U.S. Congress, at FDR's request, passed the Neutrality Act barring U.S. arms sales to Spain, a boon to the German and Italian fascists and American First sympathizers at home. Other Americans resisted. Two thousand eight hundred U.S. volunteers formed the Abraham Lincoln Brigade and traveled secretly and illegally to Spain at the request of the Spanish government to fight against fascism. American intellectuals joined the battle as well. Hemingway, Hellman and others visited Spain and brought back reports on the fighting. Hammett addressed one meeting after another, raising funds for the Republican cause. In 1937, he took the lead in organizing both the Motion Pictures Artists' Committee to Aid Republican Spain and the Hollywood Anti-Nazi League, which organized a rally that year with speakers Dorothy Parker and John Ford at L.A.'s Shrine Auditorium; 10,000 people attended to condemn Hitler's fifth anniversary in power.[44]

Hellman and Hemingway returned to America to narrate the film *The Spanish Earth* and tour the country, often with Hammett and other Hollywood notables, raising funds for the Republicans. MGM went to bat for the other side. In 1938 and '39, the company severely edited or stopped production on films that might offend Hitler or Mussolini and actually allowed the German consul in L.A. to preview films prior to their release. In at least one case, MGM sent a script, *Idiot's Delight*, to Mussolini's Rome prior to filming.[45] During the Spanish Civil War, Georg Gyssling, Nazi Consul General in Los Angeles, kept a list of fascist sympathizers. It listed Walt Disney and Gary Cooper along with Lewis Stone, who had played Andy Hardy's dad in Louis Mayer's favorite film series.[46] Franco won the war in 1939 and yet continued a war of repression, the White Terror, against his own people for the next decade. This "cleansing of society" resulted in some 50,000 summary executions and the imprisonment of 400,000 Spaniards in concentration camps.[47] George Packer wrote, "When Heinrich Himmler [Reichsfuhrer of the SS and prime architect of the Holocaust in Germany] visited Spain in 1940, a year after Franco's victory, he claimed to have been 'shocked' by the brutality of the Falangist repression."[48]

The Franco victory in Spain encouraged the fascists in Germany and Italy and soon led to World War II. But Hammett kept working. He spoke at Madison Square Garden in November 1938, at an anti–Nazi rally that attracted 22,000 inside (with another 6000 people listening outside on loudspeakers).[49] He wrote to his daughter Mary: "Your old man is becoming a talking fool: he spoke four times last week, an afternoon affair ... for Spain, at a dinner for the League for Peace and Democracy, at a Mecca Temple anti–Nazi mass meeting and over the radio for Jewish refugees.... I'm scheduled to go down to Washington for three speeches in two days."[50] In 1940, he chaired the Committee on Election Rights and in 1941 wrote letters for the Exiled Writers Committee to help anti–Nazi writers escape Germany. In 1939, he drafted the statement "In Defense of the Bill of Rights" and attracted 65 signers (scientists, writers and artists) to protest HUAC and

FBI raids on the CPUSA. He served as president of the Professionals Conference Against Nazi Persecution, protesting the treatment of Jews and other religious people in Germany. He helped launch the liberal newspaper *PM* in 1940,[51] with writers like Dorothy Parker, Lillian Hellman, I.F. Stone, Leo Huberman, James Thurber and Ben Hecht. Edited by Ralph Ingersoll and bankrolled by Marshall Field III, *PM* refused advertising in order to be free of business interests and grew to a circulation of 165,000.

The answer was in plain sight as to why Hammett stopped writing but his biographers and critics refused to take his political work seriously. He found his true calling in his work with the Communist Party and his work for racial justice. Marxism helped Hammett understand his own life and the society he lived in and to work towards the one he wanted to live in. Hellman wrote,

> For Hammett … Socialist belief had become a way of life and, although he was highly critical of many Marxist doctrines and their past and present practitioners, he shrugged them off … [H]e was a very critical Marxist, often contemptuous of the Soviet Union … [H]e said that of course a great deal about Communism worried him and always had and that when he found something better he intended to change his opinions.[52]

Hammett's life, as it unfurled during and after the international conflagration of World War II, can perhaps best be understood within the detective genre and the singular character he created: Sam Spade. Just two months before Pearl Harbor, Warner Brothers released the most famous film made from a Dashiell Hammett novel: Director John Huston's *The Maltese Falcon*, with an iconic cast of Humphrey Bogart, Mary Astor, Sydney Greenstreet and Peter Lorre. Hammett called Warners' first two Maltese Falcon movies (*The Maltese Falcon*, 1931, with Ricardo Cortez and *Satan Met a Lady*, 1936, with Warren William) "horrible jobs" in a letter to his daughter Jo[53] and much preferred the 1941 version. He wrote to his wife: "They made a pretty good picture of it this time, for a change."[54]

On-screen, Bogart immortalized Sam Spade, the detective Hammett had created, and as William Powell linked his career with Nick Charles for generations, so Bogart became Sam Spade for generations of movie fans. Bogart got his chance only because George Raft passed on the movie. The film made Bogie one of Hollywood's biggest stars. Memorable indeed are the novel's collection of villains: the femme fatale Bridget O'Shaughnessy, the gay partners in crime Joel Cairo and gunsel Wilmer Cook. They and many of the other characters are, Hammett tells us, drawn from real life, including my favorite, Kasper Gutman, as played by Greenstreet, based on someone who, Hammett wrote, "was suspected—foolishly, as most people were—of being a German secret agent in Washington, D. C., in the early days of the [World War I], and I never remember shadowing a man who bored me as much."[55] Hammett mixed fact and fiction, leaving us an indelible description of the obese Gutman (gut-man, get it?):

> The fat man was flabbily fat with bulbous pink cheeks and lips and chins, and neck, with a great soft egg of a belly that was all his torso, and pendant cones for arms and legs. As he advanced to meet Spade all his bulbs rose and shook and fell separately with each step, in the manner of clustered soap bubbles not yet released from the pipe through which they had been blown.[56]

Hammett modeled Bridget O'Shaughnessy, sexy and murderous, in part on Peggy O'Toole, who was his typist when he wrote advertising copy at Albert Samuels Jewelers in San Francisco, before breaking into fiction-writing.[57] Spade slept with O'Shaughnessy and Hammett slept with O'Toole. Mary Astor brings Bridget to seductive life. But it's Sam Spade, the hero or, more accurately, the morally conflicted anti-hero, whom we best remember. Both Spade and Bogart became synonymous with the hard-boiled, tough-talking, cynical gumshoes of all film noir literature to follow. Once again Hammett leaned on his experiences as a detective for his characters. He wrote in his introduction to the 1934 edition of the novel:

> Spade has no original. He is a dream man in the sense that he is what most of the private detectives I worked with would like to have been and in their cockier moments thought they approached. For your private detective does not—or did not ten years ago when he was my colleague—want to be an erudite solver of riddles in the Sherlock Holmes manner; he wants to be a hard and shifty fellow, able to take care of himself in any situation, able to get the best of anybody he comes in contact with, whether criminal, innocent by-stander or client.[58]

Hammett seemed to so strongly identify with Spade that he gave him his own first name of Samuel and wrote that Spade lived at 891 Post Street in San Francisco, exactly where Hammett lived when he wrote the novel and invented Spade. Spade also drinks a lot.[59] It's as if they were one and the same. While every writer puts a bit of themselves into their characters, Hammett's Spade gives us insight into the author's philosophy as do few others.

Most of us are familiar with the plot: Miss Wonderly, "a knockout," visits the office of private detective partners Miles Archer and Sam Spade ostensibly for help finding her sister Corinne, who ran away from her New York City home with one Floyd Thursby. Archer takes the case and decides to tail Thursby, who is in San Francisco. Archer is discovered shot dead in an alley, presumably by Thursby, and Spade decides to find his killer. Spade has been sleeping with Archer's wife Iva, whom he claims to detest, and, we infer, with his office secretary Effie Perine, and then with his client O'Shaughnessy. A man of seemingly little sentimentality, Spade has Archer's name scraped off his office door the day after his murder. Then Thursby is also found murdered and Spade becomes a suspect. Spade discovers that Miss Wonderly's real name is Brigid O'Shaughnessy and she leads him to her sometime accomplices Cairo, Gutman and Cook, who are each trying to cheat the other of their share in a stolen black bird statuette supposedly made of gold and precious gems. After serial double crosses, fisticuffs and another murder, they discover the Maltese Falcon is a worthless fake. Gutman takes off to find the real bird. Cook takes off to kill Gutman. Spade calls the police. He has figured out that O'Shaughnessy killed Archer because his partner would not have gone into a dark alley and turned his back on any member of this crew. She admits her guilt but claims to have fallen in love with Spade. Spade admits "Maybe you love me and maybe I love you,"[60] but, he explains, more is at stake: "When a man's partner is killed, he's supposed to do something about it."[61] He turns her over to the cops, adding "I won't play the sap for you."[62]

Some read, or, I think, misread, Spade as a sort of knight errant, a chivalrous man of honor in a world of evil. The usually hard-boiled Dorothy Parker admitted to swooning over Spade: "[I've gone] mooning about in a daze of love such as I had not known for any character in literature since I encountered Sir Launcelot at the age of nine."[63]

But Parker elides the clues in the text. It is not just that the protagonist of *The Maltese Falcon*, Spade, enters a corrupt world charged with fear, betrayal and violence, not just that the protagonist's actions, though they may solve a crime, will never change the degeneracy of the world itself, but also that the protagonist contains within himself all the contradictions, perversions and despair of the world at large. The chaos outside is the chaos within. Spade is not the usual virtuous hero; he is a deeply compromised and morally fallible human being. Drinking and smoking are outward signs of his inner morass. He cheats on his partner with Iva, has sex with Brigid even though he knows she killed Archer, and exploits Effie, even though he knows she is in love with him.

At the end of a classic detective story, a crime has been solved, a criminal apprehended, and the status quo ante has been restored: good trumps evil. But here the statue is a fake, on one level the thieves have themselves been duped, but the people they have killed to acquire this valueless bird are still quite dead. In *The Maltese Falcon*, nothing is really settled; Cairo, Cook and Brigid may be off to jail, Spade may go back to Iva, or not. The world is not a better place. Here good and evil keep co-existing and the readers' view of society as cesspool is confirmed.

Near the beginning of the novel, Hammett throws us a curve ball when Spade tells Brigid the Flitcraft story which appears in the novel but not in the movie. Like the Continental Op's dream in *Red Harvest* and the discussion of the cannibal Albert Packer in *The Thin Man*, the story does not advance the plot and seems to some critics like padding. However, we know that the Flitcraft story meant a lot to Hammett and that he had, in fact, told it earlier to his daughter Jo as they sat in the backyard of the family home, almost word for word as it would later appear in the novel.[64]

Hardboiled detective Sam Spade was created by Dashiell Hammett in his third novel, 1930's *The Maltese Falcon*. That story was filmed three times; the version we all know best is the 1941 movie directed by John Huston, with Humphrey Bogart and Mary Astor (pictured). Spade became a cultural icon.

The story, which may be based on one of Hammett's own Pinkerton cases, goes like this: A man named Flitcraft lived in Tacoma with a wife and two children and a successful real estate practice. He played golf with his business associates. One day he went out to lunch and never returned. "He went like that," Spade said, "like a fist when you open your hand."[65] Five years later, when Spade was working for a Seattle detective agency, Mrs. Flitcraft came in with news that someone had seen her husband in Spokane. Spade tracked down the man, who had changed his name to Charles Pierce. He had a wife and a baby and a successful auto sales business. He still played golf when he could.

Flitcraft tells the detective that one day just outside his Tacoma office, a steel beam fell ten stories from a construction project onto the pavement right next to him. He explained to Spade that the experience made him feel "like somebody had taken the lid off life and let him look at the works."[66] Hammett wrote:

> The life [Flitcraft] knew was a clean orderly sane responsible affair. Now a falling beam had shown him that life was fundamentally none of those things. He, the good citizen-husband-father, could be wiped out ... by the accident of a falling beam. He knew then that men died at haphazard like that, and lived only while blind chance spared them. ... Life could be ended ... at random by a falling beam; he would change his life at random by simply going away.[67]

Flitcraft took off with only the money in his wallet, wandered the northwest, then settled in Spokane, remarried and settled into a new life much like the one he had fled. Spade concludes the story with these lines: "[Flitcraft] adjusted himself to beams falling, and then no more of them fell, and he adjusted himself to them not falling."[68]

Brigid, who clearly has other things on her mind, responds in words that seem wholly insincere: "How perfectly fascinating."[69] They then drop the subject. Critics have debated the Flitcraft story ever since. Does it carry particular meaning for Hammett and Spade and, if so, what does it mean? Hammett includes hints in the story. Flitcraft is an unusual name. But a real person named A J. Flitcraft published *Flitcraft's Compendium*, an annual listing of American insurance companies, beginning in 1914. Insurance companies, of course, deal in probabilities and insurance is a form of wagering. Then, Hammett tells us in the story, Flitcraft changed his name to Charles Pierce, a fairly common first and last name, unlike Flitcraft. But the most famous person named Charles Pierce is the American philosopher (1839–1914) credited with founding the philosophical school of pragmatism. To boil down pragmatism to its essentials, this idea holds that efficacy and practical use help determine the value of a belief rather than abstract principles. Pierce also posited the thesis of Tychism, the idea that chance is a real operating force in the world.

Which leaves us with this idea: Hammett, as Spade, tells the Flitcraft story as the philosophy of detectives like themselves. Stuff happens, according to the story, and our job is to adapt to the changes wrought by it. This nicely fits the way Hammett tells the larger story: He wrote the novel from the third person limited point of view and all we read are what the characters do and say, not what they think or feel. This lends a vibrancy and verisimilitude to the characters, who remain unpredictable, just as real life is unpredictable. With the Flitcraft story, Spade is telling Brigid he knows she is lying to him and he knows she will lie to him again. She may look beautiful and she can spin fancy tales of being in jeopardy but she is also a murderess and someday he will make sure she pays a price for her crime.

Hammett shared Spade's pragmatism and his acceptance of Tychism. Though both could philander (Spade with Iva and Effie; Hammett with Laura Perelman and untold others), drink, smoke, gamble and lie, each also believed that within the seeming order but actual randomness of life are some truths worth looking for, some truths we create for ourselves, some truths worth sacrificing for. Spade sacrifices a potential relationship with the beautiful Brigid; Hammett gambles away his personal freedom to do what he believes is right even as he stands within a tiny minority. The final act of Hammett's life would have him embodying much of Spade's moral code while the man who brought Spade to filmic life, Humphrey Bogart, renounced it.

10

Three More *Thin Man* Sequels

The fourth in the Thin Man series, *Shadow of the Thin Man*, reunites collaborators from the first three movies: Powell and Loy, director W.S. Van Dyke (now credited on screen as "Major W.S. Van Dyke" due to his officer's commission in the Marine Corps), producer Hunt Stromberg and a Skippy as Asta, though no one is saying which Skippy. Hammett's name is listed in the credits as the originator of *The Thin Man* but he had nothing to do with this movie, having sold all rights to the characters of Nick and Nora to MGM for a cool $40,000. At the time, he was busy collaborating with Hellman on her anti-fascist play *Watch on the Rhine*.

Hackett and Goodrich also backed away from the project. Hackett told associates: "Finally I just threw up on my typewriter. I couldn't do it again. I couldn't write another one."[1] Goodrich added: "We had the nervous breakdown together … we said let's get out of here [and] we quit."[2] They wouldn't write another screenplay for five years. Loy shared their reluctance to return, saying of Hackett and Goodrich, "Perhaps we all should have concurred."[3] But the money was good and fans wanted more. As an MGM press release proclaimed, "Myrna Loy and William Powell are the ham and eggs, the peaches and cream, the salt and pepper of the movies. They go together as naturally as night and day."[4]

To inject new life into the formula, Stromberg chose Harry Kurnitz to write the original story and teamed him with Irving Brecher for the screenplay. Kurnitz (1908–68), originally a journalist and then a pulp mystery writer, already had four screenplays under his belt at MGM and would go on to write 30 more including *The Thin Man Goes Home*, fifth in the series. He also wrote plays, the best-known of which may be *A Shot in the Dark*, a Broadway stage success before it became a vehicle for Peter Sellers as Inspector Clouseau. Irving Brecher (1914–2008) had already written two Marx Brothers comedies, *At the Circus* (1939) and *Go West* (1940), and I am guessing he may have been largely responsible for the injection of physical humor which sets *Shadow of the Thin Man* apart from its predecessors.

We don't really watch a Thin Man to solve the mystery which is too often over-complicated and formulaic, as is the case here. A lot happens: Nick and Nora are back in San Francisco but seemingly downsized from the mansion and house staff we saw in *After the Thin Man*. Now they reside in a park-side apartment and make do with a single maid. The couple arrives at a race track as police discover a jockey dead from a bullet wound. They then take in a wrestling match which is shortly followed by two murders, making sure we get the requisite three deaths just like the earlier films. The theme of the movie seems to be corruption in the sports world though the film skims over what

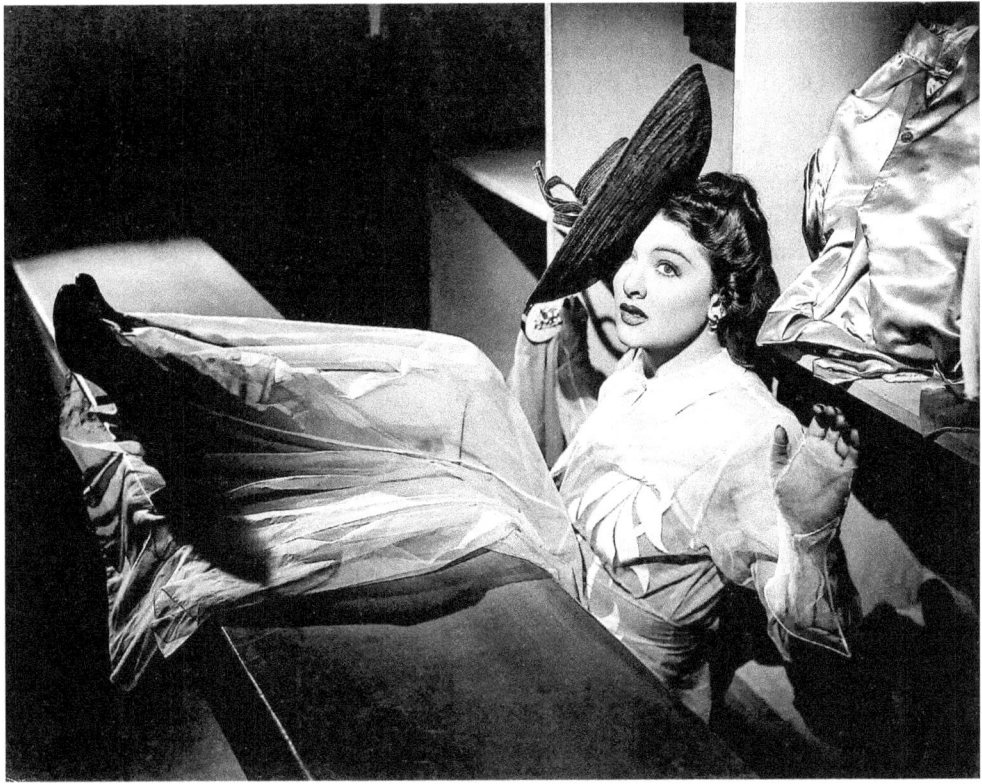

A new director and new writers may not have made the third Thin Man sequel, *Shadow of The Thin Man* (1941), better than its predecessors, but it did introduce more physical humor. Here the sophisticated and always well-dressed Nora Charles (Myrna Loy) takes a tumble.

could have been an interesting idea and reduces it to a wisecrack. When told the jockey may have been killed for throwing a race the day before, Nora says, "My, they're strict at this track."[5] Nick proves the jockey's death a suicide and, in the final scene at police headquarters, fingers the killer, as usual the least likely suspect. As he builds the tension and waits for the killer to give himself away, we get a great line:

>   NICK: "Well, gentlemen and ladies, we have our murderer."
>   NORA: "Nicky, I can't stand it. Was it me?"[6]

Like a Christmas tree upon which you hang colorful ornaments, the plot exists only for these embellishments of the sparkling Nick and Nora and the oddball collection of people who surround them. But that's just what we expect and want. Recalling the original *Thin Man* opening where Nora enters the speakeasy pulled by Asta on his leash, here we open with Nick strolling in the park, dog leash in hand. As the camera moves out, we see the leash is attached not to Asta but to a seven-year-old Nickie Jr. The camera moves back a bit more and we see that Nickie Jr. is also holding a leash … Asta's. We immediately know we are in good hands. For reasons unexplained, Nickie Jr. is wearing a military uniform. Have his parents sent him to a boarding school? Has Van Dyke chosen the costume to prepare the audience for the war to come? We know the director liked wearing his own uniform. Later we see Nickie Jr. in a sailor suit. We never learn why. Has he switched services?

Nickie Jr. is played by an earnestly cute Richard Dickie Hall, born Richard Merrill Hall in 1934, in his first film role; he went on to appear in a number of Our Gang comedies. There exists an on-set photo of Myrna Loy teaching Dickie to write during filming down time.[7] We do not know if this was mere Hollywood publicity or a regular undertaking by Ms. Loy. Hall may be the only actor from the Thin Man franchise still alive, if he *is* alive. Nick sits down on a park bench to read his son a story but quickly they shift to reading the daily racing form. When Nora, who has watched them through binoculars from their apartment balcony, begins preparing cocktails, Nick (several hundred yards away) says, "Nickie, something tells me that something important is happening somewhere and I think we should be there."[8] He leads his son home in time to snag a freshly made martini. At the table, Nora asks: "Did Daddy read you a story?"

NICKIE JR.: "Yes."
NORA: "Tell Mommy the story."
NICKIE JR.: "Son-of-a-Gun is 40 to 1."[9]

Nora tells their maid Stella (Louise Beavers), "[Nickie Jr. is] getting more like his father every day." She replies: "Yes, yesterday I found him playing with a corkscrew."[10] As the bodies begin to pile up, Nickie Jr. disappears from the film, leaving Nick and Nora room to operate.

The film offers something new, the physical humor seen here and again in *The Thin Man Goes Home*. We see Asta get stuck in a revolving door and go round and round. Later, Nick wobbles dizzily off a merry-go-round, and even Asta has to grab a fire hydrant to keep the world from spinning. Witnessing her first wrestling match, Nora gets so caught up in the ring action that she unthinkingly puts Nick, sitting beside her, in a head lock. When Nora and Molly exit a bar to follow Nick and Paul to the scene of a new murder, Nora tells the driver: "Follow that cab." He immediately does just that, driving off and leaving the two women standing on the sidewalk.[11]

We also see Nora developing as a detective in her own right. At night she follows Nick and Asta to the scene of the first killing. Later she tricks Maguire (Will Wright) into spilling the beans. At the end, when the killer grabs Nick's gun, Nora steals the scene by throwing herself between them. Then, unaware that Nick has removed the bullets from his gun, she attacks the killer to save her husband. Nora, as Hammett wrote in his original novel, really does have "hair on her chest."[12]

But for all the seriousness of the life-and-death action, the sexual banter happily remains in dialogue like this and its accompanying smirks:

NICK: "Mommy, [Nickie Jr. is] a great kid. I'm much obliged." Nora: "Oh, it was nothing. Any time."[13]

When Nora asks Nick to pick out a dress for their evening out we get this:

NORA: "Let's see if you can pick one winner for me, right now."
NICK: "What? A dress? Oh, sugar, winners are all I pick. Of course, here you are, right there. That's my favorite!"
NORA: "Oh, Nicky, that's a nightgown."
NICK: "It's still my favorite."[14]

The movie offers the usual fun in its collection of underworld misfits: the comically nervous Rainbow Benny (Lou Lubin), the hulking wrestler Jack the Ripper (Tor Johnson), Fingers (Sid Melton), Spider Webb (Joe Oakie) and the hapless mob lawyer Fenster

(Oliver Blake). Nick is seated next to Spider, a tiny, wiry, nervous little man, at the racetrack and we get this dialogue:

> "Spider" Webb: "Hiya, Nick."
> Nick: "Hiya, Spider."
> "Spider" Webb: "Where ya been? How come I ain't seen ya around?"
> Nick: "I've been around. Where you been?"
> "Spider" Webb: "I ain't been around."
> Nick: "No? In stir?"
> "Spider" Webb: "I was the victim of circumstances. The D.A. framed me, not knowin' I was guilty. Ain't that a coincidence?"
> Nick: "Yeah. Spider, I want you to meet Mrs. Charles. Dear, this is Spider Webb."
> "Spider" Webb: "You're Nick's wife?"
> Nora: "Yeah. Ain't that a coincidence?"[15]

See if you can spot future star Ava Gardner (1922–90) as an uncredited face in the crowd at that racetrack. Lieutenant Abrams returns as an inept investigator and we get to see the great stage actress and acting teacher Stella Adler in a rare film role as Claire, woman gone bad, all big eyes and beautiful, but a jailbird and another purveyor of the badger game, like Julia Wolf in the first Thin Man film. She and Nick have some nice barbed lines when he questions her movements on the night of one of the murders:

> Nick: "Why the detour?"
> Claire: "None of your business. I'm not on trial."
> Nick: "Not yet, you're not."[16]

and when she is a bit more coquettish:

> Claire Porter: "You're really not like a detective at all, Mr. Charles. You don't pound the table or shout or threaten."
> Nick: "I'm not really a detective. I just use that as an excuse to get out of the house at night."[17]

Barry Nelson as Paul Clarke and Donna Reed as Molly Ford, get none of the good lines and are dull-as-dishwater lovers.

We get also get Hollywood's usual dose of casual racism. The only black person on screen is the maid, Stella. Again we have Louise Beavers who, I have read, took the roles Hattie McDaniel didn't have time for, as if they were the only two black actresses available. They make poor Stella so dumb she says "telescope" when the word she wants is "telepathy." But never fear, Nick corrects her so we can all have a good laugh ... at her.

Shadow of the Thin Man was released in late November 1941, over the Thanksgiving holiday, and just two weeks before the attack on Pearl Harbor. The critics liked the film. According to *Variety*, "Much of the farcical flavor which characterized the earlier Thin Man films is reclaimed in the new picture. On the sentimental side, William Powell and Myrna Loy get a great deal of fun from their first appearance as parents of a four-year son [Hall was seven, according to his bio, when the film hit theaters], who has a way of asking embarrassing questions."[18] *The New York Times* critic wrote: "The Charleses, we're afraid, are settling down. Some of their former reckless *joie de vivre* is gone."[19] Looking back from 2014, Brian Eggert wrote in a review for the online site *Deep Focus*,

> Many might accuse ... *Shadow of the Thin Man* of feeling like an obligatory continuation, but the proceedings are no less delightful, funny, or suspenseful than the sequels before it.... After three entries, each following the same basic formula as the fourth, with just a change of

venue and shuffling of character, surely *Shadow of the Thin Man* doesn't feel like the freshest of sequels.[20]

According to MGM records, the film earned $1,453,000 in the U.S. and Canada and $848,000 elsewhere, resulting in a profit of $769,000. The darker John Huston version of Hammett's *Maltese Falcon*, released just weeks prior to *Shadow of the Thin Man*, made a much deeper and longer artistic impression.

Myrna Loy didn't think much of *Shadow of the Thin Man*, writing years later that she didn't remember much about it[21]: "[T]hose last three [Thin Man] films never really touched the previous ones."[22]

The lives and careers of some of the cast proved particularly colorful. Barry Nelson (1917–2007), born Robert Haakon Nielsen, the son of Norwegian immigrants, made his screen debut here, and concluded his career as the hotel manager who interviews Jack Nicholson for the job of caretaker in *The Shining* (1980).

Louise Beavers (1902–62) appeared in some 100 predominantly white-produced and -directed films, as the usual: slave, mammy, wise servant and advisor to a white employer. On TV she played the housekeeper on *The Danny Thomas Show*.

Donna Reed (1921–86), born Donna Belle Mullenger, changed her name to escape anti–German sentiment during World War II. She gained fame as James Stewart's wife in *It's a Wonderful Life* (1946) and in her eponymous TV series, which ran for eight seasons. Sickened by the War in Vietnam, she helped found Another Mother for Peace and campaigned against nuclear weapons. Like Myrna Loy, she supported anti-war candidate Senator Eugene McCarthy in his 1968 insurgent campaign against incumbent President Lyndon Johnson.

Shadow of the Thin Man was one of just three films featuring Stella Adler (1901–92), so it is really a treat to see her here. She began her career in the Yiddish theater in New York at the age of four and appeared in over 100 plays. In the 1930s, she joined Harold Clurman and Lee Strasberg in forming the Group Theater, putting on plays that spoke to contemporary social issues in a realistic way. She later taught at the New School in New York City and then founded her own acting school. Through her famous students, including Marlon Brando, she became one of the most influential acting teachers of her time.

Joseph Anthony (1912–93), born Joseph Deuster, is the weasel-faced Fred Macy. You'd never guess he was also a playwright and a stage director for several Broadway hits (he was nominated five times for Tony Awards for Best Director). He directed the play *The Rainmaker* and the 1956 movie with Burt Lancaster and Katharine Hepburn. When Anthony first went to California in the 1930s looking for acting work, he said he was "virtually penniless…, living in the countryside with a stolen stage drape for shelter and eating fruit and avocados from orchards."[23]

Adeline De Walt Reynolds (1862–1961) plays a landlady. She made her film debut in 1941 at the age of 78. *Shadow of the Thin Man* was only her second film. Born during the Civil War, Reynolds survived the San Francisco earthquake and, after raising four children as a widow, enrolled in UC Berkeley and graduated with honors at the age of 68.[24]

Tor Johnson (1902–71), born Karl Erik Tore Johansson in Sweden, appears uncredited as wrestler Jack the Ripper. He was, in fact, a professional wrestler, tipping the scales at 440 pounds. He appeared in films as a strongman, wrestler or tough guy. His most famous role was in the infamous *Plan 9 From Outer Space* (1958) as a police inspector turned zombie. This film, written, produced, edited and directed by Ed Wood, has the distinction, in the opinion of many, of having the worst script, the worst acting, the worst costumes and the worst special effects of any science fiction–horror film ever made and, therefore, it is hilarious. The story of oddball Ed Wood and his equally odd movies is told in the 1994 film *Ed Wood*.

At least one cast member came to a sad end. Frankie Burke (1915–83), born Francis Vaselle Aiello, plays a jockey. His film career lasted but three years, and his last film

The train is leaving the station and the fun is being drained from the Thin Man in sequel #4, *The Thin Man Goes Home* (1945).

role was in *Shadow of the Thin Man*. Because he bore a physical resemblance to a young Jimmy Cagney, he got the role of young Rocky in the 1938 Warner Brothers film *Angels with Dirty Faces* in which Cagney played Rocky Sullivan. His online obituary says that after his divorce, he became a hobo and rode the rails until near death. Discovered gravely ill on a train in Kansas, he was taken to a local hospital where he died.[25]

Irving Brecher (1914–2008), co-writer of *Shadow of the Thin Man,* found success in radio, television and film as a comedy writer. Working as an usher in a New York movie house as a young man, he sent one-liners to Walter Winchell and Ed Sullivan. He famously placed an ad in *Variety* looking for work, promising he could write "jokes so bad, even Milton Berle wouldn't steal them." He was promptly hired by Berle himself.[26]

I dreaded seeing *The Thin Man Goes Home*, the penultimate Thin Man, which has Nick and Nora visiting Nick's white bread WASP parents. They seem like refugees from an Andy Hardy movie. The urban and urbane Charleses are fish out of water in this whistle stop town. They even took Nick's booze away. The film's sole enduring charm lay with Myrna Loy as Nora, and William Powell as Nick, constant stars in a darkening wartime sky.

What happened to the Nick Charles of immigrant Greek parents named Charlambides who had their names changed as they disembarked at Ellis Island? Now we get Dr. Bertram Charles and his wife Marta, known to one and all as simply "Mrs. Charles" in Sycamore Springs, rather than the exotics of *Zorba the Greek* or *My Big Fat Greek Wedding.* Think of the lost possibilities. Of course, the wholesome Andy Hardy series, starring the less than wholesome Mickey Rooney, was a favorite of Louis B. Mayer, a Russian immigrant who had changed his birth name from Lazar Meir and who went around assuring everyone: "The best pictures ever were the Andy Hardy series."[27] And the movie throws in a bit of Freudian hoo-doo: Nick suffers from never having won his father's approval. The old doctor always wanted his son to follow in his medical footsteps rather than become just "a policeman." Is this why Nick drinks too much?

Robert Riskin wrote the script with his brother Everett (the latter uncredited). Robert found the job "dreadfully dull" as he wrote to his wife, actress Fay Wray.[28] Everett decided that due to wartime liquor rationing, booze would be banned from the script and replaced with … apple cider.[29] Which leads to a bit of banter:

NORA: "Nicky, do you really like cider?"
NICK: "Like it? I love it. Just the pure, natural juice of the apple. What could be better, for example?"
NORA: "A dry martini, for instance?"
NICK: "Mmmm. That horrible stuff? Almost took the lining off my stomach."
NORA: "Well, if you cared, it didn't show."[30]

As the critic Ed Sikov pointed out: "[T]he transformation of a drunken malcontent to a self-possessed man of the world is cause for celebration; in a series of dark detective comedies, it's deadening."[31]

Thank the film gods, the writers omitted Nickie Jr. He's now in kindergarten and his studies are not to be disturbed, so Nick and Nora have left him behind in the city. We don't miss him. But wouldn't Nickie Jr.'s grandparents, Nick's parents, have wanted to see him? I guess they share our sentiments since they never ask about him.

Of course, as soon as Nick and Nora hit town, every person in Sycamore Springs is sure Nick is working on a case rather than taking a vacation. But soon someone is murdered and they die just as they are approaching Nick at his father's front door.

So, naturally, Nick does go to work finding the killer. The plot involves a painting, military secrets, a local factory manufacturing war materials, spies and "Crazy Mary," a deranged woman living in a shack in the woods. As in all previous Thin Man movies, three people are murdered and Nick solves the case when he gathers all the suspects together at the end and explains the plot in mind-numbing detail. Dr. Charles has his eyes opened to his son's real skills and intelligence and, literally, pats him on the back, causing Nick to, also literally, pop a vest button in pride as father and son reconcile in mutual admiration.

Some bits work. The film opens, as do all Thin Man movies, at a train station. But America is at war: there are lots of people in uniform and the train is packed. When a conductor orders Nick and Nora to take Asta to the baggage car, they must run a gauntlet of packed aisles. Hoping to make progress, Nick asks Nora to "rub people the right way."[32] At his folks' home, Nick relaxes in a hammock while Nora struggles humorously to set up a folding chair for herself. Nick, not moving a muscle, says "Oh, I'll help you," Nora replies: "Don't bother, you might get all sweaty and die."[33]

The banter and double entendre remain as when Nick tries to retrieve the painting:

NICK: "Wait here."
NORA: "Where are you going?"
NICK: "I want to do a little business with a blonde."
NORA: "Do you think she'll give it to you?"
NICK: "Well, I can try, darling. Anything for art."[34]

But the love remains:

NICK: "A couple of weeks on this cider and I'll be a new man."
NORA: "I sort of like the old one."
NICK: "Why, darling, that's the nicest thing you've said to me since the time I got my head caught in that cuspidor at the Waldorf."

The new screenwriters get some things wrong, like a scene of Nick spanking Nora in front of his parents after she has hinted to the press that Nick is in town on a case.

NICK: "Now you're going to get it! You're going to get it."
NORA: "Oh, no, Nick, not here in front of your parents!"
NICK [bends Nora over and spanks her with a newspaper as he quotes her statement to the press]: "'But you can draw your own conclusions!'"
NORA: "Ouch! Nicky!"
NICK: "This will teach you the power of the press!"
NORA: "Oh! A fine son you brought up. A wife-beater!"
DR. CHARLES: "A brave boy! [*Laughs*] I wanted to do that to Mother for 40 years."
MRS. CHARLES: "I dare you!"[35]

If Nick ever tried this with the Nora we know from the novel and from previous movies, the next scene would feature Nora standing over his body with a knife.

Production of *The Thin Man Goes Home* had been planned for 1942, but Myrna Loy refused the role, having decided to spend all her energy and time on her war work with the USO, the Hollywood Canteen and the Red Cross. She had also recently married John D. Hertz Jr. (1908–68), heir to the Hertz car rental fortune. This, her second marriage, proved stormy in the extreme and they divorced two years later. In the meantime, MGM did their usual dance of floating names of replacement actresses, including Irene Dunne. Film critic Roger Fristoe quotes Powell recalling later, "The fans wanted Myrna, and they didn't want anyone else.... And I wanted Myrna, too. Besides the favorable reception our pictures always received, I must say it was certainly a pleasure to work with her." Powell was so delighted with the return of his co-star that he arranged to meet Loy when she arrived in Pasadena by train. He even borrowed Asta from the studio and took the pooch along for the reunion. Observing that Loy looked tired and thin, he told her that the studio might change the title of the picture to *The Thin Woman Comes Home*. When Loy arrived at MGM for her first day's work on the film, she was greeted by banners reading WELCOME HOME, MYRNA and DON'T LEAVE US AGAIN, MYRNA. "I've never seen a girl so popular with so many people," Powell recalled. "Everybody from wardrobe was over the set, everybody from makeup, everybody from property, everybody from miles around, it looked like."[36]

The Thin Man Goes Home was Loy's only wartime picture. Afterwards, she threw herself back into work with the USO and the Red Cross. In the movie, Loy is as lithe and nimble as ever, in one scene jitterbugging with Arthur Walsh, "the national jitterbug king." Loy said of the scene: "Arthur is doing all the work. I just follow him around and do a lot of faking."[37]

The other stars have aged and slowed: Skippy posed as Asta for close-ups but two younger dogs were brought in for the leaping and running about. Powell's added girth seems to make movement ponderous for him. There are two black people, a railroad porter and a maid; neither gets a word of dialogue.

Richard Thorpe directed the film. This was the first Thin Man not directed by W.S. Van Dyke, who died in 1943. Thorpe (1896–1991), like Van Dyke, worked quickly and efficiently, which saved the studio money, but he didn't have Van Dyke's eye or gift for spontaneity. Actor James Mason, who worked under Thorpe's direction on *The Prisoner of Zenda* (1952), noted of Thorpe's many forgettable movies, "His reputation for requiring only one take is why we don't remember his films."[38]

Everett Riskin replaced Hunt Stromberg, producer of the previous Thin Man films, and pressed his brother Robert into service to cowrite the screenplay with Dwight Taylor. Robert (1897–1955), who had already garnered four Oscar nominations, winning one for Best Writing Adaptation for *It Happened One Night* (1934), may have felt the material beneath him. Hollywood, as they say, is a small town and Robert had dated Carole Lombard (some suggest while she and Powell were still married[39]).

Besides Powell, Loy and Skippy the cast included a number of noted actors whose biographies open a window into Hollywood history and America's past.

Lucile Watson (1879–1962) plays Mrs. Charles, Nick's mother. Her obituary in *The Redlands Daily Facts* notes that she was known for playing formidable dowagers.[40] Watson worked primarily on stage and appeared on Broadway in nearly 40 plays, including Lillian Hellman's *Watch on the Rhine*; she was also in the film version of that play, scripted by Dashiell Hammett.

Gloria DeHaven (1925–2016) plays the ingenue Laura Ronson. She began her career as a child actor in an uncredited part in Charlie Chaplin's *Modern Times* (1936). She sang in her own nightclub act and appeared in films and on TV, including 30 episodes of *Mary Hartman, Mary Hartman* as Annie Wylie.

Anne Revere (1903–1990), who plays "Crazy Mary," is the most accomplished actor of this cast. A descendent of Paul Revere, she won an Academy Award for Best Supporting Actress for *National Velvet* in 1945 and garnered two other nominations, each for portraying mothers. She got her big break on the stage acting in Lillian Hellman's play *The Children's Hour* and later appeared in Hellman's *Toys in the Attic*, for which she won a Tony. She invoked the Fifth Amendment rather than testify before the House UnAmerican Activities Committee and was blacklisted for 11 years before being able to return to acting on TV soap operas in the 1960s. In a 1975 interview, she said of that time: "Nobody went to jail because they were Communists. They went to jail for contempt. But the awful thing about the whole bloody era was that whether you answered or didn't, cooperated or not, you were dead in the business."[41]

Helen Vinson (1907–99), born Helen Rulfs, plays Helena Draque. She first appeared on film with William Powell in *Jewel Robbery* (1932) and again with Powell in *The Kennel Murder Case* (1933). *The Thin Man Goes Home* was her final role before retirement. She was typecast as the "other woman"; her obituary in *The Guardian* describes Vinson as a "tall, slender, cool blonde."[42]

Harry Davenport (1866–1949) plays Nick's father. He appeared in some 100 films, often in starched shirt roles as a grandfather, judge, doctor or minister. According to his obituary in *The Toronto Blade*, he had the longest acting career in American history.[43] He had made his stage debut at the age of five and was still working in film at the time of his death, for a career of 78 years. He helped found Actors Equity, known as the White Rats at its inception, which struggled to win actors a six-day work week and dressing rooms with indoor plumbing.[44]

Leon Ames (1902–93), born Harry Wycoff, began acting on the stage and then made his film debut in 1931. He appeared in nearly 100 films, including the next Thin Man sequel, *Song of the Thin Man*. He took a leading role in organizing the Screen Actors Guild, upset that actors "were treated like cattle, you had no place to sit down … whoever heard of food—you bring your own lunch, if you could."[45]

Born in Scotland, Donald Meek (1878–1946) acted on stage, including on Broadway, and in 100 films including *Stagecoach* (1939) with John Wayne and in *Double Wedding* (1937) with Powell and Loy.

Edward Brophy (1895–1960), here as Brogan, was a veteran of the first Thin Man movie, where he played shady character Joe Morelli. He appeared in many of the Falcon series of detective movies and some 150 films in all over a 40-year career (1920 to 1960).

Lloyd Corrigan (1900–69) appeared in some 100 films but also directed another 14 and wrote 30 more, including three of the Fu Manchu movies.

Irish-born Anita Sharp-Bolster (1895–1985) appeared in some 80 films. In his book *The Films of Agnes Moorehead*, Axel Nissen calls Bolster "one of the most riveting human gargoyles in Hollywood films," noting the actress' "distinctively sharp nosed face and angular physiognomy."[46]

Ralph Brooks (1904–1991), born Charles Emil Muller, was a supporting actor or extra in over 350 movies and TV shows. He achieved film immortality in 1953 as Private Wilhelm in *The Charge at Feather River* who was shot in the leg with an arrow and let out a distinctive piercing scream. Motion picture sound designer Ben Burtt discovered the original recording and named it "The Wilhelm Scream," and it has now been used as a stock sound effect in film and on TV, including all the *Star Wars* movies.

Donald MacBride (1893–1957) began his career as a teenage singer in vaudeville, appeared on stage and then moved to films, often portraying a detective, usually a comic one. He also had comedy roles opposite the Marx Brothers and Abbott and Costello.

Morris Ankrum (1896–1964), born Morris Nussbaum, began his career teaching Economics at USC, switched to teaching Drama and then began acting in films and on

TV. He had a recurring role on the TV show *Mackenzie's Raiders* and was seen in 22 episodes of *Perry Mason* as the judge.

Nora Cecil (1878–1951) began on the stage, appearing first in London at the age of 19. She was in nearly 100 Hollywood films, including the John Wayne in *Stagecoach*.

Character actor Minor Watson (1889–1965) acted on the Broadway stage and appeared in 111 films. He played Clark Lewis in 1934's *Mister Dynamite*, based on a story by Dashiell Hammett.

The Thin Man Goes Home premiered in New York City on November 21, 1944, with wide release in early 1945. It's interesting that Thin Man releases often occurred over the Thanksgiving or Christmas holidays. According to MGM records, it earned $1,770,000 in the U.S. and Canada, and $1,044,000 elsewhere, resulting in a profit of $501,000. No *Thin Man* picture ever lost money. But, the critics grew weary of the repetitive material. *Variety* opined: "Production as a whole ... lacks much of the sophistication and smartness which characterized the early Thin Man films. Deficiency is mainly in the dialog and other business provided for the two leads.... Myrna Loy, while graceful and piquant for the most part, photographs unattractively in a number of sequences."[47] *Time Magazine* opined, "[T]he fifth time around the three of them [Powell, Loy and Asta] still guarantee a pleasant excuse for putting off household repairs and serious reading."[48]

The Thin Man series came to an end with *Song of the Thin Man* in 1947. During its run (1934-47), the world had passed through the depths of the Depression, fought World War II, entered the nuclear age and then a new Cold War that threatened the very future of life on Earth. Nick and Nora Charles struggled to survive before an American audience beginning its love affair with television as the movie industry faced court judgments to break up their vertical monopolies from studios to theaters. Dashiell Hammett had mustered out of honorable service in the U.S. Army for the second time and tumbled into a political witch hunt.

In an effort to adapt to changing times, while retaining all the previous charms of the series, MGM made several missteps that ultimately insured the end of the franchise. Powell and Loy returned but the studio sought a new producer, a new director and new writers, and there was a misguided attempt at cultural relevancy through "hep cat" jazz musicians. But the use of hipster slang from 1947 limited the shelf life of the film.

MGM tapped Nat Perrin (1905–98) to produce. Perrin did a bit of everything in Hollywood: gag writer to the Marx Brothers, screenwriter of some 25 films, producer and director; his longest gig was as TV producer working on *Death Valley Days* (1952–70) and *The Addams Family* (1964–66). He also co-wrote *Song of The Thin Man* with Steve Fisher from a story by Stanley Roberts.

To ingratiate Nick and Nora with a postwar audience, the writers leaned on real life jazz pianist Harry "The Hipster" Gibson (1915–91), born Harry Raab, as the model for the movie's cool cat supporting character Clarence "Clinker" Krause, played by Keenan Wynn as a jive-talking bebop musician who ushers a decidedly unhip Nick and Nora into the beatnik *demimonde*. Though classically trained at Juilliard, Gibson found his *métier* in the clubs and on the streets of Harlem. He put a white face on black music and made it acceptable to a white audience. In 1946, Gibson recorded the hilarious "Who Put the Benzedrine in Mrs. Murphy's Ovaltine?" which got him banned from several radio stations.[49] However the contemporaneity of the film's jazz argot and music just emphasized how out-of-date and out-of-place Nick and Nora had become in the postwar era.

10. Three More Thin Man Sequels

Keenan Wynn gives out with some jive... loads of laughs... and some clues... in the newest Thin Man adventure!

The Thin Man franchise wheezed to a collapse in the fifth and final sequel, *Song of The Thin Man* (1947), as MGM kept aging parents Nick and Nora out all night in supposed jazz dens and buried them in jive talk and hipster slang—all of it obsolete by the time the film hit the theaters. In the foreground, from left, are William Powell, Myrna Loy and Keenan Wynn.

The film opens with Nick and Nora attending a charity benefit on the gambling ship S.S. *Fortune*. We see a host of handsome musicians and a very attractive singer, Fran Page (Gloria Grahame). Bandleader Tommy Drake (Phillip Reed) tells *Fortune* owner Phil Brant (Bruce Cowling) that he is leaving for a better job. Tommy soon turns up dead. Who did it? Investigators Nick and Nora have a raft of suspects who all seem to have motives and complex interrelationships. Then Fran Page is murdered with a knife in the back. For the sixth time in six films, we will wind up at the end with the three murders—but for a change, not all are the work of a single killer.

Powell's girth means Nick can no longer be mistaken for the Thin Man of the title and he appears old enough to be Nickie Jr.'s *grand*father. More attention is paid to the detecting in this script, with more mystery and red herrings. The cool young Nick and Nora of the first films are now older, "out of it," and they no longer stay up all night clubbing. Someone fires into the Charleses' apartment trying to kill Brant, but hits a champagne bottle instead. When police arrive and ask if everyone is all right, Nick replies "No ... an old friend went to pieces."[50]

This film featuring jazz musicians, singers and audiences in smoky after-hours jazz clubs features no black performers. Loy called *Song of the Thin Man* "a lackluster finish to a great series. I hated it. The characters had lost their sparkle for Bill and me, and the people who knew what it was all about were no longer involved. Woody Van Dyke was dead. Dashiell Hammett and Hunt Stromberg had gone elsewhere. The Hacketts were writing other things."[51] Even Skippy was gone, having died the year before. He was replaced by Skippy Jr. or Skippy III, and doubled by brother Zip. He still had his own dressing room.[52] In one nostalgic shot, Asta rises on his rear legs and, planned or not, we see his erection, reminding us of Nick's censored response to wrestling with Mimi in Hammett's novel that began it all.

The jive talk dates the production. This is Keenan Wynn as Clinker:

NICK CHARLES: "Where can I find this whacked-up character?"
CLARENCE "CLINKER" KRAUSE: "Oh, he's been bouncin' around from place to place lately. You'll probably dig him in one of the jam joints."
NICK: "Come again?"
"CLINKER": "Dig him in one of the jam joints! Where the boys go after closin' and really ride. Just for cats and intellectuals. The rooty-toots and bobbysoxers verboten. Solid."
NICK: "Well, I don't wear bobbysox; but, would you say I'm a rooty-toot?"
"CLINKER": "Strictly. But I guess I can ace you in."[53]

But the connubial *double entendres* still works:

NICK: "If the party gets rough, duck."
NORA: "I'm practically under the table now, but not the way I like to be."[54]

And when Nick and Nora encounter the beautiful Phyllis Talbin:

NORA [looking at Phyllis Talbin]: "Stunning jewelry. Those earrings."
NICK [also looking]: "Very attractive!"
NORA: "The earrings are higher up."[55]

But their own spark still flames:

NICK: "I got a great idea."
NORA: "What is it?"
NICK: "Let's go home."
NORA: "What's at home?"
NICK: "You, my pipe, my slippers."
NORA: "Nicky, you're slipping."
NICK: "Darling, give me my pipe, slippers and a beautiful woman … and you can keep the pipe and slippers."[56]

Nick still runs into mugs of the lower order, as when two ex-cons case the gambling ship:

MUG #1: "Gee, we sure get a gentrier plateau with these charity shindigs."
MUG #2: "Especially the dames. What class! What refinement! What cultured tomatoes! Hey, get a load of that one. Yoo-hoo!"
NICK CHARLES [turning around to face the mugs]: Boys, boys, in polite society, we don't say, 'Yoo-hoo.' We say 'Yoo-whom.'"[57]

At the breakfast table reading the comics, we see that Nickie Jr. takes after his old man in several ways:

NICKIE JR.: "I knew Roy shouldn't have trusted that Arsenic Annie. She's a man dressed in woman's clothes."

NICK: "Annie's a man?"
NICKIE JR.: "Sure. It's a dead giveaway. A dame would never pass a mirror like that without looking to see if her slip was showing."
NORA: "Dame?"
NICKIE JR.: "Well, that's what Daddy always says."
NICK: "I never say *dame*. I always say *doll*—eh, *dish*. Well, anyway, it was a very shrewd deduction."[58]

As Nick and Asta hunt the murderer:

ASTA [sniffing the floor while Nick searches for clues]: "Arrr. Arrrrrrrrrr."
NICK: "What's the excitement, boy? Huh? It's just a razor blade. No. No, it couldn't have been Somerset Maugham."[59]

Get it? *The Razor's Edge,* the 1944 Maugham novel! How many in the movie theater had read that?

The film's last lines prove prescient as the franchise lurches to its conclusion:

NICK: "Now Nick Charles is going to retire."
NORA: "Are you through with crime?"
NICK: "No, I'm going to bed."[60]

And that was all they wrote.

The cast featured notable actors, especially Keenan Wynn (1916–86), born Francis Xavier Aloysius James Jeremiah Keenan Wynn. He was the son of one of my favorite actors, Ed Wynn. Keenan appeared on the Broadway stage and in hundreds of movies and TV shows, on occasion sharing billing with his father. According to later reporting, Wynn "was involved in one of the strangest *menage a trois* in film history when his wife Eve Abbott divorced him and immediately married his best friend and fellow actor Van Johnson." Decades later, Abbott claimed that MGM had persuaded her to marry Johnson, one of their top stars of the '40s. "They needed their 'big star' to be married to quell rumors about his sexual preferences," she said, "and unfortunately, I was 'It'—the only woman he would marry."[61]

Dean Stockwell (1936–2021), here as Nick Charles, Jr., had 15 movies under his belt by the age of 15. His other films included *Gentleman's Agreement, Compulsion, Paris, Texas, Dune* and *Married to the Mob,* for which he received a Best Supporting Actor nomination. Of his work on *Song of The Thin Man*, he recalled: "[Powell and Loy] were very sweet people, especially Myrna Loy. And that cute little Asta. I liked that little dog."[62] Overall, however, he did not enjoy his time as a child actor, telling one interviewer: "I had no friends, except for my brother, and I never did what I wanted to do. I had one vacation in nine years."[63]

Patricia Moriso (1915–2018), born Ursula Eileen Patricia Augustus Fraser Morrison, appears as the beautiful Phyllis. She transitioned from an early career as a singer to film acting and often played a femme fatale. She appeared in director Henry Hathaway's thriller *Kiss of Death* (1947) but her character was raped and then killed herself; the Production Code would not allow rape or suicide to be shown on film and therefore her scenes were cut.[64] Some of her greatest triumphs came on stage where she created the role of Lilli Vanessi/Kate in *Kiss Me Kate*, the Cole Porter musical (1000 performances). In retirement she took up painting but returned to the stage for special events at the age of 97 and 99. She died at age 103. On the whole, these film actors lived long lives, perhaps due to their financial status and access to good medical care.[65]

Gloria Grahame (1923–1981), born Gloria Hallward, is here as singer Fran Ledue Page, though her singing voice was dubbed by Carol Arden. *Song of the Thin Man* was just her sixth of 40 film roles; she won an Academy Award for Best Supporting Actress for MGM's *The Bad and the Beautiful*. Grahame was typecast as a femme fatale; critic Rex Reed said of her: "She was sultry, sexy, beautiful and very, very bad.... When she was good she was great but when she was bad she was even better."[66] Grahame joined Myrna Loy in campaigning for Adlai Stevenson for president in 1952. Her possibly preventable death at age 58 lies at the center of the book and film *Film Stars Don't Die in Liverpool*.

Jayne Meadows (1919–2015), born Jayne Meadows Cotter, was the daughter of American missionaries in China. She acted in some 100 films and TV shows. In her obituary, *The New York Times* called her "a glamorous redheaded actress."[67] Her younger sister Audrey achieved a level of TV immortality as Alice Kramden on the iconic show *The Honeymooners* playing the wife of bus driver Ralph Kramden (Jackie Gleason); Jayne, married in real life to comic Steve Allen, also succeeded on TV as a panelist on *I've Got a Secret* and as a guest on the popular shows *Fantasy Island*, *Hawaii Five-0* and *The Love Boat*.

Leon Ames appeared in many films, including *Meet Me in St. Louis* and *The Postman Always Rings Twice*. His last role was in *Peggy Sue Got Married* as the grandfather to Kathleen Turner's Peggy Sue. He once said he thought William Powell was bored with his role in *Song of the Thin Man*.[68] Ames helped found the Screen Actors Guild and served a term as its president. He joined the cast of the TV show *Mister Ed* as Colonel Gordon Kirkwood, neighbor to the talking horse's owner Wilbur Post. Ames and his wife made the tabloid headlines when they were kidnapped in a home invasion in 1964 but were released unhurt upon payment of a $50,000 ransom.[69]

Ralph Morgan (1883–1956), born Raphael Kuhner Wuppermann, graduated from Columbia Law School but, after two years of legal practice, left the profession for a show business career. Another co-founder of the Screen Actors Guild, he appeared in *Star of Midnight* with Powell and Ginger Rogers. As Ralph's career took off, his younger brother Frank assumed the stage name of Morgan as well and entered films, playing the Wizard in *The Wizard of Oz*.

Also in the cast is Bess Flowers (1898–1984). She ultimately became known as "The Queen of the Hollywood Extras" for her small roles in more than 1000 films. She helped found the Screen Extras Guild. Connie Gilchrist (1895–1985) appeared in some 100 films and also joined Myrna Loy in campaigning for Adlai Stevenson.

Henry Nemo (1909–1999) appears as "The Neem," a composer and bandleader. He showcased his jive talk in the 1940 movie *The Neem* and may have been the model for the hip fish Charlie in the "Sorry, Charlie" StarKist Tuna TV commercials.[70]

Director Edward Buzzell (1897–1985) started as an actor and moved behind the camera. He directed two Marx Brothers films, *At the Circus* and *Go West*, but no films of real distinction.

Song of the Thin Man made less money than the other Thin Man movies and MGM decided to retire the franchise. It cost a million dollars to make and returned a profit of $500,000 but half a million dollars wasn't what it had been 13 years earlier.[71] Loy wrote that she thought the film actually lost money for MGM.[72] *The New York Times* offered a lukewarm review: "William Powell and Myrna Loy exhibit the same old zest and bantering affection they have always brought to their performances of the Charleses.... While *Song of the Thin Man* is no world beater, it still is a mighty pleasant picture to have around."[73] Looking back 60 years later Brian Eggert in *Deep Focus Review* lauded the film:

> [It] belongs among the best of Metro-Goldwyn-Mayer's six-film franchise, ranking just behind *The Thin Man* and its first sequel, *After the Thin Man*. With its tightly constructed mystery and witty repartee standing as some of the best in the series, this sixth entry of "mirth and murder" disproves the theory that sequels only get worse as they go on.... Albeit an unofficial goodbye, the series could've hardly asked for a finer send-off.[74]

Loy also wrote,

> According to the *Hollywood Reporter*, "Most of the cricks gave a cordial welcome to old-timers Bill Powell and Myrna Loy." I know that only because Bill sent me the article with "old-timers" circled in pencil and this note scrawled at the top of the page: "Dear old girl! I know you wouldn't want to miss this! Love, Willy (old boy)."[75]

Nick and Nora found life in other media, first in radio via *The Adventures of the Thin Man* (1941–50) for some 300 episodes. On TV, NBC's *The Thin Man* ran two seasons (1957 to 1959) with Peter Lawford and Phyllis Kirk as Nick and Nora. There were 72 episodes. The show included Asta, but wisely dropped Nickie Jr. and featured less drinking. In 1975, Craig Stevens and Jo Ann Pflug starred in the made-for-TV movie *Nick and Nora*, part of the *Wide World of Mystery* series of TV movies. The pilot was not picked up as a series. But fans still saw plenty of imitation Nicks and Noras on the TV shows *McMillan & Wife* and *Hart to Hart*, which aped Hammett's creation of a crimefighting husband-wife duo.

In 1991, veteran Broadway writer Arthur Laurents joined lyricist Richard Maltby, Jr., and composer Charles Strouse to create the musical *Nick and Nora*. Barry Bostwick played Nick, Joanna Gleason played Nora, and the show bombed and folded after just nine performances. Theater critic Pat Collins wrote, "If anything would drive an audience to drink it would be this ... [C]liche plot and dull score."[76] A stage production of *The Thin Man* opened in 2009 at the City Literature Theatre in Chicago; in 2018, Vertigo Theatre in Calgary, Canada, premiered an adaptation of *The Thin Man* by playwright Lucia Frangione. Neil Simon wrote a spoof of the noir genre, the 1976 movie *Murder by Death* with David Niven as detective Dick Charleston and Maggie Smith as his wife Dora.

In 2011, a Warner Brothers film version of *The Thin Man* with Johnny Depp as Nick was in development. The part of Nora had not been cast when the project was shelved. Hammett could never have imagined the long and illustrious careers of Nick and Nora when he created that "insufferably smug" couple 90 years ago.

11

Hammett, Act IV

Hollywood had a Hitler problem in the 1930s. By and large, Jews ran the studios and owned the chains of movie theaters but they, like all American businessmen, knew that Germany, even under the Nazis, was a valuable market for American goods. The U.S. studios shipped 20 to 60 new American films each year to the Third Reich right up until Germany and the U.S. went to war.[1] Hitler loved American movies and watched a movie every night before going to bed.[2] The Nazis not only watched U.S. films, they had the clout to censor them as well. They organized a boycott of the pacifist film *All Quiet on the Western Front* as early as 1930, before even coming to power, until Universal made cuts in it to satisfy them. In fact, to keep Hitler happy, Universal made cuts in the film in screenings all around the world. That began a trend, Ben Urwand wrote in his book *The Collaboration: Hollywood's Pact with Hitler*: "[A]ll the Hollywood studios started making deep concessions to the German government."[3]

It got worse with the Nazis in power after 1933. They sent a special consul, Georg Gyssling, a member of the Nazi Party, to L.A. to work with the U.S. studios. In 1933, under pressure, U.S. film companies pulled Jewish sales employees from Germany.[4] *Variety* reported: "US Film Units Yield to Nazis on Race Issue."[5] That same year, U.S. studios sold 65 films in Germany. To serve the peculiarities of this market, some films were censored and some were simply shelved. Herman J. Mankiewicz wrote the anti–Hitler movie *The Mad Dog of Europe* in 1933, while on leave from MGM. Producer Sam Jaffe bought the rights with the intention of making a film that would warn the world about the looming danger of Naziism. Louis B. Mayer got wind of the project and tried to shoot it down. He told people he did it because "we have interests in Germany; I represent the picture industry here in Hollywood … we have terrific income in Germany … this picture will never be made."[6] The Hays Office and their chief hatchet man (and anti–Semite) Joseph Breen weighed in with the most absurd of assertions: that anti–Semites had feelings too. "It is to be remembered," said Breen, "that there is strong pro–German and anti–Semitic feeling in this country, and, while those who are likely to approve of an anti–Hitler picture may think well of such an enterprise, they should keep in mind that millions of Americans might think otherwise."[7] *The Mad Dog of Europe* was never made.

Another film Hollywood didn't make, twice, was *It Can't Happen Here*, based on the 1935 Sinclair Lewis novel. Lewis had won the Pulitzer Prize for *Elmer Gantry* in 1927 and the Nobel Prize in 1930, the first American writer to do so. Artistically, *It Can't Happen Here* is a lesser novel than his *Main Street*, *Babbitt* or *Dodsworth* but read it today and you tap into the raw fear of seeing fascism come to America in the person of Berzelius "Buzz" Windrip, a populist schemer who, in this counterfactual story, defeats FDR for the Democratic nomination in 1936, then defeats the Republican nominee, only to disband Congress, arm a personal militia, burn newspaper offices and open concentration camps for political opponents. It all reads like *opera bouffe* until the midpoint: Dr. Fowler, who has come to the jail to protest the imprisonment of newspaper editor Doremus Jessup, is led outside. Doremus hears: "From the courtyard, the sound of a rifle volley, a terrifying wail, one single emphatic shot, and nothing after."[8] It is the unadorned casualness of this murder by government agents, without charge or trial, that grabs the reader by the throat. Lewis was thinking about Hitler and Mussolini but also about homegrown populists like Huey Long, Charles Lindbergh, Father Charles Coughlin, Fritz Kuhn, Gerald L.K. Smith. The very name of his antagonist Buzz Windrip seems inspired by the anti–Semitic evangelist who ran for the U.S. Senate in Kansas in 1938, Gerald Burton Winrod, known as "the Kansas Hitler." The novel sold 340,000 copies. Critics called it "the most important anti–fascist work to appear in the United States in the 1930s."[9] The Trump years make it worth reading once again.

Sam Marx bought the rights to the novel for MGM. MGM hired Pulitzer Prize–winning playwright Sidney Howard to adapt it, cast Lionel Barrymore as Doremus Jessup and Wallace Beery as President Buzz Windrip and put the movie into production. Then Breen stepped in to ask MGM to cancel the project, calling it "inflammatory" and "filled with dangerous material."[10] After cancellation, Lewis said, "I wrote *It Can't Happen Here* but I begin to think it certainly can."[11]

Hollywood saw money to be made in cooperation with Italian fascists. In the 1930s, producer Hal Roach struck up a friendship with Vittorio Mussolini (1916–1997), second son of dictator Benito. As a pilot in the Italian Air Force, Vittorio fought in Ethiopia as the fascists invaded and in the Italian intervention in the Spanish Civil War on the side of fascist General Francisco Franco. According to *Time* magazine, Vittorio, nicknamed "Il Duce Jr." and "the Fascist Prince," described bombs as "budding roses," and called killing "exceptionally good fun."[12]

In 1937, Roach guided Vittorio around Hollywood for two weeks in anticipation of a joint U.S.-Italian production company to be called R.A.M., for Roach and Mussolini. Roach managed to praise the fascist Italian leader: "Benito Mussolini is the only square politician I've ever seen."[13] Things did not go according to plan, however, and the Mussolini and Roach tour was dogged by anti-fascist protests. According to *The Hollywood Reporter*: "Loew's chairman Nicholas Schenck was so upset he canceled Roach's MGM deal." The *Reporter* ascribed RAM Films' demise to "violent protests against the deal ... organizations opposed to Fascism and Nazism made the whole thing a bit too perilous for Roach."[14] Vittorio went home empty-handed but did fly combat missions for the Axis and against the U.S. in World War II.

American film companies began exiting Germany in 1936 but MGM, Paramount and 20th Century–Fox remained. The studios dropped from movie credits the names of cast and crew members the Nazis found objectionable, e.g., Jewish.[15] Movie sales by American studios continued in Germany through violent government-instigated anti–Semitic attacks, including Kristallnacht. *Boxoffice* reported, "MGM will make pictures without regard to politics and with only box-office and entertainment in mind."[16] MGM even donated copies of *After the Thin Man* and ten other popular films to the German war relief effort after Germany's 1939 invasion of Poland, which set off World War II in Europe.[17]

Hollywood finally began producing anti–Nazi films in 1939 with *Confessions of a Nazi Spy*, which said not a word about the persecution of the Jews. Charlie Chaplin's *The*

Great Dictator followed in 1940, distributed by United Artists, which did no business in Germany. MGM made the anti-Nazi film *The Mortal Storm* in 1940, without mentioning the word "Jews" but referring to them as "non-Aryans." As a result, the Nazis expelled MGM from German distribution. After Pearl Harbor and a U.S. declaration of war against Germany, Hollywood turned patriotic and made 800 feature films dealing with the war (1942–45), 242 of which were explicitly anti-Nazi.[18]

Another fascist dropped by Hollywood for a visit in 1938, filmmaker and Hitler confidante and, possibly, his lover, Leni Riefenstahl (1902–2003). Trained as a dancer, athlete and actress, she found her greatest success as a filmmaker, pioneering new film techniques and producing the groundbreaking documentaries *Triumph of the Will* (1935), celebrating Hitler as a new German god, and *Olympia* (1938), covering the Olympic Games held that year in Germany and filled with many scenes of Hitler and his adoring crowds offering the "Heil Hitler" salute. She traveled from New York to L.A. on a Nazi government-sponsored trip, making appearances along the way. Winfield Sheehan, the former head of Fox, put her up in his Palm Springs home while columnist Hedda Hopper trumpeted her work.[19] While others shunned her, the far-right Walt Disney gave her a three-hour tour of his studio.[20] But then Disney wouldn't hire Jews.[21] In 2022, Disney heiress Abigail Disney recalled her grand uncle's politics saying: "He bordered on rabid fascism."[22]

New York papers quoted Riefenstahl saying, "The Jews are backing the Negroes politically. Under their influence the Negroes will become Communists and so the Jew and the Negro will bring bolshevism to America."[23] When she arrived in L.A., demonstrations followed her every appearance. The Hollywood Anti-Nazi League took out a full-page *Hollywood Reporter* ad under the headline: "There is No Room in Hollywood for Leni Riefenstahl."[24] Looking for distribution deals for *Olympia*, Riefenstahl faced mounting public backlash as news of Kristallnacht broke. A *New York World-Telegram* headline read: "Mobs Wreck 10,000 Jewish Shops in Nazis' 14-hour Reign of Terror."[25] Riefenstahl hightailed it back to Germany with no deals to show for her trip.

As Nazi power grew in Germany, the U.S. experienced its own growth of fascist and anti-Semitic groups like the Silver Shirts, the Friends of the New Germany, the German American Bund, America First, the Lode Star Legion, the American National Party, the Ku Klux Klan, the Defenders of the Faith, the Black Legion, the Association of American Gentiles, the Christian American Patriots, National Socialist Teutonia Association, Gauleitung-USA, the Friends of Germany, the Paul Reveres, the Crusader White Shirts, the Christian Mobilizers, the religious right and far-right domestic politicians. From 1933 to 1940, an estimated 121 American groups stepped forth to preach fascist, pro-Nazi, anti-Semitic beliefs.[26] Some of these groups had Hollywood roots.

Behind them all, like a venomous spider in his web, doling out cash, ideas and propaganda, was a man in Detroit, one of the world's richest and most vicious anti-Semites: industrialist Henry Ford (1863–1947). I can find no single incident that bent Ford towards this monomania but he enlisted in the racial wars early. In 1919, he told *The New York World*, "International financiers are behind all war … they're what is called the International Jew: German Jews, French Jews, English Jews, American Jews … the Jew is a threat."[27] Having built the Model T in 1908 and the Model A in 1927, Ford amassed a huge fortune. He purchased *The Dearborn Independent* and for 20 years railed against "the International Jew: the world's problem." The paper issued a drum beat of anti-Semitic bile targeting a vast Jewish conspiracy undermining all areas of American life,

Henry Ford, Miracle Maker

May 1, 1920   INDEPENDENT CORPORATION   10 Cents

Automotive industrialist Henry Ford had more on his mind than Model T's. He was worried about a worldwide Jewish conspiracy, so he bought *The Dearborn Independent* and filled it with anti-Semitic rants that endeared him to a young Adolf Hitler and still reverberate online for new generations of haters.

from baseball to the Democratic Party, to New York theaters, to ... motion pictures. Chapter 31 of this collected hate, published as a four-volume, 80-chapter anthology, claimed:

> The movies are of Jewish production. If you fight filth then fight the carrier ... the Jewish camp.... Whenever an attempt is made to control the tumultuous indecency ... which the movies ceaselessly pour out night and day upon the American public the opponents thereto is Jewish.... There lies the whole secret of the movies' moral failure—they are not American and their producers are racially unqualified to reproduce the American atmosphere.[28]

Racially unqualified?!

One could turn this into a joke about one bitter old man ... except for the extraordinary reach of his hatred. Copies of *The Independent* were distributed at all Ford dealerships and the car salesmen were instructed to put effort into selling the paper. For a 1931 interview in Munich, an American reporter was ushered into Adolf Hitler's office where he found the future Fuhrer seated with a large portrait of Henry Ford behind his desk. He told the reporter: "I regard Henry Ford as my inspiration."[29] The Max Wallace book *American Axis* quoted a Ron Rosenbaum book, *Explaining Hitler*: "One could make the case that without Ford's inspiration and (probably) cash contributions, Hitler and his movement might not have been able to commit mass murder."[30]

Ford considered running for president in 1924 and again in 1928.[31] Some in Hollywood fought back. William Fox, head of Fox Pictures, told Ford he would compile footage "from hundreds of cameramen all over the country of accidents and fatalities involving Ford cars. The resulting newsreel would be projected [in his theaters] before every one of his studio's films."[32]

Jews boycotted Ford cars across the country and Hollywood executives banned Ford cars and trucks from their studio lots. In 1926, an activist Jewish lawyer, Aaron Sapiro, sued Ford for libel, forcing Ford to apologize for his anti–Semitism, cease publication of the *Dearborn Independent* and publicly ask forgiveness.[33] All of which rang hollow when, on his 75th birthday in July 1938, Ford accepted from Hitler the Grand Cross of the Supreme Order of the German Eagle, complete with four small swastikas, the highest honor Germany could award a foreigner.[34] Ford gave annual birthday gifts to Hitler.[35] Ford German factories, Ford-Werke-AG, using forced labor after the war began, kept producing during the war and one estimate suggested 15 percent to 20 percent of all vehicles used by the German Army were built by Ford.[36] After the German invasion and the fall of France, a Ford plant near Paris turned out aircraft engines, military trucks and other vehicles for the German military.[37]

Another American who received the high Nazi medal was Ford's friend and political protégé, Charles Augustus Lindbergh (1902–74). "Lucky" Lindy had successfully flown non-stop across the Atlantic alone in 1927, becoming the biggest celebrity in the world. He also had a Hitler problem as he became a spokesman for isolationism and the America First movement which he and Ford founded, stating in one radio address:

> Our bond with Europe is a bond of race and not of political ideology.... Racial strength is vital—politics is a luxury. If the white race is ever seriously threatened it may then be time to take our part in its protection, to fight side by side with the English, French, and Germans, but not with one against the other to our mutual destruction.[38]

In a *Reader's Digest* article, Lindbergh explained that aviation in Western nations served "as a barrier between the teeming millions of Asia and the Grecian inheritance of

Europe ... which permits the White race to live at all in a pressing sea of Yellow, Black, and Brown."[39] And somehow Lindy brought it back to the movies again: "Most of the Jewish interests in the country are behind war, and they control a huge part of our press and radio, and most of our motion pictures."[40] Columnist Walter Winchell called Lindbergh "the leader of the American Nazi movement"[41] as the America First Committee grew to 800,000 members.

Out in California, parts of the movie industry succumbed to the siren call of European fascism. Marie Dressler (1868–1934), who appeared with Jean Harlow in *Dinner at Eight* and was reportedly Louis B. Meyer's favorite actress at MGM, thought fascism a good idea and Mussolini an attractive leader.[42] Hollywood screenwriter William Dudley Pelley (1890–1965), who worked on two Lon Chaney features, organized the Silver Legion of America in 1933, modeled on the Nazi Brown Shirts, the S.A. or *Sturmabteilung*. Pelley offered a blend of anti-communism and anti–Semitism and described the Silver Shirts' goal as "a wholesale and drastic ousting of every radical from the United States."[43] His Silver Shirts attracted 15,000 members. Among their goals, "African-Americans would be re-enslaved and Jews would be excluded from the nation."[44]

In 1933, actor Victor McLaglen (1886–1959) who appeared in some 120 movies and won the Academy Award for his role in "The Informer," formed the California Light Horse Regiment to fight "the enemy opposed to the American idea."[45] The Light Horse established branches in Pasadena, Long Beach and Oakland. In December 1934, McLaglen led his troops into downtown L.A. to the *Examiner* building "to honor the newspaper" and then on to Olympic Stadium where McLaglen made a speech on the subject of America for Americans," looking, wrote *The Los Angeles Times*, "like a combination of a Canadian Mounted Policeman, General Goering, and Mussolini."[46] In an account for the *L.A. Times Sunday Magazine* (August 5, 1934), E.C. Van Aiken waxed poetic on the Light Horse: "They are a strange and colorful body of Los Angeles men—veterans of a thousand battlefields scattered over the face of the earth, heroes of deathless charges. This is the story of the dragoons, lancers, hussars, and Yankee doughboys—known as the California Light Horse Regiment."[47] Headlining his report "Lancers Who Ride at Night," Allen revived echoes of those other night riders, the Ku Klux Klan.

By 1936, McLaglen claimed to have an air force of 50 planes and 800 men under arms. He told *The New York Times*: "We're organized to fight. We consider an enemy anything opposed to the American idea ... if that includes the communists in this country, why, we're organized to fight them too."[48] A Hollywood screenwriter (and a World War I hero), Arthur Guy Empey (1883–1963) defected from McLaglen's Light Horse in 1935, and with politically far right actors Gary Cooper and Ward Bond formed his own paramilitary force, the Hollywood Hussars, funded by William Randolph Hearst. One contemporary press report stated: "[The Hussars] were armed to the teeth and ready to gallop on horseback within an hour to cope with any emergency menacing the safety of the community—fights or strikes, floods or earthquakes, Japanese invasions, Communist revolutions, or whatnot."[49]

But by far the biggest American fascist organization of the 1930s, the German American Bund, evolved in Detroit. Founded in 1936 by World War I German veteran Julius "Fritz" Kuhn (1896–1951), who had joined the Nazi Party at its inception, the Bund worked publicly for a fascist and Jew-free America. Arriving in America in 1928, Kuhn went to work for Henry Ford's car company. The Bund grew quickly to a paramilitary force of 5000 and a total membership between 10,000 and 30,000, and sought alliances with the Ku Klux Klan and the Silver Shirts. They established summer camps and had American children goose-stepping and Heil Hitler-ing[50] at a Nazi retreat, Camp Siegfried on Long Island, "a pro–Nazi mini-resort for family getaways,"[51] as well as at Camp Nordland in New Jersey, Camp Hindenburg in Wisconsin (a paramilitary training camp) and Hindenburg Park in La Crescenta, outside Los Angeles. An L.A. branch of the Bund targeted the Hollywood Jews in the Bund publications *Liberation* and *Silver Ranger*.[52] In February 1939, the Bund held a George Washington birthday bash at Madison Square Garden with 22,000 Nazis in attendance and 1700 New York City cops on hand to keep out an equal number of anti–Nazi demonstrators. Arriving to speak, Kuhn told a reporter, "The Jews have plotted to get hold of almost everything especially in New York and Hollywood."[53] *The New York Times* covered the rally on its front page: "[T]he Garden was decorated with ... a thirty foot picture of George Washington behind the speaker's stand, Bund flags and many banners, most of them derogatory to the Jews. 'Wake up America—Smash Jewish Communism,' said one."[54] *The Los Angeles Times* reported, "All the trappings of the spectacular mass assemblies familiar to Nazi Germany adorned the occasion. Storm troopers strode the aisles.... Arms snapped out in the Nazi salute."[55]

In 2017, filmmaker Marshall Curry released the scariest horror film I've ever seen, though it features no vampires or "walking dead." It's called, innocently enough, *A Night at the Garden* and it is a mere seven minutes of film shot that night in Madison Square Garden as the Nazis parade and the sold-out crowd of Americans offered the Nazi salute. It should be seen by every person in the United States so that they have some idea how fragile democracy can be. And it shows how to fight back. The film contains footage of one man rushing the stage when Kuhn tells the crowd he hopes for a "white Gentile–ruled America."[56] Nazi troopers on stage grab and pummel the man and lift him bodily off the stage and into the arms of police, his clothing half ripped from his body as the crowd cheers.[57] The man, Isidore Greenbaum, just 26 and working as a plumber's helper to support himself, his wife and young son, yells "Down with Hitler!" as the police carry him away. The next day in court, Greenbaum told the judge that he went to the Garden "without any intention of interrupting, but being that they talked so much against my religion and there was so much persecution I lost my head and I felt it was my duty to talk."

"Don't you realize that innocent people might have been killed?" the judge asked.

"Do you realize that plenty of Jewish people might be killed with their persecution up there?" Greenbaum replied.[58] Greenbaum paid a $25 fine. Two years later, he was in the Navy fighting Nazis again.

People in the movie industry fought back too, at least some of them. In 1936, they formed the Hollywood Anti-Nazi League for the Defense of American Democracy. Like other Popular Front organizations pre–World War II, the HANL brought together New Dealers, liberals, socialists and communists, using film stars to educate the public about the menace of Naziism and to agitate against American collaboration. Writers Dashiell Hammett, Lillian Hellman, Dorothy Parker and Donald Ogden Stewart, director John Ford and actors Myrna Loy, Fredric March, Eddie Cantor, Melvyn Douglas, Edward G. Robinson and Bette Davis joined with some 5000 others. The group picketed Leni Riefenstahl on her Hollywood visit in 1938, organized a large anti–Nazi rally at L.A.'s Shrine Auditorium in 1936, published the weekly paper the *Hollywood Anti-Nazi News*, hosted educational lectures, held public rallies against the fascists, boycotted German imports and marched outside German-American Bund events.

Joseph Breen, Father Coughlin and the House UnAmerican Activities Committee chair Martin Dies all attacked the HANL as a Communist front. Responded Fredric March: "Every time during the last few years that I have felt impelled to protest an injustice ... or to espouse some social reform, I have been called a communist. [I insist upon the right to] be recognized as a loyal American."[59] In 1937, the HANL office on Hollywood Boulevard was trashed and burglarized by, among others, Leopold McLaglen (1884–1951), brother of actor Victor of the Hussars. Leopold was an actor in his own right, earning fourth billing in the 1920 film *Bars of Iron*. He traveled the world as a martial arts instructor and wrote books on the subject. Turning up in Hollywood and trying to cash in on his brother's fame, Leopold sued Victor for slander and lost. Somehow he then fell into a Nazi plot to kill 24 prominent Hollywood Jews including Charlie Chaplin, Al Jolson and Eddie Cantor with a combination of machine-guns and explosives. When apprehended, Leopold claimed to have attacked the HANL office at the behest of millionaire sportsman Philip Chancellor, who had hired Leopold as a jiujitsu instructor. Chancellor claimed that Leopold was blackmailing him. Asked to choose between leaving town and serving a jail stretch, Leopold headed to England, his fare home paid by his estranged brother.[60]

Pearl Harbor and then the subsequent German declaration of war on the U.S. on December 11, 1941, silenced for a time most American Nazis and America Firsters who now rushed to prove their patriotism. After the end of the war, the battle of Right vs. Left resumed in new and ugly ways, leaving ruined lives in its wake.

Dashiell Hammett attempted to rejoin the Army. He was already a veteran of World War I and still on Disability from that war. The military turned him down. Army regulations kept men over 45 out of combat, and Hammett was 47. He attempted to enlist three more times. When a recruiter told him his rotten teeth blocked his enlistment, he had them pulled.[61] Finally the Army relaxed its standards and in September 1942, at the age of 48, Hammett was accepted into the Army as a private. He hoped to see combat duty with the Signal Corps but never did. The odds were always against him as the military needed nine men and women in the rear for supply, occupation, logistics, motor pool, etc., for every man or woman at the front. Only ten percent of active-duty military ever saw frontline action. Three members of my family served in World War II: My father, as a mechanic in the Army Air Corps, served on bases in California, Texas and Pennsylvania and never went overseas. His brother served in India as a radio man, helping coordinate military flights over the Himalayas, and never saw front line duty. My mother's brother wound up in the South Pacific fighting alongside the Marines from island to island and saw action he would rarely talk about.

The Army shipped Hammett to Pennsylvania's Camp Shenango, later Camp Reynolds, with other "political undesirables." This camp, like others, was racially segregated, and racial animosities sparked a race riot, which some called a massacre, that left tens of black soldiers dead in July 1943 (contemporaneous reports claimed that one black soldier died).[62] By this time, Hammett was long gone but he resisted segregation at his next posting.

When First Lady Eleanor Roosevelt learned how the Army was sequestering enlistees at Camp Shenango, she intervened with FDR and the Army dispersed the men off to other postings. Hammett's assignment was no plum: the Aleutian Islands, a thousand-mile-long archipelago off the coast of Alaska. At the beginning of the war, the Japanese had briefly occupied several of the islands until being dislodged in battles at Dutch Harbor and Attu. Though it seemed unlikely they would return, the Army posted 15,000 GIs there to make sure they didn't. In a tactic reminiscent of the mainland internment of Japanese-Americans, U.S. forces forcibly removed the indigenous Aleut population who had lived on the islands for hundreds of years. According to the National Park Service:

> They were herded from their homes onto cramped transport ships, most allowed only a single suitcase. Heartbroken, Atka villagers watched as US servicemen set their homes and church afire so they would not fall into Japanese hands. The Unangax̂ were transported to Southeast Alaska and there crowded into "duration villages": abandoned canneries, a herring saltery, and gold mine camp—rotting facilities with no plumbing, electricity or toilets.[63]

By the time Hammett arrived, the fighting was over and the Aleut were gone. The island hosted 5000 service personnel in an unattractive climate of cold, foggy weather "on the 275-square mile volcanic rock, with its moss, snow, fog and the Williwaw, that treacherous hurricane force wind that blows across the Bering Sea."[64] Hammett described the conditions in a letter to daughter Jo:

> We live in Quonset huts—those semi cylindrical metal things you have seen in pictures—strung out down along both steep walls of a little valley, close to the walls, half dug in sometimes and spaced well apart so that if some dope wants to bomb us he can't bag too many of us with one shot.... My hut is so well concealed under sod, tundra, and stuff, spread over chicken wire, that little light comes in.... Our beds are the regular metal Army cot.[65]

When the base commander made newly promoted Corporal Hammett editor of the camp newspaper, a four-page mimeographed daily called *The Adakian,* Hammett was writing again. By the time he was done, *The Adakian* "was considered by many as the best military service newspaper produced during World War II."[66] To make it work, Hammett recruited a team of eight men, including Bernard Kalb, who after the war spent decades reporting from around the world on TV. Also on the team was Bill Glackin, who wrote about the arts for the *Sacramento Bee* for five decades. Hammett also recruited two African American soldiers, Alba Morris as printer and Don Miller as illustrator. According to Miller's *New York Times* obituary, he spent his life "interpreting the black experience in the United States, the West Indies and Africa."[67] In 1986, he painted the 12 foot by seven foot mural, known as the "King Mural," in the main lobby of the Martin Luther King, Jr., Memorial Library in Washington, D.C.[68]

Significantly, Hammett integrated his team while the Army was still segregated.[69] Kalb described work on the *Adakian*: "[W]e were on the job from before midnight to breakfast, assembling the incoming news, monitoring shortwave broadcasts, typing our copy, cutting cartoon stencils—and running six thousand copies through a mimeograph machine."[70] In 1944, Hammett and fellow soldier Robert Colodny found time to research and write *Battle of the Aleutians: A Graphic History, 1942–1943*. The Army printed 100,000 copies and distributed them among the troops to build morale.[71]

Hammett turned his thoughts to life after the Army in a March 27, 1944, letter sent to Hellman:

> Nearly everybody in the Army thinks a good deal about what they'd like to do after the war. Being, as you know, very slow on some things, I've just recently got around to that. It's still kind of an idle game in which I've not yet involved myself very deeply, but I think maybe politics. I mean politics of an office-holding—or at least office-running-for-with-a-chance-of-getting-in—kind. What does Madam think? Would

Madam speak to me when I was, say, a City Council member in Detroit, for instance, or a legislator in California? It would, of course, be best—or, in any event, would make me feel I was being a shrewder jobbie—if I picked whatever geographical spot seemed to offer the best pickings for an earnest left winger who was willing to spend a year or two digging in. There is always the chance that I may have forgotten all about this by the time you reply, but, on the other hand, things like this sometimes sneak up on me and stick, and this may be one of them.[72]

In September 1945, soon after the war's end, the Army honorably discharged Hammett. In addition to his other life-long lung problems, he also suffered from emphysema. Now he would have a chance to take the national political stage in a way he had never imagined. Meanwhile, the FBI had been hard at work growing a file on Master Sergeant Dashiell Hammett.[73]

In many ways, Hammett found the world changed upon his discharge. His health was worse than ever. He went from Alaska back to New York and back to drinking. Things got so bad that in 1948, his housekeeper had to call an ambulance. A doctor sat down with him and explained his two options: stay sober or die. And just like that, Hammett never took another drink.[74] He went back to political work. He spoke at meetings allied with the Communist Party, headlined petitions and taught at the Jefferson School of Social Science in Lower Manhattan. Established by the CPUSA in 1944, the school offered adult education and a Marxist approach to social issues, accumulated a library of 30,000 volumes and attracted 5000 students at its peak. The Red hunters hounded the school to register with the Subversive Activities Control Board (SACB) as a Communist controlled-entity. Running low on funding and publicly pilloried as a Communist front organization, the school closed in 1956. (The U.S. Supreme Court gutted the powers of the SABC in 1965 and Congress abolished it in 1972.) Hammett had taught classes, not very subversive at all, in detective fiction there.

The world at large had also changed and in dangerous ways. The Great Red Scare (1947-60) was not just a mindless outburst of anti-Communist hysteria but a conscious and strategic political attack by conservative Republicans and segregationist Southern Democrats on the New Deal policies of FDR, the advancement of political and economic democracy, the rising power of women and black and brown people, and the United Nations. Representative John Elliot Rankin (1882–1960) of Mississippi helped make HUAC a standing committee of Congress. Offering his view on the House floor, Rankin stated: "I have no quarrel with any man about his religion. Any man who believes in the fundamental principles of Christianity and lives up to them, whether he is a Catholic or Protestant, deserves the respect and confidence of mankind."[75] He seems to have skipped over several other religions here.

In the 1946 midterm elections, the Republicans captured control of the House and the Senate and began battering President Truman, who had ascended to the presidency upon the death in office of four-term President Franklin Delano Roosevelt. To protect himself from charges of being soft on Communism, Truman issued Executive Order 9835 on March 25, 1947, instituting a Loyalty Program to rid the government of "subversives." According to author David McCullough, a Pulitzer Prize winner for his 1992 Truman biography, the Order meant that all 2,000,000 federal employees

> were to be subject to loyalty investigations whatever their jobs.... Anyone found to be disloyal could no longer hold a government job. Dismissal would be based merely on "reasonable grounds for belief that the person is disloyal," yet the term "disloyal" was never defined. ...

Moreover those accused would be unable to confront those making charges against them, or even know who they were or what exactly the charges were.[76]

It became a crime, in the words of Attorney General Tom Clark, to "conspire to divide our people, to discredit our institutions and to bring about disrespect for our government."[77] And who might interpret those nebulous crimes? White House Counsel (and future Secretary of Defense to LBJ) Clark Clifford said later, "It was a political problem. Truman was going to run in '48 and that was it ... the whole thing was manufactured."[78]

With Congress and the president now on the same page, HUAC headed to Hollywood in search of headlines. HUAC member Rankin announced that HUAC was not out to hound legitimate producers or writers, "but we are out to expose those elements that are insidiously trying to spread subversive propaganda, poison the minds of our children, distort the history of our country and discredit Christianity."[79] He added, "One of the most dangerous plots ever instigated for the overthrow of this government has its headquarters in Hollywood.... The information we get is that this is the greatest hotbed of subversive activities in the United States. We're on the trail of the tarantula now, and we're going to follow through."[80]

In Hollywood, Myrna Loy saw what was coming:

> All you had to do was know someone of questionable political persuasion and you were labeled a "Commie." There were perhaps six or seven hard core Communists in Hollywood then, and they were not dangerous people.... I woke up one morning to find myself listed in *The Hollywood Reporter* as "part of the Communist fifth column in America" along with Edward G. Robinson, Orson Welles, Burgess Meredith, James Cagney ... most of us just good liberals.[81]

Loy sued the *Reporter* for libel and a million dollars in damages and they retracted the story.

Over four years of Hollywood hearings, HUAC made as many careers as it destroyed. Friendly witnesses before HUAC and supporters of the committee were Robert Taylor, Robert Montgomery, Ronald Reagan, Gary Cooper, George Murphy, Adolphe Menjou, Ward Bond, Walter Brennan, Cecil B. DeMille, Victor Fleming, John Ford, Clark Gable, Cedric Gibbons, Hedda Hopper, Leo McCarey, Ginger Rogers, Barbara Stanwyck, Sterling Hayden, Lee J. Cobb, King Vidor, Hal B. Wallis, John Wayne and Walt Disney. They prospered. Song-and-dance man Murphy made it to the U.S. Senate; actor Reagan made it all the way to the White House.

Those who pushed back, especially those who had organized Hollywood unions like the Screen Writers Guild, faced the blacklist and the end of their lucrative careers—and even faced jail. Meeting at the Waldorf-Astoria in New York City on November 24 and 25, 1947, the Hollywood studio heads, reacting to boycott threats from groups like the American Legion, the Legion of Decency, the Daughters of American Revolution, the Veterans of Foreign Wars and the Knights of Columbus, blacklisted actors with Communist ties even though it was no crime to be a Communist or to belong to the Communist Party. The studios made their moves to suit public opinion. *Variety* reported in August 1948 that the studios "are continuing to drop plans for 'message' pictures like hot coals."[82] Some 600 workers, blacklisted in the film, TV and radio industries, found themselves out of jobs and, in many cases, out on the street.[83]

HUAC, Senator Joe McCarthy et al. all wanted names. They'd call in witnesses, ask them to confess their political sins and name some of their confederates. Naming names was a ritual, a publicity stunt, an act of obeisance to those with power. In his biography of Roy Cohn, Nicholas van Hoffman described composer–harmonica player Larry Adler's meeting with Cohn, who was then serving as counsel to McCarthy's Senate subcommittee. Cohn told Adler, "It'll be a secret session [with McCarthy's subcommittee]. Now I already know, you don't want to name names. We've worked a special deal for you. I've prepared a list; there are people who have been named before, we already know them. You just read the list out to us, remember you're not giving us any information, therefore you're not hurting anybody."

Adler responded: "Mr. Cohn, what is the sense of me reading you a list of names you already have?"

Cohn went to the window, looked out, then turned back to Adler. "Go fight City Hall," he said, spreading his hands, "We're all trying to get you back to work and you won't help us."[84]

In all his investigations, in all his hearings, in all his taking of testimony, "[McCarthy] did not discover a single Communist."[85] In reality, a committed Communist subversive, saboteur or spy could simply deny being a Commie under oath before these investigating committees and walk away to spy some more. Principled people refused to answer questions, believing their personal political beliefs were their private business. The rules of the game meant that if you did answer that you had been a Communist or attended a meeting, you legally then had to reveal who else had been a Party member or who else attended a meeting. If you said that you had never been a Communist or knowingly attended a Communist meeting, you had legitimized the Committee's right to question your political affiliation or political activities. If you refused to answer the question citing the First Amendment, Congress could hold you in contempt and send you to jail. If you cited the Fifth Amendment against self-incrimination, you avoided jail but the studios blacklisted you. To avoid the blacklist, you had to admit to being a former Communist and then rat out all your friends, which many people were willing to do. Then you escaped the blacklist but your former friends might not.

Naming names, no matter how well known they aleady were, often destroyed the souls of those naming them. When screenwriter Ring Lardner, Jr., was hauled before HUAC, Chair J. Parnell Thomas, Republican of New Jersey, asked him the standard question: "Are you now or have you ever been a member of the Communist Party?" Lardner replied, "I could answer ... but if I did, I'd hate myself in the morning."[86] Thomas had him removed from the witness stand. Lardner was blacklisted for 15 years and spent a year in prison as one of the Hollywood Ten (the other nine were Alvah Bessie, Herbert J. Biberman, Lester Cole, Edward Dmytryk, John Howard Lawson, Albert Maltz, Samuel Ornitz, Adrian Scott and Dalton Trumbo). Lardner bounced back to write the movie *M*A*S*H* (1970) and win an Academy Award.

In the 1950s, Congressman Thomas was sent to the same prison housing Lardner and other Hollywood Ten members. Thomas was in for fraud. Ironically, he had taken the Fifth at his own trial, a recourse he had long attacked his opponents for using. According to screenwriter Lester Cole, Lardner saw Thomas at the prison chicken coop and said to him: "Well, Parnell, still handling the chicken shit, I see."[87] Cole had screen credits in 35 films prior to being blacklisted and afterwards wrote six films under pseudonyms, including the ironically titled *Born Free* (1966).

According to Cole, on the eve of his HUAC testimony he was called into the office of MGM's Louis B. Mayer, for whom he had made a lot of money writing and doctoring films. Discussing the Committee subpoena he'd received, Cole told Mayer:

> "It looks like we have the law on our side." Mayer: "I don't give a shit about the law. It's them goddam commies that you're tied up with. Break with them. Stick with us. With me ... you'll do what you want. Direct your own pictures? Say so.... Dough means nothing ... we'll double your salary. You name it, you can have it. Just make the break.... I know about Communism. I know what happens to men like that. Take that Communist Roosevelt! A hero, a man of the people! And what happened five minutes after they shoveled dirt on his grave? The people pissed on it. That what you want, Lester? Be with us, be smart. You got kids, think of them."
> [When Cole refused:] Goddam crazy Commie! Get out! Goddam it, get out!"[88]

The witch hunters came for Thin Man screenwriters Hackett and Goodrich. The FBI had compiled a file on the meetings they attended and the petitions they signed. MGM asked them to write a letter to the studio abjuring their activities or their contract would be canceled. They replied: "We feel that if we write such a letter we would be violating every principle of democracy and freedom in which we believe.... Our patriotism, our love and loyalty for our Country ... [have] never been questioned and cannot now be questioned."[89] They didn't write the letter and somehow kept on working.

All this hysteria broke out when the Communist Party USA was already at its nadir: down from 90,000 members in 1939 to just 30,000 in 1952,[90] a large number of which were FBI agents and informers. Henry R. Luce, owner of *Life*, *Time* and *Fortune* et al., in a commencement address at Temple University in 1953, warned graduates, "We in America have developed a form of brainwashing under the name anti–Communism."[91] Everyone was afraid of being called a "Red." Even baseball teams: "[T]he Cincinnati Reds went by the [name] Redlegs in the 1950's to distance themselves from any connection to communism."[92] Speaking of Communist subversion in Hollywood, Stefan Cantor wrote in his book *Journal of the Plague Years*: "'There was no subversion in films, there never had been ... [M]ost of the comrades' time was spent trying to refurbish the screen's mean and farcical treatment of the Jew and Negro. None of the Communists had written a scene more offensive than that of a Russian girl teaching an American how to drive a tractor—and that had been excised by 20th Century-Fox."[93]

My cousin, actor Jeff Corey, born Arthur Zwerling, was blacklisted during the McCarthy era. He told me about the informers who came forward to denounce their former friends and save their own skins:

> I categorically ascribe their activities to the rankest kind of opportunism and they will admit it: that none of them testified against their colleagues out of principle. They did it for expediency's sake. It was clear: mention the names of people who had been mentioned before and add two names and you could work. It was as simple as that. It was saving their necks and getting on the bandwagon and making names for themselves as anti–Communist heroes. But they all knew the people they were informing on had never done anything anti–American or illegal.[94]

Corey felt the temptation to inform as well, if it meant he could continue his career:

> I had a dream one night where a friend of mine came in the dream and he was then my very best friend and I was very sad to hear him say that he intended to inform. I urged him: "You can't do this." He said, "No, I am going to do it." I told this dream to an analyst friend of mine who said: "You know, there's a saying that you're your own best friend." So obviously in my dream I was trying to reconcile taking such a stand, because I cared a lot about my career. But

happily I couldn't.... I remember my father comforting me and saying: "In Jewish tradition an informer cannot be buried with other people."[95]

Corey worked in 36 films from 1941 to 1951. After he took the Fifth before HUAC in 1951, no one would hire him for movies, for radio, or for TV work until 1962. He was out of work for 11 years.[96]

Hollywood organized to fight back.

Myrna Loy understood the HUAC fixation with the film industry: "It was always good publicity for those crusaders to attack Hollywood."[97] So, fresh off wringing a retraction from *The Hollywood Reporter*, she helped form the Committee for the First Amendment. "Can you believe such a thing?" she wrote, "having to form a defense for the First Amendment?"[98] The new organization, founded in September 1947, attracted a galaxy of stars including directors John Huston and William Wyler and actors Lucille Ball, Lauren Bacall, Humphrey Bogart, Joseph Cotten, Dorothy Dandridge, Bette Davis, Melvyn Douglas, Henry Fonda, John Garfield, Judy Garland, June Havoc, Sterling Hayden, Paul Henreid, Katharine Hepburn, Lena Horne, Marsha Hunt, Danny Kaye, Gene Kelly, Burt Lancaster, Groucho Marx, Burgess Meredith, Edward G. Robinson, Robert Ryan, Frank Sinatra and Jane Wyatt. In October 1947, many of its members flew to Washington, D.C., to confront HUAC and take their case to the American people. They also broadcast two 30-minute radio programs called *Hollywood Fights Back* in which 50 prominent members spoke out about the meaning of the First Amendment and the sanctity of freedom of speech and expression. On their November 2, 1947, broadcast, Loy said, "We are here to combat the menace of the UnAmerican committee."[99] Humphrey Bogart stated: "We sat in the committee room and saw for ourselves ... it can happen here. We saw American citizens denied the right to speak ... we saw police take citizens from the witness stand like criminals because they'd been denied the right to defend themselves. We saw the gavel of the Committee Chairman cutting off the words of free Americans. And every time that gavel struck, it hit the First Amendment of the Constitution of the United States."[100]

But things went downhill quickly. The Hollywood Ten were each ejected from the HUAC hearing room and accused of contempt on November 24, 1947. Studios instituted the first informal film blacklist the following day. Over the next ten years, hundreds of Hollywood actors, writers and crew members found themselves out of work because of their presumed political sympathies. Referring to the 1947 HUAC hearings for *Screen Writers Guild* magazine, in an editorial titled "The Judas Goats," Lillian Hellman wrote:

> A sickening, sickening, immoral and degraded week. And why did it take place? It took place because those who wish war have not the common touch. Highly placed gentlemen are often not really gentleman, and don't know how to go about these things. Remember that when it was needed, in Europe, they had to find the house painter [Hitler] and the gangster to make fear work and terror acceptable to the ignorant. Circuses will do it, and this was just such a circus; hide the invasion of the American Constitution with the faces of movie actors; pander to ignorance by telling people that ignorance is good, and lies even better; bring on the millionaire movie producer and show that he too is human, he too is frightened and cowardly. Take him away from his golden house and make him a betrayer and a fool and for those who like such shows and enjoy such moral degradation.... But why this particular industry? These particular people? Has it anything to do with Communism? Of course not. There has never been a single line or word of Communism in any American picture at any time.[101]

Hellman too would be blacklisted.

After November 1947, according to the Larry Ceplair–Steven England book *The Inquisition in Hollywood*, "[L]iberal resistance [to red baiting] virtually ceased to exist. Few … challenged the right of HUAC to exist … a mere handful … fought the blacklist."[102]

In self-protection, Hollywood started churning out anti–Communist films: *Rogue's Regiment* (1948), *The Red Menace* (1949), *The Big Lift* (1950), *I Was a Communist for the FBI* (1951), *Diplomatic Courier* (1952), *My Son John* (1952), *Target Hong Kong* (1953), *The Bamboo Prison* (1954), *Blood Alley* (1955), *China Gate* (1957), *The Beast of Budapest* (1958), *The Quiet American* (1958), *Battle Flame* (1959), *Satan Never Sleeps* (1962), *The Manchurian Candidate* (1962), etc. Only a handful of them were worthy of critical acclaim. But quality wasn't the point; the point was getting on the right side of the prevailing political winds.

All of this no doubt left Dashiell Hammett feeling exposed. But if he felt vulnerable, it didn't slow him down. After the War, he remained involved in dozens of organizations that would be labeled Communist fronts, like the Joint Fascist Refugee Committee, the Veterans of the Abraham Lincoln Brigade, the American Committee for the Protection of the Foreign Born and the Civil Right Congress, founded in 1946 with Hammett as its New York State president. On the faculty at the Jefferson School of Social Science, Hammett taught a weekly writing course. History professor Marvin Gettleman said of the Jefferson School:

> Its pedagogy represented some of the left's most creative cultural work in the period. With a faculty that included distinguished scholars, writers, artists and musicians, the School attracted thousands of mainly adult student-workers each term. It offered them a wide array of courses, lectures and cultural programs mostly on Marxism, trade union issues and related topics, along with teaching about practical applications to the day's political struggles. Art, music, dance and literature were also essential components of the curriculum.[103]

The 1950s found the FBI investigating 4.5 million Americans, launching 27,000 full-scale investigations. They led to government employees, librarians, university professors and others losing their jobs. One hundred fifty loyalty and security boards sprung up to deal with alleged subversives.[104] The character of individuals can be judged by their response to the enveloping fear and suspicion. Perhaps the era can even be understood at the micro level: How did Sam Spade (Humphrey Bogart) and Nick Charles (Dashiell Hammett) respond?

In our mind's eye, Sam Spade is Bogie. He's the ultimate tough guy detective come to life in *The Maltese Falcon*, living with a code of his own in a world that has lost its moral compass, sacrificing love and safety to do the right thing. But actors and the characters they play on the silver screen are rarely the same. Bogie was the ultimate star of Hollywood's 1930s–1950s golden era, appearing in such classics as *Casablanca*, *The Big Sleep*, *The Treasure of the Sierra Madre* and *The African Queen*.

The FBI, our consummate internal spy network, began a file on Bogart in 1936; they called him one of 21 members of the Screen Actors Guild "with strong Communist leanings."[105] His FBI file grew to hundreds of pages.

Martin Dies (1900–72) was a Democrat Congressman from Texas, first chair of the House UnAmerican Activities Committee (1937–44) and, like succeeding HUAC stalwarts Parnell Thomas and John Rankin, a diehard segregationist. He first took his committee on the road to Hollywood in 1940. "Dies … had no use for the New Deal, organized labor, blacks, or Jews."[106] HUAC became an instrument for entrenching a right-wing ideology and rolling back New Deal reforms.

Bogart went before the Committee and denied allegations of Communist influence in Hollywood and in his own politics, saying under oath: "I know of no Communist activities in Hollywood.... I've been born an American. I've always been a loyal citizen. I have great love for my country."[107]

The Committee for the First Amendment (CFA) delivered its petition to the House of Representatives decrying HUAC abuse of Constitutional rights. Representative John Rankin waved a copy of the petition from the CFA, substituting the original Jewish names of the stars into the record: Danny Kaye as David Daniel Kaminsky, Edward G. Robinson as Emmanuel Goldenberg, etc., and then in an anti–Semitic statement no one could miss, he stated, "They are attacking the Committee for doing its duty ... to save the American people from the horrible fate the Communists have meted out to the unfortunate Christian people of Europe."[108]

A right-wing backlash developed and William Randolph Hearst called for "the Federal censorship of motion pictures" in a front-page editorial in all his papers.[109] The studios fired and blacklisted the Hollywood Ten. A boycott of Bogart movies and a letter-writing campaign against the star began. Studio heads panicked. Wrote Bogart: "[Ed] Sullivan looked at me as if I had two heads. 'Look, Bogie,' he said.... 'the American public is beginning to think you're a Red.'"[110] What did Bogie do, this actor who had played so many tough guys, from Sam Spade to Duke Mantee (*The Petrified Forest*) to Rick Blaine (*Casablanca*)? He wilted like week-old lettuce under the bright lights of HUAC scrutiny. He called a press conference. Warner Brothers studio chief (and friendly HUAC witness) Jack Warner[111] helped him write a retraction of all he had done. Bogie told the press: "I went to Washington because I thought fellow Americans were being deprived of their Constitutional rights and for that reason alone. That trip was ill-advised, even foolish, I am very ready to admit.... I have absolutely no use for Communism nor for anyone who serves that philosophy."[112] Then, to further his *mea culpa*, he wrote an article for *Photoplay* in May 1948. The magazine put his picture on the cover with the words "I'm No Communist." He wrote of his work with the CFA: "We may not have been very smart in the way we did things, may have been dopes in some people's eyes, but we were American dopes! Actors and actresses always go overboard about things.... As I said, I'm no Communist. If you thought so, you were dead wrong. But, brother, in this democracy, no one's going to shoot you for having thought so."[113]

In response, an Indiana newspaper columnist wrote, "All right, Humphrey. You can get up off your knees."[114] But the studio was satisfied. Wired Jack Warner in all caps to the New York Office: "THEY ARE PLENTY FRIGHTENED" and "BOTH BOGART AND BACALL ARE BENDING BACKWARDS BEYOND THE FLOOR."[115] This was Humphrey Bogart, not Sam Spade; real life, not art. Bogart saved his career but may have paid a non-monetary price. His friend Richard Brooks, screenwriter of Bogart's *Key Largo* (in which gangsters stood in for the anti–Communist witch hunters), said, "Bogie was never the same again."[116] But what would you have done if your career was on the line? Hammett would have to answer that question for himself.

Mustered out of the service, Hammett moved back to Hellman and their 130-acre Hardscrabble Farm in Westchester, an hour from New York City. He also took an apartment in Manhattan to be near the Jefferson School of Social Science, where he taught from 1946 to 1950 (and served on the Board of Trustees from 1949 until it closed in 1956).

It looks like Humphrey Bogart as Sam Spade is about to punch Mary Astor, Brigid O'Shaughnessy, in 1941's *The Maltese Falcon*. Bogart often played tough guys, whether as detectives or gangsters, but in real life he folded before the Red hunters in Hollywood.

He was also involved with the Civil Rights Congress. The CRC had 60 chapters and 10,000 members at its peak and Hammett became president of the New York State office. Formed in 1946, the Congress defended voting rights and free speech, while opposing lynching and the Smith Act. It combined legal defense with anti-racist publicity campaigns and may be best remembered for its accusatory pamphlet *We Charge Genocide*, submitted to the United Nations; it charged the U.S. government with genocide against its black citizens by an entrenched system of white supremacy.

We see the way that Hammett had not only changed from an agent for the strike-breaking Pinkerton Agency to become a committed Marxist, but also from a casual racist to a civil rights activist. He looked for political, collective solutions rather than individual, personal responses to a rapacious capitalist system. In a letter to his teenage daughter Mary in 1936, he offered this political advice:

> Be in favor of what's good for the workers and against what isn't. Follow that and you may not be the most brilliant person in the world, but you'll at least be able to hold your head up when you look at yourself in the mirror.[117]

Hammett stayed busy with his political work after the war. As he wrote to daughter Mary:

> [I have] a full schedule of meetings and other doings for the Civil Rights Congress ... on behalf of the Jews, Negroes, trade unionists, Communists, pseudo-communists, suspected

Communists, imaginary communists, and god knows who all the Trumans, Tom Clarks [attorney general], Tom Deweys [governor of New York], Vandenburgs [Republican Senator], Bilbos [Mississippi Senator and leading segregationist], Rankins [HUAC] , Hoovers [FBI Director], big and little and other so-and-sos of that sort [who] choose to jump on.[118]

Hammett's FBI file, begun in 1934, grew to 278 pages by 1951. Agents shadowed him and broke into Hardscrabble Farm when Hellman and Hammett were away, for a surreptitious and illegal search, hoping to find incriminating documents.[119]

The FBI and Army Intelligence kept an eye on Hammett:

"[C]onfidential informants kept track of his activities" and "a casual surveillance" was maintained on him during his service in the Aleutians.... FBI agents spied on Hammett and Hellman at their Hardscrabble Farm—his political activities were reported in the right wing Hearst press "indicating they were being fed information because they were friendly newspapers." ... He was also a target of *Red Channels* [their report on "Communist Influence on Radio and Television" accused 151 artists of manipulating entertainment for purposes of Communist propaganda].[120]

The FBI also watched Hammett's partner Lillian Hellman. "[The] FBI file on Hellman had 307 pages, including mail intercepts and on one wartime air flight her baggage was searched without her knowledge and the books she had packed noted including *The Little Oxford Dictionary* and *The King's English*, and her bank accounts were checked."[121]

Eventually the government secret forces struck using the infamous Smith Act. Signed into law by President Roosevelt in 1940, the Smith Act made it a federal crime to "teach and advocate the overthrow of the United States government by force and violence." Over 200 Americans were indicted, fascists and Communists. Many were convicted and sentenced to years in prison. In 1957, the Supreme Court ruled that the First Amendment guarantee of freedom of speech was a defense against the Smith Act and that there was a clear difference between teaching the idea of revolution and actually plotting the overthrow of the government. At that time, courts threw out most of the convictions.

But that was 1957; Hammett ran afoul of the law in 1951.

As president of the Civil Rights Congress, Hammett was also a trustee of its bail fund which had raised contributions totaling $750,000 from some 5000 people to bail out defendants waiting trial or prison on political charges.[122] Money from the fund was used to bail out Smith Act defendants. When some of them skipped bail, the government demanded to know the names of bail fund contributors claiming they needed the names to see if any of the contributors might be sheltering the fugitives, an absurd argument that would allow them to smear anyone who might have contributed, though it was no crime to do so. The sole aim was to deter others from contributing.

Hammett and three other CRC Bail Fund trustees were hauled before District Court Judge Sylvester Ryan in July 1951. Hellman suggested that Hammett simply tell the judge he didn't know the names or addresses of the bail fund contributors, which may or may not have been true. Hellman wrote that he replied: "I hate this damn kind of talk, but maybe I'd better tell you that if it were more than jail, if it were my life, I would give it for what I think democracy is, and I don't let cops or judges tell me what I think democracy is."[123]

Hammett and the others invoked their Fifth Amendment right against self-incrimination and refused to testify or turn over the lists of contributors. Judge

Ryan held them in contempt. "Samuel Dashiell Hammett, have you anything to say as to why judgment should not be pronounced on you by this court?" Ryan asked.

"Not a thing," replied Hammett.[124]

The judge sentenced him to six months in prison or "until he purged himself of contempt." Daughter Jo added: "Fat chance, I thought, knowing that 'purging' wasn't an option for Papa, that his decision had been no decision at all. Papa had lots of faults, God knows, buckets of faults, but ratting on people who trusted him with their money and names wasn't one of them."[125]

It got crazier. While Hammett awaited prison, Supreme Court Justice Learned Hand ordered that the men be allowed to bail themselves out. Hammett's secretary showed up at the jail with a cash bail. The G-Men ordered her to reveal the source of the funds, which was legally none of their business. When she refused, they denied bail. And no money from the CRC bail fund might be used since it was considered "evidence" in the case. They packed Hammett off to Ashland Federal Penitentiary in Ashland, Kentucky, where he became Prisoner PMB8416. He served five months, from July 9 to December 9, 1951. He wrote to his daughter: "[A]s the boys say, you can do five months without taking your shoes off,"[126] explaining in another letter a few days later: "Sweeping, wall-washing, dusting, window-washing and brass polishing keep me indoors most of the day." Due to his age and bearing, even the prison guards addressed him as "sir."[127] An FBI report described Hellman as a member of Communist front organizations and so the warden barred her from visiting.

The right-wing press piled on. Water Winchell, called "the single most powerful man in American entertainment,"[128] advised his national newspaper and radio audience: "Call him Dashiell Hammett and sickle … call him Samovar Spade."[129] Said *The Knickerbocker News*: "He took crime out of the gutter, and now it looks as though he has followed it there."[130] *The New York Guide* wanted to hit Hammett in the pocketbook, and anywhere else they could: "There is no law that requires any American to add one dollar to Hammett's revenue and patriotic Americans will refuse to read or listen to a line that has ever come from that guy."[131]

Prison took its toll. Claudia Roth Pierpont wrote in *The New Yorker*:

> Lillian Hellman said she found it irritating when Hammett told people, as he always did, that his time in jail had not been bad at all; the conversation was no sillier than at a New York cocktail party, he liked to say; the food was awful but one could drink milk; and it was possible to be proud of work well done even when that work was cleaning toilets. In fact, the months that Hammett spent in jail … entirely broke his health; he was fifty-seven when he went in, and an old man when he came out. Returning to New York, he couldn't get down the ramp of the plane without stumbling and stopping to rest. (Hellman, who went to meet him at the airport, says she stayed out of sight for a while so he wouldn't see her see him.)[132]

Payback for his stand didn't end there. The IRS, the government arm best used for political punishment, delivered Hammett a tax bill of $111,008.60 in back taxes, well over a million dollars in today's dollars.[133] But Hammett was broke and blacklisted. Three of his income streams, long-running radio shows and newspaper comic strips, written by others but using his name, were cancelled. His books went out of print. No one wanted his services as a screenwriter or play doctor. By May 1952, all the money he had in the world amounted to less than $3000.[134] Hellman, also blacklisted and broke, sold their beloved Hardscrabble Farm. And yet Hammett stood up to the witch hunters bravely and with a moral code of his own, just like the protagonists of his novels.

According to Jo: "[H]e plunged right back into the battle, organizing and writing public statements of one sort or another. Much of this activity was directed against the Smith Act, which had been used as a means of jailing Communists."[135]

The Red hunters didn't quit either. In 1953, Joe McCarthy set out to clean up the U.S. Voice of America and 200 U.S. State Department Information Centers (libraries, in other words) in 63 countries and make some new headlines. Historian Richard Reeves write:

> In response, the State Dept. ordered "the banning of all books, music, paintings of 'Communists, fellow travelers, etcetera' from the Voice of America and ordering overseas librarians to remove all publication by controversial authors from their shelves." ...McCarthy charged that there were over 30,000 volumes in agency libraries by "Communist" authors. The figure was actually obtained by listing individual copies of books by 418 authors [including Hammett, Arthur Schlesinger, Jr., John Dewey, Edna Ferber and Stephen Vincent Benet]. ... [I]n the madness that followed nervous librarians discarded and even burned books.[136]

McCarthy, Chair of the U.S. Senate Subcommittee on Permanent Investigations, subpoenaed Hammett to testify. Hammett once again invoked his Fifth Amendment right against self-incrimination but did answer some questions:

> **McCarthy:** "Have you ever engaged in espionage again the United States?"
> **Hammett:** "No."
> **McCarthy:** "Have you ever engaged in sabotage?"
> **Hammett:** "No."

Finally McCarthy asked one question too many and Hammett took him to school:

> **McCarthy:** "If you were spending, as we are, over a hundred million dollars a year on an information program allegedly for the purpose of fighting Communism, would you purchase the works of some 75 Communist authors?"
> **Hammett:** "If I were fighting Communism, I don't think I would do it by giving people any books at all."[137]

As Voice of America libraries began removing Hammett's novels and short stories from their library shelves, a funny thing happened. President Eisenhower, no crusading liberal himself, said publicly that he saw no threat posed to the United States as he didn't suppose Nick Charles was a Commie. The Voice of America returned Hammett's books to their shelves.[138] Hammett wrote to his daughter, tongue in cheek no doubt: "[S]o I stick to my original hope that the publicity will help my sales. I don't see what else could be in it for anybody."[139]

Also in 1953, Hellman, worried that Hammett's continuing relationship with the Thomas Jefferson School of Social Science might lead to another prison sentence, shared her fear as they walked down 52nd Street in Manhattan. She says Hammett responded:

> "Lilly, when we reach the corner you are going to have to make up your mind that I must go my way.... I'm trouble and a nuisance to you. I won't ever blame you if you say goodbye to me now. But if you don't, we must never have this conversation again." When we got to the corner, I began to cry and he looked as if he might. I was not able to speak, so he touched my shoulder and turned downtown. I stood on the corner until I couldn't see him anymore and then I began to run. When I caught up to him, he said, "I haven't thought about a drink in years. But I'd like one. Anyway, let's go buy one for you."[140]

In August 1955, Hammett suffered a heart attack. Hellman moved him into her New York City apartment. He never really recovered and died in 1961 at 66 years of age,

Dashiell Hammett, the original Thin Man, served his country by enlisting in the military during World War I and II. Red-hunter Senator Joe McCarthy tried and failed to block Hammett's burial at the Arlington National Cemetery (Photograph by Astrochemist, Wikimedia Commons).

suffering from lung cancer and diseases of the liver, heart, kidneys, spleen and prostate after a lifetime of dissolution.[141] New York literati, including Dorothy Parker, Bennett Cerf, Leonard Bernstein and Lionel Trilling, attended his small private funeral. In her eulogy, Hellman called Hammett "a man, funny, witty. Most of his life was wide open and adventurous, and most of it he enjoyed. He learned and acted on what he learned. He believed in man's right to dignity and never in all the years did he play anybody's game but his own.... He was a man of simple honor and bravery."[142]

Hammett's books still sell well in some 68 translations[143] and he has been himself the subject of more than 20 books. At the last moment, FBI Chief J. Edgar Hoover tried to prevent Hammett from being buried at Arlington National Cemetery. Hoover failed; Hammett, a veteran of two American wars, now lies in that hallowed ground.

Epilogue
Who Was the Thin Man?

After one novel, six feature films and various radio, TV and stage spinoffs, the identity of the Thin Man seems to have been lost. Clearly he was Clyde Wynant at the beginning but only as a dismembered corpse buried in lime in the *Thin Man* novel. We are told of sightings, phone calls and letters from Wynant but these reports, from Mimi, Macaulay and Gilbert respectively, are lies. Wynant is the title character of the novel whom we never encounter. In the *Thin Man* movie, Wynant gets about five minutes of screen time before his disappearance. But James Wong Howe's black and white deep focus photography as Wynant walks down the street and his shadow lengthens and lengthens leaves no doubt in our minds that Wynant is the Thin Man.

But the dead are quickly forgotten as both novel and film dazzle us with the extraordinary relationship of Nick and Nora and Nick's own tough-mindedness and physical prowess with gun and fists. If there is a Thin Man around who holds our attention, it is Nick. And in the first three films, we believe actor William Powell is Nick Charles: his cockiness, quick comebacks and even his svelte waistline convince us he could be the Thin Man. Sadly, by movies four through six, his growing girth defeats that illusion. Powell's off-screen conventionality, political silence and 25-year retirement seclusion left Nick Charles far behind and forgotten. What we have left is "the plaid coat in which he was often seen as he puttered around Palm Springs.... The coat is now on display at the Palm Springs Historical Society."[1]

That photo of Dashiell Hammett, thin and dapper, on the cover of the first edition of *The Thin Man,* walking stick in his right hand, left hand in his pocket (perhaps concealing a revolver), pocket handkerchief in place and hat pulled down just a tad above his right eye, tie tightly knotted, personifies the very figure of Nick Charles our imagination conjures. The drinking and womanizing, the contempt for authority, the courage against long odds, and the struggle for redemption are also of a piece. Nick and Dash, each the Thin Man, do live on, their lives inspirational for many.

Chapter Notes

Chapter 1

1. Tom Soter, *Investigating Couples: A Critical Analysis of* The Thin Man, The Avengers, *and* The X Files (Jefferson, NC: McFarland, 2002), p. 4.
2. Raymond Chandler, *The Simple Art of Murder*, mysteryfictions.web.unc.edu/wp-content/uploads/sites/17139/2018/08/Chandler-Simple-Art-of-Murder.pdf.
3. *Ibid.*
4. *Ibid.*
5. Carl D. Malmgren, "The Crime of the Sign: Dashiell Hammett's Detective Fiction," *Twentieth Century Literature: A Scholarly and Critical Journal* 45.3 (1999): 371. https://core.ac.uk/download/pdf/216834408.pdf.
6. Julian Symons, *Mortal Consequences: A History from the Detective Story to the Crime Novel* (New York: Harper & Row, 1972), p. 111.
7. *Ibid.*
8. Howard Haycraft, *Murder for Pleasure: The Life and Times of the Detective Story* (New York: D. Appleton-Century, 1941), p. 165.
9. *Ibid.*, p. 166.
10. Richard Layman, *Shadow Man: The Life of Dashiell Hammett* (New York: Harcourt Brace Jovanovich, 1981), p. 80.
11. S.S. Van Dine, *The Benson Murder Case*, Chapter 1. https://www.fadedpage.com/showbook.php?pid=20131113.
12. John Douglas Eames, *The MGM Story: The Complete History of Over Fifty Roaring Years* (New York: Crown, 1975), p. 122.
13. Haycraft, p. 169.
14. *Ibid.*, p. 171.
15. Ross Macdonald, "The Writer as Detective Hero," *The Stacks Reader*, January 1965. http://www.thestacksreader.com/the-writer-as-detective-hero/.
16. George J. Thompson, "Rhino," *Hammett's Moral Vision* (San Francisco: Vince Emery Productions, 1972), p. 170.
17. Dashiell Hammett, *Five Complete Novels* (New York: Avenel Books, 1962), p. 591.
18. *Ibid.*, p. 592.
19. *Ibid.*
20. *Ibid.*, p. 595.
21. Dennis Dooley, *Dashiell Hammett* (New York: Frederick Ungar, 1984), p. 12.
22. Frederick Lewis Allen, *Since Yesterday: 1929–1939* (New York: Bantam, 1940), p. 25.
23. *Prohibition*, dir. Lynne Novick and Ken Burns, PBS Documentary, 2011, Episode 1, "A Nation of Drunkards."
24. Paula Bren, "Sex and the City," *The New York Times*, December 5, 2021, Book Reviews, p. 16.
25. Dashiell Hammett, *Five Complete Novels*, p. 693.
26. Michael Turback, *Nick and Nora: The Couple Who Taught America How to Drink* (N.p.: History Company, 2018), p. 7.
27. *Ibid.*, p. 2.
28. *Ibid.*, p. 4.
29. Dashiell Hammett, *Five Complete Novels*, p. 598.
30. *Ibid.*
31. *Ibid.*
32. Ken Fuller, *Hardboiled Activist: The Work and Politics of Dashiell Hammett* (Glasgow: Praxis Press, 2017), p. 109.
33. Dashiell Hammett, *Five Complete Novels*, p. 599.
34. *Ibid.*, p. 602.
35. *Ibid.*, p. 634.
36. *Ibid.*, p. 602.
37. *Ibid.*, p. 607.
38. *Ibid.*, p. 605.
39. *Ibid.*, p. 652.
40. *Ibid.*, p. 691.
41. Layman, *Shadow Man*, p. 145.
42. *Ibid.*
43. Dashiell Hammett, *Five Complete Novels*, p. 632.
44. *Ibid.*, p. 649.
45. Marissa Gerken, "Wisconsin Department of Health warns against eating the 'cannibal sandwich,' a traditional holiday dish in the state," CNN, December 14, 2020. https://www.cnn.com/2020/12/14/us/cannibal-sandwich-wisconsin-trnd/index.html.
46. Dashiell Hammett, *Five Complete Novels*, p. 636.
47. *Ibid.*
48. Layman, *Shadow Man*, p. 145.
49. Anna P. Kelly, "Scorched Earth: Expressions of Modernity in Dashiell Hammett's Pulp Fiction," a Thesis in the Field of English Literature for the Degree of Master of Liberal Arts in

Extension Studies, Harvard University, November 2017. http://nrs.harvard.edu/urn-3:HUL.InstRepos:37799762.
50. William Marling, *Dashiell Hammett* (Boston: Twayne, 1983), p. 104.
51. Dooley, p. 122.
52. Dashiell Hammett, *Five Complete Novels*, p. 719.
53. *Ibid.*, p. 720.
54. *Ibid.*, p. 722.
55. *Ibid.*, p. 723.
56. *Ibid.*, p. 726.
57. *Ibid.*
58. *Ibid.*
59. *Ibid.*, p. 608.
60. *Ibid.*, p. 609.
61. *Ibid.*
62. *The Thin Man*, dir. W.S. Van Dyke, perf. William Powell and Myrna Loy, MGM, 1934.
63. Dashiell Hammett, *Five Complete Novels*, p. 648.
64. *Ibid.*
65. *Ibid.*, p. 665.
66. *Ibid.*, p. 641.
67. Adam Cohen, "Rock of Ages," *The New York Times*, September 28, 2003. https://www.nytimes.com/2003/09/28/books/rock-of-ages.html.
68. Dashiell Hammett, *Five Complete Novels*, p. 645.
69. The Library of Congress, https://www.loc.gov/classroom-materials/united-states-history-primary-source-timeline/great-depression-and-world-war-ii-1929-1945/race-relations-in-1930s-and-1940s/.
70. Isaac Anderson, "New Mystery Stories," *The New York Times*, January 7, 1934. https://timesmachine.nytimes.com/timesmachine/1934/01/07/94481846.pdf?pdf_redirect=true&ip=0.
71. "The Criminal Record," *The Saturday Review of Literature*, January 13, 1934. https://www.unz.com/print/SaturdayRev-1934jan13-00412a03/.
72. Layman, *Shadow Man*, p. 147.
73. *Ibid.*
74. Raymond Chandler, *The Simple Art of Murder*, http://www.en.utexas.edu/Classes/Bremen/e316k/316kprivate/scans/chandlerart.html.
75. NPR Staff, "Nick and Nora (and Asta) Return in the Thin Man Novellas," NPR, November 3, 2012. https://www.npr.org/2012/11/03/164195799/nick-nora-and-asta-return-in-thin-man-novellas.
76. Don Herron, *The Dashiell Hammett Tour* (San Francisco: City Lights, 1991), p. 38.
77. Lillian Hellman, *Three* (Boston: Little, Brown, 1979), p. 290.
78. Christine Doudna, "A Conversation with Lillian Hellman: A Still Unfinished Woman," *Rolling Stone*, February 24, 1977. https://www.rollingstone.com/culture/culture-features/a-conversation-with-lillian-hellman-50202/.
79. Dashiell Hammett, *Five Complete Novels*, p. 589.
80. Joe Gioia, "The Garden of Curses: Down on the Farm with S.J. Perelman and Nathanael West," *Humor in America*, September 29, 2016. https://humorinamerica.wordpress.com/2016/09/29/the-garden-of-curses-down-on-the-farm-with-s-j-perelman-and-nathanael-west/.
81. Dashiell Hammett, *Five Complete Novels*, p. 675.

Chapter 2

1. Eve Zilbart, "Dashiell Hammett, Hard-Boiled &," *The Washington Post*, October 6, 1982. https://www.washingtonpost.com/archive/lifestyle/1982/10/06/dashiell-hammett-hard-boiled-38/5679d60c-96a0-4362-9e3f-e0d39c7b4abc/.
2. Don Herron, *The Dashiell Hammett Tour* (San Francisco: City Lights, 1991), p. 3.
3. Richard Layman, *Shadow Man: The Life of Dashiell Hammett* (New York: Harcourt Brace Jovanovich, 1981), p. 3.
4. Nathan Ward, *The Lost Detective: Becoming Dashiell Hammett* (New York: Bloomsbury, 2015), p. 40.
5. *Ibid.*, p. 8.
6. James Mackay, *Allan Pinkerton: The First Private Eye* (Edison, NJ: Castle Books, 2007), p. 7.
7. *Ibid.*, pp. 97–105.
8. S. Paul O'Hara, *Inventing the Pinkertons or Spies, Sleuths, Mercenaries, and Thugs* (Baltimore: Johns Hopkins University Press, 2016), p. 20.
9. *Ibid.*, p. 7.
10. *Ibid.*, p. 73.
11. *Ibid.*
12. *Ibid.*, p. 11.
13. William Marling, *Dashiell Hammett* (Boston: Twayne, 1983), p. 5.
14. Leo Huberman, *The Labor Spy Racket* (New York: Modern Age Books, 1937), p. 5.
15. *Ibid.*, p. 6.
16. *Ibid.*, p. 7.
17. *Ibid.*, p. 9.
18. *Ibid.*, p. 24.
19. *Ibid.*, p. 26.
20. *Ibid.*, p. 68.
21. *Ibid.*, p. 46.
22. Evan Osnos, "The Violent Style," *The New Yorker*, November 16, 2020, p. 34.
23. Ralph Chaplin, *Wobbly: The Rough and Tumble Story of an American Radical* (Chicago: University Chicago Press, 1948), p. 210.
24. Lillian Hellman, *Three* (Boston: Little, Brown, 1979), pp. 613–614.
25. Herron, p. 9.
26. Ward, p. 36.
27. Herron, p. 8.
28. Layman, *Shadow Man*, p. 36.
29. J.A. Zumoff, "Politics and the 1920's Writings of Dashiell Hammett," *Journal of American Studies* 52.1 (2012): 77–98, 88. https://journals.ku.edu/amsj/article/view/4413/4140.

30. *Ibid.*, p. 83.
31. Jo Hammett, *Dashiell Hammett: A Daughter Remembers*, ed. Richard Layman with Julie M. Rivett (New York: Carroll & Graf, 2001), p. 43.
32. Neely Tucker, "Stories That Will Beat You to a Bloody Pulp," *The Washington Post*, December 27, 2007. https://www.latimes.com/archives/la-xpm-2007-dec-27-et-pulp27-story.html.
33. Otto Penzler, ed., *The Black Lizard Big Book of Pulps* (New York: Vintage, 2007), p. xiii.
34. Don Swaim, "Bierce Duels with the Sage of Baltimore," *The Ambrose Bierce Site*, https://donswaim.com/bierce-mencken.html.
35. Claudia Roth Pierpont, "Tough Guy," *The New Yorker*, February 3, 2022. https://www.newyorker.com/magazine/2002/02/11/tough-guy.
36. Penzler, p. 15.
37. Dashiell Hammett, "From the Memoirs of a Private Detective," *The Smart Set*, March 1923. http://www.umsl.edu/~gradyf/film/Hammett.htm.
38. Albert Barrere and Charles Leland, eds., *A Dictionary of Slang, Jargon & Cant*, Volume 2 (London: George Bell and Sons, 1897), p. 120. https://books.google.com/books?id=1NjWAAAAMAAJ&pg=PA120&lpg=PA120&dq=p"r+collins+as+theater+slang&source=bl&ots=tJZeQL9XQ0&sig=ACfU3U0MsU3HyR3u7ayWDPOy681o3LD4hw&hl=en&sa=X&ved=2ahUKEwjQqJjvprPuAhVF-6wKHSnBfgQ6AEwEXoECBsQAg#v=onepage&q=p"r%20collins%20as%20theater%20slang&f=false.
39. Layman, *Shadow Man*, p. 27.
40. Julian Symons, *Dashiell Hammett* (San Diego: Harcourt Brace Jovanovich, 1985), p. 24.
41. Dashiell Hammett, *Five Complete Novels*, p. 7.
42. Cara Ellison, Brian Taylor, and Stu Horvath, "Dashiell Hammett's Red Harvest," Unwinnable, July 2, 2012. https://unwinnable.com/2012/07/02/dashiell-hammetts-red-harvest/.
43. Dashiell Hammett, *Five Complete Novels*, p. 9.
44. *Ibid.*, p. 377.
45. *Ibid.*, p. 41.
46. Anna P. Kelly, "Scorched Earth: Expressions of Modernity in Dashiell Hammett's Pulp Fiction," a Thesis in the Field of English Literature for the Degree of Master of Liberal Arts in Extension Studies, Harvard University, November 2017, p. 8. http://nrs.harvard.edu/urn-3:HUL.InstRepos:37799762.
47. Tom Nolan, "Crime Fiction's Hardboiled Revolutionary," *The Los Angles Times*, January 30, 2005. https://www.latimes.com/archives/la-xpm-2005-jan-30-bk-nolan30-story.html48.
48. James Robenalt, "If we weren't so obsessed with Warren G. Harding's sex life, we'd realize he was a pretty good president," *The Washington Post*, August 13, 2015. https://www.washingtonpost.com/posteverything/wp/2015/08/13/if-we-werent-so-obsessed-with-warren-g-hardings-sex-life-wed-realize-he-was-a-pretty-good-president/.
49. Diane Johnson, *Dashiell Hammett: A Life* (New York: Random House, 1983), p. 83.
50. Variety Staff, "The Maltese Falcon," *Variety*, September 30, 1941. https://variety.com/1941/film/reviews/the-maltese-falcon-2-1200413694/.
51. David T. Bazelon, "Dashiell Hammett's 'Private Eye': No Loyalty Beyond the Job," *Commentary*, May 1949. https://www.commentarymagazine.com/articles/david-bazelon-2/dashiell-hammetts-private-eyeno-loyalty-beyond-the-job/.
52. "Reappraisal: Dash and Don," *The Westlake Review*, March 9, 2018. https: thewestlakereview.wordpress.com/tag/dorothy-parker/.
53. Sally Cline, *Dashiell Hammett: Man of Mystery* (New York: Arcade, 2014), p. 101.
54. Johnson, p. 106.
55. Jo Hammett, p. 39.
56. Samuel Marx, *A Gaudy Spree: Literary Hollywood When the West Was Fun* (New York: Franklin Watts, 1987), p. 149.
57. *Ibid.*, p. 151.
58. Hellman, *Three*, p. 299.
59. Symons, *Dashiell Hammett*, p. 78.
60. Cline, p. 94.
61. Peter Feibleman, *Lilly: Reminiscences of Lillian Hellman* (New York: William Morrow, 1988), p. 25.
62. Jo Hammett, p. 79.
63. Johnson, p. 108.
64. Lillian Hellman, *Six Plays by Lillian Hellman* (New York: Vintage, 1979), p. 1.
65. *Ibid.*, p. 397.
66. Cline, p. 122.
67. Johnson, p. 107.
68. Cline, p. 94.
69. Layman, p. 140
70. Hellman, *Three*, p. 290.
71. Ward, p. 158.
72. Layman, *Shadow Man*, p. 141.
73. Ward, p. 160.
74. Layman, *Shadow Man*, p. 141.
75. Hellman, *Three*, p. 280.
76. Dashiell Hammett, *The Continental Op* (New York: Vintage, 1974), p. xi.
77. Jo Hammett, p. 72.
78. Sinda Gregory, *Private Investigations: The Novels of Dashiell Hammett* (Carbondale: Southern Illinois University Press, 1985), p. 174.

Chapter 3

1. Diane Johnson, *Dashiell Hammett: A Life* (New York: Random House, 1983), p. 113.
2. Jon Tuska, *The Detective in Hollywood* (Garden City, NY: Doubleday, 1978), pp. 194195.
3. *Ibid.*, p. 195.
4. Greg Mitchell, *The Campaign of the Century: Upton Sinclair's Race for Governor of California and the Birth of Media Politics* (New York: Random House, 1992), p. 243.
5. Stephen Follows, "How Long Does the Average Hollywood Movie Take to Make?" *Stephen Follows Film Data and Education*, May 7, 2018. https://stephenfollows.com/how-long-the-average-hollywood-movie-take-to-make/.

6. *The Week*, February 26, 2021, p. 10.

7. Roger Bryant, *William Powell: The Life and Films* (Jefferson, NC: McFarland, 2008), p. 3.

8. Dashiell Hammett, *Return of The Thin Man*, eds. Richard Layman and Julie M. Rivett (New York: The Mysterious Press, 2012), p. 3.

9. Frances Goodrich and Albert Hackett, "The Thin Man Screenplay," based on the novel by Dashiell Hammett, shooting draft, 1935. http://www.dailyscript.com/scripts/thethinman.html.

10. *The Thin Man*, dir. W.S. Van Dyke, Perf. William Powell and Myrna Loy. MGM, 1934.

11. *Ibid.*

12. *Ibid.*

13. Robert C. Cannom and Adela Rogers St. Johns, *Van Dyke and the Mythical City, Hollywood* (Culver City, CA: Murray & Gee, 1948), pp. 287–288.

14. Dashiell Hammett, *Five Complete Novels*, p. 592.

15. Charles Tranberg, *The Thin Man: Murder Over Cocktails* (Albany, GA: Bear Manor Media, 2009), p. 78.

16. *The Thin Man*, dir. W.S. Van Dyke.

17. *Ibid.*

18. David L. Goodrich, *The Real Nick and Nora: Frances Goodrich and Albert Hackett, Writers of Stage and Screen Classics* (Carbondale: Southern Illinois University Press, 2001), p. 76.

19. Tom Soter, *Investigating Couples: A Critical Analysis of* The Thin Man, The Avengers, *and* The X Files (Jefferson, NC: McFarland, 2002), pp. 34–35.

20. *The Thin Man*, dir. W.S. Van Dyke.

21. *The Kennel Murder Case*, dir. Dr: Michael Curtiz, Perf. William Powell and Mary Astor. Warner Brothers, 1933.

22. *The Thin Man*, dir. W.S. Van Dyke.

23. *Ibid.*

24. *Ibid.*

25. *Ibid.*

26. *Ibid.*

27. *Ibid.*

28. *Ibid.*

29. Roger Bryant, *William Powell: The Life and Films* (Jefferson, NC: McFarland, 2008), p. 10.

30. *The Thin Man*, dir. W.S. Van Dyke.

31. Samuel Marx, *A Gaudy Spree: Literary Hollywood When the West Was Fun* (New York: Franklin Watts, 1987), p. 8.

32. *Ibid.*, p. 7.

33. *The Thin Man*, dir. W.S. Van Dyke.

34. *Ibid.*

35. *Ibid.*

36. Emily Leider, *Myrna Loy: The Only Good Girl in Hollywood* (Berkeley: University of California Press, 2011), p. 115.

37. Marx, *A Gaudy Spree*, p. 78.

38. Bryant, p. 8.

39. *The Thin Man*, dir. W.S.Van Dyke.

40. *Ibid.*

41. Dashiell Hammett, *Five Complete Novels*, p. 610.

42. *The Thin Man*, dir. W.S. Van Dyke.

43. *Ibid.*

44. James Kotsilibas-Davis and Myrna Loy, *Myrna Loy: Being and Becoming* (New York: Alfred A. Knopf, 1987), p. 149.

45. "'The Thin Man': THR's 1934 Review," *The Hollywood Reporter*, May 25, 2018. https://www.hollywoodreporter.com/review/thin-man-review-1934-movie-1096779.

46. Mordaunt Hall, "A Nonchalant Criminologist," *The New York Times*, June 30, 1934. https://www.nytimes.com/1934/06/30/archives/a-nonchalant-criminologist.html.

47. Roger Ebert, "The Thin Man," RogerEbert.com, December 22, 2002. https://www.rogerebert.com/reviews/great-movie-the-thin-man-1934.

48. Bryant, p. 11.

49. Diana Johnson, *Dashiell Hammett: A Life* (New York: Random House, 1983), p. 117.

50. Robert C. Cannom and Adela Rogers St. Johns, *Van Dyke and the Mythical City, Hollywood* (Culver City, CA: Murray & Gee, 1948), p. 369.

51. Elizabeth Weitzman, "The Depression-era gems at 1930's prices," *The Daily News*, February 6, 2009. https://www.nydailynews.com/entertainment/tv-movies/depression-era-gems-1930s-prices-article-1.389208.

52. John Douglas Eames, *The MGM Story: The Complete History of Over Fifty Roaring Years* (New York: Crown, 1975), p. 8.

53. *Ibid.*, p. 19.

54. Edward Sorel, *Mary Astor's Purple Diary: The Great American Sex Scandal of 1936* (New York: Liveright, 2016), p. 17.

55. Charles Higham, *Merchant of Dreams: Louis B. Mayer, M.G.M. and the Secret Hollywood* (New York: Donald I. Fine, 1993), p. 70.

56. Eames, p. 40.

57. Neal Gabler, *An Empire of Their Own: How the Jews Invented Hollywood* (New York: Crown, 1988), pp. 1–2.

58. *Ibid.*, p 2.

59. *Ibid.*, p. 277.

60. Diana Altman, *Hollywood East: Louis B. Mayer and the Origins of the Studio System* (New York: Birch Lane Press, 1992), p. 284.

61. *Ibid.*, p. 4.

62. Gabler, p. 84.

63. Jan Whitaker, "Prices," *Restaurant-ing Through History*. https://restaurant-ingthroughhistory.com/restaurant-prices/.

64. *Variety* LXXXXVIII, no. 8. p. 3. https://archive.org/details/variety87-1927-09/page/n2/mode/1up?view=theater.

65. Douglas Gomery, *The Hollywood Studio System: A History* (London: British Film Institute, 2005), p. 31.

66. Altman, p. xii.

67. *Variety* LXXXXVIII, no. 8. p. 3. https://archive.org/details/variety87-1927-09/page/n2/mode/1up?view=theater.

68. Manohla Dargis, "Lion of Hollywood: The Life and Legend of Louis B. Mayer," *The New York Times*, July 6, 2005. https://www.nytimes.

com/2005/07/06/style/lion-of-hollywood-the-life-and-legend-of-louis-b-mayer.html.
 69. Gabler, p. 116.
 70. *Ibid.*, p. 125.
 71. Bosley Crowther, *Hollywood Rajah: The Life and Times of Louis B. Mayer* (New York: Holt, Rinehart and Winston, 1960).
 72. Gomery, p. 3.
 73. "Louis B. Mayer, Film Maker, Dies," *The New York Times*, October 30, 1957, p. 29b. https://timesmachine.nytimes.com/timesmachine/1957/10/30/107173004.html?auth=login-email&pageNumber=29.
 74. Crowther, *Hollywood Rajah*, p. 6.
 75. Larry Ceplair and Steven Englund, *The Inquisition in Hollywood: Politics in the Film Community 1930–60* (Urbana: University of Illinois Press, 2003), p. 2.
 76. Andrew Sarris, *You Ain't Heard Nothin' Yet: The American Talking Film, History and Memory, 1927–1949* (Oxford: Oxford University Press, 1998), p. 22.
 77. *Going Attractions: The Definitive Story of the Movie Palace*, dir. April Wright, prod. Rachael Pond and April Wright, distributed by Passion River, 2019,.
 78. Gomery, p. 102.
 79. "A to Z Quotes Louis B. Meyer," https://www.azquotes.com/author/28531-Louis_B_Mayer.
 80. Charles Higham, *Merchant of Dreams: Louis B. Mayer, M.G.M. and the Secret Hollywood* (New York: Donald I. Fine, 1993), p. 423.
 81. Karina Longworth, *Seduction: Sex, Lies and Stardom in Howard Hughes's Hollywood* (New York: Custom House, 2018), p. 5.
 82. Marx, *A Gaudy Spree*, p. 86.
 83. *Ibid.*
 84. Budd Schulberg, What Make Sammy Run? (New York: Random House, 1941), p. 5.
 85. *Ibid.*, p. 272.
 86. *Ibid.*, p. 322.
 87. Carolyn Kellogg, "Budd Schulberg: Blinded by his gift," *The Los Angeles Times*, August 6, 2009. https://www.latimes.com/archives/blogs/jacketcopy/story/2009-08-06/budd-schulberg-blinded-by-his-gift.
 88. Jeremy Geltzer, *Dirty Words and Filthy Picture: Film and the First Amendment* (Austin: University of Texas Press, 2016), p. 9.
 89. Jane Addams, *Twenty Years at Hull House* (New York: New American Library, 1960), p. 267.
 90. Erica Gunderson, "New Book Traces History of Cinema's Censorship," WTTW PBS Chicago, March 21, 2016. https://news.wttw.com/2016/03/21/new-book-traces-history-cinemas-censorship.
 91. *Ibid.*
 92. "Arizona State University Appendix 1: The Motion Picture Production Code as published 31 May, 1930," Arizona State University, https://www.asu.edu/courses/fms200s/total-readings/MotionPictureProductionCode.pdf.
 93. Geltzler, p. 95.
 94. Bob Mondello, "Remembering Hollywood's Hays Code, 40 Years On," *All Things Considered*, NPR, August 8, 2008. https://www.npr.org/templates/story/story.php?storyId=93301189.
 95. *Ibid.*
 96. Thomas Doherty, *Hollywood's Censor: Joseph I. Breen & the Production Code Administration* (New York: Columbia University Press, 2017), p. 87.
 97. John Gallagher, "Martin Scorsese and Warner Brother Gangsters," *National Board of Review*, February 2005. https://web.archive.org/web/20121206113921/http://www.nbrmp.org/features/MartinScorsese.cfm.
 98. Doherty, *Hollywood's Censor*, p. 113.
 99. Thomas Doherty, "Was Hollywood's Famed Censor an Anti-Semite?" *Forward*, December 11, 2007. https://forward.com/culture/12234/was-hollywood-s-famed-censor-an-antisemite-00948/.
 100. Doherty, *Hollywood's Censor*, p. 172.
 101. *Ibid.*
 102. Higham, p. 144.
 103. *Ibid.*, p. 158.
 104. *Ibid.*, p. 177.
 105. *Hollywood: The Dream Factory*, writ. Irwin Rosten, narr. Dick Cavett, MGM, 1972.
 106. Higham, p. 335.
 107. Thelma Adams, "Casting-Couch Tactics Plagued Hollywood Long Before Harvey Weinstein," *Variety*, October 17, 2017. https://variety.com/2017/film/features/casting-couch-hollywood-sexual-harassment-harvey-weinstein-1202589895/.
 108. *Ibid.*
 109. Suyin Haynes, "The True Story Behind the Movie 'Judy,'" *Time*, September 26, 2019. https://time.com/5684673/judy-garland-movie-true-story/.
 110. Donald Bogle, *Hollywood Black: The Stars, The Films, The Filmmakers* (Philadelphia: Running Press, 2019), p. 24.
 111. Crowther, *Hollywood Rajah*, p. 197.
 112. Frederick Lewis Allen, *Since Yesterday: 1929–1939* (New York: Bantam, 1940), p. 50.
 113. Spencer Moon, *Reel Black Talk: A Sourcebook of 50 American Filmmakers* (Westport, CT: Greenwood Press, 1997), p. 24.
 114. Gabler, p. 329.
 115. Joe Morella and Edward Z. Epstein, *Gable & Lombard & Powell & Harlow* (New York: Dell, 1975), p. 121.
 116. Lester Cole, *Hollywood Red: The Autobiography of Lester Cole* (Palo Alto: Ramparts Press, 1981), p. 127.
 117. Higham, p. 167.
 118. Cole, p. 128.
 119. *Ibid.*
 120. Higham, p. 236.
 121. Leslie Frewin, *The Late Mrs. Dorothy Parker* (New York: Macmillan, 1986), p. 79.
 122. Dorothy Parker, *The Portable Dorothy Parker* (New York: Penguin, 1973), p. xvii.
 123. Debby Applegate, *Madam: The Biography*

of Polly Adler, Icon of the Jazz Age (New York: Doubleday, 2021), p. 194.
124. Parker, p. xxiv.
125. Robert L. Gale, *A Dashiell Hammett Companion* (Westport, CT: Greenwood Press, 2000), p. 199.
126. Marx, *A Gaudy Spree*, p. 45.
127. *Ibid.*, p. 46.
128. Frewin, p. 261.
129. Jeff Greenfield, "The Hollywood Hit Movie That Urged FDR to Become a Fascist," *Politico Magazine*, March 25, 2018. https://www.politico.com/magazine/story/2018/03/25/gabriel-over-the-white-house-fdr-inauguration-217349/.
130. Mordaunt Hall, "Walter Huston as President of the United Sates Who Proclaims Himself A Dictator," *The New York Times*, April 1, 1933. https://www.nytimes.com/1933/04/01/archives/walter-huston-as-a-president-of-the-united-states-who-proclaims.html.
131. Greenfield, "The Hollywood Hit Movie That Urged FDR to Become a Fascist."
132. Nicholas Karolides, *Banned Books: Literature Suppressed on Political Grounds* (New York: Facts on File, 2006), p. 266.
133. *Ibid.*, p. 267.
134. Higham, p. 292.
135. Ben Urwand, "The Chilling History of How Hollywood Helped Hitler," *The Hollywood Reporter*, July 31, 2013. https://www.hollywoodreporter.com/news/general-news/how-hollywood-helped-hitler-595684/.
136. *Ibid.*
137. Tom Brook, "Did Hollywood Studios Help the Nazis?" BBC, October 21, 2014. https://www.bbc.com/culture/article/20130930-did-hollywood-help-the-nazis.
138. Greg Mitchell, *The Campaign of the Century: Upton Sinclair's Race for Governor of California and the Birth of Media Politics* (New York: Random House, 1992), p. xiii.
139. *Ibid.*, p. 63.
140. *Ibid.*, p. xi.
141. *Ibid.*, p. 300.
142. *Ibid.*, p. 63.
143. Ceplair and Englund, p. 91.
144. Terry Christensen and Peter J. Haas, *Projecting Politics: Political Messages in American Films* (London: M. E. Sharpe, 2005), p. 82.
145. Mitchell, "What Really Happened in 1934 California."
146. Mitchell, *The Campaign of the Century*, p. 243.
147. *Ibid.*, p. 107.
148. Samuel Marx, *Mayer and Thalberg: The Make-Believe Saints* (New York: Random House, 1975), p. 236.
149. Donald T. Critchlow, *When Hollywood Was Right: How Movie Stars, Studio Moguls, and Big Business Remade American Politics* (New York: University of Cambridge Press, 2013), p. 28.
150. Mitchell, *The Campaign of the Century*, p. 561.
151. *Ibid.*
152. *Ibid.*
153. *Ibid.*
154. Mitchell, "What Really Happened in 1934 California."
155. Brooks Barnes, Nicole Sperling and Karen Weise, "Amazon Roars with MGM Deal," *The New York Times*, May 27, 2021, p. B1.

Chapter 4

1. James Kotsilibas-Davis and Myrna Loy, *Myrna Loy: Being and Becoming* (New York: Alfred A. Knopf, 1987), p. 69.
2. Joe Morella and Edward Z. Epstein, *Gable & Lombard & Powell & Harlow* (New York: Dell, 1975), p. 33.
3. *William Powell: A True Gentleman*, dir. Rudy Behlmer, narr. Michael York, Warner Home Video, 2005.
4. *Ibid.*
5. Charles Francisco, *Gentleman: The William Powell Story* (New York: St. Martin's Press, 1985), Acknowledgements.
6. *William Powell: A True Gentleman.*
7. Francisco, p. 237.
8. Jon Tuska, *The Detective in Hollywood* (Garden City, NY: Doubleday, 1978), p. 202.
9. Franciso, p. 67.
10. Charles Tranberg, *The Thin Man: Murder Over Cocktails* (Albany, GA: Bear Manor Media, 2009), p. 11.
11. Roger Bryant, *William Powell: The Life and Films* (Jefferson, NC: McFarland, 2008), p. 61.
12. Fay Wray, *On the Other Hand* (New York: St. Martin's Press, 1989), p. 104.
13. Bryant, p. 64.
14. *Ibid.*, p. 87.
15. Roger Ebert, "The Thin Man," RogerEbert.com, December 22, 2002. https://www.rogerebert.com/reviews/great-movie-the-thin-man-1934.
16. Bryant, p. 38.
17. *Jewel Robbery*, dir. William Dieterle, perf. William Powell and Kay Francis, Warner Brothers, 1932.
18. Bryant, p. 90.
19. "Gladys Hall, 86, Writer for Film Fan magazines," *The New York Times*, September 22, 1977, https://www.nytimes.com/1977/09/22/archives/gladys-hall-86-writer-for-filmfan-magazines.html.
20. Bryant, p. 78.
21. Wes D. Gehring, *Carole Lombard: The Hoosier Tornado* (Indianapolis: Indiana Historical Society Press, 2003), p. 84.
22. *Ibid.*, p. 86.
23. *Ibid.*, pp. x–xi.
24. Larry Swindell, *Screwball: The Life of Carole Lombard* (New York: William Morrow, 1975), p. 104.
25. *Ibid.*, p. 126.
26. Chrystopher J. Spicer, *Clark Gable:*

Biography, Filmography, Bibliography (Jefferson, NC: McFarland, 2002), p. 95.
  27. *Ibid.*
  28. Fay M. Jackson, "Dainty Theresa in Gang Film," *The Afro-American*, August 28, 1937. https://news.google.com/newspapers?nid=2211&dat=19370828&id=chomAAAAIBAJ&pg=3976,428148.
  29. *Private Detective 62*, dir. Michael Curtiz, perf. William Powell and Margaret Lindsay, Warner Brothers, 1933.
  30. Francisco, p. 170.
  31. *Star of Midnight*, dir. Stephen Roberts, perf. William Powell and Ginger Rogers, RKO Radio Pictures, 1935.
  32. *Ibid.*
  33. *Ibid.*
  34. Andre Sennwald, "'Star of Midnight,' a Humorous Murder Mystery, with William Powell, at the Radio City Music Hall," *The New York Times*, April 12, 1935. https://www.nytimes.com/1935/04/12/archives/star-of-midnight-a-humorous-murder-mystery-with-william-powell-at.html.
  35. Bryant, p. 105.
  36. *Rendezvous*, dir. William K. Howard, perf. William Powell and Rosalind Russell, MGM, 1935.
  37. *The Ex-Mrs. Bradford*, dir. Stephen Roberts, perf. William Powell and Jean Arthur, RKO Radio Pictures, 1936.
  38. *Ibid.*
  39. Bryant, p. 110.
  40. Frank Nugent, "Two Slight Cases of Murder: 'The Ex-Mrs. Bradford,' at the Rivoli, and 'The Case Against Mrs. Ames,'" *The New York Times*, May 28, 1936. https://www.nytimes.com/1936/05/28/archives/two-slight-cases-of-murder-the-exmrs-bradford-at-the-rivoli-and-the.html.
  41. Bryant, p. 108.
  42. Emily Leider, *Myrna Loy: The Only Good Girl in Hollywood* (Berkeley: University of California Press, 2011), p. 121.
  43. Karina Longworth, *Seduction: Sex, Lies and Stardom in Howard Hughes's Hollywood* (New York: Custom House, 2018), p. 85.
  44. David Stenn, *Bombshell: The Life and Death of Jean Harlow* (New York: Doubleday, 1993), p. 92.
  45. *Double Whoopee*, dir. Lewis Foster, perf. Stan Laurel, Oliver Hardy, Jean Harlow, MGM, 1929.
  46. *Hell's Angels*, dir. Howard Hughes, perf. Jean Harlow, United Artists, 1930.
  47. Stenn, *Bombshell*, p. 56.
  48. *Ibid.*, p. 66.
  49. Irving Shulman, *Harlow: An Intimate Biography* (New York: Dell, 1964), p. 100.
  50. *Ibid.*, p. 102.
  51. *Ibid.*, p. 75.
  52. *Red Headed Woman*, dir. Jack Conway, perf. Jean Harlow, MGM, 1932.
  53. Shulman, *Harlow*, p. 273.
  54. Samuel Marx, *Mayer and Thalberg: The Make-Believe Saints* (New York: Random House, 1975), p. 128.
  55. Samuel Marx, *A Gaudy Spree: Literary Hollywood When the West Was Fun* (New York: Franklin Watts, 1987), p. 66.
  56. Anne Helen Petersen, *Scandals of Classic Hollywood: Sex, Deviance, and Drama from the Golden Age of American Cinema* (New York: Plume, 2014), p. 82.
  57. Joe Morella and Edward Z. Epstein, *Gable & Lombard & Powell & Harlow* (New York: Dell, 1975), p. 67.
  58. *Ibid.*, p. 93.
  59. *Ibid.*, p. 70.
  60. Stenn, *Bombshell*, p. 113.
  61. Dwight Garner, "Relishing the High Life, and Taking Notes," *The New York Times*, November 9, 2021, p. C6.
  62. Stenn, *Bombshell*, p. 133.
  63. *Variety*, January 31, 1931.
  64. Stenn, *Bombshell*, p. 98.
  65. *Ibid.*, p. 242.
  66. Spicer, p. 88.
  67. *Red Dust*, dir. Victor Fleming, perf. Clark Gable and Jean Harlow, MGM, 1932.
  68. Lakshmi Gandhi, "A History of Indentured Labor Gives 'Coolie' Its Sting," NPR, November 25, 2013. https://www.npr.org/sections/codeswitch/2013/11/25/247166284/a-history-of-indentured-labor-gives-coolie-its-sting.
  69. Longworth, p. 134.
  70. Barbara Stepko, "From Platinum Blonde to Nearly Bald: Jean Harlow's Horrifying Hair Routine," *The Vintage News*, June 12, 2018. https://www.thevintagenews.com/2018/06/12/jean-harlow/.
  71. *Bombshell*, dir. Victor Fleming, perf. Jean Harlow, MGM, 1933.
  72. "Bombshell Facts About Jean Harlow, Hollywood's Platinum Blonde," *Factinate*, https://www.factinate.com/people/50-bombshell-facts-about-jean-harlow-hollywoods-platinum-blonde/.
  73. *Bombshell*, dir. Victor Fleming.
  74. Stenn, *Bombshell*, p. 162.
  75. *Ibid.*, p. 280.
  76. *Ibid.*, p. 176.
  77. *Ibid.*
  78. "Virginia Verrill, Unseen Voice Of Hollywood's Singing Stars, 82," *The New York Times*, January 25, 1999, Section A, p. 21. https://www.nytimes.com/1999/01/25/arts/virginia-verrill-unseen-voice-of-hollywood-s-singing-stars-82.html.
  79. Shulman, p. 304.
  80. Spicer, p. 318.
  81. *Ibid.*, p. 125.
  82. Christopher Andersen, *An Affair to Remember: The Remarkable Love Story of Katherine Hepburn and Spencer Tracy* (New York: William Morrow, 1997), p. 586.
  83. *Libeled Lady*, dir. Jack Conway, perf. Jean Harlow, William Powell, Myrna Loy, and Spencer Tracy, MGM, 1936
  84. Anthony Slide, *Hollywood Unknowns: A History of Extras, Bit Players, and Stand-Ins*

(Jackson: University of Mississippi Press, 2012), p. 196.
85. Stenn, *Bombshell*, pp. 180–181.
86. Slide, *Hollywood Unknowns*, p. 200.
87. "Otto Yamaoka," National Archives, https://aad.archives.gov/aad/record-detail.jsp?dt=3099&mtch=86&tf=F&q=Yamaoka&bc=&rpp=10&pg=1&rid=103578&rlst=103563,103564,103565,103568,103569,103576,103578,103584,103586,103588.
88. Shulman, p. 334.
89. Bryant, p. 123.
90. Stenn, *Bombshell*, p. 199.
91. *Ibid.*, p. 203.
92. Shulman, p. 328.
93. "William Powell," *Los Angeles Morgue Files: All Things Living and Dying in the City of Angels*, Thursday, March 5, 2015. http://lamorguefiles.blogspot.com/2015/03/thin-man-actor-william-powell-1984.html.
94. Tranberg, p. 19.
95. Emily Leider, *Myrna Loy: The Only Good Girl in Hollywood* (Berkeley: University of California Press, 2011), p. 191.
96. Bryant, p. 135.
97. Variety Staff, "The Hoodlum Saint," *Variety*, December 31, 1945. https://variety.com/1945/film/reviews/the-hoodlum-saint-1200414678/.
98. Francisco, p. 217.
99. Bryant, pp. 158–159.
100. *Ibid.*, p.158.
101. *Ibid.*, p. 172.
102. Kotsilibas-Davis and Loy, p. 20.
103. Clyde Gilmour, "Maclean's Movies," *Maclean's Magazine*, June 15, 1953. https://archive.macleans.ca/article/1953/6/15/macleans-movies.
104. Bryant, p. 173.
105. We see no Black sailors in the movie. This is, sadly, entirely appropriate and true to life since the Navy was strictly segregated. See Thomas W. Fleming, "The Navy's Journey from Racial Segregation to Equality," *Navy Times*, July 23, 2019. https://www.navytimes.com/news/your-navy/2019/07/24/the-navys-journey-from-racial-segregation-to-equality/.
106. Variety Staff, "Mister Roberts," *Variety*, December 31, 1954. https://variety.com/1954/film/reviews/mister-roberts-1200417871/.
107. *Mister Roberts*, dir. John Ford *and Mervyn LeRoy, perf.* Henry Fonda, James Cagney and William Powell, Warner Brothers, 1955.
108. Bryant, p. 174.
109. *Ibid.*, p. 173.
110. *Ibid.*, p. 174.
111. *Ibid.*, p. 322.
112. *Ibid.*
113. Tranberg, p. 3.
114. Bryant, p. 181.
115. *William Powell: A True Gentleman*.

Chapter 5

1. Emily Leider, *Myrna Loy: The Only Good Girl in Hollywood* (Berkeley: University of California Press, 2011), p. 7.
2. "About Names: Despite its dubious roots, Myrna's popularity grew thanks to star power," American Name Society, https://www.americannamesociety.org/about-names-despite-its-dubious-roots-myrnas-popularity-grew-thanks-to-star-power/.
3. James Kotsilibas-Davis and Myrna Loy, *Myrna Loy: Being and Becoming* (New York: Alfred A. Knopf, 1987), p. 47.
4. Lieder, p. 55.
5. *Ibid.*, p. 13.
6. Frank Beacham, "Myrna Loy was born 116 years ago today," *Frank Beacham's Journal*, August 2, 2021. https://www.beachamjournal.com/journal/2021/08/myrna-loy-was-born-116-years-ago-today.html.
7. Kotsilibas-Davis and Loy, p. 32.
8. Leider, p. 46.
9. Kotsilibas-Davis and Loy, p. 33.
10. Lieder, p. 57.
11. Tom Soter, *Investigating Couples: A Critical analysis of* The Thin Man, The Avengers, *and* The X Files (Jefferson, NC: McFarland, 2002), p. 36.
12. Leider, p. 57.
13. *Ham and Eggs at the Front*, dir. Roy Del Ruth, perf. Myrna Loy. https://www.imdb.com/title/tt0017958/.
14. Jesse Holland, "5 things to know about the racist history of blackface," Associated Press, February 5, 2019. https://www.wiscnews.com/news/national/5-things-to-know-about-the-racist-history-of-blackface/collection_cc300efb-8979-52db-9cf8-270d3398ac7c.html#2.
15. Kotsilibas-Davis and Loy, p. 52.
16. *The Squall*, IMDb, https://www.imdb.com/title/tt0020446/mediaviewer/rm2130590464?ref_=ttmi_mi_all_pos_13.
17. *Ibid.*
18. Kotsilibas-Davis and Loy, p. 60.
19. Leider, p. 79.
20. *Thirteen Women*, dir. George Archainbaud, perf. Myrna Loy and Irene Dunne, RKO Radio Pictures, 1932.
21. Gregory William Mank, *Hollywood Cauldron: Thirteen Horror Films From the Genre's Golden Age* (Jefferson, NC: McFarland, 1994), p. 54.
22. *Ibid.*, p. 61.
23. *Ibid.*, p. 67.
24. *Ibid.*, p. 55.
25. Rob Baker, "'The Only Good Girl in Hollywood'—Pictures of the Beautiful Myrna Loy," *Flashbak*, April 2, 2019. https://flashbak.com/the-only-good-girl-in-hollywood-pictures-of-the-beautiful-myrna-loy-413948/.
26. *The Mask of Fu Manchu*, dir. Charles Brabin, screen. Sax Rohmer, perf. Myrna Loy and Boris Karloff, MGM, 1932.
27. *Ibid.*
28. Mank, p. 83.
29. *Ibid.*
30. Kelly Ng, "'Yellowface': An Exploration of

Hollywood's Film History with the Yellow Race," Honors College Thesis, Pace University, May 9, 2019, p. 2. https://digitalcommons.pace.edu/cgi/viewcontent.cgi?article=1243&context=honorscollege_theses.
31. Elizabeth Lee, "The Evolution of Chinese and Asian Faces in Hollywood," *Voice of America*, October 20, 2019. https://www.voanews.com/arts-culture/evolution-chinese-and-asian-faces-hollywood.
32. *The Barbarian*, dir. Sam Wood, perf. Myrna Loy and Ramon Novarro, MGM, 1933.
33. Lieder, p. 102.
34. *Ibid.*, p. 101.
35. Lori Johnston, "The Halloween Murder of Ramon Novarro," Media.com, True Crime Edition, July 13, 2020. https://medium.com/the-true-crime-edition/the-halloween-murder-of-ramon-novarro-d9b6861da2ae.
36. D.B. Mathews, "Flying for Fun," *Model Aviation* Magazine, July, August, and September 2004. https://www.modelaircraft.org/sites/default/files/files/DennyReginaldLeigh.pdf.
37. Kotsilibas-Davis and Loy, p. 83.
38. "Max Baer Biography," *IMDb*, https://www.imdb.com/name/nm0046368/bio?ref_=nm_ov_bio_sm.
39. Mordaunt Hall, "Max Baer, Myrna Loy and Walter Huston in 'The Prizefighter and the Lady,'" *The New York Times*, November 11, 1933. https://www.nytimes.com/1933/11/11/archives/max-baer-myrna-loy-and-walter-huston-in-the-prizefighter-and-the.html.
40. *Ibid.*
41. *Ibid.*
42. Kotsilibas-Davis and Loy, pp. 86–87.
43. *Ibid.*, p. 88.
44. Leider, p. 110.
45. Cliff Aliperti, "Manhattan Melodrama (1934) Starring Clark Gable, William Powell, Myrna Loy," *Immortal Ephemera*, April 29, 2015. https://immortalephemera.com/58482/manhattan-melodrama-1934/.
46. "Manhattan Melodrama Trivia," *IMDb*, https://www.imdb.com/title/tt0025464/trivia.
47. Thomas Doherty, "Tracing the Hollywood career of J. Edgar Hoover," Museum of the Moving Image, November 16, 2011. http://www.movingimagesource.us/articles/all-the-way-to-the-fbi-20111116.
48. *Manhattan Melodrama*, dir. W.S. Van Dyke, Perf. William Powell, Myrna Loy and Clark Gable, MGM, 1934.
49. *Seeing Red: Stories of American Communists*, dir. James Klein and Julia Reichert. https://www.learnoutloud.com/Free-Audio-Video/History/American-History/Seeing-Red/79329.
50. Kotsilibas-Davis and Loy, p. 88.
51. Soter, p. 39.
52. Kotsilibas-Davis and Loy, p. 91.
53. *Ibid.*, p. 88.
54. *Ibid.*, p. 92.
55. Soter, p. 51.
56. Leider, p. 116.
57. Danny Reid, ed., *Thoughts on The Thin Man: Essays on the Delightful Detective Work of Nick and Nora Charles* (CreateSpace, 2014), p. 15.
58. Budd Schulberg, "Louis B. Mayer: Lion of Hollywood," *Time Magazine*, December 7, 1998. http://content.time.com/time/subscriber/article/0,33009,989771,00.html.
59. Leider, p. 169.
60. Kotsilibas-Davis and Loy, p. 125.
61. *Petticoat Fever*, dir. George Fitzmaurice, perf. Robert Montgomery and Myrna Loy, MGM, 1936.
62. *Ibid.*
63. *Ibid.*
64. Christopher Andersen, *An Affair to Remember: The Remarkable Love Story of Katherine Hepburn and Spencer Tracy* (New York: William Morrow, 1997), p. 138.
65. *Ibid.*, p. 12.
66. *Ibid.*
67. *Ibid.*, p. 86.
68. Leider, p. 124.
69. Bosley Crowther, "William Powell and Myrna Loy Back Together in 'I Love You Again,' at the Capitol," *The New York Times*, August 16, 1940. https://www.nytimes.com/1940/08/16/archives/the-screen-william-powell-and-myrna-loy-back-together-in-i-love-you.html?rref=collection%2Fcollection%2Fmovie-guide.
70. Bryant, p. 138.
71. *Love Crazy*, dir. Jack Conway, perf. William Powell and Myrna Loy, MGM, 1941.
72. Kotsilibas-Davis and Loy, p. 123.
73. *Ibid.*, p. 160.
74. *Myrna Loy: So Nice to Come Home To*, dir. Richard Schickel, narr. Kathleen Turner, Turner Entertainment, 2005.
75. Kotsilibas-Davis and Loy, p. 182.
76. Leider, p. 239.
77. Kotsilibas-Davis and Loy, p. 173.
78. Tranberg, p. 45.
79. Kotsilibas-Davis and Loy, p. 197.
80. Carol Easton, *The Search for Sam Goldwyn: A Biography* (New York: William Morrow, 1976), p. 237.
81. *Ibid.*, p. 238.
82. *Ibid.*, p. 239.
83. Monika Bartyzel, "Girls on Film: How 'The Thin Man's' Nora Charles became Hollywood's 'perfect wife,'" *The Week*, January 8, 2015. https://theweek.com/articles/446570/girls-film-how-thin-mans-nora-charles-became-hollywoods-perfect-wife.
84. Charles Higham, *Merchant of Dreams: Louis B. Mayer, M.G.M. and the Secret Hollywood* (New York: Donald I. Fine, 1993), p. 209.
85. *Mr. Blandings Builds His Dream House*, dir. H.C. Potter, perf. Mona Loy and Cary Grant, RKO Radio Pictures, 1948.
86. Lieder, p. 260.
87. Charles Kaiser, *1968 in America: Music, Politics, Chaos, Counterculture, and the Shaping of*

a Generation (New York: Grove/Atlantic, 1988), p. 93.
88. Kotsilibas-Davis and Loy, p. 311.
89. Tranberg, p. 26.
90. Associated Press, "Myrna Loy: Oscar Winner and Outspoken Activist," *The Christian Science Monitor*, December 20, 1993. https://www.csmonitor.com/1993/1220/20162.html.
91. Leider, p. 297.

Chapter 6

1. "Van Dyke, the Trouble Shooter," *The New York Times*, August 14, 1938. https://timesmachine.nytimes.com/timesmachine/1938/08/14/96834628.html?pageNumber=130.
2. *Ibid.*
3. Lael Morgan, *Eskimo Star: From the Tundra to Tinseltown, the Ray Mala Story* (Kenmore, WA: Epicenter Press, 2011), p. 73.
4. "Van Dyke, the Trouble Shooter."
5. Alicia Mayer, "W.S. Van Dyke—the trusted director, star maker, party host, and patriot, with one of Hollywood's saddest endings," *The Film Colony*, December 24, 2012. https://hollywoodessays.com/2012/12/24/w-s-van-dyke-the-trusted-director-star-maker-party-host-and-patriot-who-would-not-wait-for-death/.
6. Morgan, p. 92.
7. *Ibid.*, p. 16.
8. *Ibid.*, p. 7.
9. *Ibid.*
10. *Ibid.*, p.74.
11. Peter Freuchen, *Vagrant Viking: My Life and Adventures* (New York: J. Messner, 1953), p. 186.
12. *Ibid.*, p. 187.
13. Morgan, p. 12.
14. *Ibid.*, p. 16.
15. Michelle Theriault Boots, "Remains of Alaska movie star Ray Mala come home 65 years after his death," *Alaska Life*, August 20, 2018. https://www.adn.com/alaska-life/2018/08/20/alaskas-movie-star-ray-mala-returns-home-65-years-after-his-death/.
16. Morgan, p. 17.
17. *Ibid.*, p. 94.
18. *Ibid.*, p. 108.
19. *Ibid.*, p. 142.
20. Andrew Sarris, *The American Cinema: Directors and Directions, 1929–1968* (New York: Da Capo Press, 1996), p. 267.
21. Danny Reid, ed., *Thoughts on The Thin Man* (CreateSpace, 2014), p. 24.
22. J.A. Aberdeen, "Hunt Stromberg," Hollywood Renegades Archive, The Society of Independent Motion Picture Producers. http://www.cobbles.com/simpp_archive/hunt_stromberg.htm.
23. Charles Tranberg, *The Thin Man: Murder Over Cocktails* (Albany, GA: Bear Manor Media, 2009), p. 116.
24. John Baxter, *Hollywood in the Thirties* (New York: Paperback Library, 1970), p. 119.
25. David L. Goodrich, *The Real Nick and Nora: Frances Goodrich and Albert Hackett, Writers of Stage and Screen Classics* (Carbondale: Southern Illinois University Press, 2001), title page.
26. *Ibid.*, p. 38.
27. *Ibid.*, p. 75.
28. *Ibid.*, p. 79.
29. James Lileks, "The famous dog that bit 'Thin Man' co-star Myrna Loy," *Star Tribune*, March 8, 2019. https://www.startribune.com/pets-the-famous-dog-who-bit-myrna-loy/506881262/.
30. Tranberg, p. 81.
31. I.S. Mowis, "Asta biography," *IMDb*, https://www.imdb.com/name/nm1208817/bio?ref_=nm_ov_bio_sm.
32. Kotsilibas-Davis and Loy, p. 91.
33. Myron Fagan, "Drive the Reds Out of Hollywood," Archive.org. https://archive.org/details/myron-fagan-compl"-works/How%20Our%20Patriots%20Die%20Mysteriously%20NO.158-MyronFagan/page/19/mode/2up.
34. Myron Fagan, "Red Stars in Hollywood," *Patriotic Tract Society*, Archive.org. https://archive.org/details/RedStarsInHollywood1949/mode/2up.
35. Frances Goodrich and Albert Hackett, "The Thin Man Screenplay," https://www.dailyscript.com/scripts/thethinman.html.
36. "Natalie Moorhead Is Fascinating," *Kenosha News*, June 30, 1930, p. 14. https://www.newspapers.com/image/595854417/.
37. "Lace, Ribbons, Chiffon Irresistible-Natalie," *Richmond Times Dispatch*, November 17, 1929, p. 47. https://www.newspapers.com/image/?clipping_id=42196108&fcfToken=eyJhbGciOiJIUzI1NiIsInR5cCI6IkpXVCJ9.eyJmcmVlLXZpZXctaWQiOjYxNTQwMjk2NSwiaWF0IjoxNjExNjE1MzEwLCJleHAiOjE2MTE3MDE3MTB9.TWhJZgG9xwRf7-ACJRRza8yP1s7IRvT-1H1iEGLy2GQ.
38. "The Thin Man Full Cast and Crew," *IMDb*, https://www.imdb.com/title/tt0025878/fullcredits.
39. J.Y. Smith, "A. Philip Randolph Dies at 90," *The Washington Post*, May 17, 1979. https://www.washingtonpost.com/archive/politics/1979/05/17/a-philip-randolph-dies-at-90/6a7a22aa-75cd-4842-8a69-29f0cb7cf91a/.
40. Beatrice Loayza, "Racism as a Crucible for a Career in Film," *The New York Times*, May 31, 2022, p. C4.
41. John Hopwood, "James Wong Howe," *IMDb*, https://www.imdb.com/name/nm0002146/bio?ref_=nm_ov_bio_sm.

Chapter 7

1. *Ham and Eggs at the Front*, IMDb, https://pro.imdb.com/title/tt0017958/.
2. James Kotsilibas-Davis and Myrna Loy, *Myrna Loy: Being and Becoming* (New York: Alfred A. Knopf, 1987), p. 663.
3. *Ibid.*, p. 68.
4. "The Connected City," The National Museum

of American History, https://americanhistory.si.edu/america-on-the-move/connected-city

5. Russell Leigh Sharman, *Moving Pictures: An Introduction to Cinema* (Fayetteville: University of Arkansas Press, 2020), pp. 281, 283.

6. Anthony Slide, *Incorrect Entertainment or Trash from the Past: A History of Political Incorrectness and Bad Taste in Twentieth Century American Popular Culture* (Albany, GA: Bear Manor Media, 2007), p. 7.

7. Miriam Petty, *Stealing the Show: African American Performers and Audiences in 1930's Hollywood* (Oakland: University of California Press, 2016), p. 3.

8. Ibid., p. 27.

9. Hadley Hall Meares, "The Icon and the Outcast: Hattie McDaniel's Epic Double Life," *Vanity Fair*, April 26, 2021. https://www.vanityfair.com/hollywood/2021/04/hattie-mcdaniel-gone-with-the-wind-oscars-autobiography.

10. Donald Bogle, *Toms, Coons, Mulattoes, Mammies, and Bucks: An Interpretive History of Blacks in American Films* (New York: Continuum, 2001), p. 63.

11. "ECTU and the Mammy Monument Proposal," *Eastern Carolina University Chronicles*, https://collectio.ecu.edu/chronicles/About/Mammy-Monument-Proposal.

12. Tony Horwitz, "The Mammy Washington Almost Had," *The Atlantic*, May 31, 2013. https://www.theatlantic.com/national/archive/2013/05/the-mammy-washington-almost-had/276431/.

13. Ibid.

14. John Hope Franklin, "'Birth of a Nation': Propaganda as History," *The Massachusetts Review* 20, no. 3 (Autumn 1979), p. 431. https://blogs.dal.ca/ww1/files/2015/10/John-Hope-Franklin-Birth-of-a-Nation.pdf.

15. Wil Haygood, *Colorization: One Hundred Years of Black Films in a White World* (New York: Alfred A. Knopf, 2021), p. 88.

16. Cheryl Wetzstein, "Black side of silver screen: Filmmaker Oscar Micheaux paved his own path to Hollywood," *The Washington Times*, April 30, 2014. https://www.washingtontimes.com/news/2014/apr/30/black-side-of-silver-screen-filmmaker-oscar-michea/.

17. Haygood, p. 36.

18. *Oscar Micheaux: The Superhero of Black Film*, dir. Francesco Zippel, Quoiat Films, 2021.

19. Spencer Moon, *Reel Black Talk: A Sourcebook of 50 American Filmmakers* (Westport, CT: Greenwood Press, 1997), p. 247.

20. Langston Hughes, "Limitations of Life," *Black Theatre U.S.A*, eds. James V. Hatch and Ted Shine (New York: The Free Press, 1974), p. 631.

21. Ibid., p. 632.

22. Manohla Dargis and A.O. Scott, "28 Days, 28 Films for Black History Month," *The New York Times*, February 1, 2018. https://www.nytimes.com/interactive/2018/02/01/movies/28-essential-films-black-history-month.html.

23. Ean Wood, *The Josephine Baker Story* (London: Sanctuary, 2000), pp. 30–31.

24. *Josephine Baker: The Story of an Awakening*, dir. Ilana Navaro, perf. Josephine Baker, ARTE, Centre National du Cinéma et de l'Image Animée, Hellenic Radio & Television (ERT), 2018.

25. Phil Baker and Antony Clayton, eds., *Lord of Strange Deaths: The Fiendish World of Sax Rohmer* (London: Strange Attractor Press, 2015), p. 79.

26. Hua Hsu, "The End of White America?" *The Atlantic*, January/February 2009. https://www.theatlantic.com/magazine/archive/2009/01/the-end-of-white-america/307208/

27. Nancy Davis, "The Life of Afong Moy, the First Chinese Woman in America: Contending with the Orientalist Fears and Fantasies of a Young Nation," *Literary Hub*, August 2, 2019. https://lithub.com/the-life-of-afong-moy-the-first-chinese-woman-in-america/.

28. Robert Barde, "An Alleged Wife: One Immigrant in the Chinese Exclusion Era," *National Archives* 36, no. 1 (Spring 2004). https://www.archives.gov/publications/prologue/2004/spring/alleged-wife-1.html.

29. "Chinese Immigration to California," *New York Daily Tribune*, September 29, 1854. https://www.newspapers.com/clip/21187143/chinese-immigration-to-california-29/.

30. *The Chinese Exclusion Act*, dir. Ric Burns and Li-Shin Ya, *American Experience*, PBS, May 29, 2018.

31. Mari Uyehara, "The Western Strategy," *The Nation*, August 23–30, 2021, p. 17.

32. Snejana Farberov, "Levi's jeans from 1880s with racist slogan sold at auction for $76K," *The New York Post*, October 13, 2022. https://nypost.com/2022/10/13/levis-jeans-from-1880s-with-racist-slogan-sold-for-76k/,

33. The Chinese Exclusion Act was repealed in 1943, and in 2011, the U.S. Congress passed a Resolution "expressing regret for the passage of discriminatory laws against the Chinese in America, including the Chinese Exclusion Act."

34. Dashiell Hammett, *The Big Knockover: Selected Stories and Short Novels*, ed. Lillian Hellman (New York: Vintage, 1972), p. 213.

35. Ibid., p. 208.

36. Ibid., p. 220.

37. Ibid., p. 227.

38. Ibid., p. 249.

39. Sax Rohmer, *The Mask of Fu Manchu* (London: Cassell, 1973), p. 99.

40. *The Mask of Fu Manchu*, dir. Charles Brabin, screen. Sax Rohmer, perf. Boris Karloff and Myrna Loy, MGM, 1932.

41. Laura Johnson (Laura Renee), "Asian and Asian American Representations in American Film," Western Washington University Honors Program Senior Projects, 2004, p. 6. https://cedar.wwu.edu/wwu_honors/210.

42. Ron Stoneman, "Far East Fu fighting: The Yellow Peril—Dr Fu Manchu and the Rise of Chinophobia," *Irish Times*, November 8, 2014. https://www.irishtimes.com/culture/books/far-east-fu-fighting-the-yellow-peril-dr-fu-manchu-and-the-rise-of-chinophobia-1.1988872.

43. Anthony Slide, *Hollywood Unknowns: A History of Extras, Bit Players, and Stand-Ins* (Jackson: University of Mississippi Press, 2012), p. 195.
44. Lael Morgan, *Eskimo Star: From the Tundra to Tinseltown, the Ray Mala Story* (Kenmore, WA: Epicenter Press, 2011), p. 72.
45. Carey McWilliams, *Prejudice: Japanese Americans, Symbol of Racial Intolerance* (Boston: Little, Brown, 1944), p. 19.
46. Tom Sugimura, "Herd 'em Up, Pack 'em Off," *Pastor Tom's Blog*, July 26, 2020. https://www.nlcwh.org/content.cfm?page_content=blogs_include.cfm&blog_id=1537.
47. *Ibid.*
48. Bradford Pearson, *The Eagles of Heart Mountain: A True Story of Football, Incarceration, and Resistance in World War II America* (New York: Atria, 2021), p. 89.
49. *Betrayed: Surviving An American Concentration Camp*, dir. Ron Banyard, writ. Sara Krass, PBS, 2022.
50. "Senate votes to study treatment of Germans during World War II," *USA Today*, June 9, 2007. https://usatoday30.usatoday.com/news/nation/2007-06-09-internment_N.htm.
51. "German and Italian detainees," *Densho Encyclopedia*, https://encyclopedia.densho.org/German_and_Italian_detainees/.
52. Sugimura.
53. Pearson, p. 98.
54. Richard Reeves, *Infamy: The Shocking Story of the Japanese American Internment in World War II* (New York: Henry Holt, 2015), p. xiv.
55. *Betrayed: Surviving An American Concentration Camp.*
56. "Otto Yamaoka," National Archives, https://aad.archives.gov/aad/display-partial-records.jsp?f=624&mtch=1&q=Otto+Yamaoka&cat=all&dt=3099&tf=F.
57. Greg Robinson, "The Ichioka Women—Part 2: Achievement and Conflict," *Discover Nikkei*, July 8, 2022. http://www.discovernikkei.org/en/journal/2022/7/8/ichioka-women-2/.
58. Pearson, p. 122.
59. *Ibid.*, p. 98.
60. *Ibid.*, p. 123.
61. Yoshiko Uchida, *Desert Exile: The Uprooting of a Japanese-American Family* (Seattle: University of Washington Press, 1982), pp. 70–71.
62. *The Week*, March 4, 2022, p. 10.
63. Pearson, p. 147.
64. Duncan Ryuken Williams, "The Karma of a Nation," *Harvard Divinity Bulletin*, Spring/Summer 2022, p. 43.
65. Reeves, p. 131.
66. Ilene Olson, "Heart Mountain Lesson: Never Again," *Powell Tribune*, August 23, 2011. https://www.powelltribune.com/stories/heart-mountain-lesson-never-again,7627.
67. Robert McFadden, "Norman Y. Mineta, First Japanese American Cabinet Officer, Dies at 90," *The New York Times*, May 4, 2022, p. A23.
68. Reeves, p. 177.
69. "Remembering racism and war hysteria at Heart Mountain Japanese Internment Camp," *Just Go Places*. https://www.justgoplacesblog.com/heart-mountain-japanese-internment-camp/#Daily_Life_at_the_Heart_Mountain_Japanese_Interment_Camp.
70. "George Yamaoka, lawyer named to post by MacArthur, dies at 78," *The New York Times*, November 22, 1981. https://www.nytimes.com/1981/11/22/obituaries/george-yamaoka-lawyer named bymacarthur-dies-at-78.html.
71. "Former Film Star Iris Yamaoka Dies in New York," *Shin Nichi Bei*, December 20, 1960.
72. Bob Okazaki, "Oriental Atmosphere," *Pacific Citizen*, September 21, 1956, p. 3.
73. *Betrayed: Surviving An American Concentration Camp.*
74. Jeanne Wakatsuki Houston and James D. Houston, *Farewell to Manzanar* (New York: Random House, 1973), p. 130.
75. *Ibid.*, p. 131.
76. *Betrayed: Surviving An American Concentration Camp.*
77. Bilal Qureshi, "From Wrong to Right: A U.S. Apology for Japanese Internment," *All Things Considered*, NPR, August 9, 2011. https://www.npr.org/sections/codeswitch/2013/08/09/210138278/japanese-internment-redress.
78. *Little Tokyo USA*, dir. Otto Brower, perf. Preston Foster and Brenda Joyce, 20th Century–Fox, 1942.

Chapter 8

1. Dashiell Hammett, *Return of The Thin Man*, eds. Richard Layman and Julie M. Rivett (New York: The Mysterious Press, 2012), p. 4.
2. *Ibid.*, p. 6.
3. Charles Tranberg, *The Thin Man: Murder Over Cocktails* (Albany, GA: Bear Manor Media, 2009), p. 119.
4. Frances Goodrich and Albert Hackett, "After the Thin Man," Scripts.com, STANDS4, 2022. September 13, 2022. https://www.scripts.com/script/after_the_thin_man_2297.
5. Dashiell Hammett, *Return of The Thin Man*, pp. 16–17.
6. Goodrich and Hackett, *After the Thin Man*, p. 14.
7. Dashiell Hammett, *Return of The Thin Man*, p. 18.
8. *After The Thin Man*, dir. W.S. Van Dyke II, perf. William Powell and Myrna Loy, Metro Goldwyn Mayer, 1936.
9. *Ibid.*
10. James Kotsilibas-Davis and Myrna Loy, *Myrna Loy: Being and Becoming* (New York: Alfred A. Knopf, 1987), p. 144.
11. "Filming Locations; Coit Tower." *IMDb*, https://www.imdb.com/search/title/?locations=Coit%20Tower,%20San%20Francisco,%20California,%20USA

12. Danny Reid, ed., *Thoughts on The Thin Man* (CreateSpace, 2014), p. 17.
13. *After The Thin Man, dir.* Woodbridge Strong Van Dyke III.
14. Dashiell Hammett, *Return of The Thin Man*, eds. Richard Layman and Julie M. Rivett (New York: The Mysterious Press, 2012), p. 52.
15. *Ibid.*, p. 53.
16. *Ibid.*, p. 57.
17. David L. Goodrich, *The Real Nick and Nora: Frances Goodrich and Albert Hackett, Writers of Stage and Screen Classics* (Carbondale: Southern Illinois University Press, 2001), p. 113.
18. Tranberg, p. 119.
19. *Ibid.*
20. *Hollywood Tea Party, dir.* Roy Rowlan, perf. Elissa Landi, MGM, 1937.
21. Stephanie Nolasco, "'30's star Elissa Landi left Hollywood for this reason, book reveals: 'I wasted 7 good years of my life there,'" Fox News, February 3, 2021. https://www.foxnews.com/entertainment/30s-star-elissa-landi-scott-obrien-book.
22. David Stenn, "It Happened One Night ... at MGM," *Vanity Fair*, April 1, 2003. https://www.vanityfair.com/news/2003/04/mgm200304.
23. Stephen Galloway, "How a Hollywood Studio Got Away with Rape," *The Hollywood Reporter*, November 13, 2017. https://www.hollywoodreporter.com/movies/movie-news/how-a-hollywood-studio-got-away-rape-1937-1057432/.
24. *Girl 27, dir.* David Stenn, Red Envelope Entertainment, 2007.
25. Galloway.
26. *Girl 27.*
27. "Alan Marshall, Actor, 52, Dead," *The New York Times,* July 10, 1961. https://timesmachine.nytimes.com/timesmachine/1961/07/10/97678922.html?pageNumber=21.
28. Tranberg, p. 130.
29. "William Law Biography," *IMDb*, https://www.imdb.com/name/nm0492406/bio?ref_=nm_ov_bio_sm.
30. MeTV Staff, "A shocking accident as a young boy made Paul Fix extra-protective of Johnny Crawford on The Rifleman," *MeTV*, July 14, 2021. https://www.metv.com/stories/a-shocking-accident-as-a-young-boy-made-paul-fix-extra-protective-of-johnny-crawford-on-the-rifleman.
31. "Hunt Stromberg, Filmmaker, Dead," *The New York Times,* August 25, 1968. https://timesmachine.nytimes.com/timesmachine/1968/08/25/91290614.html?pageNumber=88.
32. Goodrich, p. 112.
33. *After The Thin Man, dir.* W.S. Van Dyke.
34. William H. Mooney, *Dashiell Hammett and the Movies* (New Brunswick: Rutgers University Press, 2014), p. 61.
35. Frank Nugent, "The Capitol's 'After the Thin Man' Is an Amusing Sequel—'Gold Diggers' at the Strand—'Janosik,'" *The New York Times*, December 25, 1936. https://www.nytimes.com/1936/12/25/archives/the-capitols-after-the-thin-man-is-an-amusing-sequel-gold-diggers.html.
36. Variety Staff, "After the Thin Man," *Variety*, December 31, 1935. https://variety.com/1935/film/reviews/after-the-thin-man-1200411263/.
37. Roger Bryant, *William Powell: The Life and Films* (Jefferson, NC: McFarland, 2008), p. 117.
38. Emily Leider, *Myrna Loy: The Only Good Girl in Hollywood* (Berkeley: University of California Press, 2011), p. 134.
39. Dashiell Hammett, *Return of the Thin Man*, p. 9.
40. Bryant, p. 134.
41. *Ibid.*, p. 4.
42. Tranberg, p. 163.
43. Lieder, p. 191.
44. Bryant, p. 131.
45. *Ibid.*
46. *Ibid.*, p. 130.
47. *Ibid.*, p. 131.
48. Jo Hammett, *Dashiell Hammett: A Daughter Remembers*, ed. Richard Layman with Julie M. Rivett (New York: Carroll & Graf, 2001), p. 107.
49. *After the Thin Man, dir.* W.S. Van Dyke.
50. *Ibid.*
51. *Ibid.*
52. *Ibid.*
53. *Ibid.*
54. *Ibid.*
55. Dashiell Hammett, *Return of The Thin Man*, p. 220.
56. Charles Francisco, *Gentleman: The William Powell Story* (New York: St. Martin's Press, 1985), p. 194.
57. *Ibid.*, p. 201.
58. Tranberg, p. 172.
59. Joe Morella and Edward Z. Epstein, *Gable & Lombard & Powell & Harlow* (New York: Dell, 1975), p. 146.
60. "William Poulsen," *IMDb*, https://www.imdb.com/name/nm0693725/bio.
61. Danny Reid, ed., *Thoughts on The Thin Man: Essays on the Delightful Detective Work of Nick and Nora Charles* (CreateSpace, 2014), p. 160.
62. Frank Nugent, "The Screen in Review; Post-Turkey Reports on 'Another Thin Man,'" *The New York Times*, November 24, 1939. https://www.nytimes.com/1939/11/24/archives/the-screen-in-review-postturkey-reports-on-another-thin-man-at-the.html.
63. Bryant, p. 133.
64. Tranberg, p. 161.
65. Lieder, p. 192.

Chapter 9

1. Richard Layman and Julie M. Rivett, eds., *Dashiell Hammett: Selected Letters, 1921–1960* (Washington, D.C.: Counterpoint, 2002), pp. vii–viii.
2. *Ibid.*, p. ix.
3. Mark Ford, "Swinging It," *London Review of Books* 10, no. 13, July 7, 1988. https://www.lrb.co.uk/the-paper/v10/n13/mark-ford/swinging-it.

4. Joe Gioia, "The Garden of Curses: Down on the Farm with S.J. Perelman and Nathanael West," *Humor in America*, September 29, 2016. https://humorinamerica.wordpress.com/2016/09/29/the-garden-of-curses-down-on-the-farm-with-s-j-perelman-and-nathanael-west/.
5. Deborah Martinson, *Lillian Hellman: A Life with Foxes and Scoundrels* (New York: Counterpoint, 2005), p. 84.
6. Gioia, "The Garden of Curses."
7. Layman and Rivett, eds., *Dashiell Hammett*, p. 129.
8. Christine Doudna, "A Conversation with Lillian Hellman: A still Unfinished Woman," *Rolling Stone*, February 24, 1977. https://www.rollingstone.com/culture/culture-features/a-conversation-with-lillian-hellman-50202/.
9. Alice Kessler-Harris, *A Difficult Woman: The Challenging Life and Times of Lillian Hellman* (New York: Bloomsbury, 2012), p. 47.
10. Ibid., p. 49.
11. Sinda Gregory, *Private Investigations: The Novels of Dashiell Hammett* (Carbondale: Southern Illinois University Press, 1985), p. 7.
12. Ibid., p. 8.
13. Layman and Rivett, eds., *Dashiell Hammett*, p. 71.
14. Jo Hammett, *Dashiell Hammett: A Daughter Remembers, ed.* Richard Layman with Julie M. Rivett (New York: Carroll & Graf, 2001), p. 171.
15. Dashiell Hammett, *The Big Knockover: Selected Stories and Short Novels*, ed. Lillian Hellman (New York: Vintage, 1972), p. 352.
16. Peter Feibleman, *Lilly: Reminiscences of Lillian Hellman* (New York: William Morrow, 1988), p. 23.
17. Ken Fuller, *Hardboiled Activist: The Work and Politics of Dashiell Hammett* (Glasgow: Praxis Press, 2017), p. 156.
18. Lillian Hellman, *Six Plays by Lillian Hellman* (New York: Vintage, 1979), p. 1.
19. Fuller, p. 158.
20. Sally Cline, *Dashiell Hammett: Man of Mystery* (New York: Arcade, 2014), p. 150.
21. Fuller, p. 167.
22. Cline, p. 155.
23. Variety Staff, "Watch on the Rhine," *Variety*, December 31, 1942. https://variety.com/1942/film/reviews/watch-on-the-rhine-1200413959/.
24. Lillian Hellman, *Six Plays by Lillian Hellman*, p. 395.
25. Ibid., p. 463.
26. Ibid., p. 438.
27. Ibid., p. 467.
28. Robert L. Gale, *A Dashiell Hammett Companion* (Westport, CT: Greenwood Press, 2000), p. 111.
29. Cline, p. 148.
30. "Lillian Hellman, playwright, author and rebel, dies at 79," *The New York Times*, July 1, 1984. https://www.nytimes.com/1984/07/01/obituaries/lillian-hellman-playwright-author-and-rebel-dies-at-79.html.
31. Ibid.
32. Ibid., p. 236.
33. Deborah Martinson, *Lillian Hellman: A Life with Foxes and Scoundrels* (New York: Counterpoint, 2005), p. 163.
34. Ibid., p. 164.
35. Jo Hammett, *Dashiell Hammett*, p. 90.
36. Dashiell Hammett, *Five Complete Novels* (New York: Avenel Books, 1962), p. 645.
37. Richard Layman, *Shadow Man: The Life of Dashiell Hammett* (New York: Harcourt Brace Jovanovich, 1981), p. 130.
38. Matthew Bernstein, "Diamonds and Racism in Dashiell Hammett's The Dain Curse: An Intertextual Study," *Clues: A Journal of Detection* 36, no. 1 (Spring 2018).
39. "Hammett elected by Writers League; Resolutions by Group Generally Follow Communist Party Line," *The New York Times*, June 9, 1941. https://timesmachine.nytimes.com/timesmachine/1941/06/09/87620647.html?pageNumber=17.
40. *Scottsboro: An American Tragedy*, dir. Barak Goodman and Daniel Anker, WGBH, 2001.
41. Ibid.
42. Leonard Pitts, *The Miami Herald*, May 15, 2018. https://www.miamiherald.com/opinion/opn-columns-blogs/leonard-pitts-jr/article211223209.html.
43. Cline, p. 174.
44. Emily Leider, *Myrna Loy: The Only Good Girl in Hollywood* (Berkeley: University of California Press, 2011), p. 204.
45. Higham, p. 277.
46. Ibid., p. 256.
47. "The Spanish Civil War," *Holocaust Encyclopedia*, the United Staes Holocaust Memorial Museum. https://encyclopedia.ushmm.org/content/en/article/spanish-civil-war.
48. George Packer, "The Spanish Prisoner," *The New Yorker*, October 23, 2005. https://www.newyorker.com/magazine/2005/10/31/the-spanish-prisoner.
49. Layman and Rivett, eds., *Dashiell Hammett*, p. 143.
50. Ibid., p. 144.
51. Fuller, pp. 254–255.
52. Lillian Hellman, *Three* (Boston: Little, Brown, 1979), pp. 133 and 284.
53. Layman and Rivett, p. 605.
54. Ibid., p. 173.
55. Dashiell Hammett, "The Maltese Falcon. 1934," *The Thrilling Detective*. https://thrillingdetective.com/2018/08/03/dashiell-hammetts-introduction-to-the-maltese-falcon/.
56. Dashiell Hammett, *Five Complete Novels*.
57. Gale, p. 195.
58. Dashiell Hammett, *The Maltese Falcon*, 1934.
59. "Maltese Falcon Alleyway," *Atlas Obscura*, https://www.atlasobscura.com/places/place-where-miles-archer-died.
60. Dashiell Hammett, *Five Complete Novels*, p. 438.

61. *Ibid.*
62. *Ibid.*, p. 439.
63. Claudia Roth Pierpont, "Tough Guy: The Mystery of Dashiell Hammett," *The New Yorker*, February 3, 2002. https://www.newyorker.com/magazine/2002/02/11/tough-guy.
64. "Joe Gores on The Maltese Falcon," *MarkCoggins.com*, Fall 2007. https://www.markcoggins.com/joe-gores-on-the-maltese-falcon/.
65. Dashiell Hammett, *Five Complete Novels*, p. 335.
66. *Ibid.*
67. *Ibid.*, p. 336.
68. *Ibid.*
69. *Ibid.*

Chapter 10

1. William H. Mooney, *Dashiell Hammett and the Movies* (New Brunswick: Rutgers University Press, 2014), p. 72.
2. Roger Bryant, *William Powell: The Life and Films* (Jefferson, NC: McFarland, 2008), p. 141.
3. *Ibid.*
4. Emily Leider, *Myrna Loy: The Only Good Girl in Hollywood* (Berkeley: University of California Press, 2011), p. 112.
5. *The Shadow of The Thin Man*, dir. W.S. Van Dyke II, perf. William Powell and Myrna Loy, Metro Goldwyn Mayer, 1941.
6. *Ibid.*
7. https://www.pinterest.com/pin/423338433695619244/.
8. *The Shadow of the Thin Man*, dir. W.S. Van Dyke II
9. *Ibid.*
10. *Ibid.*
11. Charles Tranberg, *The Thin Man: Murder Over Cocktails* (Albany, GA: Bear Manor Media, 2009), p. 199.
12. Dashiell Hammett, *Five Complete Novels* (New York: Avenel Books, 1962), p. 609.
13. *The Shadow of the Thin Man*, dir. W.S. Van Dyke II.
14. *Ibid.*
15. *Ibid.*
16. *Ibid.*
17. *Ibid.*
18. Variety Staff, "Shadow of the Thin Man," *Variety*, December 31, 1940. https://variety.com/1940/film/reviews/shadow-of-the-thin-man-1200413512/.
19. Leider, p. 225.
20. Brian Eggert, "Shadow of the Thin Man," *Deep Focus Review*, May 16, 2014. https://deepfocusreview.com/reviews/shadow-of-the-thin-man/.
21. James Kotsilibas-Davis and Myrna Loy, *Myrna Loy: Being and Becoming* (New York: Alfred A. Knopf, 1987), p. 167.
22. *Ibid.*, p. 162.
23. Bruce Lambert, "Joseph Anthony, 80, a Director and Stage and Film Actor, Dies," *The New York Times*, January 22, 1993. https://www.nytimes.com/1993/01/22/arts/joseph-anthony-80-a-director-and-stage-and-film-actor-dies.html.
24. "Adeline De Walt Reynolds Biography," *IMDb*, https://www.imdb.com/name/nm0212339/bio?ref_=nm_ov_bio_sm.
25. "Francis 'Frankie Burke' Aiello," Parting-Wishes.com, https://www.partingwishes.com/memorials/view?id=20658.
26. "Youth Pens Radio Gags: Fellow Who Jibbed Milt Berle Becomes His Author for Network Show," *The Pittsburgh Press*, March 21, 1937. https://news.google.com/newspapers?id=GycbAAAAIBAJ&sjid=C0wEAAAAIBAJ&pg=2144%2C2189535.
27. Charles Higham, *Merchant of Dreams: Louis B. Mayer, M.G.M. and the Secret Hollywood* (New York: Donald I. Fine, 1993), p. 423.
28. Leider, p. 243.
29. *Ibid.*
30. *The Thin Man Goes Home*, dir. Richard Thorpe, perf. William Powell and Myrna Loy, Metro Goldwyn Mayer, 1944.
31. Leider, p. 243.
32. *The Thin Man Goes Home*, dir. Richard Thorpe.
33. *Ibid.*
34. *Ibid.*
35. *Ibid.*
36. Roger Fristoe, "The Thin Man Goes Home," Turner Classic Movies, August 25, 2004. https://www.tcm.com/tcmdb/title/2621/the-thin-man-goes-home#articles-reviews?articleId=81422.
37. Tranberg, p. 233.
38. *Ibid.*, p. 223.
39. "Carole and the Screenwriter," Carole & Co., https://carole-and-co.livejournal.com/8177.html.
40. UPI, "Famed Actress Dies at 83," *Redlands Daily Facts*, June 26, 1962. https://www.newspapers.com/clip/4621725/redlands-daily-facts/.
41. Peter B. Flint, "Anne Revere, 87, Actress, Dies; Was Movie Mother of Many Stars," The New York Times, December 19, 1990. https://www.nytimes.com/1990/12/19/obituaries/anne-revere-87-actress-dies-was-movie-mother-of-many-stars.html.
42. Ronald Bergan, "Helen Vinson," *The Guardian*, November 11, 1999. https://www.newspapers.com/image/?clipping_id=39790131&fcfToken=eyJhbGciOiJIUzI1NiIsInR5cCI6IkpXVCJ9.eyJmcmVlLXZpZXctaWQiOjI1OTYxNjkzNiwiaWF0IjoxNjQlODQzNzU4LCJleHAiOjE2NDU5MzAxNTh9.ScW90A0peUkMmJX_6fbvuYvmzOkuymHLm2dvA-pwO5U.
43. "Harry Davenport Has Long Career," *The Toledo Blade*, August 10, 1949. https://news.google.com/newspapers?id=oXpOAAAAIBAJ&pg=5373,6556423&dq=harry+davenport&hl=en.
44. Tranberg, p. 237.
45. *Ibid.*, p. 235.
46. Axel Nissen, *The Films of Agnes Moorhead* (Lanham, MD: Scarecrow Press, 2013), p. 112.

47. Variety Staff, "The Thin Man Goes Home," *Variety*, December 31, 1943. https://variety.com/1943/film/reviews/the-thin-man-goes-home-1200414202/.
48. Tranberg, p. 247.
49. Morgan Wright, "Harry Gibson was the wildest of the mid-1940's boogie woogie piano players," *Blues and Rhythm* 237, March 2009. http://www.hyzercreek.com/blues_and_rhythm.htm.
50. *Song of The Thin Man*, dir. Edward Buzzell, perf. William Powell and Myrna Loy, Metro Goldwyn Mayer, 1947.
51. Tom Soter, *Investigating Couples: A Critical Analysis of* The Thin Man, The Avengers, *and* The X Files (Jefferson, NC: McFarland, 2002), p. 144.
52. Jon Tuska, *The Detective in Hollywood* (Garden City, NY: Doubleday, 1978), p. 204.
53. *Song of The Thin Man*, dir. Edward Buzzell.
54. *Ibid.*
55. *Ibid.*
56. *Ibid.*
57. *Ibid.*
58. *Ibid.*
59. *Ibid.*
60. *Ibid.*
61. Tom Vallance, "Evie Wynn Johnson Actress and Ambitious Hollywood Wife," *The Independent*, October 10, 2011. https://www.independent.co.uk/news/obituaries/evie-wynn-johnson-550363.html.
62. Tranberg, p. 271.
63. Michael Buckley, "Dean Stockwell: An Interview," *Films in Review*, January 1985. https://stockwellsassies.tripod.com/articles/Dean_Stockwell_An_Intervie.html.
64. "Patricia Morison obituary," *The Guardian*, May 21, 2018. https://www.theguardian.com/stage/2018/may/21/patricia-morison-obituary.
65. *Ibid.*
66. Tranberg, p. 265.
67. Michael Pollak, "Jayne Meadows, Actress and Steve Allen's Wife and Co-Star, Dies at 95," *The New York Times*, April 27, 2015. https://www.nytimes.com/2015/04/28/arts/jayne-meadows-dies-at-95-actress-played-opposite-steve-allen-for-half-a-century.html.
68. Tranberg, p. 262.
69. Ron Rieder, "Kidnap, Free Mrs. Leon Ames," *Van Nuys News*, February 13, 1964. https://www.newspapers.com/image/?clipping_id=3148034&fcfToken=eyJhbGciOiJIUzI1NiIsInR5cCI6IkpXVCJ9.eyJmcmVlLXZpZXctaWQiOjIyOTY3NDg5LCJpYXQiOjE2NDY1MzI2ODQsImV4cCI6MTY0NjYxOTA4NH0.Bvf0EqI9DO8L7j8oo7yALe77bkzw8d7UMblgU5XB95w.
70. Jane Ellyn Aaron, "'Sorry, Charlie' reminiscent of 1940s yet steadily fades from modern speech," *The Lincoln Journal*, April 4, 2006. https://web.archive.org/web/20171107020949/http://www.lincolnjournalonline.com/news/2017-04-06/Front_Page/Sorry_Charlie_reminiscent_of_1940s_yet_steadily_fa.html.
71. Tranberg, p. 264.
72. Kotsilibas-Davis and Loy, p. 22.
73. T.M.P., "Myrna Loy and William Powell Exhibit Same Old Zest in the New Nick Charles Thriller at Capitol, 'Song of Thin Man,'" *The New York Times*, August 29, 1947. https://www.nytimes.com/1947/08/29/archives/myrna-loy-and-william-powell-exhibit-same-old-zest-in-the-new-nick.html.
74. Brian Eggert, "Song of The Thin Man," *Deep Focus Review*, May 23, 2014. https://deepfocusreview.com/reviews/song-of-the-thin-man/.
75. *Ibid.*
76. Danny Reid, ed., *Thoughts on The Thin Man: Essays on the Delightful Detective Work of Nick and Nora Charles* (CreateSpace, 2014), p. 192.

Chapter 11

1. Ben Urwand, *The Collaboration: Hollywood's Pact with Hitler* (Cambridge: Harvard University Press, 2013), p. 7.
2. *Ibid.*, p. 8.
3. *Ibid.*, p. 37.
4. *Ibid.*, p. 61.
5. *Ibid.*, p. 62.
6. *Ibid.*, p. 74.
7. Sydney Ladensohn Stern, "The Anti-Hitler Movie That Was Never Made," *Commentary Magazine*, December 2019. https://www.commentary.org/articles/sydney-ladensohn-stern/the-anti-hitler-movie-that-was-never-made/.
8. Sinclair Lewis, *It Can't Happen Here* (New York: Dell, 1961), p. 206.
9. Urwand, *The Collaboration*, p. 161.
10. *Ibid.*, p. 171.
11. *Ibid.*, p. 157.
12. "World War: CASUALTIES: Bruno's Last Flight," *Time Magazine*, August 18, 1941. http://www.time.com/time/magazine/article/0,9171,802107,00.html#ixzz0rkj0X52M.
13. Anthony Slide, *Incorrect Entertainment or Trash from the Past: A History of Political Incorrectness and Bad Taste in Twentieth Century American Popular Culture* (Albany, GA: Bear Manor Media, 2007), p. 195.
14. Bill Higgins, "Long Before Gadhafi, Mussolini tried to muscle into the movies," *The Hollywood Reporter*, March 16, 2011. www.hollywoodreporter.com/movies/movie-news/80-years-hollywood-reporter-167559/.
15. Urwand, *The Collaboration*, p. 145.
16. *Ibid.*, p. 209.
17. *Ibid.*, p. 210.
18. *Ibid.*, p. 225.
19. *Ibid.*, p. 308.
20. Slide, *Incorrect Entertainment*, p. 197.
21. Neal Gabler, *An Empire of Their Own: How the Jews Invented Hollywood* (New York: Crown, 1988), p. 364.
22. Alexandra Steigrad, "Disney heiress slams great-uncle Walt: 'He bordered on rabid fascism,'" *New York Post*, October 19, 2022. https://nypost.

com/2022/10/03/abigail-disney-calls-great-uncle-walt-disney-a-fascist/.

23. Slide, *Incorrect Entertainment*, p. 196.
24. *Ibid.*, p. 197.
25. Urwand, *The Collaboration*, p. 303.
26. Max Wallace, *The American Axis: Henry Ford, Charles Lindbergh, and the Rise of the Third Reich* (New York: St. Martin's Press, 2003), p. 135.
27. *Ibid.*, p. 7.
28. Henry Ford, "The International Jew—The World's Foremost Problem," *The Dearborn Independent*, February 12, 1921. https://archive.org/details/TheInternationalJewTheWorldsForemostProblemhenryFord1920s/page/n11/mode/2up.
29. Wallace, p. 2.
30. *Ibid.*, p. 57.
31. *Ibid.*, p. 35.
32. *Ibid.*, p. 147.
33. Victoria Saker Woeste and Susan Radomsky, "Suing Henry Ford," *Legal Affairs*, July/August 2003. https://www.legalaffairs.org/issues/July-August-2003/review_woeste_julaug03.msp.
34. Wallace, p. 145.
35. Bradley W. Hart, *Hitler's American Friends: The Third Reich's Supporters in the United States* (New York: St. Martin's Press, 2018), p. 137.
36. *Ibid.*
37. *Ibid.*
38. Wallace, p. 209.
39. *Ibid.*, p. 212.
40. *Ibid.*, p. 277.
41. *Ibid.*, p. 284.
42. Charles Higham, *Merchant of Dreams: Louis B. Mayer, M.G.M. and the Secret Hollywood* (New York: Donald I. Fine, 1993), p. 123.
43. Wallace, p. 310.
44. Jason Daley, "The Screenwriting Mystic Who Wanted to Be the American Führer," *The Smithsonian Magazine*, October 3, 2018. https://www.smithsonianmag.com/history/meet-screenwriting-mystic-who-wanted-be-american-fuhrer-180970449/.
45. Slide, *Incorrect Entertainment*, p. 193.
46. *Ibid.*
47. E.C. Van Aiken, "Lancers Who Ride at Night," *Los Angeles Times Sunday Magazine*, August 5, 1934. https://www.newspapers.com/image/?clipping_id=35049210&fcfToken=eyJhbGciOiJIUzI1NiIsInR5cCI6IkpXVCJ9.eyJmcmVlLXZpZXctaWQiOjM4MDM4MDY4MiwiaWF0IjoxNjIxNzI1NDM1LCJleHAiOjE2MjE4MTE4MzV9.26kpGhHwnGwPyrzRXO3oRahDij9TIEW1PUrbZFJ789Q.
48. "McLaglen's 'Troop' Adds an Air Force," *The New York Times*, October 31, 1936. https://timesmachine.nytimes.com/timesmachine/1936/11/01/85432684.html?pageNumber=130.
49. Slide, *Incorrect Entertainment*, p. 193.
50. Hart, p. 35.
51. Arnie Bernstein, *Swastika Nation: Fritz Kuhn and the Rise and Fall of the German-American Bund* (New York: St. Martin's Press, 2013), p. 78.
52. Gabler, p. 340.
53. Bernstein, p. 220.
54. "22,000 Nazis Hold Rally in Garden; Police Check Foes," *The New York Times*, February 21, 1939. https://timesmachine.nytimes.com/timesmachine/1939/02/21/94680980.html?pageNumber=1.
55. Hart, p. 44.
56. *A Night At the Garden*, dir. Marshall Curry, Field of Vision, 2017. https://anightatthegarden.com.
57. *Ibid.*
58. Philip Bump, "When Nazis Rallied in Manhattan one working class Jewish man from Brooklyn took them on," *The Washington Post*, January 20, 2019. https://www.washingtonpost.com/news/politics/wp/2017/10/17/when-american-nazis-rallied-in-manhattan-one-working-class-jewish-man-from-brooklyn-took-them-on/.
59. John Simkin, "Hollywood Anti-Nazi League," Spartacus Educational, September 1997. https://spartacus-educational.com/USAantinazi.htm.
60. "The Martial Shenanigans of Leopold McLaglen," *Bartitsu Society*, December 20, 2020. http://bartitsusociety.com/the-martial-shenanigans-of-leopold-mclaglen/.
61. Martinson, p. 184.
62. "One Soldier Killed in Racial Outbreak," *The New York Times*, July 13, 1943. https://www.nytimes.com/1943/07/13/archives/one-soldier-killed-in-racial-outbreak-six-negroes-also-wounded-at.html.
63. "Unangax̂ (Aleut) Evacuation and Internment during World War II," U.S. National Park Service, https://www.nps.gov/articles/000/unangax-internment.htm.
64. Stan Trybulski, "A Dash of Class: The wartime Dashiell Hammett," *Mean Streets*, January 18, 2014. https://stantrybulski.com/2014/01/dash-class-war-time-hammett/.
65. Richard Layman and Julie M. Rivett, eds., *Dashiell Hammett: Selected Letters, 1921–1960* (Washington, D.C.: Counterpoint, 2002), p. 232.
66. Trybulski.
67. "Donald L. Miller, 69, Painter and Illustrator," *The New York Times*, February 10, 1993. https://www.nytimes.com/1993/02/10/obituaries/donald-l-miller-69-painter-and-illustrator.html.
68. Desson Howe, "The Muralist's March with King," *The Washington Post*, January 20, 1986. https://www.washingtonpost.com/archive/lifestyle/1986/01/20/the-muralists-march-with-king/9a918cd8-ae7f-432a-b5cb-fc5dfeaaaa3a/.
69. Johnson, p. 180.
70. Trybulski.
71. Robert L. Gale, *A Dashiell Hammett Companion* (Westport, CT: Greenwood Press, 2000), p. 16.
72. "This Day in Letters March 27, 1944. Dashiell Hammett to Lillian Hellman," The American Reader, https://theamericanreader.com/27-march-1944-dashiell-hammett-to-lillian-hellman/.
73. Diane Johnson, *Dashiell Hammett: A Life* (New York: Random House, 1983), p. 184.

74. Iain Russell, "Dashiell Hammett," *Scotchwhiskey.com*, June 13, 2008. https://scotchwhisky.com/magazine/famous-whisky-drinkers/19438/dashiell-hammett/.
75. Gabler, p. 355.
76. David McCullough, *Truman* (New York: Simon & Schuster, 1992), p. 552.
77. Philip Zwerling, "Rituals of Repression," *The 1985 Minns Lectures* (delivered at the First Unitarian Church of Los Angeles, First and Second Church in Boston, and Kings Chapel House in Boston), Spring 1985, p. 12.
78. McCullough, p. 553.
79. Gabler, p. 356.
80. Simkin.
81. Kotsilibas-Davis and Loy, p. 205.
82. Larry Ceplair and Steven Englund, *The Inquisition in Hollywood: Politics in the Film Community 1930–60* (Urbana: University of Illinois Press, 2003), p. 340.
83. *Ibid.*, p. 438.
84. Nicholas Von Hoffman, *Citizen Cohn: The Life and Times of Roy Cohn* (New York: Doubleday, 1988), p. 164.
85. Thomas C. Reeves, *The Life and Times of Joe McCarthy: A Biography* (New York: Stein and Day, 1982), p. 675.
86. Lester Cole, *Hollywood Red: The Autobiography of Lester Cole* (Palo Alto: Ramparts Press, 1981), p. 9.
87. *Ibid.*, p. 131.
88. *Ibid.*, p. 272.
89. David L. Goodrich, *The Real Nick and Nora: Frances Goodrich and Albert Hackett, Writers of Stage and Screen Classics* (Carbondale: Southern Illinois University Press, 2001), p. 199.
90. Herbert S. Parmet, *Eisenhower and the American Crusades* (New York: Macmillan, 1972), p. 228.
91. *Ibid.*, p. 227.
92. Benjamin Hoffman, "Naps? Spiders? Molly Maguires?" *The New York Times*, December 15, 2020, p. B-7.
93. Stefan Kanfer, *A Journal of the Plague Years* (New York: Atheneum, 1973), p. 141.
94. Zwerling, p. 85.
95. *Ibid.*
96. David Caute, *The Great Fear: The Anti-Communist Purge Under Truman and Eisenhower* (New York: Simon & Schuster, 1978), p. 558.
97. Kotsilibas-Davis and Loy, p. 164.
98. *Ibid.*, p. 216.
99. "Hollywood Fights Back," *ABC Radio*, November 2, 1947. YouTube https://www.youtube.com/watch?v=l6IIpeyPjYxI.
100. *Ibid.*
101. William Wright, *Lillian Hellman: The Image, The Woman* (New York: Simon & Schuster, 1986), pp. 212–214.
102. Ceplair, p. 433.
103. Marvin Gettleman, "No Varsity Teams: New York's Jefferson School of Social Science, 1943–1956," *Society and Science* 66, no. 3 (Fall 2002), pp. 336–359. https://www.jstor.org/stable/40404006.
104. Alice Kessler-Harris, *A Difficult Woman: The Challenging Life and Times of Lillian Hellman* (New York: Bloomsbury, 2012), p. 236.
105. Stefan Kanfer, *Tough Without a Gun: The Life and Extraordinary Afterlife of Humphrey Bogart* (New York: Alfred A. Knopf, 2011), p. 130.
106. *Ibid.*, p. 131.
107. *Ibid.*, pp. 132–133.
108. *Ibid.*, p. 381.
109. *Ibid.*, p. 390.
110. Ceplair, p. 289.
111. Kanfer, *Tough Without a Gun*, p. 399.
112. *Ibid.*, p. 397.
113. Humphrey Bogart, "I'm No Communist," *Photoplay*, May 1948. http://www.oldmagazinearticles.com/1948-Humphrey_Bogart_on_Hollywood_Blacklist_editorial-pdf.
114. Kanfer, *Tough Without a Gun*, p. 399.
115. *Ibid.*, p. 400.
116. *Ibid.*, p. 406.
117. Kessler, p. 115.
118. Layman and Rivett, p. 484.
119. *Ibid.*, p. 550
120. Herbert Mitgang, *Dangerous Dossiers: Exposing the Secret War Against America's Greatest Authors* (New York: Donald I. Fine, 1988), pp. 122–123.
121. *Ibid.*, pp. 155–156.
122. Richard Layman, *Shadow Man: The Life of Dashiell Hammett* (New York: Harcourt Brace Jovanovich, 1981), p. 219.
123. Hellman, *Three*, p. 282.
124. Joan Mellen, "Dashiell Hammett Lecture," *Cumberland County Public Library*, March 5, 2009. http://joanmellen.com/wordpress/literary-matters/dashiell-hammett-lecture/.
125. Jo Hammett, *Dashiell Hammett: A Daughter Remembers*, ed. Richard Layman with Julie M. Rivett (New York: Carroll & Graf, 2001), p 147.
126. Richard Layman and Julie Rivett, eds., *Dashiell Hammett: Selected Letters, 1921–1960* (Washington, D.C.: Counterpoint, 2002), p. 565.
127. Dennis Dooley, *Dashiell Hammett* (New York: Frederick Ungar, 1984), p. 2.
128. "Walter Winchell: The Power of Gossip," dir. Ben Loeterman, *American Masters*, PBS, 2020.
129. Diane Johnson, *Dashiell Hammett: A Life* (New York: Random House, 1983), p. 9.
130. *Ibid.*
131. *Ibid.*, p 10.
132. Claudia Roth Pierpont, "Tough Guy: The Mystery of Dashiell Hammett," *The New Yorker*, February 3, 2002. https://www.newyorker.com/magazine/2002/02/11/tough-guy.
133. Richard Layman and Julie M. Rivett, eds., *Dashiell Hammett: Selected Letters, 1921–1960* (Washington, D.C.: Counterpoint, 2002), p. 577.
134. Mellen, p. 301.
135. Jo Hammett, p. 158.
136. Reeves, p. 480.

137. Johnson, p. 269.
138. Martin Duberman, *Paul Robeson: A Biography* (New York: Ballantine, 1989), p. 491.
139. Richard Layman and Julie Rivett, eds., *Dashiell Hammett: Selected Letters, 1921–1960* (Washington, D.C.: Counterpoint, 2002), p. 595.
140. Hellman, *Three*, p. 134.
141. Sally Cline, *Dashiell Hammett: Man of Mystery* (New York: Arcade, 2014), p. 202.
142. Johnson, pp. 333–334.
143. Richard Layman, *Shadow Man: The Life of Dashiell Hammett* (New York: Harcourt Brace Jovanovich, 1981), p. 239.

Epilogue

1. Roger Bryant, *William Powell: The Life and Films* (Jefferson, NC: McFarland, 2008), p. 180.

Bibliography

"About Names: Despite its dubious roots, Myrna's popularity grew thanks to star power." American Name Society, https://www.americannamesociety.org/about-names-despite-its-dubious-roots-myrnas-popularity-grew-thanks-to-star-power/.

Adams, Thelma. "Casting-Couch Tactics Plagued Hollywood Long Before Harvey Weinstein." *Variety*, October 17, 2017. https://variety.com/2017/film/features/casting-couch-hollywood-sexual-harassment-harvey-weinstein-1202589895/.

Addams, Jane. *Twenty Years at Hull House*. New York: New American Library, 1960.

After The Thin Man. Dir. W.S. Van Dyke II. Perf. William Powell and Myrna Loy. Metro Goldwyn Mayer, 1936.

"Alan Marshall, Actor, 52, Dead." *The New York Times*, July 10, 1961. https://timesmachine.nytimes.com/timesmachine/1961/07/10/97678922.html?pageNumber=21.

Allen, Frederick Lewis. *Since Yesterday: 1929–1939*. New York: Bantam, 1940.

Altman, Diana. *Hollywood East: Louis B. Mayer and the Origins of the Studio System*. New York: Birch Lane Press, 1992.

Andersen, Christopher. *An Affair to Remember: The Remarkable Love Story of Katharine Hepburn and Spencer Tracy*. New York: William Morrow, 1997.

Anderson, Isaac. "New Mystery Stories." *The New York Times*, January 7, 1934. https://timesmachine.nytimes.com/timesmachine/1934/01/07/94481846.pdf?pdf_redirect=true&ip=0.

Another Thin Man. Dir. W.S. Van Dyke II. Perf. William Powell and Myrna Loy. Metro Goldwyn Mayer, 1939.

Applegate, Debby. *Madam: The Biography of Polly Adler, Icon of the Jazz Age*. New York: Doubleday, 2021.

Associated Press. "Myrna Loy: Oscar Winner and Outspoken Activist." *The Christian Science Monitor*, December 20, 1993. https://www.csmonitor.com/1993/1220/20162.html.

Aurora. "Robert Riskin and the Thin Man Goes Home." *Once Upon a Screen*, February 23, 2019.

Baker, Phil, and Antony Clayton, eds. *Lord of Strange Deaths: The Fiendish World of Sax Rohmer*. London: Strange Attractor Press, 2015.

The Barbarian. Dir. Sam Wood. Perf. Myrna Loy and Ramon Novarro. MGM, 1933.

Barde, Robert. "An Alleged Wife: One Immigrant in the Chinese Exclusion Era." *National Archives* 36, no. 1 (Spring 2004). https://www.archives.gov/publications/prologue/2004/spring/alleged-wife-1.html.

Bartyzel, Monika. "Girls on Film: How *The Thin Man*'s Nora Charles became Hollywood's 'perfect wife.'" *The Week*, January 8, 2015. https://theweek.com/articles/446570/girls-film-how-thin-mans-nora-charles-became-hollywoods-perfect-wife.

Baxter, John. *Hollywood in the Thirties*. New York: Paperback Library, 1970.

———. *Sixty Years of Hollywood*. Cranberry, NJ: A.S. Barnes, 1973.

Bazelon, David T. "Dashiell Hammett's Private Eye: No Loyalty Beyond the Job." *Commentary Magazine*, May 1949. https://www.commentarymagazine.com/articles/david-bazelon-2/dashiell-hammetts-private-eye-no-loyalty-beyond-the-job/.

Beacham, Frank. "Myrna Loy was born 116 years ago today." *Frank Beacham's Journal*, August 2, 2021. https://www.beachamjournal.com/journal/2021/08/myrna-loy-was-born-116-years-ago-today.html.

Bentley, Eric, ed. *Thirty Years of Treason: Excerpts from the Hearings Before the House Committee on Un-American Activities, 1938–1968*. New York: Viking, 1971.

Bergan, Ronald. "Helen Vinson." *The Guardian*, November 11, 1999. https://www.newspapers.com/image/?clipping_id=39790131&fcfToken=eyJhbGciOiJIUzI1NiIsInR5cCI6IkpXVCJ9.eyJmcmVlLXZpZXctaWQiOjI1OTYxNjkzNiwiaWF0IjoxNjQ1ODQzNzU4LCJleHAiOjE2NDU5MzAxNTh9.ScW90A0peUkMmJX_6fbvuYvmzOkuymHLm2dvA-pwO5U.

Bernstein, Arnie. *Swastika Nation: Fritz Kuhn and the Rise and Fall of the German-American Bund*. New York: St. Martin's Press, 2013.

Bernstein, Matthew. "Diamonds and Racism in Dashiell Hammett's The Dain Curse: An Intertextual Study." *Clues: A Journal of Detection* 36, no. 1 (Spring 2018).

The Best Years of Our Lives. Dir. William Wyler. Perf. Myrna Loy and Frederick March. Samuel Goldwyn Company, 1946.

Betrayed: Surviving an American Concentration Camp. Dir. Ron Banyard. PBS, 2022.

Bogart, Humphrey. "I'm Not a Communist." *Photoplay*, May 1948. http://www.oldmagazinearticles.com/1948-Humphrey_Bogart_on_Hollywood_Blacklist_editorial-pdf.

Bogle, Donald. *Hollywood Black: The Stars, the Films, the Filmmakers*. Philadelphia: Running Press, 2019.

———. *Toms, Coons, Mulattoes, Mammies, and Bucks: An Interpretive History of Blacks in American Films*. New York: Continuum, 2001.

Bombshell. Dir. Victor Fleming. Perf. Jean Harlow. MGM, 1933.

"Bombshell Facts About Jean Harlow, Hollywood's Platinum Blonde." *Factinate*. https://www.factinate.com/people/50-bombshell-facts-about-jean-harlow-hollywoods-platinum-blonde/.

Bosworth, Allan R. *America's Concentration Camps*. New York: W.W. Norton, 1967.

Bren, Paula. "Sex and the City." *The New York Times*, Book Reviews, December 5, 2021.

Brook, Tom. "Did Hollywood Studios Help the Nazis?" *BBC*, October 21, 2014. https://www.bbc.com/culture/article/20130930-did-hollywood-help-the-nazis.

Bryant, Roger. *William Powell: The Life and Films*. Jefferson, NC: McFarland, 2008.

Bump, Philip. "When Nazis Rallied in Manhattan one working class Jewish man from Brooklyn took them on." *The Washington Post*, January 20, 2019. https://www.washingtonpost.com/news/politics/wp/2017/10/17/when-american-nazis-rallied-in-manhattan-one-working-class-jewish-man-from-brooklyn-took-them-on/.

Cannom, Robert C., and Adela Rogers St. Johns. *Van Dyke and the Mythical City, Hollywood*. Culver City, CA: Murray & Gee, 1948.

"Carole and the Screenwriter." *Carole & Co.* https://carole-and-co.livejournal.com/8177.html.

Caute, David. *The Great Fear: The Anti-Communist Purge Under Truman and Eisenhower*. New York: Simon & Schuster, 1978.

Ceplair, Larry, and Steven Englund. *The Inquisition in Hollywood: Politics in the Film Community 1930–60*. Urbana: University of Illinois Press, 2003.

Chandler, Raymond. "The Simple Art of Murder." University of Texas at Austin. http://www.en.utexas.edu/Classes/Bremen/e316k/316kprivate/scans/chandlerart.html.

Chaplin, Ralph. *Wobbly: The Rough and Tumble Story of an American Radical*. Chicago: University Chicago Press, 1948.

"The Chinese Exclusion Act." Dir. Ric Burns and Li-Shin Ya. *American Experience*, PBS, May 29, 2018.

"Chinese Immigration to California." *New York Daily Tribune*, September 29, 1854. https://www.newspapers.com/clip/21187143/chinese-immigration-to-california-29/.

Christensen, Terry, and Peter J. Haas. *Projecting Politics: Political Messages in American Films*. London: M.E. Sharpe, 2005.

Cline, Sally. *Dashiell Hammett: Man of Mystery*. New York: Arcade, 2014.

Coggins, Mark. "Interview with Joe Gores on the Maltese Falcon." MarkCoggins.com, Fall 2007. https://www.markcoggins.com/joe-gores-on-the-maltese-falcon/.

Cohen, Adam. "Rock of Ages." *The New York Times*, September 28, 2003. https://www.nytimes.com/2003/09/28/books/rock-of-ages.html.

Cole, Lester. *Hollywood Red: The Autobiography of Lester Cole*. Palo Alto: Ramparts Press, 1981.

"The Criminal Record." *The Saturday Review of Literature*, January 13, 1934. https://www.unz.com/print/SaturdayRev-1934jan13/.

Critchlow, Donald T. *When Hollywood Was Right: How Movie Stars, Studio Moguls, and Big Business Remade American Politics*. New York: University of Cambridge Press, 2013.

Crowther, Bosley. *Hollywood Rajah: The Life and Times of Louis B. Mayer*. New York: Holt, Rinehart and Winston, 1960.

———. "William Powell and Myrna Loy Back Together in 'I Love You Again,' at the Capitol." *The New York Times*, August 16, 1940. https://www.nytimes.com/1940/08/16/archives/the-screen-william-powell-and-myrna-loy-back-together-in-i-love-you.html?rref=collection%2Fcollection%2Fmovie-guide.

Daley, Jason. "The Screenwriting Mystic Who Wanted to Be the American Führer." *The Smithsonian Magazine*, October 3, 2018. https://www.smithsonianmag.com/history/meet-screenwriting-mystic-who-wanted-be-american-fuhrer-180970449/.

Dargis, Manohla. "Lion of Hollywood: The Life and Legend of Louis B. Mayer." *The New York Times*, July 6, 2005. https://www.nytimes.com/2005/07/06/style/lion-of-hollywood-the-life-and-legend-of-louis-b-mayer.html.

Davis, Nancy. "The Life of Afong Moy, the First Chinese Woman in America: Contending with the Orientalist Fears and Fantasies of a Young Nation." *Literary Hub*, August 2, 2019. https://lithub.com/the-life-of-afong-moy-the-first-chinese-woman-in-america/.

Des Amis, Socibetbe, and the American Friends Service Committee. *Anatomy of Anti-Communism: A Report Prepared for the Peace education Division of the American Friends Service Committee*. New York: Hill & Wang 1969.

Dick, Bernard F. *Hellman in Hollywood*. Rutherford. Fairleigh Dickinson University, 1982.

Dinner at Eight. Dir. George Cukor. Perf. Jean Harlow and Lionel Barrymore. MGM, 1933.

Doherty, Thomas. *Hollywood and Hitler, 1933–1939*. New York: Columbia University Press, 2013.

———. *Hollywood's Censor: Joseph I. Breen & the Production Code Administration*. New York: Columbia University Press, 2017.

———. "Tracing the Hollywood Career of J. Edgar

Hoover." Museum of the Moving Image, November 16, 2011. http://www.movingimagesource.us/articles/all-the-way-to-the-fbi-20111116.
"Donald L. Miller, 69, Painter and Illustrator." *The New York Times*, February 10, 1993. https://www.nytimes.com/1993/02/10/obituaries/donald-l-miller-69-painter-and-illustrator.html.
Dooley, Dennis. *Dashiell Hammett*. New York: Frederick Ungar, 1984.
Double Wedding. Dir. Richard Thorpe. Perf. William Powell and Myrna Loy. MGM, 1937.
Double Whoopee. Dir. Lewis Foster. Perf. Stan Laurel, Oliver Hardy, and Jean Harlow. MGM, 1929.
Doudna, Christine. "A Conversation with Lillian Hellman: A still unfinished woman." *Rolling Stone*, February 24, 1977. https://www.rollingstone.com/culture/culture-features/a-conversation-with-lillian-hellman-50202/.
Douglass, Frederick. "The Hutchinson Family—Hunkerism." *The North Star*, October 27, 1848. http://utc.iath.virginia.edu/minstrel/miar03bt.html.
Duberman, Martin. *Paul Robeson: A Biography*. New York: Ballantine, 1989.
Eames, John Douglas. *The MGM Story: The Complete History of Over Fifty Roaring Years*. New York: Crown, 1975.
Easton, Carol. *The Search for Sam Goldwyn: A Biography*. New York: William Morrow, 1976.
Ebert, Roger. "'The Thin Man.'" RogerEbert.com, December 22, 2002. https://www.rogerebert.com/reviews/great-movie-the-thin-man-1934.
"ECTU and the Mammy Monument Proposal." Eastern Carolina University Chronicles. https://collectio.ecu.edu/chronicles/About/Mammy-Monument-Proposal.
Eggert, Brian. "Shadow of the Thin Man." *Deep Focus Review*, May 16, 2014. https://deepfocusreview.com/reviews/shadow-of-the-thin-man/.
Ellison, Cara, Brian Taylor, and Stu Horvath. "Dashiell Hammett's Red Harvest." *Unwinnable*, July 2, 2012. https://unwinnable.com/2012/07/02/dashiell-hammetts-red-harvest/.
Eskimo. Dir. W.S. Van Dyke. Perf. Ray Mala. MGM, 1934.
The Ex-Mrs. Bradford. Dir. Stephen Roberts. Perf. William Powell and Jean Arthur. RKO Radio Pictures, 1936.
Farberov, Snejana. "Levi's jeans from 1880s with racist slogan sold at auction for $76K." *The New York Post*, October 13, 2022. https://nypost.com/2022/10/13/levis-jeans-from-1880s-with-racist-slogan-sold-for-76k/.
Feibleman, Peter. *Lilly: Reminiscences of Lillian Hellman*. New York: William Morrow, 1988.
Flint, Peter B. "Anne Revere, 87, Actress, Dies; Was Movie Mother of Many Stars." *The New York Times*, December 19, 1990. https://www.nytimes.com/1990/12/19/obituaries/anne-revere-87-actress-dies-was-movie-mother-of-many-stars.html.
Ford, Henry. "The International Jew—The World's Foremost Problem." *The Dearborn Independent*, February 12, 1921. https://archive.org/details/FordHenryTheInternationalJewTheWorldsForemostProblemEN2003496P./mode/2up.
"Former Film Star Iris Yamaoka Dies in New York." *Shin Nichi Bei*, December 20, 1960.
Francisco, Charles. *Gentleman: The William Powell Story*. New York: St. Martin's Press, 1985.
Franklin, John Hope. "'Birth of a Nation': Propaganda as History." *The Massachusetts Review* 20, no. 3 (Autumn 1979). https://blogs.dal.ca/ww1/files/2015/10/John-Hope-Franklin-Birth-of-a-Nation.pdf.
Freuchen, Peter. *Vagrant Viking: My Life and Adventures*. New York: J. Messner, 1953.
Frewin, Leslie. *The Late Mrs. Dorothy Parker*. New York: Macmillan, 1986.
Fuller, Ken. *Hardboiled Activist: The Work and Politics of Dashiell Hammett*. Glasgow: Praxis Press, 2017.
Gabler, Neal. *An Empire of Their Own: How the Jews Invented Hollywood*. New York: Crown, 1988.
Gale, Robert L. *A Dashiell Hammett Companion*. Westport, CT: Greenwood Press, 2000.
Galloway, Stephen. "How a Hollywood Studio Got Away with Rape." *The Hollywood Reporter*, November 13, 2017. https://www.hollywoodreporter.com/movies/movie-news/how-a-hollywood-studio-got-away-rape-1937-1057432/.
Gandhi, Lakshmi. "A History of Indentured Labor Gives 'Coolie' Its Sting." *NPR*, November 25, 2013. https://www.npr.org/sections/codeswitch/2013/11/25/247166284/a-history-of-indentured-labor-gives-coolie-its-sting.
Gehring, Wes D. *Carole Lombard: The Hoosier Tornado*. Indianapolis: Indiana Historical Society Press, 2003.
Geltzer, Jeremy. *Dirty Words and Filthy Picture: Film and the First Amendment*. Austin: University of Texas Press, 2016.
"George Yamaoka, lawyer named to post by MacArthur, dies at 78." *The New York Times*, November 22, 1981. https://www.nytimes.com/1981/11/22/obituaries/george-yamaoka-lawyer-named-by-macarthur-dies-at-78.html.
Gerken, Marika. "Wisconsin Department of Health warns against eating the 'cannibal sandwich,' a traditional holiday dish in the state." CNN, December 14, 2020. https://www.cnn.com/2020/12/14/us/cannibal-sandwich-wisconsin-trnd/index.html.
"German and Italian detainees." *Densho Encyclopedia*. https://encyclopedia.densho.org/German_and_Italian_detainees/.
Gettleman, Marvin. "No Varsity Teams: New York's Jefferson School of Social Science, 1943–1956." *Society and Science* 66, no. 3 (Fall 2002): 336–359. https://www.jstor.org/stable/40404006.
Gioia, Joe. "The Garden of Curses: Down on the Farm with S.J. Perelman and Nathanael West." *Humor in America*, September 29, 2016. https://humorinamerica.wordpress.com/2016/

09/29/the-garden-of-curses-down-on-the-farm-with-s-j-perelman-and-nathanael-west/.
Girl 27. Dir. David Stenn. Red Envelope Entertainment, 2007.
The Girl Who Had Everything. Dir. Richard Thorpe. Perf. Elizabeth Taylor, Fernando Lamas, and William Powell. MGM, 1953.
"Gladys Hall, 86, Writer for Film Fan Magazines." *The New York Times*, September 22, 1977. https://www.nytimes.com/1977/09/22/archives/gladys-hall-86-writer-for-filmfan-magazines.html.
Going Attractions: The Definitive Story of the Movie Palace. Dir. April Wright. Prod. Rachael Pond and April Wright. Passion River, 2019.
Gomery, Douglas. *The Hollywood Studio System: A History.* London: The British Film Institute, 2005.
Goodrich, David L. *The Real Nick and Nora: Frances Goodrich and Albert Hackett, Writers of Stage and Screen Classics.* Carbondale: Southern Illinois University Press, 2001.
Goodrich, Frances, and Albert Hackett. "The Thin Man Screenplay." Based on the novel by Dashiell Hammett. Shooting draft, 1935. http://www.dailyscript.com/scripts/thethinman.html.
Gore, Steve. "Unbecoming Dashiell Hammett." *The Los Angeles Review of Books*, September 15, 2015. https://lareviewofbooks.org/article/unbecoming-dashiell-hammett/.
Grady, Cynthia. *Write to Me: Letters from Japanese American Children to the Librarian They Left Behind.* Watertown, MA: Charlesbridge, 2018.
The Great Ziegfeld. Dir. Robert Z. Leonard. Perf. William Powell and Myrna Loy. MGM, 1936.
Greenfield, Jeff. "The Hollywood Hit Movie That Urged FDR to Become a Fascist." *Politico Magazine*, March 25, 2018. https://www.politico.com/magazine/story/2018/03/25/gabriel-over-the-white-house-fdr-inauguration-217349/.
Gregory, Sinda. *Private Investigations: The Novels of Dashiell Hammett.* Carbondale: Southern Illinois University Press, 1985.
Gunderson, Erica. "New Book Traces History of Cinema's Censorship." WTTW PBS Chicago, March 21, 2016. https://news.wttw.com/2016/03/21/new-book-traces-history-cinemas-censorship.
Hall, Mordaunt. "Max Baer, Myrna Loy and Walter Huston in 'The Prizefighter and the Lady.'" *The New York Times*, November 11, 1933. https://www.nytimes.com/1933/11/11/archives/max-baer-myrna-loy-and-walter-huston-in-the-prizefighter-and-the.html.
_____. "Walter Huston as President of the United Sates Who Proclaims Himself a Dictator." *The New York Times*, April 1, 1933. https://www.nytimes.com/1933/04/01/archives/walter-huston-as-a-president-of-the-united-states-who-proclaims.html.
"Ham and Eggs at the Front." *IMDb.* https://www.imdb.com/title/tt0017958/.
Hammett, Dashiell. *The Big Knockover: Selected Stories and Short Novels.* Ed. Lillian Hellman. New York: Vintage, 1972.

_____. *The Continental Op.* New York: Vintage, 1974.
_____. *Five Complete Novels.* New York: Avenel Books, 1962.
_____. "From the Memoirs of a Private Detective." *The Smart Set*, March 1923. http://www.umsl.edu/~gradyf/film/Hammett.htm.
_____. *Return of The Thin Man.* Ed. Richard Layman and Julie M. Rivett. New York: The Mysterious Press, 2012.
Hammett, Jo. *Dashiell Hammett: A Daughter Remembers.* Ed. Richard Layman with Julie M. Rivett. New York: Carroll & Graf, 2001.
"Harry Davenport Has Long Career." *The Toledo Blade*, August 10, 1949. https://news.google.com/newspapers?id=oXpOAAAAIBAJ&pg=5373,6556423&dq=harry+davenport&hl=en.
Haycraft, Howard. *Murder for Pleasure: The Life and Times of the Detective Story.* New York: D. Appleton-Century, 1941.
Haygood, Wil. *Colorization: One Hundred Years of Black Films in a White World.* New York: Alfred A. Knopf, 2021.
Haynes, John Earl. *Red Scare or Red Menace? American Communism and Anticommunism in the Cold War Era.* Chicago: Ivan R. Dee, 1996.
Haynes, Suyin. "The True Story Behind the Movie 'Judy.'" *Time Magazine*, September 26, 2019. https://time.com/5684673/judy-garland-movie-true-story/.
Heart, Bradley W. *Hitler's American Friends: The Third Reich's Supporters in the United States.* New York: St. Martin's Press, 2018.
Hellman, Lillian. *Six Plays by Lillian Hellman.* New York: Vintage, 1979
_____. *Three.* Boston: Little, Brown, 1979.
Hell's Angels. Dir. Howard Hughes. Perf. Jean Harlow. United Artists, 1930.
Herron, Don. *The Dashiell Hammett Tour.* San Francisco: City Lights Books, 1991.
Higgins, Bill. "Long Before Gadhafi, Mussolini tried to muscle into the movies." *The Hollywood Reporter*, March 16, 2011. www.hollywoodreporter.com/movies/movie-news/80-years-hollywood-reporter-167559/.
Higham, Charles. *Merchant of Dreams: Louis B. Mayer, M.G.M. and the Secret Hollywood.* New York: Donald I. Fine, 1993.
Hoberman, J. "Fictitious Tales, Actual Odysseys." *The New York Times*, October 9, 2015. https://www.nytimes.com/2015/10/11/movies/homevideo/fictitious-tales-actual-odysseys.html.
Hoffman, Benjamin. "Naps? Spiders? Molly Maguires?" *The New York Times*, December 15, 2020, p. B-7.
"Hollywood Fights Back." ABC Radio, November 2, 1947. https://www.youtube.com/watch?v=i6HpeyPjYxl.
Hollywood Tea Party. Dir. Roy Rowlan. Perf. Elissa Landi. MGM, 1937.
Hollywood: The Dream Factory. Writ. Irwin Rosten. Narr. Dick Cavett. MGM, 1972.

The Hoodlum Saint. Dir. Norman Taurog. Perf. William Powell, Angela Lansbury and Esther Williams. MGM, 1946.

Horwitz, Tony. "The Mammy Washington Almost Had." *The Atlantic*, May 31, 2013. https://www.theatlantic.com/national/archive/2013/05/the-mammy-washington-almost-had/276431/.

Houston, Jeanne Wakatsuki, and James D. Houston. *Farewell to Manzanar*. New York: Random House, 1973.

Howe, Desson. "The Muralist's March with King." *The Washington Post*, January 20, 1986. https://www.washingtonpost.com/archive/lifestyle/1986/01/20/the-muralists-march-with-king/9a918cd8-ae7f-432a-b5cb-fc5dfeaaaa3a/.

Hsu, Hua. "The End of White America?" *The Atlantic*, January/February 2009. https://www.theatlantic.com/magazine/archive/2009/01/the-end-of-white-america/307208/.

Huberman, Leo. *The Labor Spy Racket*. New York: Modern Age Books, 1937.

Hughes, Langston. "Limitations of Life." *Black Theatre U.S.A.* Eds. James V. Hatch and Ted Shine. New York: The Free Press, 1974.

I Love You Again. Dir. W.S. Van Dyke II. Perf. Myrna Loy and William Powell. MGM, 1940.

Irving Thalberg: Prince of Hollywood. Dir. Robert Trachtenberg. Turner Entertainment Co., 2005.

Jackson, Fay M. "Dainty Theresa in Gang Film." *The Afro-American*, August 28, 1937. https://news.google.com/newspapers?nid=2211&dat=19370828&id=chomAAAAIBAJ&pg=3976,428148.

Jewel Robbery. Dir. William Dieterle. Perf. William Powell and Kay Francis. Warner Brothers, 1932.

Johnson, Diane. *Dashiell Hammett: A Life*. New York: Random House, 1983.

Johnson, Laura (Laura Renee). "Asian and Asian American Representations in American Film." WWU Honors Program Senior Projects, 2004. https://cedar.wwu.edu/wwu_honors/210.

Johnson, Paul. *Intellectuals*. New York: HarperCollins, 1988.

Johnston, Lori. "The Halloween Murder of Ramon Novarro." Media.com, True Crime Edition, July 13, 2020. https://medium.com/the-true-crime-edition/the-halloween-murder-of-ramon-novarro-d9b6861da2ae.

Josephine Baker: The Story of an Awakening. Dir. Ilana Navaro. Perf. Josephine Baker. ARTE, Centre National du Cinéma et de l'Image Animée, Hellenic Radio & Television (ERT), 2018.

Julia. Dir. Fred Zinnemann. Perf. Jane Fonda and Jason Robards. 20th Century–Fox, 1977.

Kaiser, Charles. *1968 in America: Music, Politics, Chaos, Counterculture, and the Shaping of a Generation*. New York: Grove/Atlantic, 1988.

Kanfer, Stefan. *A Journal of the Plague Years*. New York: Atheneum, 1973.

_____. *Tough Without a Gun: The Life and Extraordinary Afterlife of Humphrey Bogart*. New York: Alfred A. Knopf, 2011.

Karolides, Nicholas. *Banned Books: Literature Suppressed on Political Grounds*. New York: Facts on File, 2006.

Kellogg, Carolyn. "Budd Schulberg: Blinded by his gift." *The Los Angeles Times*, August 6, 2009. https://www.latimes.com/archives/blogs/jacket-copy/story/2009-08-06/budd-schulberg-blinded-by-his-gift.

Kelly, Anna P. "Scorched Earth: Expressions of Modernity in Dashiell Hammett's Pulp Fiction." A Thesis in the Field of English Literature for the Degree of Master of Liberal Arts in Extension Studies, Harvard University, November 2017. https://dash.harvard.edu/bitstream/handle/1/37799762/KELLY-DOCUMENT-2018.pdf?sequence=1&isAllowed=y.

The Kennel Murder Case. Dir. Michael Curtiz. Perf. William Powell and Mary Astor. Warner Brothers, 1933.

Kessler-Harris, Alice. *A Difficult Woman: The Challenging Life and Times of Lillian Hellman*. New York: Bloomsbury, 2012.

Kotsilibas-Davis, James, and Myrna Loy. *Myrna Loy: Being and Becoming*. New York: Alfred A. Knopf, 1987.

Krutnik, Frank, Steve Neale, Brian Neve, and Peter Stanfield, eds. *Un-American Hollywood: Politics and Film in the Blacklist Era*. New Brunswick: Rutgers University Press, 2007.

Lacayo, Richard. "All Time 100 Novels." *Time Magazine*, January 6, 2010. https://entertainment.time.com/2005/10/16/all-time-100-novels/.

Lacey, Robert. *Ford: The Men and the Machine*. New York: Ballantine, 1986.

Lambert, Bruce. "Joseph Anthony, 80, a Director And Stage and Film Actor, Dies." *The New York Times*, January 22, 1993. https://www.nytimes.com/1993/01/22/arts/joseph-anthony-80-a-director-and-stage-and-film-actor-dies.html.

Lang, Cady. "Silent No More." *Time Magazine*, March 29–April 5, 2021.

Lardner, Ring, Jr. *I'd Hate Myself in the Morning*. New York: Thunder Mouth Press, 2000.

Layman, Richard. *Shadow Man: The Life of Dashiell Hammett*. New York: Harcourt Brace Jovanovich, 1981.

_____, and Julie M. Rivett, eds. *Dashiell Hammett: Selected Letters, 1921–1960*. Washington, D.C.: Counterpoint, 2002.

Lee, Elizabeth. "The Evolution of Chinese and Asian Faces in Hollywood." *Voice of America*, October 20, 2019. https://www.voanews.com/arts-culture/evolution-chinese-and-asian-faces-hollywood.

Leider, Emily. *Myrna Loy: The Only Good Girl in Hollywood*. Berkeley: University of California Press, 2011.

Lewis, Sinclair. *It Can't Happen Here*. New York: Dell, 1961.

Libeled Lady. Dir. Jack Conway. Perf. Jean Harlow, William Powell, Myrna Loy, and Spencer Tracy. MGM, 1936.

Lileks, James. "The famous dog that bit 'Thin Man' co-star Myrna Loy." *Star Tribune*, March 8, 2019.

https://www.startribune.com/pets-the-famous-dog-who-bit-myrna-loy/506881262/.
Little Tokyo USA. Dir. Otto Brower. Perf. Preston Foster and Brenda Joyce. 20th Century–Fox, 1942.
Longworth, Karina. *Seduction: Sex, Lies and Stardom in Howard Hughes's Hollywood.* New York: Custom House, 2018.
"Louis B. Mayer, Film Maker, Dies." *The New York Times*, October 30, 1957. https://timesmachine.nytimes.com/timesmachine/1957/10/30/107173004.html?auth=login-email&pageNumber=29.
Love Crazy. Dir. Jack Conway. Perf. William Powell and Myrna Loy. MGM, 1941.
Luo, Michael. "Arrivals: When the Chinese joined the gold rush, they were welcomed. That Changed." *The New Yorker*, August 30, 2021.
Lynd, Robert S., and Helen Merrell Lynd. *Middletown: A Study in American Culture.* New York: Harcourt, Brace, 1929.
MacCambridge, Michael. *America's Game: The Epic Story of How Pro Football Captured a Nation.* New York: Random House, 2004.
Macdonald, Ross. "The Writer as Detective Hero" *The Stacks Reader*, January 1965. http://www.thestacksreader.com/the-writer-as-detective-hero/.
Mackay, James. *Allan Pinkerton: The First Private Eye.* Edison, NJ: Castle Books, 2007.
Mahon, Elizabeth Kerri. "Uncivil Wars: Lillian Hellman and Mary McCarthy and the Question of Julia." *Scandalous Woman*, August 12, 2008. http://scandalouswoman.blogspot.com/2008/08/uncivil-wars-lillian-hellman-vs-mary.html.
Malmgren, Carl D. "The Crime of the Sign: Dashiell Hammett's Detective Fiction." *Twentieth Century Literature: A Scholarly and Critical Journal* 45, no. 3 (1999): 371–384. https://core.ac.uk/download/pdf/216834408.pdf.
The Maltese Falcon. Dir. John Huston. Screen. John Huston. Perf. Humphrey Bogart and Mary Astor. Warner Brothers, 1941.
"Maltese Falcon Alleyway." Atlas Obscura. https://www.atlasobscura.com/places/place-where-miles-archer-died.
Manhattan Melodrama. Dir. W.S. Van Dyke II. Perf. Clark Gable, William Powell, and Myrna Loy. MGM, 1934.
Mank, Gregory William. *Hollywood Cauldron: Thirteen Horror Films From the Genre's Golden Age.* Jefferson, NC: McFarland, 1994.
Manning, Robert John. "Re-Examining the Maladjusted Text: Post-War America, the Hollywood Left and the Problem with Film Noir." PhD thesis, University of East Anglia School of Film, Television and Media Studies, October 2015.
Marling, William. *Dashiell Hammett.* Boston: Twayne, 1983.
"The Martial Shenanigans of Leopold McLaglen." Bartitsu Society, December 20, 2020. http://bartitsusociety.com/the-martial-shenanigans-of-leopold-mclaglen/.

Martinson, Deborah. *Lillian Hellman: A Life with Foxes and Scoundrels.* New York: Counterpoint, 2005.
Marx, Samuel. *A Gaudy Spree: Literary Hollywood When the West Was Fun.* New York: Franklin Watts, 1987.
_____. *Mayer and Thalberg: The Make-Believe Saints.* New York: Random House, 1975.
Masaoka, Mike, with Bill Hosokawa. *They Call Me Moses Masaoka: An American Saga.* New York: William Morrow, 1987.
The Mask of Fu Manchu. Dir. Charles Brabin. Screen. Sax Rohmer. Perf. Boris Karloff and Myrna Loy. MGM, 1932.
Mathews, D.B. "Flying for Fun." *Model Aviation Magazine*, July, August, and September 2004. https://www.modelaircraft.org/sites/default/files/files/DennyReginaldLeigh.pdf.
McCullough, David. *Truman.* New York: Simon & Schuster, 1992.
McFadden, Robert. "Norman Y. Mineta, First Japanese American Cabinet Officer, Dies at 90." *The New York Times*, May 4, 2022, p. A23.
"McLaglen's 'Troop Adds an Air Force." *The New York Times*, October 31, 1936. https://timesmachine.nytimes.com/timesmachine/1936/11/01/85432684.html?pageNumber=130.
McWilliams, Carey. *Prejudice Japanese-Americans: Symbol of Racial Intolerance.* Boston: Little, Brown, 1945.
Meares, Hadley Hall. "The Icon and the Outcast: Hattie McDaniel's Epic Double Life." *Vanity Fair*, April 26, 2021. https://www.vanityfair.com/hollywood/2021/04/hattie-mcdaniel-gone-with-the-wind-oscars-autobiography.
Mellen, Joan. "Dashiell Hammett Lecture." Cumberland County Public Library, March 5, 2009. http://joanmellen.com/wordpress/literary-matters/dashiell-hammett-lecture/.
_____. *Hellman and Hammett: The Legendary Passion of Lillian Hellman and Dashiell Hammett.* New York: HarperCollins, 1996.
Metress, Christopher, ed. *The Critical Response to Dashiell Hammett.* Westport, CT: Greenwood Press, 1994.
MeTV Staff. "A shocking accident as a young boy made Paul Fix extra-protective of Johnny Crawford on The Rifleman." MeTV, July 14, 2021. https://www.metv.com/stories/a-shocking-accident-as-a-young-boy-made-paul-fix-extra-protective-of-johnny-crawford-on-the-rifleman.
Mr. Blandings Builds His Dream House. Dir. H.C. Potter. Perf. Mona Loy and Cary Grant. RKO Radio Pictures, 1948.
Mister Roberts. Dir. John Ford and Mervyn LeRoy. Perf. Henry Fonda, James Cagney and William Powell. Warner Brothers, 1955.
Mitchell, Greg. *The Campaign of the Century: Upton Sinclair's Race for Governor of California and the Birth of Media Politics.* New York: Random House, 1992.
_____. "What Really Happened in 1934

California." *The New York Times*, December 30, 2020, p. C4.

Mitgang, Herbert. *Dangerous Dossiers: Exposing the Secret War Against America's Greatest Authors*. New York: Donald I. Fine, 1988.

Moon, Spencer. *Reel Black Talk: A Sourcebook of 50 American Filmmakers*. Westport, CT: Greenwood Press, 1997.

Mooney, William H. *Dashiell Hammett and the Movies*. New Brunswick: Rutgers University Press, 2014.

Morella, Joe, and Edward Z. Epstein. *Gable & Lombard & Powell & Harlow*. New York: Dell, 1975.

Morgan, Lael. *Eskimo Star: From the Tundra to Tinseltown, the Ray Mala Story*. Kenmore, WA: Epicenter Press, 2011.

Morgan, Ted. *Reds: McCarthyism in the Twentieth Century*. New York: Random House, 2003.

Mowis, I.S. "Asta biography." *IMDb*. https://www.imdb.com/name/nm1208817/bio?ref_=nm_ov_bio_sm.

Murphy, Mary Jo. "A Hollywood White House for Interesting Times." *The New York Times*, June 10, 2016. https://www.nytimes.com/2016/06/10/arts/design/a-hollywood-white-house-for-interesting-times.htm.

My Man Godfrey. Dir. Gregory de La Cava. Perf. William Powell and Carole Lombard. Universal Pictures, 1936.

Myrna Loy: So Nice to Come Home To. Dir. Richard Schickel. Narr. Kathleen Turner. Turner Entertainment Co., 2005.

Navasky, Victor S. *Naming Names*. New York: Viking, 1980.

Ng, Kelly. "'Yellowface': An Exploration of Hollywood's Film History with the Yellow Race." Honors College Thesis Pace University, Spring 2019. https://digitalcommons.pace.edu/cgi/viewcontent.cgi?article=1243&context=honorscollege_theses.

"Nick and Nora (and Asta) Return in the Thin Man Novellas." NPR, November 3, 2012. https://www.npr.org/2012/11/03/164195799/nick-nora-and-asta-return-in-thin-man-novellas.

A Night at the Garden. Dir. Marshall Curry. Field of Vision, 2017.

Nissen, Axel. *The Films of Agnes Moorhead*. Lanham, MD: Scarecrow Press, 2013.

Nolan, Tom. "Crime Fiction's Hardboiled Revolutionary." *The Los Angeles Times*, January 30, 2005. https://www.latimes.com/archives/la-xpm-2005-jan-30-bk-nolan30-story.html.

Nugent, Frank. "The Capitol's 'After the Thin Man' Is an Amusing Sequel—'Gold Diggers' at the Strand—'Janosik.'" *The New York Times*, December 25, 1936. https://www.nytimes.com/1936/12/25/archives/the-capitols-after-the-thin-man-is-an-amusing-sequel-gold-diggers.html.

_____. "The Screen in Review; Post-Turkey Reports on 'Another Thin Man.'" *The New York Times*, November 24, 1939. https://www.nytimes.com/1939/11/24/archives/the-screen-in-review-postturkey-reports-on-another-thin-man-at-the.html.

_____. "Two Slight Cases of Murder: 'The Ex-Mrs. Bradford,' at the Rivoli, and 'The Case Against Mrs. Ames.'" The New York Times, May 28, 1936. https://www.nytimes.com/1936/05/28/archives/two-slight-cases-of-murder-the-exmrs-bradford-at-the-rivoli-and-the.html.

O'Hara, S. Paul. *Inventing the Pinkertons or Spies, Sleuths, Mercenaries, and Thugs*. Baltimore: Johns Hopkins University Press, 2016.

Okazaki, Bob. "Oriental Atmosphere." *Pacific Citizen*, September 21, 1956, p. 3.

Olson, Ilene. "Heart Mountain Lesson: Never Again." *Powell Tribune*, August 23, 2011. https://www.powelltribune.com/stories/heart-mountain-lesson-never-again,7627.

"One Soldier Killed in Racial Outbreak." *The New York Times*, July 13, 1943. https://www.nytimes.com/1943/07/13/archives/one-soldier-killed-in-racial-outbreak-six-negroes-also-wounded-at.html.

One Way Passage. Dir. Tay Garnett. Perf. William Powell and Kay Francis. Warner Brothers, 1932.

Oscar Micheaux: The Superhero of Black Film. Dir. Francisco Zippel. Quoiat Films, 2021.

Osnos, Evan. "The Violent Style." *The New Yorker*, November 16, 2020.

Packer, George. "The Spanish Prisoner." *The New Yorker*, October 23, 2005. https://www.newyorker.com/magazine/2005/10/31/the-spanish-prisoner.

Parker, Dorothy. *The Portable Dorothy Parker*. New York: Penguin, 1973.

Parmet, Herbert S. *Eisenhower And the American Crusades*. New York: Macmillan, 1972.

"Patricia Morison obituary." *The Guardian*, May 21, 2018. https://www.theguardian.com/stage/2018/may/21/patricia-morison-obituary.

Patterson, Haywood, and Earl Conrad. *Scottsboro Boy*. New York: Bantam, 1950.

Pearson, Bradford. *The Eagles of Heart Mountain: A True Story of Football, Incarceration, and Resistance in World War II America*. New York: Atria, 2021.

Pegram, Thomas. *One Hundred Percent American: The Rebirth and Decline of the Ku Klux Klan in the 1920s*. Chicago: Ivan R. Dee, 2011.

Penzler, Otto, ed. *The Black Lizard Big Book of Pulps*. New York: Vintage, 2007.

Petersen, Anne Helen. *Scandals of Classic Hollywood: Sex, Deviance, and Drama from the Golden Age of American Cinema*. New York: Plume, 2014.

Petticoat Fever. Dir. George Fitzmaurice. Perf. Robert Montgomery and Myrna Loy. MGM, 1936.

Petty, Miriam. *Stealing The Show: African American Performers and Audiences in 1930's Hollywood*. Oakland: University of California Press, 2016.

Phillips, Michael. "A Curio for the Trump Era: 'Gabriel Over the White House.'" *The*

Chicago Tribune, February 2, 2017. https://www.chicagotribune.com/entertainment/movies/ct-gabriel-over-white-house-mov-0203-20170202-column.html.

Pierpont, Claudia Roth. "Tough Guy: The Mystery of Dashiell Hammett. *The New Yorker*, February 3, 2002. https://www.newyorker.com/magazine/2002/02/11/tough-guy.

Pilgrim, David. "The Picaninny Caricature." Jim Crow Museum of Racist Memorabilia at Ferris State University, October 2000. https://www.ferris.edu/HTMLS/news/jimcrow/antiblack/picaninny/homepage.htm.

Plan Nine from Outer Space. Dir. Edward D. Wood. Perf. Tor Johnson. Reynolds Pictures, Inc., 1959.

Pollak, Michael. "Jayne Meadows, Actress and Steve Allen's Wife and Co-Star, Dies at 95." *The New York Times*, April 27, 2015. https://www.nytimes.com/2015/04/28/arts/jayne-meadows-dies-at-95-actress-played-opposite-steve-allen-for-half-a-century.html.

Princess Tam Tam. Dir. Edmond T. Gréville. Perf. Josephine Baker. Productions Arys, 1935.

Private Detective 62. Dir. Michael Curtiz. Perf. William Powell and Margaret Lindsay. Warner Brothers, 1933.

The Prizefighter and the Lady. Dir. W.S. Van Dyke. Perf. Myrna Loy and Max Baer. MGM, 1933.

Prohibition, Episode 1, "A Nation of Drunkards." Dir. Lynne Novick and Ken Burns. PBS, 2011.

The Public Enemy. Dir. William Wellman. Perf. James Cagney and Jean Harlow. Warner Brothers, 1931.

Qureshi, Bilal. "From Wrong to Right: A U.S. Apology for Japanese Internment." *All Things Considered*, NPR, August 9, 2011. https://www.npr.org/sections/codeswitch/2013/08/09/210138278/japanese-internment-redress.

Race Relations in the 1930s and 1940s. *Library of Congress*. https://www.loc.gov/classroom-materials/united-states-history-primary-source-timeline/great-depression-and-world-war-ii-1929-1945/race-relations-in-1930s-and-1940s/.

"Race Relations in the 1930s and 1940s." *The Library of Congress*. https://www.loc.gov/classroom-materials/united-states-history-primary-source-timeline/great-depression-and-world-war-ii-1929-1945/race-relations-in-1930s-and-1940s/.

Red Dust. Dir. Victor Fleming. Perf. Clark Gable and Jean Harlow. MGM, 1932.

Red Headed Woman. Dir. Jack Conway. Perf. Jean Harlow. MGM, 1932.

Red Stars Over Hollywood. Patriotic Tract Society, n.d. https://archive.org/details/RedStarsInHollywood1949/mode/2up.

Reeves, Richard. *Infamy: The Shocking Story of the Japanese American Internment in World War II*. New York: Henry Holt, 2015.

Reeves, Thomas C. *The Life and Times of Joe McCarthy: A Biography*. New York: Stein and Day, 1982.

Reid, Danny, ed. *Thoughts on The Thin Man: Essays on the Delightful Detective Work of Nick and Nora Charles*. CreateSpace, 2014.

"Remembering racism and war hysteria at Heart Mountain Japanese Internment Camp." Just Go Places. https://www.justgoplacesblog.com/heart-mountain-japanese-internment-camp/#Daily_Life_at_the_Heart_Mountain_Japanese_Interment_Camp.

Rendezvous. Dir. William K. Howard. Perf. William Powell and Rosalind Russell. MGM, 1935.

Riskin, Victoria. *Fay Wray and Robert Riskin: A Hollywood Memoir*. New York: Pantheon, 2019.

Robinson, Greg. *By Order of the President: FDR and the Internment of Japanese Americans*. Cambridge: Harvard University Press, 2001.

Rohmer, Sax. *The Mask of Fu Manchu*. London: Cassell, 1973.

Saratoga. Dir. Jack Conway. Perf. Clark Gable and Jean Harlow. MGM, 1937.

Sarris, Andrew. *The American Cinema: Directors and Directions, 1929–1968*. New York: Da Capo Press, 1996.

_____. *You Ain't Heard Nothin' Yet: The American Talking Film, History and Memory, 1927–1949*. Oxford: Oxford University Press, 1998.

Schulberg, Budd. "Louis B. Mayer: Lion of Hollywood." *Time Magazine*, December 7, 1998. http://content.time.com/time/subscriber/article/0,33009,989771,00.html

_____. *What Make Sammy Run?* New York: Random House, 1941.

Scottsboro: An American Tragedy. Dir. Barak Goodman and Daniel Anker. WGBH, 2001.

Seeing Red: Stories of American Communists. Dir. James Klein and Julia Reichert. https://www.learnoutloud.com/Free-Audio-Video/History/American-History/Seeing-Red/79329.

"Senate votes to study treatment of Germans during World War II." *USA Today*, June 9, 2007. https://usatoday30.usatoday.com/news/nation/2007-06-09-internment_N.htm.

Sennwald, Andre. "'Star of Midnight,' a Humorous Murder Mystery, with William Powell, at the Radio City Music Hall." *The New York Times*, April 12, 1935. https://www.nytimes.com/1935/04/12/archives/star-of-midnight-a-humorous-murder-mystery-with-william-powell-at.html.

The Shadow of The Thin Man. Dir. W.S. Van Dyke II. Perf. William Powell and Myrna Loy. Metro Goldwyn Mayer, 1941.

Sharman, Russell Leigh. *Moving Pictures: An Introduction to Cinema*. Fayetteville: University of Arkansas Press, 2020.

Shulman, Irving. *Harlow: An Intimate Biography*. New York: Dell, 1964.

Simkin, John. "Hollywood Anti-Nazi League." Spartacus Educational, September 1997. https://spartacus-educational.com/USAantinazi.htm.

Slide, Anthony. *Hollywood Unknowns: A History of Extras, Bit Players, and Stand-Ins*. Jackson: University of Mississippi Press, 2012.

_____. *Incorrect Entertainment or Trash From the Past: A History of Political Incorrectness and Bad Taste in Twentieth Century American Popular Culture*. Albany, GA: Bear Manor Media, 2007.

Song of The Thin Man. Dir. Edward Buzzell. Perf. William Powell and Myrna Loy. Metro Goldwyn Mayer, 1947.

Sorel, Edward. *Mary Astor's Purple Diary: The Great American Sex Scandal of 1936*. New York: Liveright, 2016.

Soter, Tom. *Investigating Couples: A Critical Analysis of* The Thin Man, The Avengers, *and* The × Files. Jefferson, NC: McFarland, 2002.

"The Spanish Civil War." Holocaust Encyclopedia, The United States Holocaust Memorial Museum. https://encyclopedia.ushmm.org/content/en/article/spanish-civil-war.

Sperber, A.M., and Eric Lax. *Bogart*. New York: William Morrow, 1997.

Spicer, Chrystopher J. *Clark Gable: Biography, Filmography, Bibliography*. Jefferson, NC: McFarland, 2002.

Star of Midnight. Dir. Stephen Roberts. Perf. William Powell and Ginger Rogers. RKO Radio Pictures, 1935.

Steigrad, Alexandra. "Disney heiress slams great-uncle Walt: 'He bordered on rabid fascism.'" *New York Post*, October 19, 2022. https://nypost.com/2022/10/03/abigail-disney-calls-great-uncle-walt-disney-a-fascist/.

Stenn, David. *Bombshell: The Life and Death of Jean Harlow*. New York: Doubleday, 1993.

_____. "It Happened One Night … at MGM." *Vanity Fair*, April 1, 2003. https://www.vanityfair.com/news/2003/04/mgm200304.

Stepko, Barbara. "From Platinum Blonde to Nearly Bald: Jean Harlow's Horrifying Hair Routine." *The Vintage News*, June 12, 2018. https://www.thevintagenews.com/2018/06/12/jean-harlow/.

Stern, Sydney Ladensohn. "The Anti-Hitler Movie That Was Never Made." *Commentary Magazine*, December 2019. https://www.commentary.org/articles/sydney-ladensohn-stern/the-anti-hitler-movie-that-was-never-made/.

Stoneman, Ron. "Far East Fu fighting: The Yellow Peril—Dr Fu Manchu and the Rise of Chinophobia." *Irish Times*, November 8, 2014. https://www.irishtimes.com/culture/books/far-east-fu-fighting-the-yellow-peril-dr-fu-manchu-and-the-rise-of-chinophobia-1.1988872.

Sugimura, Tom. "Herd 'em Up, Pack 'em Off." *Pastor Tom's Blog*, July 26, 2020. https://www.nlcwh.org/content.cfm?page_content=blogs_include.cfm&blog_id=1537.

Swindell, Larry. *Screwball: The Life of Carole Lombard*. New York: William Morrow, 1975.

Symons, Julian. *Dashiell Hammett*. San Diego: Harcourt Brace Jovanovich, 1985.

_____. *Mortal Consequences: A History from the Detective Story to the Crime Novel*. New York: Harper & Row, 1972.

Takei, George, Justin Eisiger, and Steven Scott. *They Called Us Enemy*. Art by Harmony Becker. Marietta, GA: Top Shelf Productions, 2019.

Test Pilot. Dir. Victor Fleming. Perf. Clark Gable and Myrna Loy. MGM, 1938.

The Thin Man. Dir. W.S. Van Dyke II. Perf. William Powell and Myrna Loy. Metro Goldwyn Mayer, 1934.

The Thin Man Goes Home. Dir. Richard Thorpe. Perf. William Powell and Myrna Loy. Metro Goldwyn Mayer, 1944.

Thirteen Women. Dir. George Archainbaud. Perf. Myrna Loy and Irene Dunne. RKO Radio Pictures, 1932.

"This Day in Letters March 27, 1944. Dashiell Hammett to Lillian Hellman." *The American Reader*. https://theamericanreader.com/27-march-1944-dashiell-hammett-to-lillian-hellman/.

Thompson, David. *Humphrey Bogart*. New York: Faber & Faber, 2009.

Thompson, George J. "Rhino." *Hammett's Moral Vision*. San Francisco: Vince Emery Productions, 1972.

T.M.P. "Myrna Loy and William Powell Exhibit Same Old Zest in the New Nick Charles Thriller at Capitol, 'Song of Thin Man.'" *The New York Times*, August 29, 1947. https://www.nytimes.com/1947/08/29/archives/myrna-loy-and-william-powell-exhibit-same-old-zest-in-the-new-nick.html.

Tranberg, Charles. *The Thin Man: Murder Over Cocktails*. Albany, GA: Bear Manor Media, 2009.

Trybulski, Stan. "A Dash of Class: The War-Time Dashiel Hammett." *Mean Streets*, January 18, 2014. https://stantrybulski.com/2014/01/dash-class-war-time-hammett/

Tucker, Neely. "Stories That Will Beat You to a Bloody Pulp." *The Washington Post*, December 27, 2007. https://www.latimes.com/archives/la-xpm-2007-dec-27-et-pulp27-story.html.

Turback, Michael. *Nick and Nora: The Couple Who Taught America How to Drink*. N.p.: History Company, 2018.

Tuska, Jon. *The Detective in Hollywood*. Garden City, NY: Doubleday, 1978.

Uchida, Yoshiko. *Desert Exile: The Uprooting of a Japanese-American Family*. Seattle: University of Washington Press, 1982.

"Unangax̂ (Aleut) Evacuation and Internment during World War II." U.S. National Park Service. https://www.nps.gov/articles/000/unangax-internment.htm.

UPI. "Famed Actress Dies at 83." *Redlands Daily Facts*, June 26, 1962. https://www.newspapers.com/clip/4621725/redlands-daily-facts/.

"Upton Sinclair's End Poverty in California Campaign." University of Washington Civil Rights and Labor History Consortium. https://depts.washington.edu/epic34/.

Urwand, Ben. "The Chilling History of How Hollywood Helped Hitler." *The Hollywood Reporter*, July 31, 2013. https://www.hollywoodreporter.com/news/general-news/how-hollywood-helped-hitler-595684/.

_____. *The Collaboration: Hollywood's Pact with Hitler.* Cambridge: Harvard University Press, 2013.

Uyehara, Mari. "The Western Strategy." *The Nation*, August 23–30, 2021, p. 17.

Vallance, Tom. "Evie Wynn Johnson Actress and Ambitious Hollywood Wife." *The Independent*, October 10, 2011. https://www.independent.co.uk/news/obituaries/evie-wynn-johnson-550363.html.

Van Dine, S.S. *The Benson Murder Case.* Faded Page. https://www.fadedpage.com/showbook.php?pid=20131113.

Variety. "Marcus Loew." *Variety* LXXXXVIII, no. 8. September 7, 1927. https://archive.org/details/variety87-1927-09/page/n2/mode/1up?view=theater.

Variety Staff. "After the Thin Man." *Variety*, December 31, 1935. https://variety.com/1935/film/reviews/after-the-thin-man-1200411263/.

_____. "Shadow of the Thin Man." *Variety*, December 31, 1940. https://variety.com/1940/film/reviews/shadow-of-the-thin-man-1200413512/.

_____. "The Thin Man Goes Home." *Variety*, December 31, 1943. https://variety.com/1943/film/reviews/the-thin-man-goes-home-1200414202/.

"Virginia Verrill, Unseen Voice of Hollywood's Singing Stars, 82." *The New York Times*, January 25, 1999, Section A, p. 21. https://www.nytimes.com/1999/01/25/arts/virginia-verrill-unseen-voice-of-hollywood-s-singing-stars-82.html.

von Hoffman, Nicholas. *Citizen Cohn: The Life and Times of Roy Cohn.* New York: Doubleday, 1988.

"W.S. Van Dyke Dies, Film Director, 53." *The New York Times*, February 6, 1943. https://timesmachine.nytimes.com/timesmachine/1943/02/06/85626547.html?pageNumber=13.

Wallace, Max. *The American Axis: Henry Ford, Charles Lindbergh, and the Rise of The Third Reich.* New York: St. Martin's Press, 2003.

"Walter Winchell: The Power of Gossip." *PBS American Masters*, October 20, 2020. Written, produced and directed by Ben Loeterman.

Ward, Nathan. *The Lost Detective: Becoming Dashiell Hammett.* New York: Bloomsbury, 2015.

Weitzman, Elizabeth. "The Depression-era gems at 1930's prices." *The Daily News*, February 6, 2009. https://www.nydailynews.com/entertainment/tv-movies/depression-era-gems-1930s-prices-article-1.389208.

"William Law Biography." *IMDb.* https://www.imdb.com/name/nm0492406/bio?ref_=nm_ov_bio_sm.

William Powell: A True Gentleman. Dir. Rudy Behlmer. Narr. Michael York. Warner Home Video, 2005.

Williams, Duncan Ryuken. "The Karma of A Nation." *Harvard Divinity Bulletin*, Spring/Summer 2022, p. 43.

Woeste, Victoria Saker, and Susan Radomsky. "Suing Henry Ford." *Legal Affairs*, July/August 2003. https://www.legalaffairs.org/issues/July-August-2003/review_woeste_julaug03.msp.

Wolfe, Peter. *Beams Falling: The Art of Dashiell Hammett.* Bowling Green: Bowling Green University, 1980.

Wood, Ean. *The Josephine Baker Story.* London: Sanctuary, 2000.

"World War Casualties: Bruno's Last Flight." *Time Magazine*, August 18, 1941. http://www.time.com/time/magazine/article/0,9171,802107,00.html#ixzz0rkj0X52M.

Wray, Fay. *On the Other Hand.* New York: St. Martin's Press, 1989.

Wright, Morgan. "Harry Gibson was the wildest of the mid–1940's boogie woogie piano players." *Blues and Rhythm Magazine* 237, March 2009. http://www.hyzercreek.com/blues_and_rhythm.htm.

Wright, William. *Lillian Hellman: The Image, the Woman.* New York: Simon & Schuster, 1986.

Zilbart, Eve. "Dashiell Hammett, Hard-Boiled &." *The Washington Post*, October 6, 1982. https://www.washingtonpost.com/archive/lifestyle/1982/10/06/dashiell-hammett-hard-boiled-38/5679d60c-96a0-4362-9e3f-e0d39c7b4abc/.

Zinn, Howard. *The People's History of the United States, 1492–Present.* New York: HarperCollins, 1995.

Zumoff, J.A. "Politics and the 1920's Writings of Dashiell Hammett." *Journal of American Studies* 52.1 (2012): 77–98 https://journals.ku.edu/amsj/article/view/4413/4140.

Zwerling, Philip. "Rituals of Repression." *The 1985 Minns Lectures.* First Unitarian Church of Los Angeles, First and Second Church in Boston, and Kings Chapel House in Boston, Spring 1985.

Index

Numbers in ***bold italics*** indicate pages with illustrations

Abraham Lincoln Brigade 148
The Adakian 178
Addams, Jane 48
Adler, Larry 181
Adler, Stella 157–158
Adventures of the Thin Man 169
After the Thin Man ***3***, 64, 68, 78, 101, 127–***128***, 133–135, 138, 171
Ajón, Ramona 139
The Aleutian Islands 177–178
All Quiet on the Western Front 170
America First 148, 174
Ames, Leon 163, 168
Anderson, Ernest 78–79
Andrews, Dana 99
Ankrum, Morris 163
Another Thin Man 18, 91, 101, 108, 127, 136–***137***, 139–141
Anthony, Joseph 158
Arnold, Edward 88
Arthur, Jean 67, 78
Asta ***3***, 4, 9, 19, 37, 41, 64, 97, 107, 129, 131, 136, 138, 142, 154, 161–162, 166
Astor, Mary 36, 72, 79, 149–***151***
The Autumn Garden 145

Baer, Dorothy 74
Baer, Max 74, 91
Baer, Max, Jr. 91
Baker, Josephine 116–***117***
Bankhead, Tallulah 72
The Barbarian 88–90
Barrymore, Lionel 171
Battle of the Aleutians: A Graphic History, 1942–1943 178
Beavers, Louise 73, 112–***113***, 115, 156–158
Bellaver, Harry 140–141
The Benson Murder Case 8, 64, 120
Bern, Paul 71–72, 78
The Best Years of Our Lives 98
Betrayal: Surviving an American Concentration Camp 125
Biberman, Abner 138–139
Birth of a Nation 44, 114
Black Mask 23, 24, 25, ***26***, 29
The Black Watch 83–84, 110
Blackface 83, 110–111
Blake, Oliver 157

Bogart Humphrey 36, 149, 153, 183–***186***
Bolger, Ray 69
Bombshell 73, 91, 113
Bond, Ward 175
Brecher, Irving 154, 160
Breen, Joseph Ignatius 49, 93, 129, 170–171
Brooks, Ralph 163
Brophy, Edward 108, 163
Bruce, Virginia 78
Brush, Katherine 71
Burke, Billie 70
Burke, Frankie 159
Buzzell, Edward 168

Cagney, James 49, 71, 79–81
Calleia, Joseph 130, 134
Camp Shenango 177
The Canary Murder Case 7, 8, 60, 64
Carnera, Primo 91
Carrillo, Leo 93
Cecil, Nora 164
Celebrated Criminal Cases of America 13
Chandler, Raymond 6–7, 17–18
Chase, Charlie 132
The Children's Hour 144
China Slaver 121
Chinese Exclusion Act 87
City Streets 28
Civil Rights Congress 147, 184, 186
Cody, Iron Eyes 104
Cohn, Harry 42
Cohn, Roy 181
Colbert, Claudette 115
Cole, Lester 52, 181–182
Colodny Robert 178
Committee for the First Amendment 183, 185
The Communist Party, USA 145–147, 149, 182
Confessions of a Nazi Spy 171–172
The Continental Op 23, 26, 27, 119
Cook, Elisha, Jr. 97
Cooper, Gary 175, 180
Corey, Jeff 182–183
Corrigan, Lloyd 163
Cortez, Ricardo 85, 149

Costello, Don 140
The Cotton Club 92, 94
Cowling, Bruce 165
The Crimson City 84
Cukor, George 59
Curry, Marshall 176

The Dain Curse 28, 146
Davenport, Harry 163
Dead Yellow Women 119, 146
Dees, Mary Ella 78
DeHaven, Gloria 162
Denny, Reginald 88, 90
The Desert Song 110
Dewitt, John L. 121–122
The Diary of Anne Frank 105
Dies, Martin 184–185
Dieterle, William 61
Dillinger, John 93
Disney, Walt 172, 180
Double Wedding 39, 78, 81, 134
Double Whoopee 70
Douglas, Melvyn 99
Douglas, Patricia 133
Douglass, Frederick 83
Doyle, Buddy 69
Dressler, Marie 175
Dunne, Irene 85

East, Henry 107
Ebert, Roger 41, 61
Empey, Arthur Guy 175
Entwistle, Millicent Lillian "Peg" ***85***
Equality 147
Eskimo 95, 102–***103***
Eskimo 96, 102–104, 121
Evelyn Prentice 81
The Ex-Mrs. Bradford 67

Fagan, Myron C. 107
The Farewell Murder 135
Film Stars Don't Die in Liverpool 168
Fitzgerald, F. Scott 71, 101
Fix, Paul 134
Fleming, Victor 72–73
Flowers, Bess 168
Folies Bergère 117
Fonda, Henry 79
A Fool That Was 84
Ford, Henry 43, 172–175

223

Index

Ford, John 83
Fountain of Education 82
Fox, William 42
Francis, Kay 61–62
Franco, Francisco 147–148, 171
Freuchen, Peter 103
Fung, Willie 87

Gable, Clark 41, 64–65, 72, 75–76, 92–93, 140, 180
Gabriel Over the White House 54–55
Garbo, Greta 91
Gardner, Ava 157
Garland, Judy 50–51
Gentlemen Prefer Blondes (novel) 90
The German-American Bund 175
Gibson, Harry "The Hipster" 164
Gilchrist, Connie 168
Girl 27 133
The Girl Who Had Everything 79
The Glass Key (movie) 134
The Glass Key (novel) 14, 29, 31
Goldwyn, Samuel 74, 98, 144
The Goldwyn Follies 74
Gombell, Mina 107
Gone with the Wind 93, 113
Goodrich, Francis 4, 16, 32, 39, 40, 90, 97, 105, 127–128, 131–132, 134–136, 141, 144, 154, 182
Gordon, Phyllis 138, 140
Grahame, Gloria 165, 168
Grant, Cary 99
Grease 82
The Great Dictator 172
The Great Ziegfeld 65, 68–**69**, 75, 78, 81
Greenbaum, Isidore 176
Greene, Graham 72
The Greene Murder Case 64
Grey, Virginia 138, 140
Griffith, D.W. 101
Guillén, René Ramon 139
Gyssling, Georg 56, 148, 170

Hackett, Albert 4, 16, 32, 39, 40, 52, 90, 97, 105, 107, 127–128, 131–132, 134–136, 141, 144, 154, 182
half-breed 103–104
Hall, Mordaunt 41
Hall, Porter 108
Hall, Richard Dickie 56
Halsey, Betty 74
Ham and Eggs at the Front 83–**84**, 110, 116
Hammett, Dashiell **3**, 4, 5, 7, 8, 10, 11, 20, 21, 22, 23, 25, 27, 28, 29, 30, 31, 32, 41, 52, 64, 70, 72, 76, 82, 97, 101, 116, 119, 122, 127, 131, 135–136, 139, 142–154, 164, 170–174, 177, 184–190
Hammett, Jo (Josephine) 29, 30, 31, 142–144, 146, 151, 188–189
Hammett, Josie 29
Hammett, Mary 142
Harlow, Jean 60, 65, 70–76, 91, 96, 129, 134

Harris, Theresa 64
Hart, Teddy 134
Hawks, Howard 91
Haycraft, Howard 6, 8
Hays, Will 48–49
Hays Office 48, 56, 63, 88, 90, 170
Hearst, William Randolph 54–55, 57, 133, 175, 185
Heart Mountain Camp 123–125
Hellman, Lillian 5, 18, 19, 21, 22, 29, 30, 39, 41, 52, 76, 105, 122, 142–145, 148–149, 154, 176, 183–184, 186–190
Hell's Angels 70
Henry, William 108
Highsmith, Patricia 72
Hitler, Adolf 170, 174
Hold Your Man 76
Hollywood Anti-Nazi League for the Defense of American Democracy, HANL 148, 172, 176–177
Hollywood Tea Party 132
Hollywood Ten 181, 183, 185
The Hoodlum Saint 78
Hopper, Hedda 91, 172
Hornblow, Arthur 97
House Un-American Activities Committee (HUAC) 52–53, 79, 91, 122, 149, 180, 183–184
Howard, Shemp 138
Howard, Sidney 171
Howe, James Wong 99, 109
Huber, Harold 108
Hughes, Howard 49, 70
Hughes, Langston 116
Hurst, Fannie 115
Hussey, Ruth 136, 140
Huston, John 158
Huston, Walter 91
Hutchinson, Muriel 138, 140

I Love You Again 56, 81, 97
Igloo (Manna) 104
Imitation of Life 115
The Industrial Workers of the World 22
The Insidious Dr. Fu Manchu 86
It Can't Happen Here (movie) 55, 170
It Can't Happen Here (novel) 66, 170
It Happened One Night 41

Jaffe, Sam 170
Japanese-American Citizen's League 87
Jefferson School of Social Science 179, 184
Jewel Robbery 61
Johnson, Nunnally 79
Johnson, Tor 156, 158
Jolson, Al 111–**112**
Joy, Leatrice 72

Kalb, Bernard 178
Kantor, MacKinlay 98
Karloff, Boris 85–86, 120, 122

Kaufman, George S. 79
The Kennel Murder Case, 36, 64
Knowles, Patric 140
Kruger, Otto 91–92
Ku Klux Klan 114
Kuhn, Julius "Fritz" 175–176
Kurnitz, Harry 154

La Cava, Gregory 54
Ladies' Man 62
Laemmle, Carl 42
Lamas, Fernando 79
Landi, Elissa 129, 132–133
Lansbury, Angela 78
Lardner, Ring, Jr. 181
Larkin, John 108–109
The Last of the Pagans 104
The Last Tycoon 101
Law, William 134
Lawson, John Howard 52
The League of American Writers 147
Lemmon, Jack 80–81
Leo the Lion 42
Leonard, Sheldon 138, 140
Levene, Sam 134
Lewis, Diana 78, 139
Lewis, Sinclair 55, 170
Libeled Lady 74–75, 77–78, 81, 96, 113, 120
Life with Father 78
Limitations of Life 116
Lindbergh, Charles Augustus 171, 174-
Lindsay, Margaret 64
Little, Frank 22
The Little Foxes 144
Little Men 49
Little Tokyo U.S.A. **126**
Loew, Arthur 56
Loew, Marcus 32, 44–46, 101
Lombard, Carole 60, 62–63, **65**, 76, 162
Long, Lotus 102
Loos, Anita 71, 90
Lord, F. Daniel A. 48
Love Crazy 81, 97
Loy, Myrna 4, 38, 39–42, 56, 60, 65–68, 74–75, 77–79, 81–101, 104, 107, 110, 116, 120, 127, 129, 132, 135–136, 154–**155**, 161–169, 180, 183
Lubin, Lou 156
Luce, Henry R. 182

MacBride, Donald 163
The Mad Dog of Europe 170
Madam (novel) 10
Main, Marjorie 140
The Maltese Falcon (novel) 13, 14, 28, 151
The Maltese Falcon (3rd movie version) 36, 97, 149–151
Mammy 112–**113**
Man of the World 62
The Man Who Broke a Thousand Chains 97
Manhattan Melodrama **65**, 81, 92–93, 111

March, Frederic 58, 99, 177
Marie Antoinette 101
Marshal, Alan 134
Marx, Samuel 29, 32, 38–39, 41, 47, 53, 57, 72, 171
The Mask of Fu Manchu 85–87, 111, 116, 119–120
Mason, James 162
Mayer, Louis B. 4, 32, 41–45, 50, 52, **55**–58, 72, 76, 93–97, 101, 132–133, 136, 145, 160, 170, 182
Mayo, Virginia 99
McCarthy, Eugene 158
McCarthy, Joseph 79, 189
McDaniel, Hattie 73, 76, 112–113
McDaniel, Sam 93
McLaglen, Leopold 177
McLaglen, Victor 175, 177
McNulty, Dorothy 134
Meadows, Jayne 168
Meek, Donald 63
Melton, Sid 156
Metro-Goldwyn-Mayer (MGM) **3**, 18, 29, 31, 32, 40–42, 44–46, 50, 56–59, 73, 78–79, 90–91, 93, 95, 101–105, 127, 133, 139–140, 145, 148, 154, 161, 167, 171, 182
Micheaux, Oscar 114–115
Miller, Don 178
Millette, Dorothy 72
Mineta, Norman Yoshio 124–125
Mr. Blandings Builds His Dream House 99
Mister Roberts 78–**80**
Montgomery, Robert 95, 180
Moorhead, Natalie 108
Morgan, Frank 70
Morgan, Ralph 168
Moriso, Patricia 167
The Mortal Storm 172
Moy, Afong 118
Mussolini, Vittorio 171
My Man Godfrey **63**, 78

Nazis 170
Neal, Tom 138, 140
Nelson, Barry 157–158
Nemo, Henry 168
New York Civil Rights Congress 147
Nick and Nora (stage musical) 169
Nick and Nora (TV movie) 169
A Night at the Garden 176
Nissen, Greta 70
Novarro, Ramon 88, 90

Oakie, Joe 156
Oland, Warner 121
Olympia 172
On the Waterfront 47
One Way Passage 61–62
Oscar Micheaux: The Superhero of Black Film 114
O'Sullivan, Maureen **106**–107
O'Toole, Peggy 149
The Outlaw 49
Owen, Reginald 95

Paiva, Nestor 138
Parker, Dorothy 10, 29, 52–**53**, 57, 145, 148, 150, 176
Parsons, Louella 76, 84
Patrick, Gail 97
Patterson, Haywood 147
Pelley, Dudley 175
Pendleton, Nat 70, 93, 108
Perelman, Laura 142
Perelman, S.J. 142
Perrin, Nat 164
Petticoat Fever 95, 120–121
Pinkerton, Allan 21
Plan 9 from Outer Space 158
Platinum Blonde 71
PM 149
Poe, Edgar Allan 5, 6
Potter, H.C. 99
Poulson, William Anthony 136, 140
Powell, William 3, 5, 8, 33, 36, 39, 41, 59–65, 69–70, **74**–82, 92–96, 101, 127, 135–136, 154–169
Powell, William David, Jr. 60
Princess Tam Tam 116
Private Detective 62 64
The Prizefighter and the Lady 91
The Public Enemy 49, 71

race films 114
Rainer, Louise **69**
Ralph, Jessie 130, 134
Randolph, A. Philip 108–109
Rankin, John Elliot 121, 179
Reckless 65, **74, 76**
Red Dust 72–73, 87, 120
Red Harvest (novel) 14, 26, 27, 82
Red-Headed Woman 71, 90
Redface 110
Reed, Donna 157158
Reed, Phillip 165
Rendezvous 66, 95
Revere, Anne 162–163
Reynolds, Adeline De Walt 158
Riefenstahl, Leni 172
The Rising Tide of Color Against White World-Supremacy 118
Riskin, Everett 162
Riskin, Robert 160, 162
Roach, Hal 70, 171
Roadhouse Nights 28
Roberts, Stephen 68
Rogers, Ginger 65–66, 180
Rohmer, Sax 86, 117–118, 120
Romero, Cesar 66, 107
Rooney, Mickey 44, 51, 92, 160
Ross, David 133
Ross, Shirley 94
Rosson, Hal 73, 91
Rowlan, Roy 132
Russell, Harold 99
Russell, Jane 49
Russell, Rosalind 66–67, 95
Ryan (Nixon), Pat 70

Said, Edward 86
St. Denis, Ruth 82
Santa Anita Race Track 122

Sapiro, Aaron 174
Saratoga 76, 78, 90, 113
Schenck, Nicholas 45, 92, 101, 171
Schmeling, Max 91
Schulberg, Budd 47, 56, 95
The Scottsboro Boys 147
Screen Writers Guild (SWG) 52–53, 58, 145–146, 180
screwball comedy 62–63
Selznick, David O. 72
The Senator Was Indiscreet 79, 81
Shadow of the Thin Man 101, 113, 134, 154–158
Sharp-Bolster, Anita 163
Shearing, Norma 72
Sherlock Holmes 60, 78
Shotter, Winifred 95
Simpson, Alan K. 124–125
Sinclair, Upton 56, 58, 146
Siren of the Tropics 116
Skippy 4, 37, 41, 107, 135, 154, 162, 165
Smith, C. Aubrey 90–91, 137, 140
Smith Act 187
Song of the Thin Man 164–169
Sorel, Edward 41
Spade, Sam 8, 149
The Spanish Earth 148
The Squall 83, 116
Stahl, John 115
Star of Midnight 65–66
Stein, Gertrude 31
Stewart, Donald Ogden 145, 176
Stewart, James 74–75, 132
Stockwell, Dean 167
Strickling, Howard 72–73
Stromberg, Hunt 73, 86, 90, 102, 104–105, 132, 134, 141, 154
Subversive Activities Control Board (SACB) 179
Swerling, Jo 39
Switzer, Carl 97

Takei, George 123
Tamirof, Akim 91
Tanner, Edward Elis 107–108
Taurog, Norman 78
Taylor, Elizabeth 79
Taylor, Libby 69
Taylor, Robert 95
Temple, Shirley 50
Test Pilot 96
Thalberg, Irving 41, 45, 47, 52–53, 55, 57–58, 71–72, 101
The Thin Man (movie) 4, 5, 12, **15**, 16, 17, 32, 33, **35**, 37, 38, 41, 44, 59, 61, 63, 64, 66, 78, 88, 90, 94, 97, 99–102, 105, 111, 127, 138, 146
The Thin Man (novel) 5, 8, 9, 10, 11, 13, 14, 15, 16, 18, 19, 30, 110
The Thin Man (stage play) 169
The Thin Man (TV series) 169
The Thin Man Goes Home 39, 66, 108, 154, 156, **159**–164
Thirteen Women 84, 88, 111, 116, 120
Thomas, J. Parnell 181
Thornton, Cyril 108

Thorpe, Richard 39, 79, 162
To Mary—with Love 95
Tokyo Rose 103
Tone, Franchot 73, 140
Tracy, Lee 73
Tracy, Spencer 75, 77, 79, 96, 120
Trader Horn 101
Triumph of the Will 172
Truman, Harry S. 179
Tucker, Lorenzo 115
Tulip 144
Turback, Michael 11
Twenty Years at Hull House 48

Valentino, Rudolph 83
Van Dine, S.S. 6–7, 36
Van Dyke II, Woodbridge Strong 4, 32, 36, 38, 39, 41, 57, 64, 91–94, 96, 101–104, 107, 127, 129, 132, 134–135, 141, 154
Verrill, Virginia 74
Vinson, Helen 163

Wadsworth, Henry 108
Walsh, Arthur 162
Ward, Arthur Henry 86

Warner, Harry 146
Warner, Jack 146, 185
Warner Brothers 42, 58, 82
Warren, Earl 57, 125
Washington, Freddie 115
Watch on the Rhine 144–145, 162
Watson, Lucile 162
Watson, Minor 164
We Charge Genocide 186
Weissmuller, Johnny **106**
The Wet Parade 57
What Makes Sammy Run? 47
Whipsaw 96
White, Walter 114
White Shadows in the South Seas 101
Whitewashing 88, 110–111
Wife vs. Secretary 75
William, Warren 115
Williams, Esther 78
Winchell, Walter 10, 38, 175, 188
Wing, Lulu Wong 103
Wise, Ray (Ray Mala) 103
Within Our Gates 114

Woman in the Dark (movie) 143
Woman in the Dark (short story) 143
Wong, Anna May 120, 133
Wood, Ed 159
Wood, Sam 90
Wray, Fay 60
Wright, Willard Huntington 7, 156
Wyler, William 98
Wynn, Keenan 164–**165**, 167

Yamaoka, George 125
Yamaoka, Iris 96, 103, 121–122, 125
Yamaoka, Otto 76, 96, 120, 122, 125
Yellow Peril 86, 118
Yellowface 88, 110, 119–122, 126

Zanuck, Darryl 61, 84
Ziegfeld Follies 116
Zip 166
Zucco, George 134
Zukor, Adolph 42

www.ingramcontent.com/pod-product-compliance
Lightning Source LLC
Chambersburg PA
CBHW060341010526
44117CB00017B/2924